House of Dan Curtis

House of Dan Curtis

The Television Mysteries of the *Dark Shadows* Auteur

SECOND EDITION

JEFF THOMPSON

Foreword by James Storm
Preface by Jim Pierson
Afterword by Ansel Faraj

Ideas into Books®
WESTVIEW
Kingston Springs, Tennessee

© 2020 Jeff Thompson.
All rights reserved, including the right to reproduction
in whole or in part in any form.
No part of this book may be reproduced or transmitted in any form or by any means, electronic or mechanical, including photocopying or recording, or by any information storage and retrieval system, without permission in writing from the author.

Each photograph is courtesy of
Jim Pierson and Dan Curtis Productions.

On the cover: Dan Curtis at his camera.

ISBN 978-1-62880-189-7

Printed in the United States of America on acid free paper.

IDEAS INTO BOOKS ® WESTVIEW
P.O. Box 605
Kingston Springs, Tennessee 37082

To
Sonia and E.D.
Lee Anne
Jonathan
Katy and Bruce
Madelyn
Kate and Kevin
Blakely
Mackenzie
Kameron
Kelly and Jake
Kimberly
and
to Dan Curtis

Table of Contents

Foreword by James Storm 1

Preface by Jim Pierson 3

Introduction: From Golf Shows to Miniseries 5

I. The Milestones: *Dark Shadows* in 1966-1971, 1991, 2004, and the 2010s 11

II. The Horrors: Kolchak, Norliss, Trilogies, and More 43

III. The Features: *House of Dark Shadows, Night of Dark Shadows, Burnt Offerings*, and More 71

IV. The Epics: Western, War, UFO, and More 89

V. The Dramas: Purvis, Coopers, Mrs. R, and More 189

VI. The Pilots: *The Big Easy, Johnny Ryan, Angie the Lieutenant*, and More 129

VII. The Mysteries: *Wide World Mystery, The Great Ice Rip-Off, Supertrain*, and What Might Have Been 147

Conclusion: From *Dark Shadows* to Today 159

Afterword by Ansel Faraj 203

Chapter Notes 205

Bibliography 211

Index 223

Foreword

James Storm

The first time Dan and I met was for my audition as Gerard Stiles in 1970. From the moment I entered the room and saw this guy sitting behind his desk with his feet up and twirling a front portion of his hair, which he was prone to do, I liked this guy right off the bat, and getting the job on *Dark Shadows* was a landmark event for me.

I liked Dan very much, and he believed in me and my work not only on the show but with other jobs he hired me for, such as *The Kansas City Massacre*.

The day I moved to Los Angeles, I called Dan, and without hesitation he told me to come in and see him that day. I did. He made it clear with the people around him that I was to have an agent, do two jobs for him, and told me to join him for lunch. I had a great agent the very next day.

It's not enough to say that Dan helped me get started, but he did. What I can say is he was a guy who believed in me and would, and did, do whatever he could to help me and guide me along. I owe Dan Curtis my career, for which I will forever be indebted to him.

He was a lion in every sense of the word—sometimes a little overbearing but never without heart.

The business that we know today has changed, and you don't have the Dan Curtises around anymore. Sadly.

I really miss him.

James Storm played Gerard Stiles on *Dark Shadows* and in *Night of Dark Shadows*. He later worked for Dan Curtis in *Scream of the Wolf, Wide World Mystery: The Invasion of Carol Enders, Trilogy of Terror,* and *The Kansas City Massacre*. He was an original cast member of *The Bold and the Beautiful* in the role of Bill Spencer Sr. His Internet website is **jimstormphotography.com**.

Preface

Jim Pierson

I first met Dan Curtis in the late 1980s not long after I had graduated from college. He was just finishing directing and producing the biggest dramatic program in television and film history, adapting Herman Wouk's novel *War and Remembrance*. To say that I was in awe of the man would be an understatement. I'd never met such an intimidating figure. His passion was enormous, his energy was staggering, and his sheer willpower was nothing short of supernatural. Of course, those are qualities that many friends and colleagues admired in Dan.

In addition to his legendary lack of patience, he could also scare the hell out of you. But that didn't last. Once you knew what Dan expected of you, and you knew how to make it happen, you came to realize that he was really a world-class motivator, a great mentor, and a creative genius. Dan could be tough, but once he responded with that nod of approval, or his million-dollar smile, or the words, "Good job, son," I can't imagine a more rewarding validation.

I'm grateful for all of the incredible opportunities and adventures that Dan Curtis brought to my life during the 16 years that I worked with him, until his passing in 2006. His legacy in film and television is vast and varied. He won and deserved his greatest critical acclaim with his massive World War II epics, but I think just as meaningful to viewers are Dan's wonderfully inventive and absorbing adventures with supernatural suspense and heart-stopping spookers. Starting with the original daytime version of *Dark Shadows* in 1966 and continuing with other classic chillers such as *The Night Stalker* and *Trilogy of Terror*, Dan carved out a career of genre favorites that made him the original king of television horror, inspiring future fear-inducing filmmakers such as Quentin Tarantino and Stephen King. But Dan was there first. As he often remarked, he loved "squeaking the door," and it's clear that he's left audiences with a body of work that still delivers the thrills.

Jim Pierson is a Los Angeles-based producer who served as marketing and promotions director for Dan Curtis Productions. He continues to represent the Curtis estate and oversee *Dark Shadows* projects in addition to producing DVD documentaries and public television musical specials. Jim is also active in film and television preservation.

INTRODUCTION

From Golf Shows to Miniseries

When did you start watching *Dark Shadows*? Did you first see the Gothic serial in the 1960s on ABC television, in the 1970s or 1980s in syndicated reruns, in the 1990s on VHS or on the Sci-Fi Channel, in the 2000s on DVD, or in the 2010s on streaming media or on the Decades TV channel? *Dark Shadows* is alive and well in the 2020s and ranks with *Star Trek* and *Doctor Who* as one of the greatest TV cult classics of all time.

I first saw an especially dramatic episode (#326) of *Dark Shadows* on ABC in September 1967 when I was a third grader sick at home one afternoon. I watched the show until its end in 1971 and then read Dan "Marilyn" Ross's *Dark Shadows* novels and Gold Key Comics' *Dark Shadows* comic books, collected almost all of the *Dark Shadows* TV and movie memorabilia, and began writing for such *Dark Shadows* fanzines as *The World of Dark Shadows, Shadows of the Night, The Parallel Times, Lone Star Shadows, The Collinsport Call*, and many others.

Finally, after writing my 1991 M.A. thesis about Canadian author Dan Ross (1912-1995) and my 2007 Ph.D. dissertation about American producer-director Dan Curtis (1927-2006), I wrote three books about the *Dark Shadows* creator—*The Television Horrors of Dan Curtis:* Dark Shadows, The Night Stalker, *and Other Productions, 1966-2006* (McFarland, 2009; 2nd ed., 2019); *Nights of Dan Curtis: The Television Epics of the* Dark Shadows *Auteur* (Ideas, 2016; 2nd ed., 2019); and this book, *House of Dan Curtis: The Television Mysteries of the* Dark Shadows *Auteur* (Westview, 2010; 2nd ed., 2020). In the books, I asserted that Dan Curtis could be considered an *auteur* (i.e. the predominant author of his productions and the one most responsible for their tone and vision) because of his intense involvement in numerous aspects of his works, from producing, directing, and editing to writing, script-doctoring, and set-decorating. In each book, I presented a career-overview chapter describing all four dozen of Curtis's productions, as well as information about his personal appearances and speaking engagements, his unrealized movie projects, his PGA and DGA awards, his funeral and his memorial service, and more. Then, each book focused more closely on a certain type of Curtis's productions, such as his horror movies (e.g. *Trilogy of Terror, Curse of the Black Widow*), his epics (e.g. *The Last Ride of the Dalton Gang, War and Remembrance*), or his mysteries (e.g. *Shadow of Fear, The Great Ice Rip-Off*). Each book featured rare photographs and forewords or afterwords by *Loon Lake* director Ansel H. Faraj, *Dark Shadows* star John Karlen, *My Music* producer Jim B. Pierson, and/or *CHiPs* star Larry Wilcox.

This second edition of *House of Dan Curtis* spotlights Curtis's 13+ mysteries and crime dramas—*Dead of Night: A Darkness at Blaisedon, Wide World Mystery: Frankenstein, Wide World Mystery: The Picture of Dorian Gray, Wide World Mystery: Shadow of Fear, Wide World Mystery: The Invasion of Carol Enders, Wide World Mystery: The Turn of the Screw, Wide*

World Mystery: Come Die with Me, *Wide World Mystery: Nightmare at 43 Hillcrest*, *The Great Ice Rip-Off*, *Supertrain*, *The Big Easy*, *Johnny Ryan*, and *Angie Lieutenant*—in chapters VI and VII. Chapters I, II, III, IV, and V focus, respectively, on *Dark Shadows*, Curtis's made-for-TV horror, his four feature films, his Western and *War* epics, and Curtis's often unsung dramas, from *Melvin Purvis, G-Man* and *Mrs. R's Daughter* to *The Love Letter* and *Saving Milly*.

Curtis was born Daniel Mayer Cherkoss, the only child of Mildred and Edward Cherkoss, on Friday 12 August 1927, in Bridgeport, Connecticut. He gained a half-brother from his dentist-father's second marriage after his mother's death. When Curtis dramatized his childhood in 1930s Bridgeport in two award-winning made-for-TV movies, *When Every Day Was the Fourth of July* (1978) and *The Long Days of Summer* (1980), he added a fictitious younger sister Sarah to his TV family—just as he had given Barnabas Collins of *Dark Shadows* a little sister Sarah.

After serving in the Naval Reserve in 1945, Curtis attended Syracuse University and graduated with a bachelor's degree in sociology in 1950. Two years later, he married his Syracuse classmate Norma Mae Klein, his wife until her death in March 2006 (just 20 days before Curtis's own passing). Cathy and Tracy, two of the Curtises' three daughters, survived their parents; Linda Curtis died tragically in 1975.

Beginning a career in television in the 1950s, Curtis worked in film sales (TV syndication) for NBC for eight years. "I sold *Douglas Fairbanks Presents* and *Hopalong Cassidy* reruns," as well as *Victory at Sea* and *Dragnet* reruns, Curtis explained.[1] Between 1952 and 1960, Curtis advanced from the position of Eastern field salesman to central sales manager to Eastern sales manager to regional/national sales manager and finally to director of sales. Then, he spent two years in the show-packaging department at MCA, where he sold *Union Pacific* episodes and the Grace Kelly TV special *A Look at Monaco* to local television stations. When he sold the cartoon series *Linus! the Lion-Hearted* to CBS, Curtis made a cameo voice appearance in one episode as Big-Time Talent Agent, who kidnaps a singing group led by Billie Bird (voiced by Carl Reiner). His experience in selling syndicated reruns prompted him to save all 1225 episodes of *Dark Shadows* for future sales. All but one of the episodes still exist and are available on VHS, DVD, and other media.

In 1962, the 35-year-old Curtis formed his own company, Dan Curtis Associates (soon renamed Dan Curtis Productions), and created **Challenge Golf** for ABC-TV. The 13-episode series, premiering on Saturday 12 January 1963, featured Arnold Palmer and Gary Player in a best-ball competition against a pair of challengers. In the 12th episode (Saturday 30 March), for example, Palmer and Player's opponents were Byron Nelson and Ken Venturi at the Pebble Beach golf course in California. The 13th and final episode aired on Sunday 7 April 1963.

In mid-1963, CBS, wanting to cultivate its own golf audience, asked Curtis to create and executive-produce *The CBS Match-Play Golf Classic* (later called **The CBS Golf Classic**). "CBS and I owned the show 50–50," Curtis revealed.[2] It was he who devised the practice of wiring golfers with throat microphones so that the TV audience could hear the players' immediate reactions to their shots (including occasional obscenities when they missed).

Introduction: From Golf Shows to Miniseries

Dan Curtis turns his love of golf into *The CBS Golf Classic* (CBS, 1963-1973), which he produces at the same time as *Dark Shadows* (ABC, 1966-1971). The 1965-1966 Emmy Award for Outstanding Sports Program is a three-way tie among ABC's *Wide World of Sports*, Curtis's *CBS Golf Classic*, and *Shell's Wonderful World of Golf* on NBC.

The CBS Golf Classic aired for a decade, from Saturday 28 December 1963 to Saturday 21 April 1973, and brought Curtis his first Emmy Award (for Achievement in Sports) in the 1965–1966 season. Curtis executive-produced the show until 1967; Frank Chirkinian was his producer-director. The series eventually went from one hour to 90 minutes (and from black-and-white to color), and the prize money rose from $166,000 to $225,000. Most of the tournaments took place on golf courses in California, New Jersey, and Ohio. The Emmy Award-winning Curtis, now earning $100,000 per year, was well on his way to becoming a noted television producer.

Dan Curtis's friend Ed Graham, the producer-director of *Linus! the Lion-Hearted*, remembered that Curtis asked him for an idea for a live-action TV series that they could produce together. Graham suggested Batman. In a 2010 email to me, Graham (1928-2018) recalled,

> We decided on Don Murray (*The Hoodlum Priest*) to play Batman. We also decided to go with the Rat Pack for villains, starting with Sammy Davis Jr. to play the Joker. Dan took the project to Jim Aubrey, who was head of

programming for CBS, and Aubrey decided to go with Batman in the fall of 1964—no pilot necessary. We told an excited National Periodical Publications [DC Comics] just as Aubrey was *fired* from CBS. We could not go elsewhere without a release from CBS because [attorney Dick] Barovic had granted them first refusal on any of my other projects after *Linus! the Lion-Hearted*. National Periodicals, now eager to go, made their own deal with ABC. [. . .] I think my Batman show would have been a success, but I told Jim Pierson I'm pretty sure Dan would have bought me out somewhere along the way and done an even better job, himself.[3]

No Ed Graham/Dan Curtis *Batman* series materialized, but James Aubrey and Dan Curtis notably crossed paths again when Aubrey was head of MGM (as revealed in Chapter III of this book). Meanwhile, Curtis still yearned to try his hand at dramatic television. His nightmare that became ABC-TV's *Dark Shadows* gave him that chance. Chapter I of this book chronicles the 1966-1971, 1991, and 2004 incarnations of *Dark Shadows,* as well as Tim Burton's 2012 film *Dark Shadows* and David Gregory's 2019 documentary *Master of Dan Curtis,* about Curtis's 1963-2005 television career.

As I prepare this revised second edition, I cannot overemphasize the invaluable assistance of Jim Pierson. Through his leadership of the Dark Shadows Festival and his vital involvements with Dan Curtis Productions, Big Finish Productions, MPI Home Video, and film-and-television preservation, Jim has been a major force in perpetuating *Dark Shadows* and the entire body of work of his mentor Curtis, whom Pierson has called "the ultimate fearless leader."[4] I extend a very special thank-you to Jim Pierson not only for helping me and encouraging me along the way but also for writing the preface to this book and for supplying me with every single photograph found herein. Plus, I thank Mary Catharine Nelson of www.ideasintobooks.net for her creativity, her layouts, her publishing expertise, and her friendship.

I also wish to thank Jo and Jim Addie, Anthony Ambrogio, Jeffrey Arsenault, Dr. Linda Badley, Dennis Baker, Marc Ballard, Joyce and Bill Barry, Harry Benshoff, Dr. Laura B.F. Beraha, Eileen and Marc Berger, David Bianculli, Michele Blackledge, Robert Bloch, Mark Booher & Bob Fritz, Ken Bramming, Dr. Will Brantley, Stephon Brisco, Norman Brunette, Jon Burlingame, Bill Byrge, Dale Clark, Melody Clark, Robert Cobert, Joe Collins, David Colton, Julie and Gary Conn, Dick Cowl, Dan Curtis Holdings, Jenny and Mike Darrell, Dr. Jane Davis, Mark Dawidziak, David Del Valle, Bruce Dettman, Stacey and Ben Dixon, Eileen and Keith Dunmire, Charles Ellis, Ansel H. Faraj, Eileen Farrar, Scott Farris, Robert Finocchio, Lynn and Jim Fitzwater, Jonathan Gales, Danielle S.O. Gelehrter, Chris Geny, Scott Gibson, Ed Graham, Greg Greene, Elva and John Griffin, Dr. Johnanna Grimes, Darren Gross & Phil Hansen, Dr. Karen Gupton, Guy Haines, Bruce Hallenbeck, Richard Halpern, Laraine Harford, Jonathan Harrison, Arlena Hayden, Joan Higgins, Douglas Howard, Joe Integlia, Rochelle and Scott Isaacs, Dr. Coreen Jackson, Dr. Laurel Jenkins-Crowe, Dr. Gloria Johnson, Jamie Jones, Katy and Bruce Jumper, Barbara Kannard, John Karlen, Rhonda and Brad Kavan, Mary and Gaines Kergosien, Nancy Kersey, Rod Labbe, Renae and Dave Lackey, Angelia and Curt Ladnier, Kimberly and Jonathan Lampley, Randall D. Larson, Amy and Jay Lipper, Wendy and Ira Lipper, Derek Martin, Richard Matheson, Wallace McBride, Dan McEachern, Cindy and Martin McGeachy, Dr. J. Gordon

Melton, Robby Midgett, Jeremy Miller, Dr. Samantha Morgan-Curtis, Gary Mosher, Brigid and Patrick Murphy, Phyllis Muzeroll, Phil Myers, Isaac Neel, Kelly and Jake Neel, Mary Catharine Nelson, Julie and Jerry Nidiffer, Lois and John Nixon, Jacque Nodell, Michelle and John Noel, William F. Nolan, Mary Overstreet, Kameron Parsley, Kate and Kevin Parsley, Kimberly Parsley, Jim Pierson, Cheryl and Jeff Podolsky, Dr. Luke Powers, Judy Price, Dr. Tim Quain, Dr. Jo Helen Railsback, Kathy Resch, Keith Richardson, Scott Richardson, Daryl Allan Ritchie, Marcy Robin, Marilyn and Dan Ross, Nikki and Chad Rush, Helen Samaras, Chris Schlueter, Kathryn Leigh Scott, Dan Silvio, Cindy and Brian Smith, Dr. Connie Smith, Leah and Stephen Soule, Barbara Steele, Joseph Stern, Brinke Stevens, Harriet Stich, Valerie and James Storm, Alex Sutton, Susan and Gary Svehla, Gary Swafford, Donna and Jack Thomas, Wayne Thomas, Harriet and Charlie Thompson, Lee Anne Thompson, Lisa and Boyd Thompson, Sonia and E.D. Thompson, Bob Tinnell, Sy Tomashoff, Mike Turner, Larry Underwood, Joshua Vance, Jeff Vaughn, Steve Vertlieb, Athena Victory & Hercules Invictus, Shirley and David Wadell, Marie Wallace, Dariel and Shawn Washington, Sherry Watson, Dr. Warren Westcott, Cyndi and Robert White, Larry Wilcox, Tim Wiley, Ann Wilson, Paula Underwood Winters, Emma Wisdom, Tyler Wisniewski, Ken Wright, and Reed Young.

I also thank the stars of *Dark Shadows* (whom I always enjoy seeing at the Dark Shadows Festivals); my colleagues and students at Tennessee State University (where I often show Dan Curtis's "Graveyard Rats"); my former colleagues and students at Watkins College of Art, Design, & Film (where I showed Richard Matheson's *Incredible Shrinking Man* and "Amelia" in 2009-2010); my former colleagues and students at Nashville State Community College (where I showed Curtis's *Dark Shadows* revival series in 1997-1999); my former co-workers and listeners at WAMB-AM 1200 (where I often played Robert Cobert's "Quentin's Theme" and *Winds of War* theme many times between 1981, when I began at WAMB, and 2013, when the station ended); my fellow members of Nashville's Suspense, Sci-Fi, Horror, and Fantasy Meet-Up (where I have signed books and spoken about Dan Curtis); and *you*. Finally, I thank the people to whom this book is dedicated: my parents, my sister, my son, my nieces, my nephews, my great nieces, and, of course, Dan Curtis.

The Productions of Dan Curtis

Challenge Golf (1963) in Introduction
The CBS Golf Classic (1963-1973) in Introduction
Dark Shadows (1966-1971) in Chapter I
The Strange Case of Dr. Jekyll and Mr. Hyde (1968) in Chapter II
Dead of Night: A Darkness at Blaisedon (1969) in Chapter VI
House of Dark Shadows (1970) in Chapter III
Night of Dark Shadows (1971) in Chapter III
The Night Stalker (1972) in Chapter II
The Night Strangler (1973) in Chapter II
Frankenstein (1973) in Chapter VII
The Norliss Tapes (1973) in Chapter II
The Picture of Dorian Gray (1973) in Chapter VII
Scream of the Wolf (1974) in Chapter II
Shadow of Fear (1974) in Chapter VII
Dracula (1974) in Chapter IV
The Invasion of Carol Enders (1974) in Chapter VII
Melvin Purvis, G-Man (1974) in Chapter V
The Turn of the Screw (1974) in Chapter VII
Come Die with Me (1974) in Chapter VII
Nightmare at 43 Hillcrest (1974) in Chapter VII
The Great Ice Rip-Off (1974) in Chapter VII
Trilogy of Terror (1975) in Chapter II
The Kansas City Massacre (1975) in Chapter V
Burnt Offerings (1976) in Chapter III
Dead of Night (1977) in Chapter II
Curse of the Black Widow (1977) in Chapter II
When Every Day Was the Fourth of July (1978) in Chapter V
Supertrain (1979) in Chapter VII
Mrs. R's Daughter (1979) in Chapter V
The Last Ride of the Dalton Gang (1979) in Chapter IV
The Long Days of Summer (1980) in Chapter V
I Think I'm Having a Baby (1981) in Chapter V
The Big Easy (1982) in Chapter VI
The Winds of War (1983) in Chapter IV
St. John in Exile (1986) in Chapter IV
War and Remembrance (1988, 1989) in Chapter IV
Johnny Ryan (1990) in Chapter VI
Dark Shadows (1991) in Chapter I
Angie the Lieutenant (1992) in Chapter VI
Intruders: They Are Among Us (1992) in Chapter IV
Me and the Kid (1993) in Chapter III
Trilogy of Terror II (1996) in Chapter II
The Love Letter (1998) in Chapter V
Dark Shadows (2004) in Chapter I
Alzheimer's Association PSA (2004) in Chapter V
Saving Milly (2005) in Chapter V
Our Fathers (2005) in Chapter V

CHAPTER I

The Milestones
Dark Shadows in 1966-1971, 1991, 2004, and the 2010s

In one of his final interviews, Dan Curtis (1927-2006) remarked, "I'll probably be remembered for *Dark Shadows* instead of the things I really cared about, which were the great epics that I made [*Dracula, The Last Ride of the Dalton Gang, The Winds of War, War and Remembrance, Intruders: They Are Among Us*]. *Dark Shadows* will be the thing that'll be on my gravestone—but I love *Dark Shadows*. I guess it's terrific to have somehow created something that will live forever. It *will* live forever."[1]

Curtis's spooky brainchild is thriving in the 2020s through the 1225 episodes' availability on VHS, DVD, various streaming media, and nightly on the Decades television channel. The Gothic serial has spun off into movies, novels, comic books, puzzles, games, View-Master reels, Dark Shadows Festival fan conventions, Big Finish audio dramas, and even a modern ballet.

In the mid-1960s, as *The CBS Golf Classic* was earning him $100,000 per year, Curtis yearned to try his hand at dramatic television. One night in the summer of 1965, he went to sleep and had a dream that changed the course of television popular culture and the fortunes of the third-place ABC television network. In his dream, Curtis saw a dark-haired young woman riding a train toward a house of dark shadows by the sea—and her destiny. She was a present-day Jane Eyre, soon to be caught up in the intrigues and deceptions of a wealthy, eccentric family and its secrets.

Curtis remembered that he awoke suddenly after the strange dream. "The bedroom was pitch-black, but I could see the figure in my dream clearly—as though I were watching a movie. I saw a girl with long dark hair. She was about 19, and she was reading a letter aboard a train and occasionally staring wistfully out the window." Curtis perceived that the dream girl had been hired as a governess at an old house somewhere on the New England seacoast.

"Then, the train stopped in this dark, isolated town. The girl got off the train and started walking. Finally, she came to a huge, forbidding house. At the door, she lifted a huge brass knocker and gently tapped it three times. I heard a dog howl, and then—just as the door creaked open—I woke up!"[2] Apparently, Curtis, who later mastered the daily cliffhanger on his **Dark Shadows** soap opera, *dreamed* in cliffhangers himself.

"The next morning," he continued, "I wasn't so sure. At breakfast, I told my wife about the dream. When I finished, sure enough, Norma looked at me with wide-eyed enthusiasm and said, 'Dan, that's a great idea for a TV show!' She pointed out that the dream had a Gothic flavor, something eerie and threatening."[3]

Curtis pitched his Gothic idea to ABC executives Brandon Stoddard and Leonard Goldberg. He was supposed to meet with them to discuss a different idea for a series, but his dream of the girl on the train would not leave his mind. Curtis gave ABC that idea instead, to which Goldberg replied, "Dan, haven't you just rewritten Jane *Eyre?*" Curtis's comeback was, "Is anybody doing it on TV right now?"[4]

After briefly considering it as a nighttime program, Curtis and ABC decided to present *Dark Shadows* as a daytime soap opera. It would be videotaped on designer Sy Tomashoff's sets at ABC studios in Manhattan, with Seaview Terrace in Newport, Rhode Island, serving as the exterior of the Collinwood mansion. Robert Costello (*Armstrong Circle Theatre, The Patty Duke Show*) would serve as the producer. The show's stars would be Hollywood film actress Joan Bennett, New York stage actor Louis Edmonds, and (as the governess on the train) newcomer Alexandra Moltke. In the wake of the Monday 8 November 1965 premiere of NBC-TV's *Days of Our Lives,* with classic Hollywood star MacDonald Carey heading the cast, Curtis decided to seek Bennett, an even more celebrated movie star, for the anchor role of Elizabeth Collins Stoddard. *Dark Shadows* debuted on Monday 27 June 1966. Also appearing in the early episodes of the show were Conrad Bain, Nancy Barrett, Joel Crothers, Thayer David, David Ford, Conard Fowkes, Hugh Franklin, David Henesy, Frank Schofield, and Kathryn Leigh Scott. Mitchell Ryan co-starred as Burke Devlin, an adversary of the Collins family.

Dark Shadows **producer Robert Costello (left), creator Dan Curtis, actor David Ford (background), and others attend a cast party in 1967.**

In its first ten months, *Dark Shadows* was a mysterious but tame soap opera with the flavor of the woman-in-jeopardy Gothic novels that were popular in the 1960s and 1970s. Novelists such as Dorothy Daniels, Dan "Marilyn" Ross, Phyllis A. Whitney, and Daoma Winston were filling bookstore shelves with their stories of young women working as governesses in (seemingly haunted) old, dark houses where their lives were in danger from some unseen threat. Dan Ross went on to write 32 Paperback Library novels based on *Dark Shadows* itself and a half-dozen other vampire novels. However, what made for enthralling reading was *not* generating high-spirited (or highly-rated) television. By early 1967, *Dark Shadows* was facing a danger far worse than creaking doors: cancellation.[5]

"When the show went on the air," Curtis observed, "it was the best-kept secret since Oak Ridge. Nobody was watching it."[6] In 1966 and 1967, only nine to ten million viewers (a paltry number, ratings-wise) were following the stories of the neurotic Collins family of Collinsport, Maine—a far cry from the record 16 to 18 million fans who watched the show in 1968, 1969, and early 1970.[7] What turned the show around was another Curtis innovation: a vampire.

Curtis's own daughters suggested that their father make *Dark Shadows* "scarier." As a result, what had begun as an extra-mysterious soap opera only several steps beyond *The Edge of Night* or *The Secret Storm* soon became overtly supernatural. Curtis decided to have fun with *Dark Shadows* and push the envelope since (he thought) the show was going off the air anyway. Curtis had the writers add ghosts, and the ratings increased. Next came a phoenix (Diana Millay) who rose from her ashes and lived again every 100 years. Finally, in April 1967, Curtis and the writers added the character of Barnabas Collins, an 18th-century vampire freed from his chained coffin to terrorize 20th-century Collinsport.

Curtis intended the Barnabas character to be a short-term villain who would kill a few characters and then be destroyed by a stake through the heart. However, Curtis soon realized that Barnabas's portrayer, Shakespearean actor Jonathan Frid, "brought a very Gothic, romantic quality to this role that I guess will live forever."[8] Audiences reacted passionately to the vampire Barnabas, as well as to the witch Angelique (Lara Parker), the werewolf Quentin (David Selby), and the endless stream of ghosts, sorcerers, gypsies, zombies, and mad doctors. Time travel added to the romantic exoticism of *Dark Shadows,* and in mid-1969, as the show was telling a complex tale set in the year 1897, *Dark Shadows* was the highest-rated network program on daytime television.[9] Curtis credited his show with allowing ABC to compete with NBC (*Another World, Concentration*) and CBS (*As the World Turns, Search for Tomorrow*) during the day. Watching *Dark Shadows* led viewers to ABC's other daytime offerings, including *The Dating Game, The Newlywed Game, One Life to Live,* and *Let's Make a Deal,* all of which began runs on ABC between 1965 and 1968.

"The idea was to bring a vampire on as a marauding, evil presence: a Dracula," Curtis reiterated. "There was no other intention. I went off to England to do *Dr. Jekyll and Mr. Hyde* [in 1967], and I said to cast a vampire. And they cast a vampire: they cast Jonathan Frid." Curtis continued,

> Frid was a wonderful actor to work with. He had a particular quality; he had a haunting quality about him. He was very "period" to me; he wasn't

contemporary. He somehow probably encompassed the kinds of shadings that made a Heathcliff or a Rochester or people like that attractive to women. Here's a guy who's supposed to be a vampire and supposed to terrorize people, but he started getting all this fan mail, and I realized there was something really wild going on here. We had to find a way to perpetuate a vampire—I couldn't kill him off now—and this is the way the love story started.[10]

Curtis's "love story" was Barnabas's doomed love for Josette DuPres (Kathryn Leigh Scott), the 18th-century woman who kills herself when she learns that her beloved Barnabas is a vampire. Curtis realized that this somber love story had become central to the appeal and success of his show.

Dark Shadows (1966-1971): **Jonathan Frid (as Barnabas Collins) and Grayson Hall (as Dr. Julia Hoffman) pose for a 1968 photo session.**

"The audience really cared about Barnabas," Curtis admitted, "and he became the reluctant vampire. Now, I know a lot of people have tried that since then, but you really cared about him. So we had to take him from the mode of being this horrifying terror to this guy you feel sorry for."[11]

Barnabas Collins reflected the ambivalent social consciousness and pop psychology of the 1960s in that he was not all bad or all good. The vampire was tragic and guilt-ridden, an idea previously implied in the Universal classics *Dracula's Daughter* (1936),

House of Frankenstein (1944), and *House of Dracula* (1945). A decade before Anne Rice's *Interview with the Vampire* (1976), the complex, multi-faceted, Byronic vampire/anti-hero came of age in Barnabas Collins as the turbulent times posed the questions: should wrongdoers be seen as evil and punished or be considered as victims and rehabilitated? Should Barnabas Collins be despised and staked or pitied and cured? Is vampirism curable like other social diseases? Jonathan Frid often remarked, "I played Barnabas as an alcoholic. I didn't play 'the bite.' I played his problems. He was a guy with a hang-up."[12] As a result, millions of housewives, college students, and school children sympathized with Barnabas and followed his daily exploits. Dr. Julia Hoffman (Grayson Hall) sought to find a cure for him while suffering herself—from unrequited love for the vampire.

Curtis and his writers had hit pay dirt. The ratings skyrocketed for the next several years (until 1970).

Tuxedo-clad composer-conductor Robert Cobert laughs with Dan Curtis during the filming of Cobert's cameo appearance in *War and Remembrance* (1988, 1989). Cobert is nominated for the Emmy Award for his music.

One of the many elements that made *Dark Shadows* so memorable was its distinctive music, composed by the Emmy Award-nominated composer Robert Cobert. "I met Dan Curtis in 1966," Cobert recalled, "and there was an immediate rapport, so I was hired and wrote all of the music for *Dark Shadows*"—20 hours of music cues in all.[13] As for the unforgettable theme song, Cobert said, "I whistled the whole theme to Dan as he was putting golf balls on his office floor. His face lit up, and he said, 'I love it!' We then recorded it with a five-piece orchestra"—alto flute, double bass, vibes, harp, and Yamaha synthesizer.[14]

Julliard-educated Cobert had broken into television in the early 1960s by writing music for dramatic specials (*The Scarlet Pimpernel*, *The Heiress*), game shows (*To Tell the Truth*, *The Price Is Right*), and soap operas (*The Young Marrieds*, *The Doctors*). After *Dark Shadows*, Cobert went on to compose the music for almost every Dan Curtis production. Only *When Every Day Was the Fourth of July*, *The Long Days of Summer*, *Saving Milly*, three unsold pilots, and a public-service announcement feature music scores by composers other than Cobert. In terms of their long creative partnership, Curtis and Cobert were the Alfred Hitchcock and Bernard Herrmann, or the Tim Burton and Danny Elfman, of television.

Cobert recalled, "As the rapport not only held, but grew, I did for Dan, due to his incredible versatility, an unbelievable variety of projects. The best thing about working with 'Big D' is that he'll let me try anything I want to do musically—even when he is violently opposed to my idea—and then make a truly open-minded decision."[15] Dan Curtis called Robert Cobert "the most brilliant composer around, and he's never let me down. The guy just writes dead-perfect scores."[16] A best-selling soundtrack LP of Cobert's *Dark Shadows* music was released in July 1969 and stayed on the *Billboard* music chart for 19 weeks.

"I have absolutely fond memories of *Dark Shadows*," Curtis declared. "We had a great time, and I loved all of those people; we were like a big family. We were trailblazers in those days. We gave ABC a daytime schedule. It was great fun."[17]

The convoluted storyline of *Dark Shadows* can be easily divided into segments that fans refer to as "pre-Barnabas," "1795," "1897," etc. Henry Jenkins, author of *Textual Poachers: Television Fans and Participatory Culture* (Routledge, 1992), points out that each segment "is reduced to a brief phrase, evoked for an audience which has already absorbed its local significance and fit it into the larger sense of the series's development."[18]

The 1966-1967 **pre-Barnabas** episodes concern governess Victoria Winters (Alexandra Moltke) and her exploration of the secrets of her past and their possible link to the Collins family. Burke Devlin (Mitchell Ryan) returns to Collinsport, Maine, in order to settle a score with Roger Collins (Louis Edmonds). Collins Cannery manager Bill Malloy (Frank Schofield) is murdered, and the ensuing investigation involves Roger Collins, Sam Evans (David Ford), Sam's daughter Maggie Evans (Kathryn Leigh Scott), Maggie's boyfriend Joe Haskell (Joel Crothers), Collinwood caretaker Matthew Morgan (Thayer David), and Victoria, who sees Malloy's ghost. Roger's presumed-dead wife Laura Collins (Diana Millay) returns to Collinwood and seeks custody of her and Roger's troubled son David Collins (David Henesy). Laura is a phoenix who almost succeeds in drawing David into the fire that gives her rebirth every century. Elizabeth Collins Stoddard (Joan Bennett) never wants her daughter Carolyn Stoddard (Nancy Barrett) to know what happened to Elizabeth's long-absent husband. Jason McGuire (Dennis Patrick) blackmails Liz about her husband's presumed fate.

In April **1967**, Jason's friend Willie Loomis (John Karlen) releases the vampire Barnabas Collins (Jonathan Frid) from his chained coffin. Barnabas introduces himself to Elizabeth, Roger, and Carolyn as their "cousin from England." The vampire kidnaps Maggie Evans and tries to make her over as his lost love Josette. The experience causes Maggie to suffer a mental breakdown, and she is committed to Windcliff Sanitarium. The ghost of Sarah Collins (Sharon Smyth) visits her there. Maggie's psychiatrist Dr. Julia Hoffman (Grayson Hall) discovers Barnabas's secret and offers to cure him of his vampirism. Barnabas switches his romantic attentions to Victoria. Julia, feeling rejected, intentionally ruins the experimental cure and causes Barnabas to age drastically until he bites Carolyn and rejuvenates. Elizabeth, Roger, Carolyn, Barnabas, Julia, and Victoria hold a séance that sends Vicki back in time.

The **1795** time period (late 1967-early 1968), one of the greatest stories ever told on television, reveals Barnabas's life as a mortal and dramatizes the witch Angelique's curse that caused his vampirism. Victoria finds herself living in 1795 among Barnabas, his little sister Sarah (S. Smyth), and their parents Joshua (L. Edmonds) and Naomi (J. Bennett). Josette DuPres (K.L. Scott) and her family (D. Ford, G. Hall) arrive from Martinique to prepare for Josette's wedding to Barnabas. Josette's maid Angelique (Lara Parker), who wants Barnabas for herself, bewitches Josette and Jeremiah Collins (Anthony George) into marriage and causes countless other supernatural calamities that Abigail Collins (Clarice Blackburn) and the Reverend Trask (Jerry Lacy) blame on Victoria. Angelique marries Barnabas, who still loves Josette and only Josette. Vicki stands trial for witchcraft, and she is defended by Peter Bradford (Roger Davis), who falls in love with her. Barnabas shoots Angelique, who turns him into one of the living dead—a vampire. Before Barnabas can make Josette his vampire bride, Josette jumps to her death from Widow's Hill. When fortune-hunter Lt. Nathan Forbes (J. Crothers) tells Naomi that her son is a vampire, she takes poison and dies. Barnabas kills Forbes for his treachery and walls up Trask for tormenting Vicki. Joshua chains his son in a coffin. Victoria, convicted of witchcraft, is about to be hanged when she suddenly returns to 1968.

The **1968** time period brings Cassandra Collins (actually, Angelique) to Collinwood as Roger's new wife. Dr. Eric Lang (Addison Powell) succeeds where Julia failed: he seemingly cures Barnabas of vampirism. Cassandra begins a Dream Curse that works its way through the Collinses and their friends before it reaches Barnabas and (she hopes) reinstates his vampire curse. The Dream Curse fails because of Barnabas's involvement in Dr. Lang's experiment that brings about the *Frankenstein*-like creation Adam (Robert Rodan). Nicholas Blair (Humbert Allen Astredo), a warlock, takes Adam under his wing. Peter's lookalike Jeff Clark appears in town, and Victoria is certain that he is really Peter Bradford. Nicholas falls for Maggie Evans. Adam kidnaps Carolyn. Cassandra kills Dr. Lang. Julia and Barnabas create Eve (Marie Wallace), a mate for Adam, but she is more interested in Nicholas and Jeff/Peter. Nicholas turns Angelique into a vampire, who bites handyman Tom Jennings (Don Briscoe), Tom's cousin Joe Haskell, and Barnabas. Tom, now a vampire, bites Julia before Barnabas vanquishes him. Vicki (now played, briefly, by Betsy Durkin) and Jeff/Peter vanish together into the past. (Alexandra Moltke Isles has left the TV series to have a baby.) Adam kills Eve and then leaves Collinsport with the help of Professor Stokes (T. David). Tom's brother Chris Jennings (D. Briscoe) comes to town to see his disturbed little sister Amy (Denise Nickerson). Chris has a terrible secret: he is a werewolf. David Collins and Amy Jennings become possessed by the ghosts of Quentin Collins (David Selby) and Beth Chavez (Terry Crawford). Learning that Chris and Quentin's fates are connected, Barnabas uses the I Ching wands to go back in time.

Dark Shadows (1966-1971): Alexandra Moltke (as Vicki the governess) is menaced by Lara Parker (as Cassandra the witch), Robert Rodan (as Adam, the *Frankenstein*-like creation), Jonathan Frid (as Barnabas the vampire), and Humbert Allen Astredo (as Nicholas the warlock) in 1968.

The extremely popular **1897** time period (March-November 1969) takes Barnabas (a vampire again) back to *fin-de-siècle* Collinwood to try to save the life of the werewolf Quentin Collins. Quentin and his friend Evan Hanley (H.A. Astredo), who are demonology enthusiasts, summon a demon and get Angelique, who is attracted to both Barnabas and Quentin. Quentin and his siblings Judith (J. Bennett), Edward (L. Edmonds), and Carl Collins (J. Karlen) quarrel over their inheritance. Reverend Gregory Trask (J. Lacy) establishes a school in town, but his real goal is marrying Judith and taking her share of the Collins fortune. Edward's missing wife Laura Collins (D. Millay) returns for their children Jamison (D. Henesy) and Nora (D. Nickerson). Quentin realizes that Laura is a phoenix. Angelique stops Laura from staking Barnabas. Magda (G. Hall) puts a curse on Quentin for his mistreatment of her sister Jenny (M. Wallace). Quentin becomes a werewolf. Barnabas defeats Laura and vows to help Quentin and his descendants, including Chris. Gregory's daughter Charity Trask (N. Barrett) becomes possessed by the spirit of Pansy Faye, Carl's former fiancée. Magda regrets cursing Quentin and seeks to help him by giving him a magical, severed hand. The hand's owner, Count Andreas Petofi (T. David), comes to Collinwood to take back his hand. Petofi, a powerful warlock, gives painter Charles Delaware Tate (R. Davis) the ability to bring to life whatever he paints. Quentin meets and falls in love with Amanda Harris (Donna McKechnie), a woman brought to life by Tate. Quentin's werewolf curse ends when Tate paints a *Dorian Gray*-like portrait of him. Barnabas meets Lady Kitty Hampshire (K.L. Scott), who is the reincarnation of Josette. After being tormented by Gregory, Judith turns the tables on her avaricious husband. Barnabas makes plans to go away with Kitty/Josette, but he loses his way in the woods.

Dark Shadows takes a sci-fi turn with the **Leviathan** storyline (late 1969-early 1970), in which shapeless, prehistoric entities possess Barnabas (now human again), Elizabeth, David, and Amy in order to regain their dominion over the earth. The ancient Leviathan creatures waylaid Barnabas in the woods and sent him back to 1969 with an ornate box housing the essence of the Leviathan leader who will be born into the present-day world and pave the way for the new Leviathan age. Antique-shop owners Megan and Philip Todd (M. Wallace and Christopher Bernau) become the caretakers of the essence, which grows from baby to boy to teenager to man, Jebez Hawkes (Christopher Pennock), in record time. Jeb falls for Carolyn and wants her to be his Leviathan bride. Elizabeth's husband Paul Stoddard (D. Patrick) returns to Collinwood. Paul is indebted to the Leviathans. Nicholas Blair returns to aid the Leviathan cause. Chris Jennings still suffers from the werewolf curse despite an attempt by his fiancée Sabrina Stuart (Lisa Richards) to free him through the use of a magical moon poppy. Quentin's lookalike Grant Douglas surfaces, and Barnabas and Julia realize that he is indeed Quentin Collins. When Barnabas betrays Jeb, he turns Barnabas back into a vampire. Julia seeks to cure Barnabas, whose bloodlust is becoming uncontrollable. Barnabas turns Megan into a vampire. Searching for Quentin's portrait, Julia finds Angelique, living as a mortal woman, married to millionaire Sky Rumson (Geoffrey Scott), who follows the Leviathan cause. Quentin meets Amanda's lookalike Olivia Corey and realizes that she is his lost love Amanda. However, Quentin loses her to Mr. Best (Emory Bass), the personification of death. Angelique is the keeper of Quentin's portrait, whose image has aged monstrously while Quentin has remained young. Jeb fears the werewolf (stuntman Alex Stevens), the only supernatural being that he cannot control. Carolyn marries Jeb. In the East Wing of Collinwood, Barnabas finds a room that is a portal to another world—Parallel Time. Megan bites Roger before Willie and Julia drive a stake through her heart. Jeb and Barnabas cause the Leviathans to lose their foothold on earth. Barnabas fears that he will lose control and vampirize Maggie Evans, but he feels that his cure may lie in Parallel Time. Despite Julia's warnings of the possible dangers, Barnabas enters the parallel world.

The next *Dark Shadows* storyline (April-July 1970) deals with **1970 Parallel Time**, an alternate universe in which the people of Collinsport, Maine, look the same but lead vastly different lives "because they have made different choices." In this world, Quentin is the master of Collinwood, and Elizabeth and Roger are the poor relations. Quentin, whose wife Angelique has died, returns to Collinwood with a new bride, Maggie Evans Collins. Before Barnabas can introduce himself at Collinwood, he is captured by the frustrated writer William H. Loomis and chained in a coffin while Loomis forces Barnabas to tell him his life story. (Jonathan Frid is away filming *House of Dark Shadows* during Barnabas's off-camera captivity.) Collinwood's housekeeper Miss Hoffman is fiercely loyal to Angelique Collins, even months after Angelique's death, and she despises Maggie. Suddenly, Angelique's twin sister Alexis Stokes shows up, and Hoffman and others are convinced that "Alexis" is really Angelique, returned from the dead. Quentin's friend Dr. Cyrus Longworth (C. Pennock) develops a *Jekyll & Hyde*-type serum that allows him to transform from the meek Cyrus into the cruel, lecherous John Yaeger. John abuses Buffie Harrington (Elizabeth Eis) and kills his blackmailer (John Harkins). Barnabas finally frees himself and introduces himself to Quentin, Elizabeth, and Roger as their "cousin from South America." Alexis truly is Alexis, not Angelique—but then, Angelique herself rises from the dead, kills Alexis, and takes her sister's place at Collinwood. John Yaeger kidnaps Maggie Collins. Dr. Julia Hoffman follows Barnabas to 1970 Parallel Time and kills Miss Hoffman before Hoffman can stake Barnabas. Julia takes Hoffman's place at Collinwood. Barnabas finds the kidnapped Maggie, frees her, and kills John Yaeger. Angelique discovers that "Miss Hoffman" is really Julia and imprisons her in the sub-basement of Collinwood. Barnabas finds Julia with the help of Roxanne Drew (Donna Wandrey), a psychic who is being victimized by Angelique and her father Timothy Stokes. Barnabas vanquishes the Angelique of this world, and in retaliation, Stokes sets fire to Collinwood. Barnabas and Julia become separated from Roxanne, who perishes in the flames.

Through the uncanny powers of the parallel-time portal, Barnabas and Julia instantly find themselves back in their own time band but in the future year of **1995** when Collinwood is in ruins and the Collins family is dead except for Quentin and Carolyn, who are insane. This thrilling two-week-long story arc (20-31 July 1970) is practically a two-person show as Barnabas and Julia explore the shocking ruins of Collinwood and try in vain to get answers from Carolyn and Quentin. Meanwhile, Julia becomes possessed by the ghost of Gerard Stiles (James Storm), who is haunting the ruined mansion. Barnabas and Julia also encounter the spirits of Daphne Harridge (Kate Jackson), Tad Collins (D. Henesy), and Carrie Stokes (Kathy Cody). Julia begs Barnabas to leave 1995 without her before Gerard forces her to harm him. Barnabas replies, "Not without you, Julia—*never* without you."

As suddenly as they appeared in 1995, Barnabas and Julia return to the summer of **1970** and attempt to prevent the prophesied destruction of Collinwood. The ghosts of Gerard and the others are already present in the house, and Gerard and Daphne are controlling David Collins and Hallie Stokes (K. Cody). Meanwhile, Barnabas meets a woman named Roxanne—but the Roxanne of this time band has a terrible secret that her friend Sebastian Shaw (C. Pennock) helps her hide. After Maggie Evans suffers an ordeal similar to her 1967 victimization, Sebastian drives her out of town and to Windcliff Sanitarium. (Kathryn Leigh Scott leaves the show to marry Ben Martin and move to Paris.) Through their investigations, Barnabas and Julia realize that the imminent destruction of Collinwood is linked to the events of the year 1840. The prophesied events come to pass, and Collinwood suffers doom.

Now, in the autumn of 1970, Barnabas and Julia's quest leads them, and later Professor Stokes, through time, back to **1840**, when the present-day threat to Collinwood originated with the powerful warlock Judah Zachery (Michael McGuire) and his possession of Gerard Stiles. Barnabas and Julia introduce themselves as brother and sister. Quentin Collins, having been presumed lost at sea, suddenly returns to Collinwood and his wife Samantha Collins (Virginia Vestoff), who has already married Gerard. Samantha is torn between Quentin and Gerard, both of whom are attracted to Tad's new governess, Daphne Harridge. Angelique, who is passing through town with her servant Laszlo (Michael Stroka), is shocked to find Barnabas out of the coffin, back at Collinwood, and very different from the Barnabas of 1795. Barnabas meets and falls for Roxanne Drew, but Angelique ruins the match by introducing herself at Collinwood as "Valerie Collins," Barnabas's *wife*. Desmond Collins (J. Karlen) returns from his world travels with the magical, disembodied head of Judah Zachery. The head possesses Gerard, who frames Quentin and Desmond for witchcraft. Once again, a room in the East Wing of Collinwood is discovered to be a portal to a very different 1841—a time when Barnabas lived and died a mortal man, married Josette, and had a son, Bramwell. Quentin and Desmond stand trial for witchcraft. Angelique remembers her life in 1692 as a disciple of Judah Zachery. She helps Barnabas, Julia, and Stokes defeat Judah Zachery and exonerate Quentin and Desmond, but she loses her life in the process. Barnabas realizes too late that he has felt love for Angelique all along. Barnabas chases Angelique's killer Lamar Trask (J. Lacy) into the East Wing, where he dies. Barnabas, Julia, and Stokes return to the present time and find a peaceful, happy Collinwood. The stories of the original 1966-1971 characters come to an end.

Beginning in January 1971, the final three months of *Dark Shadows* divorce themselves completely from the regular characters' time band and tell a *Wuthering Heights*-inspired story that recasts Jonathan Frid and Lara Parker. No longer the vampire and the witch, they become Bramwell and Catherine, star-crossed lovers at the Collinwood of **1841 Parallel Time**. (By this time, Frid no longer wishes to play Barnabas, and Parker finally gets her wish to portray the ingénue instead of the villainess. In 1966, she had auditioned for the role of Victoria Winters.) Bramwell is a poor Collins relation who is ambitious and driven. Catherine Harridge loves Bramwell yet marries his cousin Morgan Collins (Keith Prentice). Although the 1841 Parallel Time storyline involves a vicious ghost and a family lottery (inspired by Shirley

Jackson's 1959 novel *The Lottery*), the plot complements the pre-Barnabas episodes in its return to family dynamics, interpersonal relationships, and soap-operatic devices, such as Melanie's secret parentage, Catherine's pregnancy, and Daphne's terminal illness. As *Dark Shadows* draws to a close, Melanie (N. Barrett) learns that her birth mother is Josette Collins (Mary Cooper), and she makes plans to marry Kendrick Young (J. Karlen). Morgan Collins goes mad and dies in a fall. Bramwell and his beloved Catherine defeat the ghost of Brutus Collins (L. Edmonds), and the story ends happily for this alternate Collins family when *Dark Shadows* airs its final episode on Friday 2 April 1971.

Even in its tamer 1966 and 1841 PT days—and certainly in its heyday of vampirism, witchcraft, time travel, lycanthropy, and Leviathans—*Dark Shadows* profited from emotional, convincing, and enthralling writing. Art Wallace, who had written for *Armstrong Circle Theatre* between 1956 and 1960, plotted and scripted most of the first four months of the series (65 episodes). He based some of the characters (e.g. Elizabeth, Jason, Carolyn, Joe) on those in "The House," his television play, performed on CBS-TV's *The Web* in 1954 and again on NBC-TV's *Goodyear TV Playhouse* in 1957. Wallace went on to write the made-for-TV movies *A Tattered Web* (1971) and *She Waits* (1972). Next, screenwriter Francis Swann (*Shine on Harvest Moon*) wrote three dozen *Dark Shadows* episodes, and Ron Sproat (*Love of Life*), one of the show's major writers, turned out 214 scripts. Malcolm Marmorstein (*Peyton Place*) wrote 80 episodes, and Joe Caldwell (*Strange Paradise*) wrote 63. Sproat, Marmorstein, and Dan Curtis co-created the Barnabas Collins character.

Beginning in the fall of 1968, Gordon Russell (*A Flame in the Wind*) and Sam Hall (*Adventures in Paradise*) became the head writers of *Dark Shadows*. Russell and Hall wrote 366 and 316 episodes, respectively. They later co-wrote *One Life to Live*. Ralph Ellis (*A Flame in the Wind*) scripted two DS episodes in February 1969. In March 1969, theatrical press agent Violet Welles began writing for *Dark Shadows* and eventually wrote 84 shows. The writers took many of their story ideas from Dan Curtis himself and his love of things that go bump in the night.

Lela Swift, a director of *Studio One in Hollywood* between 1950 and 1952, directed more episodes of *Dark Shadows* than anyone else—580. They included the first and last episodes plus Curtis's one-shot nighttime *Dark Shadows*-style experiment *Dead of Night: A Darkness at Blaisedon* (1969). Swift went on to direct five episodes of *Wide World Mystery* and more than 825 episodes of *Ryan's Hope*. She passed away on Tuesday 4 August 2015.

Five hundred sixty-eight of the rest of the 1225 episodes of *Dark Shadows* were directed by either Henry Kaplan (*All My Children*), John Sedwick (*The Edge of Night*), or Dan Curtis. Seeing others direct his spooky brainchild inspired Dan Curtis the producer to become Dan Curtis the director. He remembered, "I was producing all the time, and then I finally got to the point where I said, 'This is crazy. I develop the projects; then, I bring in directors, and I tell them what to do.' And I said, 'Why don't I just cut out the middle-man, the director?'"[19]

After spending some time in England and Canada in 1967 to produce the Emmy Award-nominated *Strange Case of Dr. Jekyll and Mr. Hyde* (1968), Curtis returned to the New York studios of *Dark Shadows* and directed a total of 21 daily episodes in 1968 and

1969. "The first time I ever directed was the greatest nightmare that ever happened," Curtis insisted. "I took about two weeks on *Dark Shadows* where I taught myself how to direct—I almost sank ABC while I was doing that—but I've produced *and* directed almost everything I've done since."[20]

His first experience as a director was on episodes #457-461 in March 1968. These episodes delivered the climax of the popular storyline set in 1795-1796, revealing how and why Barnabas Collins became a vampire. Later, Curtis occupied the director's chair for another 1796 interlude, then for three 1969 episodes of the *Turn of the Screw*-like storyline introducing Quentin Collins as a ghost, and finally for six episodes in the 1897 storyline. That saga revealed how and why Quentin became a werewolf. It also changed history by preventing both Quentin's death in 1897 and his existence as a ghost in 1969. Quentin had overcome the werewolf curse and become immortal through a *Dorian Gray*-like portrait, and Dan Curtis had added *director* to his producing and writing credits. His accomplishments throughout the 1970s built on his *Dark Shadows* success and caused the *Los Angeles Times*, in 1978, to crown Curtis "the master of the macabre."[21]

But first, just as *Dark Shadows*, after the introduction of Barnabas Collins, had gone up like a rocket, it eventually came down just as abruptly. In late 1970, some of the audience—as well as Curtis himself—"became disenchanted" with the TV show, in Curtis's words.[22] Indeed, the viewership had fallen from 18 million in 1969 to 12 million in 1970-1971. Curtis admitted that he lost interest in *Dark Shadows* during the last six months of the show.[23] The final episode, set in 1841 Parallel Time, aired on Friday 2 April 1971. The 1971 MGM film *Night of Dark Shadows*, Dan "Marilyn" Ross's *Dark Shadows* novels for Paperback Library, and Gold Key Comics' *Dark Shadows* comic books kept *Dark Shadows* alive in the first half of the 1970s. Then, fanzines such as Kathy Resch's *World of Dark Shadows*, Dale Clark's *Inside the Old House*, and Marcy Robin's *Shadowgram* continued the legacy of the show.

Years later, in both 1988 and 1989, before and after the broadcasts of *War and Remembrance*, NBC entertainment president Brandon Tartikoff approached Dan Curtis about resurrecting *Dark Shadows* as a lavish nighttime dramatic serial—a kind of *Dynasty* with fangs. At first skeptical about revisiting *Dark Shadows* after two decades, Curtis ultimately decided to remake the show, this time with the luxuries of time, money, and film (instead of videotape). He resolved to produce **Dark Shadows** in the much grander, more opulent way that he "and the fans had always wanted to see the series," in his words.[24]

The new *Dark Shadows* was filmed in and around Los Angeles from March to December 1990. After directing the pilot from Monday 19 March to Wednesday 11 April 1990, Curtis directed episodes two, three, and four between Monday 23 July and Tuesday 28 August 1990. Armand Mastroianni (*Tales from the Darkside*), Paul Lynch (the 1980s *Twilight Zone*), Rob Bowman (*Star Trek: The Next Generation*), and Mark Sobel (*Quantum Leap*) directed hours six through 13, with a few retakes directed by Curtis for the 12th and 13th hours. Robert Cobert, of course, returned to furnish the show with his 1960s *Dark Shadows* music cues, as well as many new, eerie, synthesized compositions, performed by a 25-piece orchestra under his direction.

As Curtis was preparing the new *Dark Shadows* in 1989 and 1990, he drew as much inspiration from *House of Dark Shadows* as he did from the television series. With an order first for just a pilot, then for six hours, and finally for 13 hours, the director knew that he would have to condense and streamline the 1967 Barnabas storyline and the 1795 epic, which together had taken a full year's worth of daily episodes to tell. Curtis realized that he, Sam Hall (on board for the new series), and the late Gordon Russell had already condensed the original Barnabas/Maggie story for *House of Dark Shadows*, so he patterned some of the four-million-dollar pilot after that film. Curtis and Hall co-wrote the series with eight other writers: Hall's novelist son Matthew Hall, *Beauty and the Beast* writers M.M. Shelly Moore and Linda Campanelli, Jon Boorstin (*Dream Lover*), Steve Feke (*When a Stranger Calls*), William Gray (*The Changeling*), Hall Powell (*B.L. Stryker*), and Bill Taub (*Supertrain*).

Daphne Budd, the Collinwood employee whom Barnabas attacks in her car at the beginning of *House of Dark Shadows*, becomes Daphne Collins for the 1991 series. Since she is a niece to both Roger Collins (Roy Thinnes) and Elizabeth Collins Stoddard (Jean Simmons), the Roger and Elizabeth of 1991 must have a brother somewhere. Daphne Collins (Rebecca Staab) is attacked in her car by the vampire and then follows the path of the Carolyn Stoddard character in *House of Dark Shadows*. It is Daphne who becomes the vampire, and Curtis shoots her funeral, her undead appearance to young David Collins (Joseph Gordon-Levitt), and her staking by Professor Woodard (Stefan Gierasch) very similarly to the corresponding scenes in *House of Dark Shadows*.

Dark Shadows (1991): Ben Cross (*Nightlife*) stars as Barnabas Collins in NBC's prime-time revival. Star Trek fans know Cross as Sarek, Spock's father, in the 2009 film.

The new Barnabas Collins, played by Ben Cross (*The Unholy*), is more sinister and ferocious than Jonathan Frid's TV Barnabas but not quite the rampaging evildoer of the 1970 movie. Cross's Barnabas has a tortured, vulnerable, romantic side which allows him to fall in love with Victoria Winters (Joanna Going), whom he sees as the reincarnation of Josette DuPres, and which causes him to seek a cure for his vampirism from Dr. Julia Hoffman (Barbara Steele). In the new series, Victoria, not Maggie, resembles Josette and captures Barnabas's heart. In a sign of the times, the new Maggie Evans (Ely Pouget) is a New Age mystic who is having an affair with Roger Collins—something unthinkable on the original series![25] After the Harmonic Convergence in the year 1987, devotees of mysticism believed that a new era had dawned, and their New Age beliefs received a great deal of attention in various media. In a logical step in the updating of *Dark Shadows*, Dan Curtis and his writers acknowledged the new philosophy by reshaping the Maggie character into a New Age psychic.

Dark Shadows (1991): Roy Thinnes (as Roger), Joseph Gordon-Levitt (as David), and Joanna Going (as Victoria) are involved in a never-resolved subplot about David's mother Laura. In 2012, Gordon-Levitt (David Collins '91) and Gulliver McGrath (David Collins '12) play the President's sons in Steven Spielberg's *Lincoln*.

Other considerable changes occur in the characters of Willie Loomis and the Reverend Trask. Jim Fyfe portrays Willie much more comically than even John Karlen did, and Roy Thinnes unwisely plays Trask as a foppish dandy instead of as the frightening, dangerous witchfinder that Jerry Lacy had portrayed. Other surprises in Curtis's 13-hour remake of the 1967 and 1795 storylines are the death of Joe Haskell (Michael Weiss), the manner in which Barnabas becomes a vampire (Josette's doppelganger, not a bat, bites him), the family's use of a Ouija-type board (something that never happened on the original series), and Dr. Hoffman's possession by the spirit of the witch Angelique (played by Lysette Anthony of *A Ghost in Monte Carlo*). The outstanding sixth episode (Friday 1 February 1991) features a lavish costume party at Collinwood and climaxes with the séance that sends Victoria Winters back in time to 1790 and leaves Phyllis Wicke (Ellen Wheeler) in her place.

One of the hallmarks of the series is the dramatic, emotional, and tragic mood that the show almost always maintains (thus why Willie and especially Trask are so jarring). *Terror Television* (McFarland, 2001) author John Kenneth Muir notes that "a sense of overwhelming tragedy dominates this *Dark Shadows* in an almost poetic manner."[26] Except for a few missteps, *Dark Shadows* '91 is a worthy successor to the original series.

Curtis filmed much of *Dark Shadows* '91 at Greystone mansion in Beverly Hills, California. The 55-room Tudor Revival mansion on 18 acres of land was built in 1928 by the oil millionaire Edward Doheny, who earlier in the 1920s had played a role in the Teapot Dome scandal. Doheny gave the mansion to his son Ned and daughter-in-law Lucy. Ned was murdered in the house in 1929; Lucy lived there until 1955. The city of Beverly Hills assumed ownership of Greystone in 1965, and since 1971 it has opened the grounds (but not the house) as a public park. Since 1963, Greystone has been seen in countless movies and TV shows, including *The Day Mars Invaded Earth*, *The Disorderly Orderly*, *General Hospital*, *Hart to Hart*, *The Loved One*, and *Mannix*. Greystone served admirably as Collinwood for *Dark Shadows* (and would again in the 2000s). The mansion also appears in Curtis's *Winds of War*, *War and Remembrance*, and *Intruders* miniseries.

The first four hours of NBC-TV's *Dark Shadows* aired as a miniseries on Sunday-Monday 13-14 January 1991. The show garnered respectable ratings, especially from the coveted 18-34 and 25-54 demographics, and favorable reviews. The *Fort Worth Star-Telegram* called the series "dark, slick, and expertly acted and executed" and "beautifully photographed."[27] *The Hollywood Reporter* complimented the show's "wonderful sets and stately surroundings."[28] *Variety* called it "bloody good" and observed, "Fans will get a rush from the new *Dark Shadows* because, in many ways, it's faithful to the original, and new viewers looking for something to sink their teeth into won't be disappointed, either. Ben Cross and Joanna Going are excellent."[29] The *Chicago Sun-Times* proclaimed, "This Gothic chiller is bound to enchant TV viewers who are swayed by a lovingly designed experiment in style and flavor. [. . .] The vampire's kiss is irresistible!"[30]

The new *Dark Shadows* seemed destined for success—but then, fate intervened and dealt the show a mortal wound. Before the fifth hour could air in its regular Friday-night timeslot on January 18, the Persian Gulf War broke out. News coverage blanketed the TV networks for much of the week, and *Dark Shadows* was lost in the shuffle. Although the Friday 18 January episode aired on the East Coast, it was pre-empted by war coverage on the West Coast and did not air until Friday 25 January, one hour before that night's regularly scheduled episode. A nationwide pre-emption in favor of a showing of *The Empire Strikes Back* (1980) on 22 February did not help, and neither did Brandon Tartikoff's departure from NBC for Paramount Pictures. The new NBC entertainment president, Warren Littlefield, did not seem interested in *Dark Shadows,* and despite fans' "Save *Dark Shadows* Day" demonstrations across the country on Wednesday 8 May 1991, *Dark Shadows* did not appear on NBC's fall schedule. The final episode had aired on Friday 22 March 1991 and had ended with a cliffhanger: Victoria Winters returns from her travels through time with the knowledge that the Barnabas Collins of 1790 and the Barnabas of 1991 are one and the same—and a vampire.

Dan Curtis and the fans were crestfallen that a promising new beginning for *Dark Shadows* had ended so abruptly. Curtis, who had fought NBC for the go-ahead to film 13 hours instead of a mere six, considered keeping the new show alive through a made-for-TV movie or a theatrical feature, but no such sequel materialized. (The mythos of the new series did live on for another two years in the form of a comic-book series from Innovation Comics.) The TV show received the Saturn Award for Best Genre Television Presentation from the Academy of Science-Fiction, Fantasy, and Horror Films, and it won Dee-Dee Petty (*The Last Ride of the Dalton Gang, The Outsiders*) and four other stylists an Emmy Award for hairstyling for the thrilling eighth episode (Friday 15 February 1991), in which Barnabas and his brother Jeremiah (Adrian Paul) fight a duel over Josette and suffer the disastrous effects of Angelique's witchcraft. *Dark Shadows* '91 later reran several times on the Sci-Fi, TNT, and Chiller channels.

One year after the NBC-TV nighttime series, Dan Curtis, in his foreword to Jim Pierson's book, *Dark Shadows Resurrected* (Pomegranate Press, 1992), wrote,

> After a quarter of a century, no one is more surprised than I with the devotion that *Dark Shadows* still commands. I can't believe that it's been going on all these years. When the original daytime series ended in the spring of 1971 and we finished the second theatrical film shortly thereafter, I figured that *Dark Shadows* was a thing of the past.
>
> As the years passed, it became apparent that *Dark Shadows* was much more than just a fond memory. The undying fascination and loyalty for the series were astonishing, and in 1990 I found myself back in the dark corridors of Collinwood, producing a new incarnation of *Dark Shadows* for primetime, weekly television.
>
> I never intended to do *Dark Shadows* again, but the show refused to die, kept alive by legions of passionate fans. Although the new series was given a network life of only 12 episodes, I think we were able to recreate and reinvent the magic that first enthralled viewers so many years ago.[31]

Dark Shadows seized the director's attention once again in the early 2000s. Ever since the short-lived 1991 revival, Curtis had been seeking a way to reincarnate the show yet again. He had considered a theatrical film, a nighttime TV series, a daytime series, an animated series, and even a Broadway musical (with music by Robert Cobert and Rupert Holmes). In early 2002, the Fox network considered making a new, nighttime *Dark Shadows* based on a script by Eric Bernt, writer of the 2000 films *Romeo Must Die* and *Highlander: Endgame,* but Fox eventually passed on the idea.

Finally, in 2003, the WB network, which had enjoyed considerable success with its shows about vampires, super-heroes, and teenagers, greenlighted the pilot for a new, younger, hipper **Dark Shadows**. Executive producers Dan Curtis and John Wells (*ER, The West Wing*) asked Rob Bowman, one of the directors of the 1991 series, to direct the lavish, six-million-dollar pilot film. The scriptwriter was Mark Verheiden, who had written for *Timecop* (1997-1998) and *Smallville* (2001-2011).

Verheiden prepared for the job by watching some 1967 episodes of *Dark Shadows*, the two movies, and all of the 1991 series. Although Dan Curtis wanted to restage the 1967 Barnabas-out-of-the-coffin storyline and the 1795 saga, Verheiden desired a new approach, perhaps one focusing on young David Collins. His ideas brought him into conflict with both Curtis and the WB. "I hate it" is what Verheiden reported that Curtis said to him several times.[32]

Another idea that Verheiden devised was Victoria's witnessing Collinsport locals engaging in an ancient Halloween ritual around a bonfire. Verheiden explained,

> I really wanted to set it in a different world, but that collided with what the network wanted. They were very concerned that it *not* be like a different place. They wanted it to feel like this was a town in "real Maine, USA." It was a valid request but a bit hard to make come together because on *Dark Shadows*, the characters *are* in kind of a strange place—it's just the nature of the Gothic.[33]

Finally, Verheiden crafted a script that once again launched *Dark Shadows* with the arrival via train of Victoria Winters (Marley Shelton) and with Willie Loomis's release of Barnabas Collins (Alec Newman) from the chained coffin. This time, Willie (Matt Czuchry) has a girlfriend, Kelly Greer (Alexis Thorpe), who is present at the unchaining and who becomes Barnabas's first victim. Verheiden was pleased and proud when Peter Roth, head of Warner Brothers, called him and said that the script was "the best he'd read all year."[34]

The 41-minute pilot, filmed at Greystone Mansion in Beverly Hills, also introduces Roger Collins (Martin Donovan), intended to be the J.R. Ewing-like villain to Barnabas's hero; Elizabeth Collins Stoddard (Blair Brown); Carolyn Stoddard (Jessica Chastain); David Collins (Alexander Gould); Dr. Julia Hoffman (Kelly Hu); and several other Collinsport citizens. Curtis wanted to introduce even more characters in the pilot, but Verhdeiden protested that the script was overcrowded. Therefore, there is no Professor Stokes or Professor Woodard character, and there is no Maggie Evans. There is, however, Angelique (Ivana Milicevic), who for the first time is introduced simultaneously with Barnabas and Victoria. The pilot's final, unfinished scene, in which Angelique crashes through the windshield of Victoria's car, would have had to have been redone or even excised before it matched the more serious tone of the rest of the pilot.

A definite misstep is Blair Brown's wrong-headed portrayal of Elizabeth Collins Stoddard. Brown lacks the majesty of Joan Bennett and Jean Simmons, and she does further disservice to the character by playing her as wacky and scatterbrained. Her sitcom-like portrayal does not complement the more serious efforts by Donovan and Newman in their interpretations of Roger and Barnabas. In the early stages of the pilot, the Internet hummed with fans' wishes that Kathryn Leigh Scott, Marie Wallace, or Kate Jackson could have played Elizabeth. In fact, Scott, as well as Susan Sullivan, did audition for the role, but co-producer John Wells pushed for Blair Brown (*Captains and the Kings*).

Dark Shadows (2004): Ivana Milicevic and Alec Newman portray Angelique and Barnabas in the unsold pilot for the WB network. In 2006, both Milicevic (Angelique '04) and Eva Green (Angelique '12) appear in the James Bond film *Casino Royale*. In the 2010s, Newman is the voice of the adult David Collins in *Bloodlust, Bloodline,* and other *Dark Shadows* audio dramas from Big Finish Productions.

Because this is a WB television production, the young men and women are fashionably beautiful as required by the network's distinctive look. Willie Loomis and Joe Haskell (Jason Shaw) could be models, Victoria and Carolyn are extremely attractive, and even Barnabas and Julia have been made more youthful. The reduction in Barnabas's age actually is a wise move because Jonathan Frid and Ben Cross (both in their early forties when they played Barnabas) had been too old for the part. Barnabas had become a vampire when he had been a young man in his early twenties, so it is logical that he would have retained a more youthful appearance in un-death.

Director Rob Bowman had bowed out of the WB project in order to direct *Elektra* (2005), and last-minute replacement director P.J. Hogan, while able to helm an excellent version of *Peter Pan* in 2003, did not quite capture the essence of *Dark Shadows*. Mark Verheiden recalled that Hogan attempted a colorful, overly artistic, "Dario Argento/*Suspiria* look" that Verheiden called "nerve-wracking because the Argento style can be emotionally distancing."[35] Argento was the stylish Italian director of *Deep Red* (1975), *Suspiria* (1977), *Inferno* (1980), *Opera* (1987), and *Trauma* (1993). Critic Mark Dawidziak stated the situation more harshly when he observed, in his talk at the 2005 Dark Shadows Festival, that much of the pilot was "lighted like a French whorehouse." Victoria's overcoat is yellow, the side of a building is blue, and many walls are lighted red. Adding to the weird effect was the musical temp track, which temporarily scored the pilot with cues from *Klute* (1971), *Deep Red* (1975), and *Jennifer Eight* (1992). Post-production work on the pilot never progressed to the point of adding (or even commissioning) Robert Cobert's all-important compositions.

Despite these drawbacks, *Dark Shadows* '04 displayed great promise for a contemporary reinvention of the series. Most of the cast, especially the young women, played their roles very well, and Alec Newman displayed the definite potential for developing into a strong, romantic Barnabas. Having portrayed Paul Atreides in two *Dune* miniseries (2000, 2003) for the Sci-Fi Channel and Victor Frankenstein in the Hallmark Channel's superb 2004 *Frankenstein* miniseries, Newman had proven that he could play a tortured soul. Also, for the first time, the cast of *Dark Shadows* was multicultural. The original series had included only one Asian American and two African Americans in minor, short-term roles, and the 1991 remake had featured one African-American actor in the small role of a police officer. For *Dark Shadows* '04, Dr. Hoffman (Kelly Hu) was Asian-American, Sheriff George Patterson (Michael D. Roberts) was African-American, and the young housekeeper "Sophia" (Jenna Dewan)—not the middle-aged Mrs. Johnson of the two previous series—was described as Latina. Curtis looked forward to a spot for his new show on the WB's fall 2004 schedule.

Nevertheless, when Curtis and co-producer John Wells screened the unfinished pilot for Warner Brothers executives in June 2004, the executives rejected it out of hand and expressed no interest in retooling it. In July, WB chairman Garth Ancier said, "We had a new director [Hogan] come in who was accomplished in movies but frankly didn't do a particularly good job, and the rest is history." Ancier added, "The script was terrific, [but] creatively, the end result did not come out the way we'd all hoped for."[36] The WB had driven a stake through the heart of *Dark Shadows* '04. Lacking post-production, titles, and music, the pilot never was telecast or released on video or DVD. Its only public exhibitions have taken place at Dark Shadows Festival fan conventions.

Dan Curtis, although terribly disappointed, was philosophical. "*Dark Shadows* refuses to die," he declared. "I can never escape it. The new pilot didn't work out, but we're still looking at other possibilities. We've considered a stage version, and it would make a great feature film, so who knows what might happen next?"[37]

The WB later regretted its decision to shelve *Dark Shadows,* for the show's fall 2004 debut would have caught the wave of the similarly mystical and quirky *Lost* and *Desperate Housewives,* which premiered that fall, as well as *Medium* (which began in January 2005) and the *six* horror/sci-fi-themed TV series (including *Supernatural, Invasion,* and *Ghost Whisperer*) that debuted in the fall of 2005. Dan Curtis and replacement director P.J. Hogan had never quite gelled in their visions for *Dark Shadows,* and Curtis felt that a Rob Bowman-directed pilot (if not a Dan Curtis-directed one) would have stood a better chance of successfully reimagining *Dark Shadows* for the 21st century. Curtis died of brain cancer on Monday 27 March 2006—just 20 days after the passing of his wife Norma Mae Klein Curtis—before he could make any further plans for *Dark Shadows.*

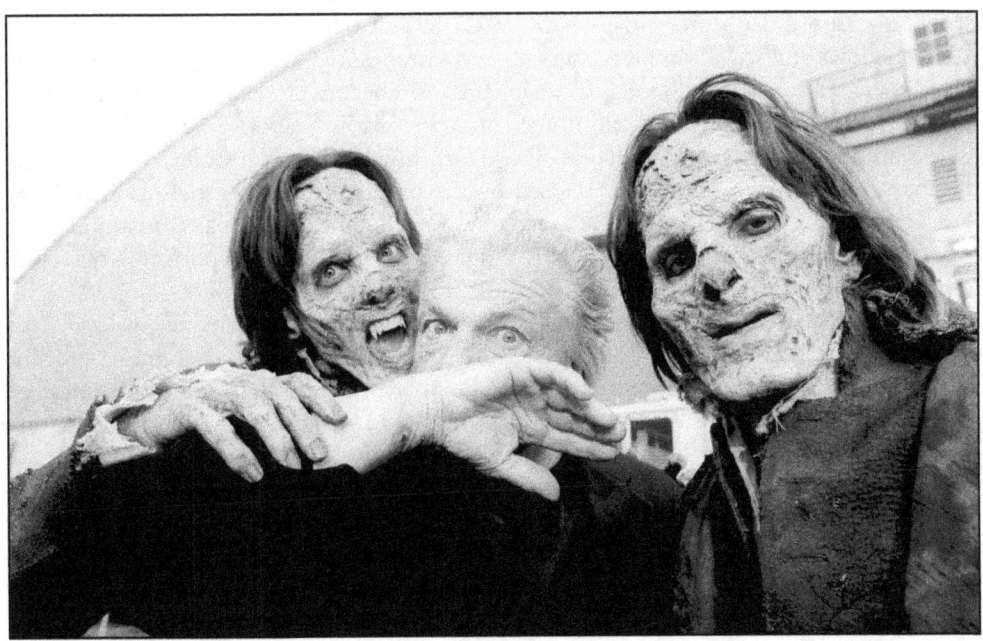

Dark Shadows **(2004): Original *Dark Shadows* actor John Karlen is attacked by "vampires" when he visits the set of the unsold pilot. Karlen does not appear in the pilot film.**

Six years after the producer-director's death, the name Dan Curtis once again flashed across movie screens when Tim Burton's May 2012 film **Dark Shadows** was "dedicated to the memory of Dan Curtis." Curtis's daughters Tracy and Cathy, as well as Jim Pierson, acted as consultants, and *Saving Milly* and *Our Fathers* producer David

Kennedy was one of the producers. Although the music score is composed by Danny Elfman (*Batman Returns, Mars Attacks!*), the very first sound in the film is a bit of Robert Cobert's *Dark Shadows* music cue "The Secret Room." Unfortunately, Cobert's *Dark Shadows* theme, Collinwood theme, Josette's Music Box theme, or other cues are *not* heard in the film, which nevertheless features a dynamic Elfman score and early-1970s-era songs by the Carpenters, Donovan, Elton John, T. Rex, and others.

After an outstanding eight-minute prologue covering the years 1760-1776 and the origin of the relationship between Barnabas Collins (Johnny Depp) and Angelique Bouchard (Eva Green), the action moves ahead to October 1972. The residents of a Collinwood in disrepair are Elizabeth Collins Stoddard (Michelle Pfeiffer), Roger Collins (Jonny Lee Miller), Carolyn Stoddard (Chloe Grace Moretz), David Collins (Gulliver McGrath), Dr. Julia Hoffman (Helena Bonham Carter), caretaker Willie Loomis (Jackie Earle Haley), and housekeeper Mrs. Johnson (Ray Shirley). For the fourth time (1966, 1991, 2004, 2012), Dan Curtis's dream of the governess riding the train is shot—only this time, the governess is Maggie Evans, who adopts the spurious name "Victoria Winters" as the Moody Blues' "Nights in White Satin" is heard. (Simon and Garfunkel's "The Sounds of Silence" was considered for this scene.)

Bella Heathcote plays "Victoria Winters" and the ghost of Josette DuPres, and Josephine Butler plays the ghost of Laura Collins. Collinwood is a cursed house of dark shadows, full of "vampires, ghosts, and witches," in the sarcastic words of an unbelieving Elizabeth Stoddard. However, Liz soon becomes a believer when Barnabas Collins returns to Collinwood and immediately reveals his secret to her and her alone. The vampire proceeds to revitalize the great house and the Collins fish-canning business, which has been all but eclipsed by the preternaturally prosperous Angel Bay Seafood, run by the ageless "Angie" (actually, Angelique). The great Christopher Lee plays an old fisherman employed by Angie until Barnabas hypnotizes him into switching sides.

What *Dark Shadows* '12 does well, it does very well. The dramatic prologue, the design of Collinwood and Collinsport, the period music and costumes, and the scattered moments of drama, romance, and horror are outstanding and in the spirit of the 1966-1971 and 1991 incarnations of *Dark Shadows*. These serious moments are remnants of the original 2008 script by John August (*Big Fish, Corpse Bride*) before Seth Grahame-Smith (*Vendettas, The Hard Times of R.J. Berger*) wrote a new, overly comical revision in late 2010. Now, Mrs. Johnson, Willie, Julia, and sometimes even Barnabas and Angelique are played for laughs. Mrs. Johnson, who never speaks, cleans around Barnabas as he hangs upside down like a bat or sleeps in cupboards. Willie and Julia are alcoholics. Barnabas befriends a group of hippies but then slaughters them. Angelique seduces Barnabas in an utterly out-of-control scene that has the lovers hurling each other against walls, breaking furniture, and rolling around on the ceiling as Barry White's 1974 song "You're the First, the Last, My Everything" blares on the soundtrack. At one point, Angelique has a lizard's tongue. "The scene doesn't even make sense," according to the *Boston Globe*.[38]

In the final 20 minutes of the film, *Dark Shadows* '12 goes completely out of all reason as Angelique spews green vomit on Barnabas, Liz totes a shotgun, the paintings and sculptures in Collinwood come to life, Angelique cracks and crumbles like a porcelain doll, Collinwood is wrecked and burned, Angelique pulls her heart out of her body, and a character turns into a werewolf! Barnabas and Victoria, whose courtship is not given nearly enough screen time, share a life-changing experience, and the final shot shows another character turning into a vampire. Most viewers are left exhausted after these head-spinning, overblown events. Justin Chang of *Variety* noted the "FX-laden climax that desperately conjures up everything from *Rebecca* to *Death Becomes Her*."[39] Ty Burr of the *Boston Globe* observed that "the last half-hour is a traffic jam of silly ideas like a werewolf out of nowhere."[40] Granted, both the original *Dark Shadows* and the 1991 revival had a few comic characters and a few funny moments (intentional or unintentional), but Dan Curtis and Art Wallace's concept of the show was that of a serious drama and not a sitcom or a farce.

A highlight of the 2012 film—in addition to the serious prologue—is the grand party that the Collins family throws at Barnabas and Carolyn's urging. Since this is 1972, Alice Cooper (playing himself) entertains the guests with his songs "No More Mr. Nice Guy" and "The Ballad of Dwight Fry." The latter song is introduced by Carolyn in a sly nod to the original show's mystery surrounding her absent father—"Mommy, where's Daddy? He's been gone for so long. Do you think he'll *ever* come home?"

Barnabas, Quentin, and the Rock Star: Jonathan Frid (left), Alice Cooper, and David Selby prepare to shoot the party scene in Tim Burton's *Dark Shadows* (2012).

At Pinewood Studios in July 2011, original *Dark Shadows* stars Jonathan Frid (left), Lara Parker, Kathryn Leigh Scott, and David Selby (standing), wearing their 1972-era costumes, are ready to shoot the party scene in Tim Burton's *Dark Shadows* (2012). Frid dies on 14 April 2012, one month before the May 11 release of Burton's film.

Fans of Curtis's original series were delighted to see Jonathan Frid, Lara Parker, Kathryn Leigh Scott, and David Selby as four party guests whom Elizabeth and Barnabas welcome. The four *Dark Shadows* stars journeyed to England in early July 2011 and filmed the party scene at Pinewood Studios where the Collinwood and Collinsport sets were housed. Jonathan Frid, the first and definitive Barnabas, died nine months after he filmed his cameo role and just one month before this film was released.

Needless to say, reactions to *Dark Shadows* '12 ran the gamut from love to indifference to disappointment to hate. Many diehard fans disliked the silly elements, but many others were more receptive to the tongue-in-cheek treatment. Some fans concluded that DS '12 succeeds as an entertaining vampire movie (especially to viewers who have no knowledge of *Dark Shadows*) but it fails as a *Dark Shadows* movie because of the rampant silliness and excess. In other words, *Dark Shadows* '12 is a typical Tim Burton movie, but it is not a *Dark Shadows* movie. At least, there are a half-dozen shots of the familiar waves crashing against the rocks (but no Cobert theme song to go with them).

The New York Times called Tim Burton's *Dark Shadows* "Mr. Burton's most pleasurable film in years" and praised the director's "exquisite detail work, his playfulness, and his macabre wit. [. . .] There is also something of a story, mostly involving Barnabas's true love, if anyone's interested, though traditional storytelling has never been Mr. Burton's specialty or perhaps interest. What counts in his work is the telling, not the tale."[41]

Variety noted, "Burton and Depp have cited Curtis's creation as a formative influence, and together with scenarist Seth Grahame-Smith, they have paid tribute to the show's legacy in predictably whimsical, irreverent fashion." Reviewer Justin Chang continued,

> With a smirk and a wink, the filmmakers have inflated an enduring relic into an extravagantly empty postmodern artifact, an object lesson in the perils of camping up a property that had no shortage of camp to begin with. [. . .] Outfitting ABC's cult-worshipped, occult-themed soap opera with super-slick production values and a tone that veers unsteadily between kooky comedy and Gothic horror, this bizarre but weirdly bloodless retro-camp exercise is neither funny nor eerie enough to seduce the uninitiated and will court bemused reactions at best from the series's still-estimable fan following. The picture's pedigree could intrigue audiences for a spell, but long-term box-office bewitchment seems unlikely.[42]

Boston Globe reviewer Ty Burr, while finding some fault with the movie, declared, "Tim Burton has got his groove back [. . .] after the cluttered pointlessness of *Alice in Wonderland* and *Charlie and the Chocolate Factory*. [. . .] *Dark Shadows* doesn't pretend to be anything more than an entertainment, but it recaptures the experience of watching the Gothic daytime soap opera with rapturous comic bliss."[43]

Michael Logan of *TV Guide* quoted *Night of Dark Shadows* star and 2012 party guest David Selby:

> Burton not only dedicates the film to Dan Curtis, the late creator of *Dark Shadows,* but he also casts some of the show's top stars in cameo roles, including Jonathan Frid (who died at 87 just last month), David Selby (Quentin), Kathryn Leigh Scott (Josette), and Lara Parker (Angelique). They have become the film's biggest boosters. "I have complete confidence in Tim Burton's vision," says Selby. "It's good to put a fresh perspective on what we did so many years ago. The fans who are upset have to remember that when we made the series, we screwed with beloved monster movies and turned them upside down! We were hardly reverent ourselves."[44]

Jay Stone, in the St. John, New Brunswick, *Telegraph-Journal,* called *Dark Shadows* "something unusual: a long and scattered romp,"[45] and Lisa Kennedy, in the *Denver Post,* dubbed the film "an often amusing, teasingly naughty lark."[46] In *Shadowgram* #122/123 (January 2014), editor Marcy Robin reported the *Entertainment Weekly* review of the movie trailer that premiered both on TV's *Ellen* and on the Internet on Thursday 15 March 2012.[47] Without even seeing the entire film, *E. Weekly* seemed to grasp its problems:

> Ultimately, it "plays for laughs" but starts as "straight-up Gothic horror: an 18th-century romance, a jealous witch, a freshly-born vampire craving blood, a hushed ghost whispering, 'He's coming.'" It then "turns on the laugh track" and "takes its source material not so seriously. When the buried undead bloodsucker Barnabas is freed from his tomb in the year 1972, he finds the time period…a little funky," and later "things even get a little kinky" with "a surreal love scene." It "sets up a kind of comedic, supernatural version of *Fatal Attraction* as Barnabas and Angelique war with each other, with his decadent Me Decade family caught in the crossfire…. Those craving serious treatment of the material may be disappointed, but fans of Burton's twisted sense of humor who don't come with major expectations may be surprised to find this movie is more farce than horror."[48]

Shades of *Night of Dark Shadows*: Burton's film seemed incomplete because certain scenes seemed to be missing. *Shadowgram* #122/123 revealed a very illuminating *Syndicated* report from Thursday 20 September 2012:

> Warner Brothers has released a set of deleted scenes. Now, we've got some idea of what happened to some of that missing character development as apparently several key scenes were cut in favor of other, more dramatic scenes or perhaps more humorous scenes. These seem like they were perhaps meant to be funny but didn't quite turn out. The character-driven scenes: 1. An important interaction between Barnabas and David as they discuss prehistoric dinosaurs and early Collins family history. 2. Dr. Hoffman is shown to hold some concern for Victoria. 3. Hoffman and Elizabeth discuss Barnabas's eccentricities, which not only deepens the relationship between these two characters but also shows a little more of the distrust for Barnabas's story that any rational person would have had in their situations. 4. The conversation between Carolyn and Victoria which is hinted at later, but we never see. It also foreshadows the transformation of her character at the film's climax, something that was sorely lacking in the final cut. 5. A scene that shows that the townspeople actually noticed that people were getting killed out in the woods. These are all outstanding, and I question the decision to remove any of them. Perhaps, the scenes showed poor pacing where they sat—it'd be hard to tell without rewatching the film with them in it—or perhaps it wasn't Burton's decision to remove any of them. Either way, even just watching them after the fact, they improve the film immensely and make the greater vision of *Dark Shadows* more apparent.[49]

Because of the film's mid-level performance at the box office (especially in the United States), no sequel to *Dark Shadows* materialized. Nevertheless, the Gothic serial has returned from the dead, time and again, in movies, novels, comic books, toys, Big

Finish CD dramas, and even a ballet, so Dan Curtis's 55-year-old dream of the governess on the train may yet resurface in multimedia. *Dark Shadows* is only one of the indelible marks that the versatile director has made on popular culture.

That impact was celebrated in 2019 with the release on DVD and Blu-Ray of ***Master of Dark Shadows: The Gothic World of Dan Curtis***. Presented by "MPI Media Group, in association with Severin Films and Dan Curtis Productions," *Master of Dark Shadows* is a feature-length work, scored to Robert Cobert's music, *about* the great producer-director and his spooky brainchild. The documentary is narrated by Dan Curtis's friend Ian McShane (*War and Remembrance, Deadwood*) and directed by David Gregory (*Plague Town, The Theatre Bizarre*). The prolific Gregory has directed more than 200 DVD/Blu-Ray extras, featuring interviews with Dario Argento, Karen Black, Christopher Lee, Richard Matheson, Franco Nero, Paula Prentiss, Charlotte Rampling, Ken Russell, Barbara Steele, Raquel Welch, and dozens of other genre luminaries. Gregory is also the director of the 2014 documentary feature *Lost Soul: The Doomed Journey of Richard Stanley's "Island of Doctor Moreau,"* about the troubled 1996 production starring Marlon Brando, Val Kilmer, and Ron Perlman.

Master of Dark Shadows (2019) features a rare ABC *Dark Shadows* promo (narrated by Paul Frees) featuring Alexandra Moltke running away from Seaview Terrace, the cliffside mansion in Newport, Rhode Island.

The 2019 Dan Curtis documentary reveals a bit of information about and pictures of the young Curtis although daughter Tracy Curtis reveals in her interview that Curtis did not talk about his early family life very often. Both she and her sister Cathy Curtis mention that their mother Norma Curtis always gave her opinions about Curtis's ideas and projects and Curtis listened to her. Tracy Curtis adds that her father was "always working—always reading scripts and books" for his next big idea. Some of those books came from his New York secretary Rita Fein, who in the late 1960s would bring horror books back to her boss from her travels. "He had a frightening intensity," Fein remembers in her interview, but she knew that Dan Curtis also was very sensitive. In fact, she mentions a moment in the mid-1960s when she looked over at him and saw that he "was crying." Barbara Steele concurs: "Behind that cloak of largesse, there was a very vulnerable person. He couldn't have been so intuitive without it."

In addition to rare family pictures and home movies, *Master of Dark Shadows* affords viewers clips of Curtis's *CBS Match-Play Golf Classic*, Art Wallace's television play "The House," ABC's early promos for *Dark Shadows*, and Jonathan Frid's public appearances. The late Frid and Curtis appear in archive footage from the 1990s and the 2000s, but the other 30 interviewees appear in new footage shot since 2016. Some of the *Dark Shadows* stars are seen sitting inside Lyndhurst in Tarrytown, New York, or the Vista Theatre in Los Angeles, California. *Dark Shadows* writer Joe Caldwell sits for his interview inside the now demolished *Dark Shadows* TV studio that stood (until September 2017) at 433 West 53rd Street in Manhattan. Robert Cobert appears in his Southern California home while his unmistakable music for *Dark Shadows, The Great Ice Rip-Off, Supertrain*, and other Dan Curtis productions artfully underscores the entire documentary.

Cobert declares that "*Dark Shadows* changed the face of daytime television." Former ABC-TV executives Michael Brockman and Leonard Goldberg further discuss the Gothic serial as do *Dark Shadows* stars Nancy Barrett, Roger Davis, John Karlen, Jerry Lacy, Lara Parker, Christopher Pennock, Kathryn Leigh Scott, David Selby, James Storm, and Marie Wallace. Pictures or clips of other *Dark Shadows* performers (including Grayson Hall) and writers (including Ron Sproat) appear in the film.

David Gregory's documentary, produced by Jim Pierson, reveals Dan Curtis to be a tireless and determined *auteur* of *Dark Shadows* and his other horror and war productions. *Dark Shadows* writer Malcolm Marmorstein, who wrote 80 episodes, claims that the writers sometimes had "24-hour story sessions" in order to keep the ideas and plots flowing, and fellow writer Joe Caldwell, who wrote 63 episodes, remembers, "Dan kept saying, 'How can we make it better?'" Lara Parker acknowledges that Dan Curtis "gave us all our starts," and James Storm insists that Curtis "was always on my side, and I really was incredibly indebted to him."

David Selby discusses his "theme song," "Quentin's Theme" (originally written by Cobert for *The Strange Case of Dr. Jekyll and Mr. Hyde*), and his gratitude for having been on *Dark Shadows* and having played the unique role of Quentin Collins. "It was a respite to go to the studio because of what was going on around us" (i.e. news of the Vietnam War, social unrest, and assassinations). Selby playfully adds, "The actors were just as eccentric as the characters they played!"

Dark Shadows star Kathryn Leigh Scott keeps the Gothic serial alive by writing books about the show, playing her *Dark Shadows* character Maggie Evans in Big Finish audio dramas, appearing in *Master of Dark Shadows,* and reading aloud Dan "Marilyn" Ross's Paperback Library *Dark Shadows* novels on compact disc.

The documentary also covers *The Winds of War, War and Remembrance*, and all incarnations of *Dark Shadows*, including the 1970, 1971, and 2012 films. Barbara Steele, Ben Cross, and director Armand Mastroiani discuss the 1991 *Dark Shadows* series, and Alec Newman and writer Mark Verheiden remember the never-aired 2004 WB pilot. Steele remarks that her co-star Cross "was great because he looks like a medieval gargoyle." Cross reveals, "I felt lucky and blessed to be on *Dark Shadows*. No one on the set worked harder than Dan Curtis, [and] if he didn't like something, boy, did you know it!"

Fifteen years after the project, Alec Newman still feels terribly disappointed that the 2004 WB pilot—"a sure thing, certain to be picked up" as a series, everyone believed—was rejected and never finished. Nevertheless, Newman says, "I loved being a tiny part of that world [of *Dark Shadows*] that people are really passionate about." Ironically, Alec Newman is the embodiment of writer Malcolm Marmorstein's vision for the character of Barnabas Collins back in 1967 when Marmorstein urged Dan Curtis to "get a young blond guy" to play the vampire! Marmorstein did *not* want "a Bela Lugosi type." The writer says that his premise was that no one in Collinsport, Maine, had ever read *Dracula* or seen a Bela Lugosi movie. Vampires were unknown there.

Also seen in *Master of Dark Shadows* are Paley Center for Media curators David Bushman and Ron Simon, former *16* magazine associate editor Nola Leone, Jonathan Frid's business partner Mary O'Leary, Dan Curtis's frequent collaborator William F. Nolan, and long-time *Dark Shadows* fan Whoopi Goldberg, who claims that the original series was "right up my alley" because "these were characters that were talking to *you*," i.e. us the young viewers. The Oscar-winning comedian admits that she loved Barnabas and Quentin. "Jonathan Frid's picture was on my wall because I wanted to get bit!" As for the werewolf, "I would have taken that bite, also," she laughs.

Master of Dark Shadows is an outstanding tribute to a producer-director who had an impact on many lives and definitely left his mark. As Nancy Barrett exclaims, "If you were in the middle of the Atlantic Ocean, in a leaky rowboat with one oar, you would want Dan Curtis in that boat with you because he would figure out a way to save your neck!" [50]

Premiere screenings of *Master of Dark Shadows*, attended by *Dark Shadows* stars and fans, took place at the Los Angeles Airport Westin Hotel on Saturday 20 October 2018 and at the Paley Center for Media in New York City on Saturday 13 April 2019. October 2018 proved to be a momentous month for all things Dan Curtis. First, the New York branch of the Miskatonic Institute of Horror Studies celebrated made-for-TV horror in general and Dan Curtis in particular. At the Brooklyn Horror-Film Festival on October 13, author and TV-movie expert Amanda Reyes presented "Big Scares on the Small Screen: A Brief History of the Made-for-TV Horror Film." Then, back at the Paley Center for Media in NYC on October 25, curator David Bushman presented "Dan Curtis: Old School/New School." Bushman discussed how the scary productions of Dan Curtis blended elements of classic horror and modern horror and went on to influence today's horror properties and their creators. Finally, on Monday 29 October 2018, the Decades television network began airing *Dark Shadows* weeknights at midnight (11:00 PM Central time).

More and more viewers in the 2020s are being exposed to *Dark Shadows*. Although the show is readily available on VHS, DVD, and various streaming media, the Decades network, like the Sci-Fi Channel 20+ years earlier, is providing fans the excitement of seeing their favorite show *on* television again. "Tune in tomorrow" is what *Dark Shadows*—and soap operas in general—are all about.

Significa from the House of Dan Curtis: Forty-five years before Barnabas Collins of *Dark Shadows* emerged from his chained coffin and found a lookalike for his lost love Josette—and ten years before a similar scenario occurred in Karl Freund's *The Mummy*—Harry Houdini wrote and starred in director Burton L. King's *The Man from Beyond*. Released on Sunday 2 April 1922, the film concerns "Howard Hillary," who comes back to life after being frozen in the Arctic for 100 years and finds a modern-day reincarnation of his lost love ("Marie," played by Nita Naldi of *Dr. Jekyll and Mr. Hyde*).[51]

Significa from the House of Dan Curtis: On ABC-TV's *Dark Shadows* (1966-1971), the interiors of the Collinwood mansion were Sy Tomashoff's beautiful sets inside the *Dark Shadows* studio at 24 West 67th Street (1966)—and later 433 West 53rd Street (1966-1971)—in New York City. The exterior of Collinwood was Seaview Terrace, now known as the Carey Mansion, on Ruggles Avenue in Newport, Rhode Island. The 65-room mansion is situated near The Breakers and other famous Gilded Age homes along Newport's seaside "Cliff Walk."

In 1927-1929, Washington DC businessman Edson Bradley built up Seaview Terrace around James Kernochan's former residence "Seaview," which had been constructed in 1885. Architect Howard Greenley designed the new house for Mr. and Mrs. Bradley. Greenley also designed the Prince George Hotel in New York City and the Corning Free Academy in Corning, New York.

For much of the 1930s, Seaview Terrace was home to the Bradleys' daughter Julia and her husband Herbert Shipman. In the 1940s, the great house became the quarters for World War II army officers, and around 1950, it became a private school for girls. In 1974, the Carey family of New York purchased Seaview Terrace and renamed it the Carey Mansion. The French Renaissance manor house still belongs to the Careys, who for decades leased it to Salve Regina University as a recital hall and a student dormitory. Then, in mid-2009, the Careys ended their affiliation with Salve Regina and turned Seaview Terrace back into a private residence. In 2009-2010, Denise Carey refurbished most of the house. In 2016, writer-director Charlie McDowell filmed part of his 2017 Netflix film *The Discovery*, starring Robert Redford and Mary Steenburgen, at Seaview Terrace.[52]

Significa from the House of Dan Curtis: The first seven *Dark Shadows* stars to say the word "vampire" on the show are, in order, Lara Parker, Thayer David, Jonathan Frid, Louis Edmonds, Joel Crothers, Addison Powell, and Grayson Hall.

From left, actor Denholm Elliott, director Charles Jarrott, and producer Dan Curtis converse on the set of *The Strange Case of Dr. Jekyll and Mr. Hyde* (1968).

CHAPTER II

The Horrors
Kolchak, Norliss, Trilogies, and More

The various incarnations of *Dark Shadows* are only a fraction of Dan Curtis's horror output from the 1960s to the 2000s. In 1967, around the time of the casting of Jonathan Frid as Barnabas Collins, Curtis took a break from *Dark Shadows* and began preparing a prestigious TV adaptation of Robert Louis Stevenson's 1886 novel, ***The Strange Case of Dr. Jekyll and Mr. Hyde.*** (Curtis and Stevenson share the curious trait that both *Dark Shadows* and *Jekyll and Hyde* came to their creators in vivid dreams.) The plan was for Rod Serling to write the script, Jason Robards to play Jekyll and Hyde, and Curtis to produce the drama in London. Suddenly, both Serling's script and Robards's services became unavailable, and Curtis had to rethink the production. He hired Jack Palance to star and moved the taping back to New York near the *Dark Shadows* studio. Then, a technicians' strike forced Curtis to move once again, this time to Toronto. Sets for the production had already been built in New York, but Curtis had to start all over with new sets in Canada.

Curtis had hired an accomplished director when he had been in London. Since 1960, Charles Jarrott had directed episodes of the BBC-TV series *Armchair Theatre*, *The Wednesday Play*, and *Haunted*. Jarrott agreed to follow Curtis's production to New York and finally to Toronto. Curtis's script writer was Ian McLellan Hunter, who had written some *Dr. Christian* and *Mr. District Attorney* movies and more recently had scripted the TV series *The Adventures of Robin Hood* (1955-1958) and *The Defenders* (1961-1965).

Hunter's script is one of the more nearly faithful adaptations of Stevenson's story, which has been filmed for movies and television six dozen times, beginning in 1908. Of course, a *completely* faithful filming has never materialized, for it would be devoid of women and probably of heterosexuality. According to critic Elaine Showalter, "While there have been over 70 films and television versions of *Dr. Jekyll and Mr. Hyde*, not one tells the story as Stevenson wrote it—that is, as a story about men."[1]

The dance-hall girls and female prostitutes who populate almost all of the screen adaptations of *The Strange Case of Dr. Jekyll and Mr. Hyde* are not found in Stevenson's novel. It is the story of the London solicitor Gabriel John Utterson, his cousin and dear friend Richard Enfield, and his secretary and confidant Mr. Guest. It is also the story of the prominent physician Dr. Henry Jekyll, his formerly close (now estranged) friend Dr. Hastie Lanyon, and his devoted butler Poole. This is a world of powerful men—doctors, lawyers, educators, even a member of Parliament—and women play little or no part in this world except as servants. Utterson and Enfield take a much-anticipated walk together every Sunday afternoon, and Dr. Jekyll often holds jovial dinner parties for the male intelligentsia of London. None of the men seem to have, need, or want women in their lives; instead, they find fulfillment in their important work and in each other's company.

Ian Hunter's script hints at this circumstance when Drs. Lanyon and Jekyll goad each other by pointing out that neither has a woman in his life, but both men quickly agree that their work makes their lives complete. What Stevenson's novel hints at more concretely (but still nebulously enough for polite reading society) is that these men make up London's hidden but quite organized homosexual community of the late 19th century and that Jekyll's alter-ego Mr. Edward Hyde represents the unbridled, socially taboo homosexual nature that these Victorian men must *hide*. In "Henry Jekyll's Full Statement of the Case," the tenth and final chapter of the novel, Jekyll never reveals the exact nature of his "irregularities" and his "profound duplicity of life," but he confesses that he "hid them with an almost morbid sense of shame."[2] In chapter nine, "Doctor Lanyon's Narrative," Jekyll's estranged friend is equally cryptic. "What he [Jekyll] told me in the next hour I cannot bring my mind to set on paper. I saw what I saw, I heard what I heard, and my soul sickened at it," Lanyon admits. "As for the moral turpitude that the man unveiled to me, even with tears of penitence, I cannot, even in memory, dwell on it without a start of horror."[3] Stevenson allows the reader to decide the exact nature of Henry Jekyll's questionable acts, which began in his youth and continued to the time of this confession and his death.

Almost all screen adaptations of *The Strange Case of Dr. Jekyll and Mr. Hyde* are based most heavily on these final two chapters, in which Jekyll's experiments and Hyde's misdeeds are revealed. The first eight chapters detail Utterson's investigation of the mystery surrounding Jekyll. Readers in 1886 did not realize that Jekyll and Hyde were the same man until the last two chapters, which provided the fantastical explanation. Only the 2004 Australian short film *The Strange Game of Hyde and Seek*, directed by Nathan Hill, approaches the story as Utterson's investigation and not chiefly as Jekyll's story. Paolo Barzman's 2008 *Jekyll and Hyde* TV-movie, set in present-day Boston, divides its time between Jekyll's activities and a female attorney's thorough investigation of Hyde's string of murders.

Of course, a straightforward presentation of the events as Dr. Jekyll experiences them first-hand is a richer cinematic construction than Utterson's mere study of the events. Therefore, the Dr. Jekyll character always is the protagonist, and Utterson, Lanyon, and especially Enfield are often not even included in the film.

Ian McLellan Hunter's Edgar Award-winning script for Curtis does include Enfield (Geoffrey Alexander), Lanyon (Leo Genn), and Utterson although the latter's name is changed to George Devlin (Denholm Elliott). While shifting the focus to Jekyll (Jack Palance), the script, set in London in 1888, remains faithful to the tone of Stevenson's novel. Devlin looks into the matter of Hyde (as Utterson does in the novel), quizzes Jekyll about him, and asks if Hyde is blackmailing Jekyll. Jekyll and Lanyon's strained friendship plays a part as does the faithfulness of Jekyll's butler Poole (Gillie Fenwick). The script also recreates the scene in which Poole summons Jekyll's solicitor to investigate Hyde's pathetic howling in Jekyll's laboratory while, in Stevenson's words in chapter eight, "the whole of the servants, men and women, stood huddled together like a flock of sheep" in their fright.[4] Although in the novel Hyde beats Sir Danvers Carew to death, in this version Hyde beats but does not kill Dr. Lanyon, and although in the novel Hyde changes back to Jekyll before Lanyon's eyes, here Hyde transforms in front of Devlin. The adaptation forgoes Jekyll's suicide for a more sensational climax, a deadly confrontation between Devlin and Hyde in the very room (the hospital amphitheatre) where the movie opens.

The Strange Case of Dr. Jekyll and Mr. Hyde (1968): Jack Palance, in Dick Smith's frightening makeup, portrays Mr. Hyde. Smith goes on to create makeup for two *Godfather* movies and two *Exorcist* movies and to win an Academy Award for *Amadeus* (1984).

In the same vein as Gabriel Utterson's investigation of Edward Hyde's actions, this Henry Jekyll must investigate Mr. Hyde's actions of the night before because Jekyll, at first, has no knowledge of what Hyde has done. This search leads Jekyll to Tessie O'Toole's Windmill music hall, a necessary invention of scriptwriter Hunter's in order to inject heterosexuality and women's roles into the teleplay. Tessie (played by Tessie O'Shea) is a chanteuse and madam who warmly welcomes Dr. Jekyll and informs him that Mr. Hyde "took a real shine to" her employee Gwyneth Thomas, a "dancer" who also privately entertains men in the upstairs "dining rooms." As Gwyneth, Billie Whitelaw (*The Flesh and the Fiends*) provides Mr. Hyde with a female object of desire. However, Hunter offers another subtle hint at Jekyll's "irregularities" when on two different occasions Gwyn offers Jekyll a "cure" for his (in her word) "shyness," which could connote sexual repression, impotence, or homosexuality.

The Strange Case of Dr. Jekyll and Mr. Hyde debuted on the Canadian Broadcasting Corporation network (CBC) on Wednesday 3 January 1968, and it first aired on the American Broadcasting Company network (ABC) on Sunday 7 January. The production received overwhelmingly positive reviews. "It was incredibly gratifying," Dan Curtis remembered. "The reviews on that thing were absolutely incredible."[5] The *Baltimore Sun* raved,

> Dan Curtis, producer of *The Strange Case of Dr. Jekyll and Mr. Hyde*, introduced on ABC last Sunday, made good on all his promises. It was indeed a version of the Robert Louis Stevenson story never before seen in photoplay or television form; it adhered closely to the book; and the artistry of Dick Smith, master of makeup, did surpass anything seen in earlier transformations. What's more, the production, co-produced by the Canadian Broadcasting Corporation, surpassed the best version hitherto offered—the one in which Fredric March played the title role [and won an Oscar for it]. Jack Palance is the new champion in this difficult assignment, and he may hold the title for a long time.[6]

The *Boston Globe* concurred: "Jack Palance, a rugged villain from way back, for my money was the best Jekyll-and-Hyde yet to come along."[7] The *Sacramento Union* added,

> With its overpowering sense of time and place, the production proved immensely effective, all very dark and shadowy and Gothic—and scary. I bow to Dan Curtis and Charles Jarrott, producer and director, for framing the yarn so adeptly. Robert Cobert's music was properly spooky, too, alive with jabs of tense foreboding.[8]

The Strange Case of Dr. Jekyll and Mr. Hyde is scored with *Dark Shadows* music—in a way. Although *Dark Shadows* fans who watch the program today recognize almost every note of music as coming from the 1968-1971 years of the TV series, these music cues actually originated in this 1968 production. Cobert later re-recorded them for use on *Dark Shadows*, and these actual cues were used as the music score of *House of Dark Shadows* two years later. The heartbreaking, operatic music heard at Jekyll and Hyde's death is the same used at the staking of Barnabas Collins at the end of the 1970 film. (The cue was used yet again at the climaxes of Curtis's 1973 adaptations of *Frankenstein* and *The Picture of Dorian Gray*.) Most remarkably, the bouncy music-hall ditties that Cobert composed for the scenes at Tessie O'Toole's music hall took on new life on the

Dark Shadows TV series as "I'm Gonna Dance for You," associated with Nancy Barrett's Pansy Faye character, and "Quentin's Theme," the hit record and Grammy Award nominee forever associated with David Selby's several Quentin Collins characters on TV and in *Night of Dark Shadows* (1971). "When Dan told me there was a new spook [Quentin] coming on *Dark Shadows* and he needed a theme song," Cobert laughed, "I said, 'You remember what I wrote for Billie Whitelaw? You loved that! Use that!'"[9]

The Strange Case of Dr. Jekyll and Mr. Hyde, which ABC reran on Wednesday 25 June 1969, was a prestigious entry into prime-time television producing for Dan Curtis. He, Charles Jarrott, Ian Hunter, and Jack Palance had created a quality production that enjoyed several TV airings and later life on VHS and DVD. According to *Cleveland Plain Dealer* film and television critic Mark Dawidziak,

> Although often overlooked because it was done for the so-called "small screen" and shot on videotape, this Curtis gem is cherished by a fiercely devoted group of horror fans, Stevenson devotees, and TV scholars. The sheer brilliance of this *Dr. Jekyll and Mr. Hyde* demands special attention in any discussion of the Curtis career and accomplishments.[10]

The television academy took notice and bestowed four technical and two major Emmy Award nominations on *Dr. Jekyll and Mr. Hyde*. Tony Award-winning Welsh music-hall entertainer Tessie O'Shea was nominated for Outstanding Supporting Actress in a Drama Series or Special but lost to Barbara Anderson for *Ironside*. *Jekyll and Hyde* was nominated for Outstanding Dramatic Program of 1967-1968 but lost to *Elizabeth the Queen*, a *Hallmark Hall of Fame* drama co-starring Judith Anderson and Charlton Heston.[11] Despite losing all six awards, the Dan Curtis production took its place in television history as an early example of Curtis's brand of "ornately atmospheric horror," in the words of *The Hollywood Reporter*.[12]

Another milestone in Curtis's horror *oeuvre* was **The Night Stalker** (ABC, Tuesday 11 January 1972), the *ABC Movie of the Week* that introduced the character of Carl Kolchak (Darren McGavin), a rumpled, seedy reporter on the trail of a vampire (Barry Atwater) in modern-day Las Vegas. Based on a novel by Jeff Rice (1944-2015), scripted by the great fantasy author Richard Matheson (*I Am Legend, The Shrinking Man, Somewhere in Time*), produced by Curtis, and directed (in August-September 1971) by John Llewellyn Moxey (*The House That Would Not Die, The Last Child, Genesis II*), *The Night Stalker* scored an enormous viewership (a 33.2 rating and a 54 share, representing 75 million viewers) and remains (as of 2020) in the top 20 highest-rated made-for-TV movies. Matheson (1926-2013) won the Edgar Award for his script. Stephen King remarked that Matheson "has written for TV with better pace and more dramatic flair than anyone since Reginald Rose" (*Playhouse 90, Studio One, The Twilight Zone*).[13]

Curtis, Matheson, and Moxey give The Night Stalker a *film-noir* feel as the movie opens on a lone man (McGavin), down on his luck and inhabiting a seedy rented room. Like many *film-noir* anti-heroes before him, Carl Kolchak narrates the film. The reporter begins,

> Chapter One. This is the story behind one of the greatest manhunts in history. Maybe you read about it, or rather what they *let* you read about it, probably in some minor item buried somewhere in a back page.

> However, what happened in that city between May 16 and May 28 of this year was so incredible that to this day the facts have been suppressed in a massive effort to save certain political careers from disaster and law-enforcement officials from embarrassment. This will be the last time I will ever discuss these events with anyone, so when you have finished this bizarre account, judge for yourself its believability and then try to tell yourself, wherever you may be, "It couldn't happen here."

Kolchak concludes the film with those same final four words. Curtis, Matheson, and Moxey were struck by the traditional yet modern nature of Jeff Rice's story, and they successfully imbued the TV-movie with that double-edged sensibility. *The Night Stalker* has the feel of docudrama or, as Matheson characterized it, *cinema verite*. The film details an entire city government's investigation, along with one determined reporter's investigation, of the crimes of a real vampire. The movie showcases the inner workings of the Las Vegas Police Department, the district attorney's office, and the *Las Vegas Daily News* as all of those agencies face this outlandish threat. Even the Las Vegas coroner's office becomes involved via an autopsy scene—from the unsettling point of view of the corpse. At Matheson and Curtis's suggestion, Moxey's camera looks *up* at the medical examiners as they point their scalpels downward. Also, what could be more modern and *real* than the sight of a vampire driving a rented car?

Kolchak humanizes the vampire's victims—Las Vegas showgirls and cocktail waitresses walking alone at night—by listing, in his narration, the dead women's names, ages, occupations, weights, dates and times of the attacks, and other vital statistics. These cold, hard facts add to the modern, clinical feel of the proceedings, as does the press conference that Kolchak attends (and disrupts). Back in the newsroom, Kolchak's altercations with his volatile editor Tony Vincenzo (Simon Oakland) set a seriocomic tone that lasts through all 22 original adventures of Carl Kolchak (*The Night Stalker*, *The Night Strangler*, and 20 episodes of producer Cy Chermak's *Kolchak: The Night Stalker*).

Another innovative technique is that *The Night Stalker* is not the story of a vampire, per se, as is the case in such films as *Nosferatu* (1922), *Dracula* (1931), *Horror of Dracula* (1958), and *House of Dark Shadows* (1970). *The Night Stalker* (1972) is the story of a reporter—a regular type of guy—and the vampire is a secondary character. Plus, the all-too-real notions of cover-ups and corruption are just as much the monsters of the story as is the vampire Janos Skorzeny. Kolchak defeats Skorzeny (Barry Atwater), but he cannot vanquish censorship or suppression of the facts.

At the same time that *The Night Stalker* demonstrates what would happen if a vampire showed up in a real city like Las Vegas, the film has a traditional side that ties it to classic horror. The story, after all, is a vampire melodrama that climaxes in that most classic of vampires' lairs—an old, dark house—in this case, a dilapidated home that Skorzeny has rented on an otherwise ordinary street on the outskirts of Las Vegas. The house, actually located near Echo Park in Los Angeles, was seen again in Curtis's *When Every Day Was the Fourth of July* (1978).

All of the classic vampire trappings are present: Skorzeny's coffin (even with the added detail of the bloodsucker's native soil inside the casket); Kolchak's explanation of the rules of vampirism; Carl's crucifix, hammer, and mallet; the sunlight that stuns Skorzeny; and the obligatory staking scene. However, another reality check is that after

Kolchak stakes the vampire, he faces *murder* charges and must flee Las Vegas! The city officials, deciding that a vampire is "bad for business," have closed ranks, covered up the truth, and either paid off or run off everyone involved. Again, this is what probably would happen if a vampire invaded Las Vegas and threatened the status quo.

Darren McGavin (left) and Simon Oakland co-star in *The Night Stalker* **(1972) and** *The Night Strangler* **(1973)—both Dan Curtis productions—as well as on the 1974-1975 television series** *Kolchak: The Night Stalker* **(a Cy Chermak production).**

John Llewelyn Moxey (1925-2019) remembered that Dan Curtis was very much a presence on the set but did not interfere. "He was very full of helpful hints. [*The Night Stalker*] had a very good script and an innovative and clever storyline with well-drawn characters and a great cast. [Curtis] was the prime mover in bringing these first-rate people together, and everybody fit his particular role perfectly." Moxey remembered the stunt team as "wonderful" and the fight scenes as "still exciting today."[14]

Moxey continued, "*The Night Stalker* was very well publicized by ABC, and the promotion was well handled. There was a certain titillation about there being a vampire in Las Vegas. It tickled the imagination to read about it, and when people started watching, they stuck with it"[15]—to the tune of a record-high TV-movie viewership.

The success of *The Night Stalker* is due not to critics, who barely previewed or reviewed it outside of Los Angeles, but to the tantalizing ABC promos telecast in early January 1972 and to the viewers who made it such a huge hit. *The New York Times* did not review *The Night Stalker* although it described the film in its TV listings as, "Newsman fights censorship, from his editor and the police, trying to prove that Las Vegas is being terrorized by a vampire."[16] In just those few words, the *Times* at least had hit upon what a multi-faceted movie *The Night Stalker* is. The refreshing mixture of humor, horror, newspapers, and *film noir* can be viewed as a reporter-fights-vampire thriller movie or as a reporter-fights-censorship message film.

Another innovative touch is Robert Cobert's double-edged music—"detective jazz," as Cobert himself called it.[17] A detective show set to jazz music is nothing new—it dates back at least to Henry Mancini and his music for *Peter Gunn* (1958-1961)—but scoring a horror movie with "detective jazz" *is* something innovative. Cobert's theme for Carl Kolchak is a modern mixture of jazz and early-1970s funk while his background music accompanying the vampire's attacks on women and battles with police evokes a classic scary-movie sound, full of shimmering strings, shocking brass, and unnerving vibraphone.

"It was spooky stuff," Cobert explained, "but it wasn't a *Dark Shadows* type of spooky. I mean, it was Las Vegas in 1971. That's the whole point. You need something that is spooky but contemporary—something with an edge to it."[18] This dichotomy of modern jazziness versus classic frightfulness perfectly captures the hybrid nature of *The Night Stalker*: realistic, scary; funny, shocking; irreverent, morbid; clinical, supernatural. At some points in *The Night Stalker*, Cobert overlays his horror chords onto his jazz beat for the ultimate effect.

After the amazing success of *The Night Stalker*, ABC clamored for a sequel, and this time, Dan Curtis produced *and* directed Matheson's script of **The Night Strangler** (ABC, Tuesday 16 January 1973), again starring Darren McGavin as reporter Carl Kolchak and Simon Oakland as editor Tony Vincenzo.

In the sequel, Kolchak and Vincenzo have moved from Las Vegas to Seattle, and the Seattle Underground is the lair of this film's killer, a Civil War-era surgeon who has prolonged his life by concocting an elixir of longevity. Lest he revert to his actual age (as Barnabas Collins does in *House of Dark Shadows*), Dr. Richard Malcolm (Richard Anderson) must replenish his elixir—with the fresh blood of young women—every 21 years. Therefore, Seattle has suffered a spate of unsolved murders for 18-day periods in 1889, 1910, 1931, 1952, and now the present day of 1973. Thus, Carl Kolchak is back on the trail of a supernatural menace.

Matheson's original title for the sequel to *The Night Stalker* was *The Time Killer*, but ABC preferred the more familiar *The Night Strangler*. Dan Curtis filmed the movie over 12 days in Seattle and Los Angeles. The producer-director captured the local flavor of Seattle by showcasing Pioneer Square, the Seattle Underground, the Space Needle, and the city's monorail system. For decades afterwards, Seattle Underground tour guides still pointed out a loveseat prop used in *The Night Strangler* and discarded there. I saw it when I toured the Underground in May 2000.

The Night Strangler opens with more of Carl Kolchak's wry narration: "This is the story behind the most incredible series of murders ever to occur in the city of Seattle,

Washington. You never read about them in your local newspapers or heard about them on your local radio or television station. Why? Because the facts were watered down, torn apart, and reassembled—in a word, falsified." Once again, an underlying theme is the people's right to know, and Kolchak is a noble crusader for that privilege.

Kolchak enlists the aid of belly dancer Louise Harper, who helps him locate Dr. Richard Malcolm in his underground laboratory. Jo Ann Pflug plays Louise with a mixture of intelligence and wackiness. Adding to the seriocomic feel of the film is the supporting cast of fondly remembered character actors: Wally Cox as an archivist, Al Lewis as a vagrant, Margaret Hamilton as a professor, and John Carradine as the *Daily Chronicle* publisher who orders Kolchak and Vincenzo out of town after he suppresses Kolchak's exclusive story of the 144-year-old murderer Malcolm. Instead, the noncommittal headline reads, KILLER FOUND—IDENTITY UNKNOWN.

Robert Cobert's "detective jazz" for *The Night Strangler* is even more aggressive in its use of saxophones and percussion for the upbeat theme, strings and vibraphone for scary interludes, and trumpets and muted trombone for weird effects. Cobert called his score "a combination of jazz and longhair music, with really wild harmonies."[19]

This time, many more critics sat up and took notice of *The Night Strangler* (viewed by 35 million TV households) and recognized a good movie when they saw one. Also, the critics noticed and commended the traditional/modern, scary/funny duality of *The Night Strangler*, a hallmark carried over from *The Night Stalker*. Kevin Thomas of the *Los Angeles Times* congratulated the sequel's "well-developed, amusing premise that places an old-style monster in a modern-day world coupled with genuine scariness, colorful characters, and sharp dialogue." Thomas continued,

> Dan Curtis, creator of the long-running horror serial *Dark Shadows*, has directed zestfully as well as produced, and once again Richard Matheson, working from characters created by Jeff Rice, has come through with a lively script. McGavin is terrific, and so is Simon Oakland, [both] well supported by delectable Jo Ann Pflug.[20]

Howard Thompson of the *New York Times* wrote, "This made-for-TV thriller is a yeasty surprise, blending laughs, local color, and real chills."[21] *The Hollywood Reporter* concurred that *The Night Strangler* "achieves its purpose: it is flat-out scary as hell."[22] Indeed, the newsroom high jinks, the Seattle scenery, and the horrific climax (in Malcolm's underground lair, full of cobwebs, test tubes, and rotting corpses) combine to deliver a realistic horror adventure equal to its groundbreaking predecessor.

Director Joe Dante (*Gremlins, Matinee, Small Soldiers*) observed, "I was a big fan of *The Night Stalker*, particularly the first two movies, and the second one, *The Night Strangler*, was surprisingly strong—much better than any sequel has a right to be. There were a lot of neat things going on in that."[23] A possible third Kolchak telefilm, *The Night Killers*, never materialized, and Curtis was not involved with ABC-TV's 20-episode series *Kolchak: The Night Stalker* (1974-1975), produced by Cy Chermak (*The Virginian, Ironside, The Bold Ones*).

Darren McGavin (as reporter Carl Kolchak) explores the Seattle Underground in *The Night Strangler* **(1973).**

One year after *The Night Strangler*, Dan Curtis, attempting to recreate the reporter-versus-the-supernatural magic of the Kolchak films, directed **The Norliss Tapes** (NBC, Wednesday 21 February 1973) from a script by William F. Nolan (*Space for Hire*). Nolan adapted *The Norliss Tapes* from a story idea by novelist Fred Mustard Stewart (*The Mephisto Waltz*). "It had something to do with a walking dead man," Nolan recalled. "Beyond that, everything in the teleplay is mine. I wrote it without any references whatever to the Stewart story."[24] Robert Cobert composed the atmospheric music.

Roy Thinnes, already a cult favorite for his starring roles in the TV series *The Long Hot Summer* (1965-1966) and *The Invaders* (1967-1968), portrays David Norliss, a brooding author who writes books debunking the occult—"fake mediums, phony astrologers," and the like. However, Norliss is in crisis because his latest investigations have brought him face to face with supernatural forces all too real. He demands a meeting at his home with his editor Sanford Evans (Don Porter), but before the editor arrives, Norliss has vanished. All that is left is a stack of audiocassette tapes containing Norliss's narrations of the paranormal events that he has witnessed. If *The Norliss Tapes* had become a weekly series, the lost protagonist might never have been seen in the present time—only in flashbacks dramatizing the events of each new cassette tape that Evans auditions.

In the pilot adventure, Evans listens as Norliss's taped voice reveals how he aids Ellen Cort (Angie Dickinson), who is convinced that her recently deceased sculptor-husband James has returned from the dead and is terrorizing Monterey, California. At one point, Norliss narrates a *Night Stalker*-esque scene in which a young woman, walking alone at night, is murdered. Claude Akins, who played Kolchak's adversary Sheriff Butcher in *The Night Stalker*, returns to portray Sheriff Hartley, a similar skeptic who blocks Norliss's investigation and who tells his men, "I'm putting a lid on this one." Clearly, Curtis and Nolan are mining the same Kolchakian vein. The title *The Norliss Tapes* even recalls the original title of the first Kolchak movie—*The Kolchak Tapes*. Blogger Christopher Loring Knowles (*Weekend Matinee*) observed, "For my money, Thinnes suits the material better; his moody, brooding demeanor adds a somber realism to the proceedings that McGavin's wiseguy act could either embellish or undermine, depending on which way the wind was blowing."[25]

Before his death, the terminally ill James Cort made a pact with the dark gods that he would return to life every night after sunset in order to sculpt a body for the demon Sargoth (Bob Schott) to inhabit. Norliss tells Ellen, "The clay mixture is 40 percent human blood." The zombified Cort (Nick Dimitri, in Fred Phillips's ghoulish gray makeup) has been draining women's blood to mix with his clay. The blood ultimately is his undoing, for just as Cort brings Sargoth to life, Norliss traps both creatures inside "a blood circle" and sets it on fire.

Screenwriter Nolan's blending of vampire, zombie, golem, and Egyptian lore was quite innovative and memorable as was the film's nod to the demonology and downbeat endings so popular in early-1970s literature and film. Telecast on the heels of *The Night Strangler*, Nolan and Curtis's *Norliss Tapes* captivated the Kolchak fans who caught it, and it made a lasting impression—for decades a mythic one because *The Norliss Tapes* had never been available on VHS and did not come to DVD until October 2006.

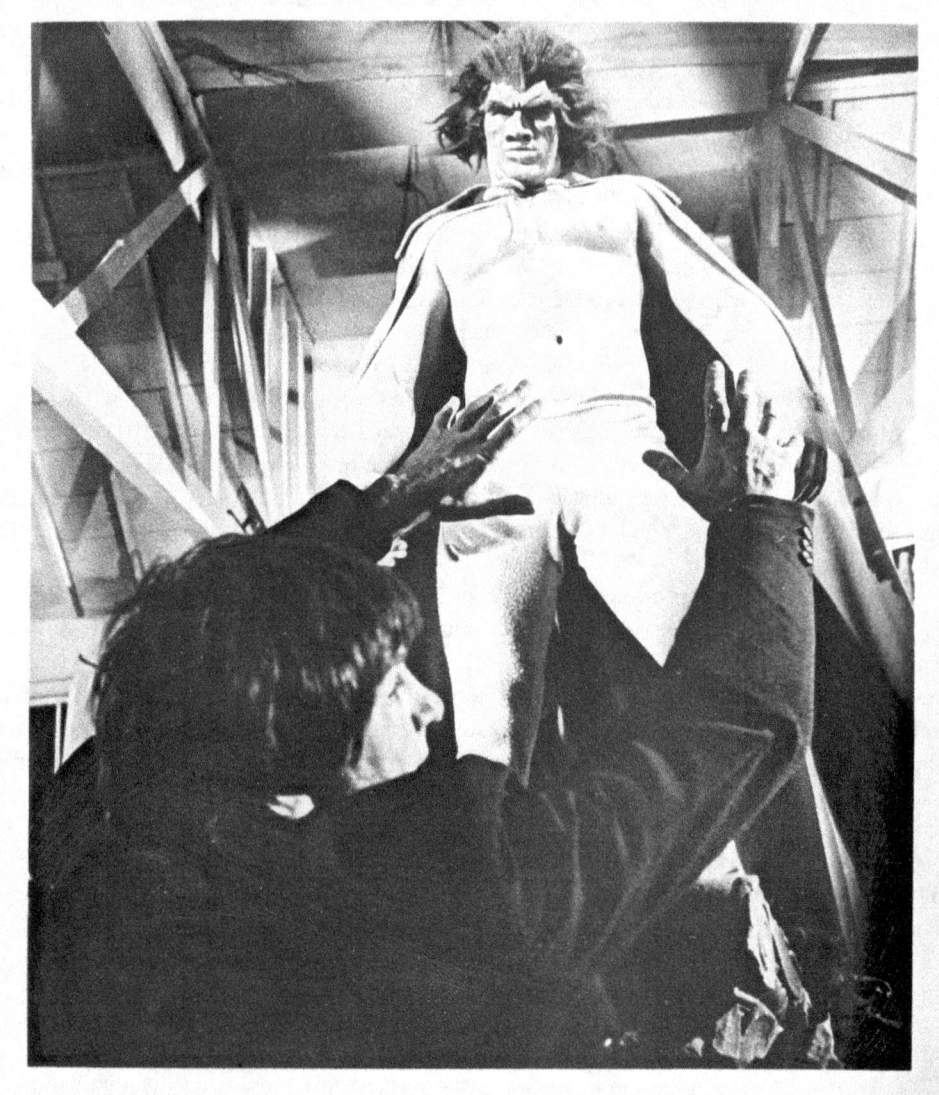

"The Norliss Tapes," a 90-minute mystery movie on Channel ___ , (day)___ at (time)___ involves the occult when a man, supposedly dead, comes to life and tries to build a demon out of clay. Roy Thinnes stars. Angie Dickinson guest stars.

The Norliss Tapes (1973): Bob Schott (as the demon Sargoth) menaces Nick Dimitri (as James Cort).

Still attuned to Kolchakian concerns, the critics took notice of *The Norliss Tapes*. *The Hollywood Reporter* wrote, "The movie is a lot of fun, with a new twist on the old vampire story."[26] *Variety* offered, "Curtis directed film with an eye to tension, and that he manages. The idea behind Nolan's script has validity, with its open dependency on the supernatural. The basic thrust, to scare, is what counts, and there Nolan, Curtis, Thinnes, and company succeed."27

The *Miami News* opined, "This program confirms one basic television truth: excellence in execution can be more important than mere originality. The professional, technical, and acting job reflected in *The Norliss Tapes* is a tribute to all those involved in its production."28

"People still talk about *The Norliss Tapes* all these years later," marveled Roy Thinnes, who worked with Curtis again on *Supertrain* (1979) and the 1991 *Dark Shadows*.79 In a 2002 interview, Curtis laughed, "*Norliss* was supposed to be a pilot for a series. I just left everyone up in the air. When they didn't pick it up as a series, I laughed my ass off. What do I think happened to [Norliss, the missing writer]? I have no idea."30

"Richard Matheson, Earl Wallace, and I were Dan's three favorite writers," William F. Nolan told me in a February 2010 telephone conversation. "After *Norliss,* Dan wanted a series. Dan and six writers [including Nolan] sat around Dan's swimming pool and discussed ideas. I came up with *The Return*."31 Nolan's promising follow-up adventure involved time travel, but a *Norliss* sequel or series never materialized. Curtis did produce (but not direct) late-night adaptations of *Frankenstein* and *The Picture of Dorian Gray* for ABC in 1973; those *Wide World Mystery* productions are discussed in Chapter VII.

Dan Curtis exploited his own Kolchakian writer-investigates-murders sub-genre one last time in **Scream of the Wolf** (ABC, Wednesday 16 January 1974), telecast one year to the day after *The Night Strangler*. Richard Matheson once again wrote the teleplay, this time from the 1969 short story, "The Hunter," by David Case, author of *Fengriffin* (1970).

This movie's picturesque setting is Malibu, California, where John Weatherby (Peter Graves) has traded his big-game-hunting days for a more leisurely life as a men's-adventure novelist. Weatherby's girlfriend is Sandy (Jo Ann Pflug, playing a totally different type than her wacky Louise in *The Night Strangler*). Living near Weatherby is his old friend Byron Douglas (Clint Walker), a troubled, reclusive big-game hunter.

The strangely nonchalant Byron is more concerned with hunting, arm-wrestling, and other manly pursuits than with the series of brutal, wolfen murders happening around town. In a change from the Kolchak adventures, all but one of the six victims are male. Sheriff Bell (Phil Carey) asks for Weatherby's help in the investigation after Byron gives Bell the brush-off. "The tracks go from four feet to two feet to nothing, period!" a baffled Weatherby observes—almost as if the wolf-like creature begins walking upright and gains enough human-like sentience to begin covering his tracks.

In a change from Claude Akins's skeptical-sheriff characterization, Sheriff Bell is just as eager to solve the mystery—whatever it turns out to be—as is Weatherby, who begins to wonder if an actual werewolf is stalking the woods. In a nod to the two *Night Stalker* movies, Bell and city officials hold a press conference, which a heckling reporter not unlike Carl Kolchak disrupts. However, in another switch, the local newspaper freely prints the headline, "WEREWOLF" KILLER STILL AT LARGE. This is one of Matheson's clever red herrings to lull the audience into the belief that a real werewolf is the culprit.

Scream of the Wolf (1974): Phil Carey (left, as Sheriff Bell), Jo Ann Pflug (as Sandy), and Peter Graves (as John) discuss the "werewolf" killings.

Curtis films the murders with his usual quick takes, low angles, and dark shadows, as well as quite a few zoom shots (popular in genre filmmaking at the time). Robert Cobert supplies suitably tense, eerie background music, plus a funky main title.

The most memorable scene in *Scream of the Wolf* is a staple of the 1970s-era woman-in-jeopardy TV-movie subgenre. The creature's frenzied chase of Sandy through her house is a precursor to Curtis and Matheson's perfection of that scenario one year later in Karen Black's *tour-de-force* dash through her apartment with the Zuni fetish doll literally on her heels in *Trilogy of Terror*. Sandy survives the attack but is convinced that Byron, who was bitten by a wolf in Canada, is to blame. The hunter's only response is, "In a way, these killings may be of benefit to everybody."

Matheson has a few more twists in store in this underrated, almost-forgotten TV-movie now relegated to public-domain DVDs. David Deal, author of *Television Fright Films of the 1970s* (McFarland, 2007), calls Clint Walker's enigmatic Byron "one of his finest performances." Deal adds,

Curtis and Matheson have fashioned a sharp, fast-moving thriller with *Scream of the Wolf.* The many fog-shrouded night scenes lend atmosphere galore, and the killings are not drawn-out stalking affairs but swift, exciting set pieces. The use of the camera from the killer's point of view—fast and low to the ground—is properly suggestive of an animal and adds considerably to the action.[32]

Dan Curtis's 1974 productions of *Dracula,* starring Jack Palance, and *The Turn of the Screw,* starring Lynn Redgrave, are discussed in Chapters IV and VII, respectively. The year 1975 brought another Curtis milestone, **Trilogy of Terror** (ABC, Tuesday 4 March 1975), another ratings smash that made a huge impression on the popular-culture consciousness. Curtis, Richard Matheson, and William F. Nolan collaborated on this anthology of three of Matheson's short stories, all starring Karen Black. The actress had come to Dan Curtis's attention when he had seen her in *The Playroom* on Broadway. He later cast her as four different women in *Trilogy of Terror.*

The first story of the trilogy is "Julie," based on Matheson's 1962 short story "The Likeness of Julie" and adapted by Nolan. Julie Eldridge (Karen Black) is a seemingly shy, mousy English professor who exerts an unexplained, wicked influence over a series of her male students, including Chad Foster (Robert "Skip" Burton, Black's husband at the time) and Arthur Moore (Gregory Harrison).

The second segment of *Trilogy of Terror* is "Millicent and Therese," based on Matheson's 1969 short story "Needle in the Heart" and adapted by Nolan. Millicent and Therese Lorimor (both Karen Black) are vastly different sisters who uneasily share their childhood home after the death of their father. Nolan retains the feel of Matheson's epistolary short story by having the prim, proper, brown-haired Millicent write entries in her diary about Therese, her blonde, libertine, immoral sibling, who corrupts Thomas Anmar (John Karlen) and confounds both women's psychiatrist, Dr. Chester Ramsay (George Gaynes).

The third segment of *Trilogy of Terror* is the one that viewers remember most strongly. "Amelia," based on Matheson's 1969 short story "Prey" and adapted by Matheson himself, is the story of a small, ferocious-looking Zuni fetish doll that comes to life and stalks Karen Black through her apartment. Black called *Trilogy of Terror* "a little legend all to itself."[33] That legend has lived on through reruns and home video in the 1980s, Curtis's *Trilogy of Terror II* in the 1990s, and a collectible Zuni fetish doll action figure in the 2000s.

With one exception, Matheson's "Amelia" teleplay is extremely faithful to his "Prey" short story. In the story, Amelia's mother and boyfriend speak several lines over the telephone; in the film, viewers hear only Amelia's side of the conversations. Karen Black declared,

> I rewrote some of the dialogue with the mother in the beginning with the director, Dan, because I wanted to make it very clear how the mother made Amelia feel. So at the end, it would be justified what she did [i.e. planned to kill her mother]. I wanted the audience to feel her suppression and the way she was made to feel inadequate. I thought that scene on the phone was very important to bring all of that out. Even though Amelia herself couldn't recognize it, the audience could.[34]

Of her director, Black added, "Dan is an excellent director and excellent at doing suspense. He knows just the right angles. Nobody is better at suspense. Dan should be applauded for his work with it."[35]

Curtis remembered that long before the days of CGI effects, he "did it all with smoke and mirrors. The Zuni doll was a little hand puppet. But it worked. The thing still holds up." Curtis explained,

> The first two stories were pretty straightforward, but when it came time to shoot the Zuni-doll story, I was scared out of my wits because I didn't know what we were going to do. How was I going to make this thing work? All we had was a hand puppet and a little model with hands and legs that could move. So what we did was to build the apartment set on risers. We cut lines into the floor that were covered by the shag carpet, and we had some idiot underneath running [and] moving the Zuni doll by means of a rod stuck up the puppet's ass. Well, forget it. It absolutely didn't work. It was the most awful thing you've ever seen. So I got the idea of chasing Karen Black with a hand-held camera about two inches off the ground. That was very effective, but I still didn't have anything with the doll. When it was over, everybody was going home, and I was sitting there in a total depression. I didn't know what to do. Then, I got one last thought, which saved the picture. I got hold of the puppeteer [Erick Von Buelow, co-creator of the Pillsbury Doughboy], and we hung a piece of black velvet. And I just shot a ton of close-ups of the doll: opening its mouth, thrashing around, exiting frame. I sent it to the lab and had it skip-framed, and before you know it, it was zipping around. I flipped the film over to make him go from left to right and right to left. The knife would jump from one hand to another, but nobody has ever noticed that! It was against black. I could cut to it any time I wanted. I edited those into the scene, and it was very effective. It absolutely saved me.[36]

So does Walker Edmiston's performance of the terrifying voice of the Zuni doll. Edmiston later portrayed General Douglas MacArthur in *War and Remembrance*. Also adding to the horrifying effect of *Trilogy of Terror* is Robert Cobert's nerve-wracking music. "I wrote some of the most abstruse music that Dan's ever allowed me to write," Cobert exclaimed. "Really far-out!"[108] Among other instruments, Cobert uses vibraphone for Julie, oboes for Millicent and Therese, and clarinet, bass clarinet, trumpet, strings, and tambourine for Amelia. Cobert's music over the closing credits builds to a shattering climax. Karen Black remarked, "He does an incredible job with the music."[37] She continued,

> It's an interesting study as to *why* [the Zuni-doll story] is *so* scary. It seems to me that maybe it's the little things in life that kill you eventually. But, of course, I'm a woman, and I think it's fine to say this in 2006, but women are afraid of *entry*—you know, vaginal entry—and that's why rats, snakes, and mice are so incredibly frightening. If you watch women draw away from them, they generally close their knees, you see! I don't know if you think that consciously, but certainly you're vulnerable in a way that a

man can't be. So I think that small things and women—and being chased by a small thing—might have something to do with why it's *so* scary.[38]

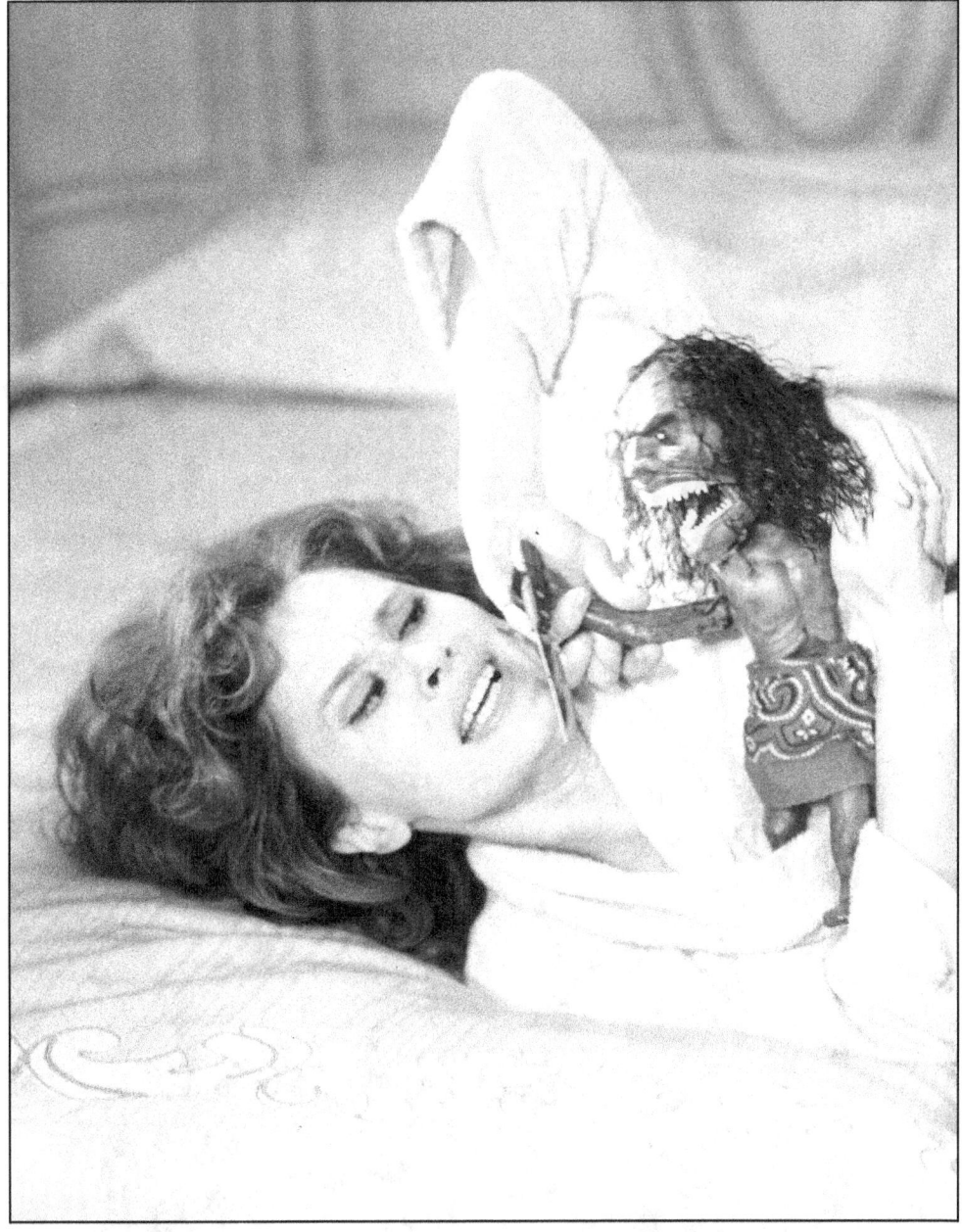

Trilogy of Terror (1975): Karen Black fights the Zuni warrior doll in this memorable scene from the climactic "Amelia" ("Prey") segment of the trilogy.

Trilogy of Terror received high ratings and high praise. *Variety* called the film "fodder for a virtuoso performance by Karen Black, who essays a quartet of women, and producer-director Dan Curtis, [who] displays his talents in the horror genre. The beginning and final scene, in which the devil doll prepares her for action, are separated by ghoulish work shrewdly manipulated, realistically managed."[39]

The year 1976 saw the release of Curtis's United Artists film *Burnt Offerings*, starring Karen Black, Oliver Reed, and Bette Davis. The Saturn Award-winning movie is discussed in Chapter III of this book.

Dead of Night (1977): In "Second Chance," Ed Begley Jr. (*Mary Hartman, Mary Hartman*) drives a restored 1923 Jordan Playboy automobile back to the year 1926 (1923 in Jack Finney's short story).

After mastering horror for more than a decade, Curtis left the genre for more than a dozen years after his two 1977 made-for-TV movies. **Dead of Night** (NBC, Tuesday 29 March) was another trilogy of terror and the final full-fledged Dan Curtis/Richard Matheson collaboration. Two of the stories (about vampirism and black magic) were Matheson's, and Matheson adapted the third, about time travel, from a short story by Jack Finney, a respected fantasy author who since the 1950s had specialized in such tales (e.g. *Time and Again, From Time to Time, The Woodrow Wilson Dime*, "The Third Level"). Curtis's filming of the 1956 Finney story, "Second Chance," is an old-fashioned, Bradbury-esque tale of a restored 1923 Jordan Playboy automobile that carries its driver (Ed Begley Jr.) back in time to 1926 (1923 in Finney's story). This is a change-of-pace sweet film from Curtis and a warm-up for his two semi-autobiographical family dramas (1978 and 1980) and, much later (1998), his sensitive filming of Jack Finney's romantic time-travel short story "The Love Letter."

The second *Dead of Night* entry is Matheson's adaptation of his 1959 short story "No Such Thing as a Vampire." This segment actually was filmed for Metromedia in 1973 as the pilot of a weekly mystery anthology series. According to Jim Pierson, "Originally titled *Inner Sanctum*, it never aired, and Dan bought back the half-hour and folded it into his *Dead of Night* TV-movie pilot."[40]

Dead of Night (1977): **Patrick Macnee (*The Avengers*) stars in "No Such Thing as a Vampire," filmed in 1973 for a project called *Inner Sanctum*.**

"No Such Thing as a Vampire" co-stars Patrick Macnee, Anjanette Comer, and Horst Bucholz as a husband, a wife, and a family friend—one of whom may be a vampire. Macnee, star of *The Avengers* (1961-1969), gleefully plays against type in this clever—and frightening—tale. Indeed, *The Hollywood Reporter* acknowledged, "All of the performances are top-rate."[41]

Much scarier still is "Bobby," the final act that attempts to recapture the killer-chases-woman phenomenon of *Trilogy of Terror*. Matheson wrote this story especially for *Dead of Night*, so it is very much in tune with the times. It incorporates demonology (in vogue at the time) and perpetuates the 1970s-era trend of real horror in an everyday setting (e.g. *The Exorcist* [1973], *The Wicker Man* [1973], *The Texas Chainsaw Massacre* [1974], *Carrie* [1976], *Halloween* [1978]) as a woman named Alma (Joan Hackett) resorts to the dark arts to bring her drowned 12-year-old son Bobby (Lee Harcourt Montgomery of *Burnt Offerings*) back from his watery grave. The Bobby that returns is horrifyingly different and poses a deadly threat to Alma. "Bobby" continues a trend of evil-child movies (e.g. *The Bad Seed* [1956], *Village of the Damned* [1960], *The Innocents* [1961], *A Little Game* [TV-1971], *The Other* [1972]), but even more importantly, it belongs to the then-current sub-genre of films expressing female anxiety about reproduction, childbirth, and children (e.g. *Rosemary's Baby* [1968], *The Exorcist* [1973], *It's Alive* [1974], Matheson's *The Stranger Within* [TV-1974], *The Brood* [1979]).

In addition to being topical, "Bobby" is an extremely frightening cat-and-mouse game that builds relentlessly to a shocking climax. As always, Curtis's direction is full of low angles, and Robert Cobert makes excellent use of music *and silence*. Whenever either begins, the effect is nerve-jangling. Like *Scream of the Wolf* three years earlier, *Dead of Night* is another underrated gem in Curtis's horror *oeuvre*.

Six months after *Dead of Night*, ABC launched its 1977-1978 season with **Curse of the Black Widow** (Friday 16 September), Curtis's homage to 1950s-era monster movies. Anthony Franciosa headed a veteran cast (June Allyson, Sid Caesar, Jeff Corey, June Lockhart, and Vic Morrow) in a tale of a private investigator, a *femme fatale*, and a giant spider. Also starring were Patty Duke Astin, Donna Mills, Max Gail, and Roz Kelly. Curtis again included his daughter Tracy, as well as his neighborhood handyman Orin Cannon, whom Curtis used in small parts in five of his films.

Writer Robert Blees created the story of *Curse of the Black Widow*, and Blees and Earl Wallace co-wrote the script (with the working titles of *Dark Destroyer* and *Spider Lady*). Blees had co-written one of the actual giant-bug movies that *Curse of the Black Widow* evokes—*The Black Scorpion* (1957), about giant scorpions in Mexico City. More recently, Blees had co-written *Dr. Phibes Rises Again* and *Frogs* (both 1972). Earl Wallace went on to write *Supertrain* and *The Last Ride of the Dalton Gang* (both 1979) for Curtis. In the 1980s, Wallace was the story editor of *The Winds of War*, and he was a full-fledged co-writer (with Dan Curtis and Herman Wouk) of *War and Remembrance*. Between the two *War* miniseries, Wallace won the Academy Award for the Best Original Screenplay of 1985 for co-writing *Witness*, directed by Peter Weir.

Dead of Night (1977): Joan Hackett (*The Last of Sheila*) plays Alma, who is so desperate to bring her drowned son "Bobby" back to life that she resorts to the dark arts.

In *Curse of the Black Widow* (1977), Mark Higbie (Tony Franciosa) is a private investigator who is drawn into a baffling series of gruesome murders somehow tied to the fraternal twins Leigh and Laura Lockwood and a mysterious brunette named Valerie Steffan. The film pays homage to *film noir* in the scene in which Leigh (Donna Mills) comes to Higbie's office and hires him. Countless *film-noir* thrillers, from *The Maltese Falcon* (1941) to *Chinatown* (1974), have included such a scene in which the beautiful, enigmatic female client hires the gumshoe. *Curse of the Black Widow* also toys with Curtis's Kolchakian formula as Higbie butts heads with Lt. Guillermo "Gilly" Conti (Vic Morrow) and delivers lines such as, "What are you guys trying to hide?" and "I'm going to stay on this thing, and I'm going to find out what you're so scared of!"

Phil "Rags" Ragsdale (Max Gail), one of Higbie's allies in the police department, surreptitiously aids Higbie in his investigation of these full-moon murders in which men's chests are ripped open and "the bodies drained of blood." "Rags" tells him of a Chinese legend of "an enchanting woman who appeared to weary travelers and took them to a cave to rest." There, she transformed into a giant spider and fed on them. He adds that certain "North American Indians" have a similar legend. Higbie and his outspoken secretary, Florence Ann "Flaps" Parsons (Roz Kelly), research a belief held by "Northern California Indians" of "a spider curse transferred down the female line" and causing transformations, from woman to spider, during the full moon.

The aforementioned characters, with their unusual names and distinctive personalities, lend texture and characterization to *Curse of the Black Widow*. Sid Caesar provides comic relief as Lazlo Cozart, Higbie's ornery neighbor in the office building. H.B. Haggerty plays Marion "Popeye" Sykes, an alcoholic gymnastics coach who witnessed one of the first documented spider-murders. Jeff Corey has a memorable scene as Aspa Soldado, a Native American who rescues Higbie after he has a terrifying accident. Dan Curtis's gymnast daughter Tracy even turns a flip in one scene.

While Mark Higbie's storyline is unfolding, the heart of *Curse of the Black Widow* is the story of the Lockwood family. "Flaps" learns that Leigh and Laura's mother gave birth to the twins in 1947 in the desert after surviving a plane crash that killed their father. Before Aspa Soldado found the woman and her newborns, one of the girls had been bitten numerous times by spiders. Leigh and Laura's mother later died under mysterious circumstances in Rome in 1965. Their family estate is now home to Olga (June Allyson), the twins' former nanny, and Jennifer (Rosanna Locke), a young girl of unspecified parentage. Jennifer calls Laura (Patty Duke Astin) "Aunt Laura" and thinks of Olga as her "grandmother." Whenever Laura stays at the house, she goes upstairs to a locked attic room and visits a shadowed figure.

Meanwhile, Leigh Lockwood, Higbie's client, lives in a fashionable beach house. At the beginning of the film, Leigh is engaged to Frank Chatham (James Storm), and Laura is engaged to Jeff Wallace (Robert "Skip" Burton). In the past, each man was linked to the opposite sister. Before the end of the film, both fiancés (and a third man, who encountered Valerie Steffan) have died from the bite of the giant spider.

This family melodrama becomes even more complicated when it is revealed that the spider-bitten twin is cursed, like a werewolf, to transform into a giant spider under the full moon—and that her mother (June Lockhart) did not die in Rome but went mad after seeing her daughter change. It is Mrs. Lockwood who languishes in the attic room. One of the twin sisters is revealed to be the spider-woman, and secrets about Valerie and Jennifer come out, too. The surprisingly layered *Curse of the Black Widow*—much more than just a giant-spider movie—is one of Curtis's most entertaining horror films.

Curse of the Black Widow (1977): Tony Franciosa (*The Name of the Game*) and Roz Kelly (*Happy Days*) flee the gigantic spider.

"Cinematically speaking," author David Deal adds, "this is actually a well photographed movie," thanks to Curtis's director of photography Paul Lohmann (*Nashville, High Anxiety, Time After Time*). In *Television Fright Films of the 1970s* (McFarland, 2007), Deal writes,

> Higbie's fall through the floor of an old house (unleashing a bevy of creepy crawlers) is nicely done, as is the shot of Olga (June Allyson) trapped in a web near the end of the film. The scenes shot from the point of view of the spider will evoke images of the fabled science-fiction films of the 1950s.[42]

Robert Cobert's music is a Kolchakian blend of "detective jazz" (a jazz-riff *leit-motif* for Higbie) and his trademark scary music (along with two disco instrumentals as source music). In a change of pace, Cobert scores one scene with solo acoustic guitar (an idea that he considered for *Night of Dark Shadows* but discarded).

Curse of the Black Widow was another ratings winner for ABC. Before receiving a deluxe VHS treatment in 1999, it was released on early home video under the softer title *Love Trap*. Patty Duke, who played Laura Lockwood, laughingly admitted that *Curse of the Black Widow* was one of her sons' favorites of her movies when they were growing up.

Dan Curtis's own personal golden age of horror (1966-1977), beginning with *Dark Shadows* and *The Strange Case of Dr. Jekyll and Mr. Hyde*, now concluded with *Dead of Night* and *Curse of the Black Widow*. Curtis felt that he had reached the point where he "didn't want to try to squeak another door."[43] He did not return to horror until the 1990s and *Dark Shadows, Intruders,* and *Trilogy of Terror II*.

Because the Zuni fetish doll had become so much a part of popular culture over the years—even being spoofed on an episode of *The Simpsons* and made into a collectible action figure—Curtis decided to film **Trilogy of Terror II** for the USA Network in 1996. It turned out to be his final horror presentation on television. (The 2004 *Dark Shadows* pilot for WB never aired.) *Trilogy of Terror II*, seen on Wednesday 30 October 1996, proved to be a powerful finale to Curtis's unique brand of horror television. This latter-day sequel is perhaps scarier than either *Trilogy of Terror* (1975) or *Dead of Night* (1977).

Stepping into Karen Black's role as the woman around whom each story is built is Lysette Anthony, Angelique from the 1991 *Dark Shadows*. The first story, adapted by William F. Nolan and Dan Curtis, is "The Graveyard Rats," based on the March 1936 *Weird Tales* story by fantasy author Henry Kuttner (*Dr. Cyclops,* "The Twonky," "Mimsy Were the Borogroves"). It tells a terrifying, *noir*-ish story of a rich old man (Matt Clark), his trophy wife (Anthony), her lover (Geraint Wyn Davies), and a gravedigger (Geoffrey Lewis), all devoured by greed, lust, or rats.

The second story is a shot-for-shot remake of "Bobby," Richard Matheson's story from *Dead of Night* (1977). Lysette Anthony assumes Joan Hackett's role of Alma. Dan Curtis faithfully follows Matheson's script and almost all of his own camera angles and shots from his earlier filming of Alma's ordeal at the hands of her demonic son. This time, however, the storm outside is even fiercer, Robert Cobert's dire music adds eerie synthesized effects, and the climax is even scarier. "Bobby" still packs a punch and explores Richard Matheson's trademark theme of one person, alone, against insurmountable odds (e.g. the last man on earth, the shrinking man, the time traveler, the motorist in *Duel*, Amelia in *Trilogy of Terror*, Bobby's mother Alma, etc.).

Lysette Anthony stars as Alma, a troubled woman who uses mystical incantations to bring her son back in "Bobby," one of three stories comprising the USA Pictures Original presentation **"Trilogy of Terror II,"** airing Wednesday, October 30, 9:00-11:00pm ET/PT.

***Trilogy of Terror II* (1996): Lysette Anthony (*Dark Shadows* '91) plays Alma in "Bobby," the second segment.**

William F. Nolan explained that Matheson was not involved with *Trilogy of Terror II*. "Dan simply reshot Matheson's 'Bobby' from his earlier script and put it in as the middle story. Then, he and I wrote the other two as a team. I had always wanted to have a crack at writing about the Zuni doll—since it was all anybody ever talked about from the first *Trilogy*—so it was very satisfying being able to do it at last."[44]

Curiously, the third story, "He Who Kills," is both a sequel to and a remake of Matheson's "Amelia" story about the Zuni fetish doll in *Trilogy of Terror*. This story begins soon after Amelia's story has ended. Amelia has died (off-camera), and the police take the charred Zuni doll to Dr. Simpson (Lysette Anthony again), a scientist who examines it at her office in a natural-history museum after hours. The Zuni doll comes back to life and stalks her through the museum, and what follows is a close remake of the original segment's frantic, bloody battle of wits between woman and doll.

In an interview in the November 1996 *Cinefantastique*, Curtis called *Trilogy of Terror II* "scarier" than the original, "and it has more humor in it."[45] *USA Today* raved that

Trilogy of Terror II is "not only the best and spookiest new offering of the TV season, but it is also a wonderful and worthy nod to an old TV classic. Revisiting *Trilogy of Terror* was a clever choice. Equally clever was casting Lysette Anthony."[46] *USA Today* also dubbed these three stories "more ambitious" than the 1975 stories and added, "From its morbid opening credits to its final shock sequence, *Trilogy of Terror II* is a treat all the way."[47]

The *New York Daily News* declared that the Zuni fetish doll had "lost none of its menace—or teeth—in the intervening years. If you enjoyed the original *Trilogy of Terror*, you'll want to scope out the sequel as well."[48] On New Year's Eve of 1996, the *N.Y. Daily News* named *Trilogy of Terror II* one of the best made-for-TV movies of '96.[49] Months later, makeup artist Rick Stratton (*Edward Scissorhands, Batman Forever*) was nominated for an Emmy Award for his *Trilogy of Terror II* makeup and prosthetics.

Trilogy of Terror II, with its strict remake of "Bobby," its loose remake of "Amelia," and its outstanding new Henry Kuttner adaptation, serves as a synthesis of *Dead of Night* and *Trilogy of Terror*, with new tips of the hat to *Weird Tales* and *film noir* as well. William F. Nolan expressed only one regret: "In my opinion, the best segment of all would have been my adaptation of Philip K. Dick's 'The Father-Thing,' but it got dropped at the last moment and replaced with Matheson's 'Bobby.' My Dick teleplay was very frightening, but no one ever got a chance to see it."[50]

In a 2010 telephone conversation with me, Nolan revealed that *Trilogy of Terror II* (1996) had been germinating for 17 years. In 1979, Dan Curtis had wanted to produce an anthology TV series called *House of Terror*, and Nolan had written the first drafts of his "Graveyard Rats" and "Father-Thing" scripts at that time. *House of Terror* never materialized, and ten years later (1989), Curtis first made plans with Nolan to make *Trilogy of Terror II*. Curtis finally made the film in early 1996. Nolan remembered that he met with Curtis in May 2000 about making another story about the Zuni doll, but they decided against it. Nolan last saw Curtis in April 2004 at the Museum of Television and Radio in Los Angeles.[51] In 2019, Nolan appeared in David Gregory's documentary *Master of Dark Shadows*, in which he called his friend Curtis "creative" and "dedicated."[52]

Significa from the House of Dan Curtis: Around the time of *The Night Stalker* in 1972, *Logan's Run* novelist William F. Nolan adapted "Slaughter House," a 1953 story by Richard Matheson, for a possible *ABC Movie of the Week* to be directed by Dan Curtis. A TV-movie never materialized. Also in 1972, Dan Curtis signed Jack Palance to host a syndicated Viacom TV series tentatively titled *Classic Mystery Ghost Stories with Jack Palance*. According to Jim Pierson, "Unfortunately, no tape seems to exist, but wraparound intros were taped with Jack Palance for a pilot presentation."[53]

Significa from the House of Dan Curtis: In 1996-1997, Dan Curtis and Morgan Creek Productions planned a theatrical version of *The Night Stalker*—with a new, perhaps younger actor to play reporter Carl Kolchak. Nick Nolte expressed an interest in playing Kolchak but was never officially cast. On Thursday 12 December 1996, the headline on the front page of *The Hollywood Reporter* proclaimed, NIGHT STALKER ON PROWL IN PIC. However, in February 1997, Morgan Creek reneged on the deal, and Kolchak hibernated for another eight-and-one-half years until the short-lived ABC-TV remake, starring Stuart Townsend, in the fall of 2005.[54]

Significa from the House of Dan Curtis: On *Dark Shadows* in 1968, Cassandra's Dream Curse, meant to return Barnabas to vampirism, goes from Maggie to Jeff to Dr. Lang to Julia (twice) to Mrs. Johnson to David to Willie to Carolyn to Prof. Stokes (with an appearance by Angelique) to Sam to Vicki to Barnabas. The Dream Curse fails because of Barnabas's connection to Adam.

CHAPTER III

The Features
House of Dark Shadows, Night of Dark Shadows, Burnt Offerings, and More

The 1970s began with Dan Curtis's direction of the September 1970 Metro-Goldwyn-Mayer theatrical feature **House of Dark Shadows** at the Lyndhurst estate in Tarrytown, New York, while the *Dark Shadows* TV series continued. In 1969, when *Dark Shadows* and its merchandising were at the peak of their popularity, Curtis had dreamed up another incarnation for his Gothic serial: a major motion picture. Curtis conceded,

> No one had ever done this before, but the show's such a big hit, so why don't we make a movie out of it? A soap opera turned into a movie! We did it, and the movie was a huge hit. We kept the show going at the same time. We juggled the scripts around. People would be brought out on buses and brought back to play on the show the next day. Those were unbelievable, wild days.[1]

House of Dark Shadows, written by Sam Hall and Gordon Russell, was shot between Monday 23 March and Friday 1 May 1970. Half of the television cast (including Jonathan Frid and Grayson Hall) filmed the movie in Tarrytown while the other half (including David Selby and Lara Parker) carried the TV show in Manhattan.

MGM rented Lyndhurst for Curtis and his 55 actors and crew members for $35,000. Curtis filmed in most of the mansion's rooms and bedrooms, all laden with antiques and paintings, and he also utilized the estate's huge coach house (glimpsed in one 1966 episode of *Dark Shadows* itself), the barren greenhouse (for a scene cut from the film), and the empty, crumbling indoor swimming pool (for one of the most frightening scenes of the movie—"If I catch this one, Carolyn isn't dead"). Curtis and his cast and crew also filmed scenes at the Sleepy Hollow Cemetery, down the street from Lyndhurst; in Scarborough, New York; and in Westport and Norwalk, Connecticut.

Curtis and the cast and crew commuted to and from Lyndhurst, only an hour's drive from Manhattan, for the nine-hour work days. Curtis filmed only during the day; he used the day-for-night lensing technique for nighttime scenes. The cast used the basement of Lyndhurst for wardrobe and screening rooms, the souvenir shop for the makeup room, and the stable for a cafeteria. Kathryn Leigh Scott remarked, "We'd worked together so long as a close-knit group, isolated in our TV studio on West 53rd Street. Filming on location at Lyndhurst seemed like a natural extension—we'd just taken our show on the road."[2]

House of Dark Shadows **(1970): Jonathan Frid stars as the vampire Barnabas Collins in the MGM feature.**

House of Dark Shadows is a bloodier, more violent retelling of the TV show's 1967 storyline, in which Willie Loomis (John Karlen) releases the 18th-century vampire Barnabas Collins (Jonathan Frid) from his chained coffin in the Collins mausoleum. Barnabas violently preys on the residents of Collinsport, Maine, and he mesmerizes Maggie Evans (Kathryn Leigh Scott), who bears an uncanny resemblance to his lost 1790s love Josette DuPres. During the course of the film, Barnabas strangles several characters to death, he cruelly beats Willie, and he vampirizes his cousin Carolyn Stoddard (Nancy Barrett), her uncle Roger Collins (Louis Edmonds), and the Collinses' friend, Professor Stokes (Thayer David).

The *Dark Shadows* TV series spotlighted Gothic mystery and doomed romance over violence and body counts, so the gory mayhem of *House of Dark Shadows* was a jarring shift in tone. Frid, who had patented the reluctant, conflicted vampire on *Dark Shadows*, now found himself playing a monster in *House of Dark Shadows*. Barnabas makes Willie his Renfield and Carolyn his slave. Lovesick Dr. Julia Hoffman (Grayson Hall) attempts to cure him of his vampirism and give him a normal life, but she intentionally gives him an overdose of her serum when she realizes that he has chosen Maggie instead of her. Barnabas ages rapidly and displays Dick Smith's horrifying old-age makeup design. Smith recalled, "We decided to make Barnabas bald with a veined, mottled, liver-spotted head, which we basically improvised, on the set."[3] Smith reworked the Old Barnabas design for Dustin Hoffman in Arthur Penn's *Little Big Man* (1970). Later, Tobe Hooper's *Texas Chainsaw Massacre* (1974) imitated Smith's makeup.

In return for her betrayal of him, Barnabas strangles Julia to death. Although in 1967 the TV Barnabas threatened Julia's life several times, he never would have gone through with such an atrocity. *House of Dark Shadows* demonstrates the diabolical trajectory that the Barnabas character would have followed if Dan Curtis had stuck to his original plan of "letting him bite and kill people for a cycle [13 weeks of soap-opera episodes] and then driving a stake through his heart."[4] Indeed, the film concludes (in a lurid scene shot on Friday 1 May 1970 at the Lockwood-Mathews Mansion in Norwalk, Connecticut) with the bloody running-through of Barnabas by the arrow from a crossbow. Barnabas's death occurs after Carolyn has been staked (in another of the film's most stunning sequences), Stokes has been shot through the heart, and Roger has been impaled on a spear. Although most of the cast has been killed, *House of Dark Shadows* manages a traditional happy ending as Jeff Clark (Roger Davis) rescues his love interest Maggie from the bloodsucker. However, it is not Jeff who is the true hero of the film but poor, hapless Willie, who gives his life to destroy his master. This shattering sequence is scored to Robert Cobert's emotional "Death of Hyde" music cue from *The Strange Case of Dr. Jekyll and Mr. Hyde* (1968).

House of Dark Shadows (1970): Thayer David (as Prof. Stokes) accuses Grayson Hall (as Dr. Hoffman) of being in love with a vampire.

Cobert wanted to write original music for the film, but Curtis wanted to reuse the TV show music. "I fought Dan tooth and nail on that decision but ultimately lost.

While the budget was part of Dan's concern, I sincerely feel that he wanted to use the existing music because the fans liked it and Dan thought they would enjoy hearing it in the film."[5]

Cobert was correct in his observation—the legions of *Dark Shadows* fans certainly did like the familiar music cues—and Curtis was correct in his decision to re-use those cues (actually Cobert's *Jekyll and Hyde* score which had been re-recorded and re-used on *Dark Shadows*). The music of *Dark Shadows* was just as much a character on the show as Barnabas or Elizabeth, and Curtis wanted the fans to have that familiar musical touchstone as a consolation to their forced adjustments to a new Collinwood (Lyndhurst), a new level of violence (gory bitings and stakings), and a somewhat new Barnabas (an out-and-out villain).

Frederick S. Clarke's *Cinefantastique* magazine—the *Time* or *Newsweek* of all things horror—declared, "The seventies have begun with an inordinate number of vampire films, [and] *House of Dark Shadows* is the superior film of the crop—a fast-paced, harrowing thriller." Clarke continued,

> The screenplay by Sam Hall and Gordon Russell is highly inventive; however, credit for the film's unqualified success must go to director Dan Curtis, who previously had exhibited his skill in the genre by producing, incomparably, the finest version of Robert Louis Stevenson's *Dr. Jekyll and Mr. Hyde* on television several seasons ago. Curtis provides *House of Dark Shadows* with a stylistic flair indelibly his own, a restless, roving visual sense, never content in projecting a static image. Curtis directs Arthur Ornitz's excellent camerawork not at a scene but into it, through it, and around it with an hypnotically fluid ebb and flow of nightmarish montage.[6]

Donald F. Glut, author of *The Dracula Book* (Scarecrow, 1975), added, "Barnabas dies in one of the most vivid stakings ever recorded on film. The fast-paced, atmospheric, and graphic film proved that Curtis was capable of transforming a television soap opera into one of the finest horror films of the year."[7] In the early 1970s, *House of Dark Shadows* was released or re-released on double bills with such diverse films as *The Brotherhood of Satan*, *Dusty and Sweets McGee*, *Every Little Crook and Nanny*, and *The Traveling Executioner*.[8]

Meanwhile, on ABC-TV, ratings for *Dark Shadows* were dropping because viewers were losing interest and switching to the new soap opera *Somerset* on NBC or to reruns of *Gomer Pyle, USMC* on CBS. In late 1970, not only some of the audience but also Dan Curtis himself "became disenchanted" with the TV show, in Curtis's words.[9] Indeed, the viewership had fallen from 18 million in 1969 to 12 million in 1970-1971. Curtis admitted that he lost interest in *Dark Shadows* during the last six months of the show.[10] The final episode, set in the vampire-less alternate universe of 1841 Parallel Time, was taped on Wednesday 24 March and aired on Friday 2 April 1971.

Five days after the 1225th and final episode had been taped, Curtis began directing **Night of Dark Shadows** (MGM, 1971) on the Lyndhurst estate. Shooting stretched through April and ended on Friday 7 May 1971, and the movie was released in August.

After Jonathan Frid refused to play a risen Barnabas, Curtis abandoned his idea of another vampire movie and, with Sam Hall, crafted a psychological ghost story similar to the TV show's 1970 Parallel Time storyline, which itself was an homage to Daphne Du Maurier's 1938 novel *Rebecca*.[11]   *Night of Dark Shadows* also bears a strong resemblance to Charles Beaumont and Roger Corman's 1963 film *The Haunted Palace*, based on H.P. Lovecraft's 1927 story "The Case of Charles Dexter Ward." Both *The Haunted Palace* and *Night of Dark Shadows* involve the public execution of a witch, significant ancestral portraits, an attempted marital rape, a husband (Vincent Price, David Selby) influenced by a ghost, his anguished wife (Debra Paget, Kate Jackson) whom he endangers, and a sinister housekeeper (Lon Chaney Jr., Grayson Hall) who exacerbates the problems.

Night of Dark Shadows (1971): **Grayson Hall (as Carlotta Drake) and David Selby (as Quentin Collins) pose outside the Lyndhurst mansion in Tarrytown, New York.**

Under the best of circumstances, *Night of Dark Shadows* faced an uphill battle. It was released four months after *Dark Shadows* had been cancelled, and it lacked the vampire angle that had defined the TV series. Furthermore, *Night of Dark Shadows* lost its soul on the cutting-room floor. As written and filmed, Curtis's follow-up to *House of Dark Shadows* would have been superior to that film and could have been at least a minor masterpiece of early-1970s horror cinema because of its numerous timely qualities (*déjà vu*, reincarnation, witchcraft, ghosts, and a downbeat ending). Instead, Curtis was forced, under a tight deadline, to cut his 129-minute film to 97 minutes. At the behest of the MPAA, the studio subsequently cut it even further, to 93.5 minutes. What is left is a confusing, often unsatisfying narrative which nevertheless delivers enough atmosphere and impact for the *Boston Globe* to call the movie "a cut above the average" and "a horror film for people who don't really like horror films."[12]

Artist Quentin Collins (David Selby) and his wife Tracy (Kate Jackson) move in to Quentin's inheritance, the Collinwood estate, sternly run by Carlotta Drake (Grayson Hall) and handyman Gerard Stiles (James Storm). Soon, Quentin begins having dreams and visions of his lookalike ancestor, Charles Collins, also a painter, who lived at Collinwood in 1810. Quentin is especially drawn to Collinwood's mysterious tower room, where Charles had an affair with Angelique (Lara Parker), his brother's wife, before her public hanging for witchcraft. Angelique's spirit still haunts Collinwood, and Carlotta tells Quentin that he is the reincarnation of Charles Collins and the vessel through which Angelique and Charles's love will live again. Carlotta declares that she herself is the reincarnation of Sarah Castle (Monica Rich), a young girl who lived at Collinwood in 1810 and who witnessed Angelique's unjust hanging.

As Quentin falls under the spell of the house and its beautiful ghost, he takes on the identity of his ancestor. He attempts to rape and later drown Tracy, whom he and Carlotta see as a threat to Angelique's plan for Quentin and Collinwood. Quentin, with the help of Tracy and their Gothic-novelist friends Claire and Alex Jenkins (Nancy Barrett and John Karlen), attempts to resist his possession. The deaths of Gerard and Carlotta seem to vanquish the ghost, and the Collinses and the Jenkinses prepare to leave Collinwood forever. Then, Quentin must go back into the house one last time to retrieve his canvases.

When Dan Curtis delivered his 129-minute opus to MGM chief James Aubrey, Aubrey demanded drastic cuts—and gave Curtis as little time as 11 hours to submit them! Aubrey, the so-called Smiling Cobra who at different times tyrannized MGM and CBS, was the basis for the ruthless television executive Robin Stone in Jacqueline Susann's 1969 novel *The Love Machine*. In his film career, Aubrey was accused of tampering with movies by Blake Edwards, Ken Russell, and Sam Peckinpah, as well as this one by Dan Curtis. Therefore, on a moment's notice, Curtis and an MGM staff editor were forced to eviscerate *Night of Dark Shadows* in order to please Aubrey.

As a result, several of Quentin's dream sequences are consolidated, thereby causing his pajamas to change from yellow to blue in the course of one night's sleep. The Jenkinses are edited out of some scenes, and much of Angelique's part is cut. As the film now stands, the audience does not know how Gerard and Carlotta are related (he is her nephew), why Tracy goes to the pool house (she had a dream about it), why Quentin/Charles tries to drown her there (Charles drowned his wife Laura in 1810), why Quentin/Charles limps (off-camera, he fell off his horse), or why Laura Collins (Diana Millay) laughs during Angelique's funeral (Angelique's body is not really in the coffin but is entombed with a still-living Charles in a secret room beneath Collinwood). The viewers also do not understand the reverend's line about Angelique's "threats" (her spoken curse on her executioners is deleted, thereby making the original title *Curse of Dark Shadows* meaningless), and they see Carlotta re-hang Angelique's portrait when they never saw it removed in the first place. Most significantly, what would have been the film's most important and powerful scene—a séance conducted by Quentin, Tracy, Alex, and Claire and the revelation that Angelique was *not* a witch—does not appear in the movie and shortchanges the effect of the ending. Nevertheless, the final moments—when the audience learns the fates of the characters—still have the power to stun. According to *Video Watchdog* editor Tim Lucas, "The material may be derivative, but it is consistently well-handled by writer-director Curtis, and the downbeat finale [. . .] is stimulating."[13]

Night of Dark Shadows **(1971): Lara Parker (as Angelique) haunts a cemetery in this publicity shot for the heavily edited film.**

When Aubrey viewed Curtis's hastily shortened film, he announced, "It's a tight little thriller." Curtis insisted, "But the film doesn't make sense any more!" Aubrey retorted, "With *your* audience, it doesn't matter!"[14]

Understandably, some reviews of the truncated *Night of Dark Shadows* were lackluster. A.H. Weiler, in the *New York Times,* pronounced the movie "a bore" but complimented the many atmospheric shots of Lyndhurst. Weiler wrote, "The attraction of this dour adventure is Lyndhurst, the Gothic Revival mansion, where the film was shot. Its many period rooms, paintings, and objects d'art are richly eye-filling. The somber story shot there, however, is strictly for the low-rent district."[15] Indeed, the titles of the two *Dark Shadows* films could be switched. The Barnabas movie is all about what happens at *night,* while the Quentin film lovingly shows off the bedrooms, stairways, second-floor gallery, and tower room of this Gothic *house* of dark shadows. The *Boston Globe* also noted the film's "visual beauty."[16]

The *San Francisco Examiner* observed, "Dan Curtis, who created the TV series, directed the film in a slow, languid style that contributes to the evocation of a menacing climate."[17] Sensing that important elements were missing from the film, Roger Ebert, in the *Chicago Sun-Times,* added, "Toward the end of the movie, not a lot goes on except for double takes, screams, and lots of bleeding."[18] Granted, the film effectively builds, but the re-edited payoff is hasty and minimal.

Even Robert Cobert's eerie music score suffers in the forced edit. Some of his cues end abruptly, and the scene that explains the film's frequent use of "Quentin's Theme" does not appear in the 93.5-minute cut. In a missing 1810 flashback, Angelique plays the unnamed melody on the piano and tells Charles that the music reminds her of him. The lovers are interrupted by the appearance of Laura, Quentin's wife. The film uses several new recordings of "Quentin's Theme," as well as weird echo effects and some unnerving chase music played on strings and bongo drums.

The love theme from *Night of Dark Shadows* is one of Cobert's most haunting melodies. The tune originated as a piano solo in the final months of the TV series. For the film, Cobert follows a piano rendition of the love theme with a refrain played on harmonica and guitar, a novel combination for Cobert but appropriate to the film's early-1970s origins. Cobert re-used the love theme in *The Invasion of Carol Enders,* a late-night ABC *Wide World Mystery* drama (Friday 8 March 1974) produced by Dan Curtis and directed by Burt Brinkerhoff (*Come Die with Me*).

Laura's intrusion upon Quentin and Angelique at the piano is one of many scenes—approximately 25 percent of the finished film—which Aubrey forced Curtis to eliminate. Other missing scenes, as evidenced in Hall and Curtis's complete shooting script, are Quentin and Tracy's picnic, Quentin's removal of Angelique's portrait, several clarifying discussions, and the all-important séance. In 1989, I wrote and directed *The Night Before,* a play that reinstated many of the missing scenes and afforded the audience at that year's Dark Shadows Festival a seriocomic feel for what the complete *Night of Dark Shadows* might have been like. In 1997, film historian Darren Gross definitively reconstructed the film in the pages of Donna and Tim Lucas's *Video Watchdog* magazine.

Then, in August 1999, Gross found the long-lost, one-and-only 129-minute color separations (footage) of *Night of Dark Shadows* in a film-storage vault in a Kansas City salt mine. Gross recalled, "Being able to finally see all the shots from this legendary [séance] sequence was such a thrilling revelation that I had to stifle any yelps of joy."[19]

Darren Gross and Jim Pierson launched an effort to reconstruct the film for a definitive DVD release. Because only 100 minutes of the soundtrack survive, all of the film's living stars re-recorded their missing dialogue. "That was the hardest I've ever worked!" David Selby told me at the 2008 Dark Shadows Festival. "We had the script, but we didn't know the *exact* words we'd said, so they brought in lip-reading specialists to help us match our dialogue to the picture."[20] Sadly, even with so much of the work toward reconstruction completed, Warner Brothers released a DVD and Blu-Ray of the familiar *cut* version of *Night of Dark Shadows* on 30 October 2012 when it also released *House of Dark Shadows* on DVD and Blu-Ray. (No extra footage of *HODS* still exists.) Perhaps, some day, Warner Brothers will add the missing *NODS* scenes, either at their correct points within the movie or as DVD extras, in a new, definitive re-release.

Later in 1971, with *Dark Shadows* seemingly behind them, Norma and Dan Curtis and their three daughters Cathy, Linda, and Tracy spent time on the West Coast before they permanently relocated from New York to California in 1972. For the next eight years (and in the following three decades), Curtis produced and/or directed a string of highly successful made-for-TV movies that captivated an entire generation of baby boomers and their parents. The unforgettable Dan Curtis productions—horror, Western, and drama in the 1970s; *The Winds of War* and *War and Remembrance* in the 1980s; *Dark Shadows* and *Intruders* in the 1990s, and *Saving Milly* and *Our Fathers* in the 2000s—were about to begin.

Curtis's third theatrical feature was the October 1976 United Artists film **Burnt Offerings**, based on Robert Marasco's 1973 Gothic-horror novel of the same name and filmed at Dunsmuir House in Oakland, California. The impressive cast included Karen Black, Oliver Reed, Bette Davis, Burgess Meredith, and Eileen Heckart. In addition to directing *Burnt Offerings*, Curtis co-wrote the script with William F. Nolan. "I took the back half" of the script, Curtis remembered, "and Nolan wrote the first half."[21]

The movie is an extremely accurate, faithful filming of the novel—up to a point. Virtually everything that is in the movie is in the book, and vice versa. The only changes of any import come at the conclusion of the film—but they are significant changes. In the novel, the father and son meet their demises at the swimming pool on the estate, but in the movie, the mother rescues them. Ultimately, no one saves them from the much gorier, more spectacular finishes that Curtis and Nolan devise for them. Nolan and Curtis forgo novelist Marasco's nebulous, abstract ending for a more cinematic conclusion, which is a cross between the climaxes of Alfred Hitchcock's *Psycho* (1960) and Curtis's own *Night of Dark Shadows* (1971). Curtis admitted,

> Someone pointed out to me that I stole the ending from what I did in *Night of Dark Shadows*—the concept of the person going back into the house and the car horn beeping outside and the whole *waiting* thing. "What's taking so long?" All I know is I think the last 15 minutes of this film—and I did a lot of scary stuff in my day—is the scariest 15 minutes I have ever seen. Nothing beats the last 15 minutes of this picture.[22]

Nevertheless, until the final moments, *Burnt Offerings* is an extremely faithful filming of the novel. Even a great deal of Marasco's actual dialogue makes it into the screenplay. In both the novel and the film, homeowners Roz Allardyce (Eileen Heckart) and her brother Arnold (Burgess Meredith) tell Marian Rolfe (Karen Black) and her husband Ben (Oliver Reed) that the house is "practically immortal."[23] The elderly Allardyce siblings offer the house to Ben and Marian—or perhaps it is vice versa—for the entire summer for only $900.00.

Burnt Offerings (1976): Oliver Reed (*The Assassination Bureau*) and Karen Black (*The Day of the Locust*) portray husband and wife in Dan Curtis's award-winning United Artists film.

At first, Ben, Marian, young David (Lee Harcourt Montgomery), and Aunt Elizabeth (Bette Davis) are overjoyed with their summer retreat, but soon, disturbing events cast a pall of uneasiness, suspicion, and even terror over 17 Shore Road. Ben tries to drown David in the pool, a rift grows between Ben and Marian, and Aunt Elizabeth loses her energy and begins to wither away. At the same time, Marian neglects her family as she becomes obsessed with caring for the house and possessively looking after the never-seen, 85-year-old Allardyce mother whom Roz and Arnold have left behind in the attic sitting room. According to Marasco's novel, "There was a malevolence in the house, and she [Marian] was being used as its agent."[24]

While a graying Marian becomes consumed by her housekeeping, Ben begins suffering a mental breakdown. These are perhaps the most frightening scenes in the film, as Ben abuses David and later Marian and suffers dreams and hallucinations involving a grim, long-ago funeral and a grinning chauffeur (Anthony James) driving a hearse-like Bentley—which now may be coming back for Ben and his failing aunt. The chauffeur's leering interest in the boy Ben (Todd Turquand) suggests a long-buried abuse which may be at the root of Ben's mistreatment of David and Marian and of the house's exploitation of Ben's fears. Bette Davis's death scene, which anticipates Sylvia Sidney's similar death scene in Don Taylor's *Damien—Omen II* (1978) by two years, is a memorable moment as Aunt Elizabeth and Ben, both terror-stricken, are paralyzed by their fear of what may be approaching the bedroom door. With each new death, the house revitalizes itself.

The ending was inconsiderately revealed in United Press International's unsigned, lackluster review of the film. UPI also called *Burnt Offerings* "torturously slow,"[25] but almost all other reviewers understood the fact that the film works *because* it is slow-moving and the frights are spaced out along the two-hour running time. The *Fort Worth Star-Telegram* realized that "Curtis, the *Dark Shadows* creator, has done a masterful job of bringing to the viewer a tangible sense of dread and then punctuating it with jabs of pure terror."[26]

Films in Review agreed, "This story of a family menaced by psychic forces which plague their summer estate succeeds because producer-director Dan Curtis has enough confidence in his material to pitch the level of suspense at a low key."[27] The *New York Times* added, "Director Curtis times his audience immersions into the ice-bath of terror with skill."[28] Rex Reed, in *Vogue*, also complimented the film's "inwardly churning horror," "visually breathtaking splendor," and "enormous style."[29]

Much of that style comes from Curtis's most frequent use of low angles in any of his horror movies. Curtis claimed,

> I was always known as "Mr. Low Angle." I never want to shoot eye-level, with rare exceptions, because I think it's boring. Either you're going to shoot low, or you're going to shoot high, or you're going to shoot raking angles. I try not to get straight-on stuff because the low angle, to me, is more involving. You somehow feel, as a viewer, that you're in the picture, and you're looking *up* at it, and you are *there*. Visually, it seems to have more depth and be more interesting. You see ceilings, for example.[30]

Another hallmark of the film is Robert Cobert's tantalizing score. Cobert infuses *Burnt Offerings* with *Dark Shadows*-style trembling violins, ominous vibraphone, and harsh brass. He adds bells when the grinning chauffeur haunts Ben, and as in *Dark Shadows* and *Dracula*, Cobert uses a music-box theme to great effect.

Burnt Offerings (1976) director Dan Curtis and camera operator Sven Walnum film Oliver Reed and Lee H. Montgomery in the swimming pool at Dunsmuir House and Gardens in Oakland, California, in August 1975.

"Little things" are what make the movie work, Curtis explained, "like finding the old, rusted bicycle by the graves and the glasses at the bottom of the pool."[31] *Burnt Offerings*, at its core, is the story of a family. Curtis and Nolan's script accentuates the family's happiness in the initial car ride to the house and the group's banter and warmth before the malevolence of the house unhinges Ben, enslaves Marian, and destroys Aunt Elizabeth. After a slowly paced build-up, the characters careen helplessly to their ghastly ends.

Burnt Offerings ranked number one at the box office for the week of 13-19 October 1976. Its business was boosted by Lawrence Van Gelder's oft-quoted blurb from the *New York Times*: "an outstanding terror movie [. . .] that does for summer houses what *Jaws* did for a dip in the surf."[32] Rex Reed called *Burnt Offerings* "an amazingly gripping horror film."[33] *Films in Review* noted, "Curtis is one of the few Hollywood producers to employ well-known sci-fi authors regularly to write scripts. This deserves applause at a time when most such movies are being entrusted to people who don't understand or respect the genre."[34] Over the years, *Burnt Offerings* has earned a reputation as being more sophisticated than most contemporary horror films. "The public loved it," William F. Nolan said.[35]

George LaVoo, in *The Old, Dark House* genre magazine, wrote, "Bette Davis outdoes them all in the role of Aunt Elizabeth. Her death scene, with the chauffeur dragging the coffin up the stairs, is by far the best scene in the movie."[36] In 1977, Davis won the Saturn Award for best supporting actress from the Academy of Science-Fiction, Fantasy, and Horror Films. *Burnt Offerings* also won Saturns for best horror film of 1976 (beating *The Omen*) and best director (Dan Curtis). Bette Davis and Oliver Reed won acting awards for *Burnt Offerings* at the Antwerp Film Festival in Belgium, and Karen Black and Burgess Meredith won acting awards at the Sitges-Catalonian Film Festival. Curtis was named the best director at that festival in Spain.

Essential to the effect and the success of *Burnt Offerings* is Karen Black, whose portrayal of Marian goes from sympathetic to ambivalent to lethal. In a 1976 interview, Dan Curtis revealed that his daughter Tracy, who had acted with Black in *Trilogy of Terror*, "threatened to leave home if I didn't cast Karen Black in *Burnt Offerings*."[37] Curtis had high praise for Black's performances in both films. "She worked her tail off and never, ever let me down."[38] Thirty years later, in a DVD interview, Karen Black insisted, "There's no one better at this genre than Dan Curtis. He has certitude and reliability."[39]

While his made-for-television accomplishments were numerous, Dan Curtis made only four theatrical films. After *House of Dark Shadows* (MGM, 1970), *Night of Dark Shadows* (MGM, 1971), and *Burnt Offerings* (UA, 1976), his fourth and final feature, **Me and the Kid** (Orion, October 1993), was a bittersweet experience for the director. Because of its uneven (but refreshing) mix of broad comedy, crime drama, and kids' adventure, *Me and the Kid* under-performed in theatres and greatly disappointed Curtis. He recalled,

> While I was doing *The Winds of War*, a fellow who worked with me, Joe Stern, came across this book called *Taking Gary Feldman*, by Stanley Cohen. He showed it to me, and I thought it was a good story although I felt certain things needed to be done to it. But we sold it to CBS, and

they developed a screenplay while I was off doing the miniseries. Unfortunately, it never worked out—the option lapsed, and that was that. But I always remembered that story. It's really a problem finding material. It limits me as it limits everybody else. And I'm very tough on material—there's not a lot of stuff I like, particularly after I finished those two giant epics, *The Winds of War* and *War and Remembrance*. I mean, everything paled by comparison, and nothing appealed to me. It was awful; I was in a very depressed state. I thought, "I'll never find anything else I want to do." Then, I remembered the *Gary Feldman* script. It was a sweet little movie, a direct departure from the epics I'd been making. So I optioned it again and developed the screenplay—without talking to any studios. I just developed the material myself, and I thought I would try to put it together and make a deal. I took it around to a few places and met a lot of people who felt the central relationship needed to be developed more, but I said, "Hold the phone; I believe this works—I'll make it myself!" And that's what happened.[40]

Curtis spent four million dollars of his own money filming *Me and the Kid* in California, New York, and New Jersey from mid-October to early December 1992. Producer-director Curtis had some input into Richard Tannenbaum's script, and Robert Cobert supplied the jaunty background music (as well as a song, "Goin' to Mexico"). Tracy Curtis served as associate producer.

Neglected by his parents (David Dukes and Anita Morris), Gary Feldman (Alex Zuckerman) is a sheltered rich boy who walks in on two inept burglars, Harry Banner (Danny Aiello) and Roy Walls (John Karlen lookalike Joe Pantoliano), cracking his father's safe. When the safe is devoid of cash, the crooks kidnap Gary instead. This is the most fun that Gary has had in his whole life! He would rather stay with the criminals, especially Harry, than return home.

After parting with the cruel Roy, the kind-hearted Harry takes Gary with him on a cross-country adventure that leads them to an out-of-the-way motel and amusement park run by Rose Farrell (Cathy Moriarty). As the police, the FBI, and Gary's parents close in, the boy does something outlandish that allows Harry to escape. The final scene takes place "six months later."

The cast of *Me and the Kid* is excellent—it also includes Demond Wilson, Abe Vigoda, Robin Thomas, Ben Stein, and Rick Aiello—but the story, of a boy who befriends a crook and travels with him, was difficult to sell. Curtis was aiming for a latter-day *Kid* (1921) or *Champ* (1931, 1979)—with elements of buddy movies, road movies, and his own 1974 *Great Ice Rip-Off* caper movie—but *Me and the Kid* became lost amid the many *Home Alone* (1990) imitations of the early 1990s. Perhaps the worst blow was that *Me and the Kid* (released on Friday 22 October 1993) appeared at essentially the same time (24 November) as Clint Eastwood's much higher-profile film *A Perfect World* (1993), which itself was the story of a boy who accompanies a criminal (Kevin Costner) on his capers.

Despite favorable audience response at early screenings, *Me and the Kid* made no impression at the box office and vanished quickly. (By Wednesday 30 March 1994, it was available on VHS. It came to DVD in 2004. I showed the movie to my Tennessee

State University students in 2007.) The *Los Angeles Times* called the film "an amiable family entertainment for the undemanding, but it has the potential to be much more."[41] *Variety* noted young Alex Zuckerman's "unaffected acting,"[42] but the *Orange County Register* criticized the film's "weak" script and "major flaws in feasibility."[43] Granted, the beginning and the end of *Me and the Kid* could be considered weak or implausible, and a nevertheless very strong, delightful middle could not counteract those flaws. The *Los Angeles Times* praised the "lovable duo" of Danny Aiello and Alex Zuckerman but lamented, "You really want their picture to be better."[44]

Me and the Kid (1993): Danny Aiello (left) shares a moment between takes with director Dan Curtis.

In a December 1993 interview, Dan Curtis blamed Orion Pictures for "opening and closing *Me and the Kid* in a week." He insisted, "The promotion was all wrong. It opened as a well-kept secret. Nobody came to see it. It broke my heart. I lost my tail on it. Never, never again will I finance a movie with my own money."[45] As *Me and the Kid* found a small cult audience on home video, Curtis put his noble experiment behind him and refocused his attention on television. Still to come were *Trilogy of Terror II* and *The Love Letter* in the 1990s and *Saving Milly* and *Our Fathers* in the 2000s.

Director Dan Curtis spends four million dollars of his own money making *Me and the Kid* (1993).

Significa from the House of Dan Curtis: *House of Dark Shadows* and *Night of Dark Shadows* first aired on network television on the *CBS Late Movie*. *HODS* aired on Friday 16 July 1976. *NODS* aired on Monday 13 June 1977 after a rerun of *Kojak*.

In *House of Dark Shadows* (1970) and *Night of Dark Shadows* (1971), the interiors and exteriors of the great house of Collinwood were filmed at Lyndhurst, the magnificent Gothic Revival mansion on the banks of the Hudson River in Tarrytown, New York. It was designed and built in 1838 by the famous 19th-century architect Alexander Jackson Davis. Earlier in the 1830s, Davis had designed the Indiana state capitol, the Federal Customs House in New York City, and several buildings on the campus of the University of Michigan.

Davis built Lyndhurst (first called "Knoll") as a country villa for William Paulding, a brigadier general in the War of 1812 and a mayor of New York in the 1820s. In 1864-1865, Davis doubled the size of the house for its second owner, George Merritt, a New York City merchant. Merritt renamed the mansion "Lyndenhurst" (soon "Lyndhurst") after the linden trees which he planted on the 67-acre estate.

Between 1880 and his death in 1892, Lyndhurst was the summer home of the railroad magnate Jay Gould, who controlled the Union Pacific Railroad, the New York Elevated Railway, and the Western Union Telegraph Company. Gould ran a spur line of his railroad behind the mansion on the riverbank. A huge portrait of Gould is seen in *House of Dark Shadows*, and Gould's railroad track is the scene of a fight to the death in *Night of Dark Shadows*. Actor Scott Brady portrayed Jay Gould in a few scenes in *The Last Ride of the Dalton Gang* (1979).

After Gould's death, Lyndhurst became the home of Gould's daughter Helen Gould Shepard and her family until her death in 1938. For the next 23 years, Gould's other daughter, Anna, Duchess of Talleyrand-Perigord, resided there. Upon her death in 1961, Lyndhurst passed to the National Trust for Historic Preservation. Nine years later, *House of Dark Shadows* became the first of several movies, including *The Worst Witch* (1986), *Reversal of Fortune* (1990), *Gloria* (1999), and *Winter's Tale* (2014), to shoot scenes at Lyndhurst—all while daily tours of the house were still conducted. *Reversal of Fortune* is notable in that both the interior of Lyndhurst and the exterior of Seaview Terrace may be glimpsed in the film.[46]

House of Dark Shadows was feted at the Sleepy Hollow International Film Festival in Tarrytown, New York, on October 10-11-12-13 of 2019. At the Tarrytown Music Hall, *Master of Dark Shadows* producer Jim Pierson and *Dark Shadows* star Kathryn Leigh Scott gave a presentation about the making of the film (at nearby Lyndhurst in 1970). Other guests included Jeffrey Combs (*Re-Animator*), Bobcat Goldthwait (*Scrooged*), and Dana Gould (*Stan Against Evil*). SHIFF celebrated the 200th anniversary of Washington Irving's story "The Legend of Sleepy Hollow" and the 70th anniversary of Walt Disney's animated short film of the same name. The film festival also commemorated the 20th anniversary of Tim Burton's *Sleepy Hollow*, the 25th anniversary of *The Crow*, the 35th anniversaries of *The Neverending Story* and *Friday the 13th The Final Chapter*, the 45th anniversary of *Phantom of the Paradise*, and the 60th anniversary of *Plan 9 from Outer Space*. Dan Curtis's *House of Dark Shadows* turned 50 years old one year later in 2020.

Significa from the House of Dan Curtis: Dan Curtis visited Karen Black on the set of Alfred Hitchcock's *Family Plot* in San Francisco and asked her to star in his United Artists film *Burnt Offerings*. Black, who died on Thursday 8 August 2013, called *Burnt Offerings* "a wonderful, scary movie."[47] It aired on television for the first time on *NBC Saturday Night at the Movies* on 23 September 1978.

Although the *Burnt Offerings* house is supposed to be somewhere on the East Coast, Curtis shot his movie at Dunsmuir House, a 37-room mansion in Oakland, California. The Neoclassical Revival home was built in 1899 by Alexander Dunsmuir, the scion of a wealthy Canadian family that had made its fortune in coal. Three years after *Burnt Offerings*, Dunsmuir House was seen again in the 1979 horror film *Phantasm*. It turned up yet again in Roger Moore's final James Bond movie, *A View to a Kill* (1985).[48]

Significa from the House of Dan Curtis: On *Dark Shadows* in 1968, the order in which the characters see Adam is Barnabas, Julia, Willie, Mrs. Johnson, Elizabeth, David, Roger, Carolyn, Vicki, Prof. Stokes, Joe, and Maggie. After Vicki sees Adam but before Stokes does, Sam and Adam re-create the classic blind-man-meets-*Frankenstein*-monster scenario (in the rare episode #509).

CHAPTER IV

The Epics
Western, War, UFO, and More

Dan Curtis's five epic productions, from *Dracula* to *Intruders,* spanned the genres of horror, Western, war, and science fiction (or is it science fact?). First, Curtis's acclaimed adaptation of the most famous vampire novel of all time took him to Yugoslavia and England, where he directed his acclaimed version of **Dracula**, based on Bram Stoker's 1897 novel. The film, sometimes known as *Bram Stoker's Dracula* or *Dan Curtis's Dracula*, aired on CBS-TV on Friday 8 February 1974, after the first episode of the new sitcom *Good Times.*[1]

Dracula was the fourth of six collaborations between Curtis and author Richard Matheson, who had written about vampires in such 1950s stories and novels as "Blood Son," "The Funeral," and *I Am Legend*. Matheson's 1959 short story "No Such Thing as a Vampire" had been filmed for the 19 April 1968 premiere of BBC-TV's *Late-Night Horror*—one of the very first BBC productions filmed in color—before Dan Curtis remade it in 1973.[2]

Matheson recalled that his and Curtis's *Dracula* aired in a two-hour timeslot. He added,

> [It] turned out quite well, I thought, but it was even better at the three hours originally shot. I wrote a script for three hours, and Dan shot a three-hour version, but the network would give us only two hours. So Dan had to edit it down. I would have loved to have seen it at three hours. It was the first one that tried to follow the book and the first one to use the Vlad the Impaler material. To this day, I think we came the closest.[3]

What Matheson includes in his adaptation *is* an accurate reproduction of Bram Stoker's novel, especially the novel's first four chapters (relating Jonathan Harker's stay at Castle Dracula), as well as the shipwreck of the *Demeter* (chapter 7), Dracula's release of a wolf from the zoo (chapter 11), Mina's drinking of Dracula's blood from an open wound (chapter 21), and Van Helsing's hypnosis of Mina (chapter 23). However, Matheson omits the characters of Quincey Morris (often absent from film adaptations), Dr. John Seward, and the mad R.M. Renfield. The adaptation works without the Seward/Renfield subplot as it focuses fully on Jonathan Harker (Murray Brown), Mina Murray (Penelope Horner), Arthur Holmwood (Simon Ward), Lucy Westenra (Fiona Lewis), Mrs. Westenra (Pamela Brown), Dr. Abraham Van Helsing (Nigel Davenport), and Count Dracula (Jack Palance).

In 1973, Jack Palance (*Oklahoma Crude*) is 54 years old when he plays Count Dracula.

Matheson, with input from Curtis, makes two significant changes, one of which makes this adaptation so distinctive and influential. In the novel, Jonathan's opening storyline leaves him (at the end of chapter 4) a prisoner of Castle Dracula and at the mercy of Dracula's three vampire brides (played in the movie by Sarah Douglas, Barbara Lindley, and Virginia Wetherell). Four chapters later, Mina receives word that Jonathan is in a hospital in Budapest. Stoker never explains exactly how Harker managed to escape the castle. In Curtis's version, Jonathan does *not* escape. When Arthur and Van Helsing arrive at Castle Dracula, they find that their friend has become a vampire.

The more important change is the revisionist explanation of why Dracula comes to England in the first place. Stoker does not offer a reason until chapter 24 when Van Helsing assumes that Dracula is "leaving his own barren land—barren of peoples—and coming to a new land where life of man teems 'til they are like the multitude of standing corn."[4] In other words, Dracula may as well relocate to the world's largest city (London) in order to have an endless supply of victims. Curtis insisted,

> Richard Matheson, who's a wonderful writer, and I adapted the Bram Stoker novel and brought to it something that wasn't in it. I ripped myself off. I took the *Dark Shadows* love story and put it in our *Dracula* because in the novel, Dracula leaves Transylvania and goes to England for no reason at all. Stoker says he's sucked virtually everybody dry down there, and he had to find new blood. We didn't do that. I always felt that was ridiculous, so we came up with the central love story to *Dracula* that never existed in the novel but that has *since*, I might add, been *copied* by other *Draculas*, the most recent one, for instance.[5]

Curtis referred to Francis Ford Coppola's *Bram Stoker's Dracula* (1992).[6] However, the animated adventures *The Batman vs. Dracula* (2005) and *Highlander: The Search for Vengeance* (2006) also fit this description. So do Fred Olen Ray's vampire serial *The Lair* (2007-2009) and the CW series *The Vampire Diaries* (2009-2017). Curtis added,

> In our movie, he [Dracula] saw a picture of a girl [Lucy] in the newspaper, and we established that she was the reincarnation of this woman he was in love with in the 1400s. She's in England, and he goes to England to get her back. It's a little *Dark Shadowy*, but it worked. It was perfect. That's why our *Dracula* was as good as it was. It brought to the monster a degree of sympathy. Instead of making him just this marauding vampire, he was a haunted figure. You really cared about him even though you were terrified of him. Jack [Palance] is extraordinary. Jack is the best Dracula there ever was. He was the most frightening Dracula that ever put on that cape.[7]

The *Los Angeles Times* agreed. "This two-hour version of the classic horror story made for television by Dan Curtis and offered tonight on CBS would chill the bones of a plaster saint. It's as flesh-crawling an experience as you've ever had."[8] The *Times* proclaimed, "If the late [Bela] Lugosi was the definitive Count Dracula, it's no longer true. It's now Jack Palance."[9]

In a 2000 DVD featurette, Palance, who died on Friday 10 November 2006, at age 87, mused that Count Dracula was "the only character I ever played that frightened me even in the doing of it. But I never thought of the character as being evil. He was someone who was trapped in a situation." Palance added that with Curtis at the helm of the movie, "I knew it would be done very well and with great authenticity."[10] Donald F. Glut, author of *The Dracula Book* (Scarecrow, 1975), agreed: "The film surely ranks with the best movie adaptations of Stoker's *Dracula*, and it firmly establishes director Curtis and actor Palance among the genre's upper echelon."[11]

That newfound "authenticity" is the other hallmark of Curtis's *Dracula*—and the other ingredient that Coppola's 1992 blockbuster appropriated from its 1974 predecessor. Except for one line in Mehmet Muktar's 1953 Turkish film *Drakula Istanbul'da (Dracula in Istanbul)*—"The locals believe that I, like my ancestor Voyvodo Drakula, am ruthless"—Curtis's *Dracula* is the first Dracula film to make an explicit connection between Count Dracula and the real-life Vlad the Impaler of the 15th century. Matheson's screenplay reflects the scholarship of the time in Raymond McNally and Radu Florescu's *In Search of Dracula* (Houghton Mifflin, 1972) and *Dracula: A Biography of Vlad the Impaler, 1431-1476* (its 1973 follow-up).

Twenty-first-century film audiences take for granted that the Dracula character is based on the real-life story of a ruthless warrior, but at the time of Curtis's *Dracula*, such an idea was just coming into the popular consciousness. Vlad Dracula, also known as Vlad Tepes, was born in Sighisoara (a.k.a. Schassburg), a village in Transylvania, in late 1430 or early 1431. His father Vlad Dracul had been prince of Wallachia and a member of the Order of the Dragon, a Christian brotherhood founded by King Sigismund I of Hungary in 1418 and dedicated to fighting the Turkish people. "Drac" is a Romanian word meaning "dragon" or "devil." Vlad Dracul's son was called Drac**ula**, or "son of the dragon" or "son of the devil." In later life, Vlad Dracula also was called "Tepes," which means "impaler," because of his penchant for skewering as many of his enemies as possible. Vlad had many of them, for he spent his life attacking the Turkish people and fighting to acquire and keep the throne of Wallachia. After putting to death 40,000 of his enemies (four times more than Ivan the Terrible), Vlad fell to an assassin in December 1476 or early January 1477.[12]

Some evidence of Count Dracula's having been patterned after Vlad Tepes exists in Bram Stoker's novel. In chapter 3, Harker notes that Dracula sounds "like a king speaking"[13] when the Count talks knowingly of his family's "guarding of the frontier of Turkey-land."[14] Dracula declares,

> Who was it but one of my own race who as Voivode crossed the Danube and beat the Turk on his own ground? This was a Dracula indeed! [. . .] Was it not this Dracula, indeed, who inspired that other of his race who in a later age again and again brought his forces over the great river into Turkey-land; who, when he was beaten back, came again, and again, and again, though he had to come alone from the bloody field where his troops were being slaughtered, since he knew that he alone could ultimately triumph! They said that he thought only of himself. Bah! What good are peasants without a leader? Where ends the war without a brain and heart to conduct it? Again, when, after the battle of Mohacs, we threw off the Hungarian yoke, we of the Dracula blood were amongst their leaders, for our spirit would not brook that we were not free.[15]

Later, in chapter 18, as Van Helsing is explaining the rules of vampirism to Mina and the others, he reports his own findings about Dracula's origins.

> Thus, when we find the habitation of this man-that-was, we can confine him to his coffin and destroy him, if we obey what we know. But he is clever. I have asked my friend Arminius, of Buda-Peth University, to make his record; and, from all the means that are, he tells me of what he has been. He must, indeed, have been that Voivode Dracula who won his name against the Turk, over the great river on the very frontier of Turkey-land. If it be so, then he was no common man; for in that time, and for centuries after, he was spoken of as the cleverest and the most cunning, as well as the bravest of the sons of the "land beyond the forest." That mighty brain and that iron resolution went with him to his grave, and are even now arrayed against us. The Draculas were, says Arminius, a great and noble race, though now and again were scions who were held by their coevals to have had dealings with the Evil One. They learned his secrets in the Scholomance, amongst the mountains over Lake Hermanstadt, where the devil claims the tenth scholar as his due. In the records are such words as "stregoic"—witch, "ordog," and "pokol"—Satan and hell; and in one manuscript, this very Dracula is spoken of as "wampyr," which we all understand too well.[16]

Van Helsing's "friend Arminius" is the real-life Hungarian historian Arminius Vambery, author of *Hungary in Ancient, Medieval, and Modern Times* (1886) and other books of history and travel. Bram Stoker met Vambery at the Beefsteak Room, behind the Lyceum Theatre, in 1890 when Stoker was 43 and Vambery was 58. (The restaurant is mentioned in *Masterpiece Theatre*'s 2007 reimagining of *Dracula*.) At the time that he met Vambery, Stoker had begun to write *Dracula*, and it is possible that Vambery told Stoker stories of Vlad the Impaler—stories that the leading Hungarian scholar doubtless knew even though he himself never wrote about Vlad Tepes in any of his own books.[17] "The land beyond the forest" refers both to the literal translation of "transylvania" and to Emily Gerard Laszowska's 1888 book, *The Land Beyond the Forest: Facts, Figures, and Fancies from Transylvania*, which Stoker is known to have read when he was gathering information about the region.

The Scholomance is a legendary school of occult sciences and necromancy—a kind of antediluvian Hogwarts—where Count Dracula studied and perhaps where he lost his soul to the powers of darkness and became a vampire. (Stoker offers no concrete explanation as to how Dracula became undead centuries ago, but he strongly hints that sorcery was involved.) Students at the Scholomance are taught by a dragon and/or the devil how to affect the weather and how to transform themselves into animals.[18] Dracula's name suggests both "dragon" and "devil."

In Curtis and Matheson's groundbreaking film, Count Dracula is seen as a medieval warrior prince in two brief flashbacks and in an enormous painting. The nameplate below the painting of the kingly soldier on horseback even names him as "Vlad Tepes, Prince of Wallachia, 1475." In one scene, Dracula refers to himself as "me, who commanded armies hundreds of years before you were born." Indeed, in the summer of 1475, Vlad had regained the throne and then led armies to Serbia and Turkey.[19]

Finally, after Van Helsing and Arthur succeed in destroying the vampire, an epigraph in red letters on the screen proclaims,

> In the 15th Century, in the area of Hungary known as Transylvania, there lived a nobleman so fierce in battle that his troops gave him the name Dracula, which means devil. Soldier, statesman, alchemist, and warrior, so powerful a man was he that it was claimed he succeeded in overcoming even physical death. To this day, it has yet to be disproven.

Richard Matheson's words echo Dr. Seward's diary entry in chapter 23 of Stoker's novel:

> He was in life a most wonderful man. Soldier, statesman, and alchemist—which latter was the highest development of the science-knowledge of his time. He had a mighty brain, a learning beyond compare, and a heart that knew no fear and no remorse. He dared even to attend the Scholomance, and there was no branch of knowledge of his time that he did not essay. Well, in him, the brain powers survived the physical death.[20]

The film takes place near Bistritz, Transylvania, in May 1897; "five weeks later" near Whitby, England; and finally, back in Transylvania. The scenes of Jonathan Harker's captivity in Castle Dracula are atmospheric and frightening. Count Dracula and his vampire brides show a feral side that is quite unnerving. The scares continue in England as a wolf attacks Arthur Holmwood and Dracula vampirizes Lucy Westenra, who seems to be the reincarnation of Dracula's lost love. The scenes of Lucy's macabre death and rainy funeral are reminiscent of the corresponding scenes with Carolyn Stoddard in *House of Dark Shadows* (1970).

One of the most chilling moments of *Dracula* is Arthur's sighting of Lucy, now a vampire, plaintively rapping on the window and begging Arthur to let her come in. Another scary highlight is the mayhem that the superhuman Count Dracula causes at the George Hotel where Mina Murray and Mrs. Westenra are staying.

One of the most shocking moments (especially for 1974-era television) is Dracula's opening a wound on his torso and forcing Mina to drink *his* blood while Arthur Holmwood and Dr. Abraham Van Helsing stand by helplessly. The overseas theatrical cut of *Dracula* is even gorier. Blood gushes from the mouths of Lucy and one of the vampire brides when they are staked, and blood bursts from Dracula's mouth when he is impaled in the sunlight. Curtis's film editor was Richard A. Harris, who also edited *Scream of the Wolf*, *The Great Ice Rip-Off*, and the two Melvin Purvis movies. Harris later won the Academy Award for editing James Cameron's *Titanic* (1997).

For *Dan Curtis's Dracula*, Robert Cobert wrote a majestic, martial fanfare for the former warrior prince, as well as a dynamic main-title theme in the key of C minor. Cobert explained, "I wrote a love theme for *Dracula* that came from a music box. [. . .] I was the first composer to write a love theme for Dracula because Dan's *Dracula* had a love story in it.[21] [. . .] I wrote something modal, with a Romanian accent, the kind of music box that he might have had."[22] By "modal," Cobert meant something evocative of medieval church music.

"In a number of movies we did," Cobert added, "I had a music box somewhere."[23] Indeed, *House of Dark Shadows* (1970), *Come Die with Me* (1974), and *Burnt Offerings* (1976) feature music-box themes, continuing a practice begun on the *Dark Shadows* TV series with Josette's Music Box. "When I wrote the Dracula music-box theme, I played it for Dan, and at first he didn't like it. He said, 'It sounds sad.' I said, 'Of course it sounds sad. He's Dracula. He's sad!' It was a Hungarian music box rather than a Mozartian music box. Then, that music-box theme becomes the love theme, with full orchestra, and it morphs into danger halfway through."[24]

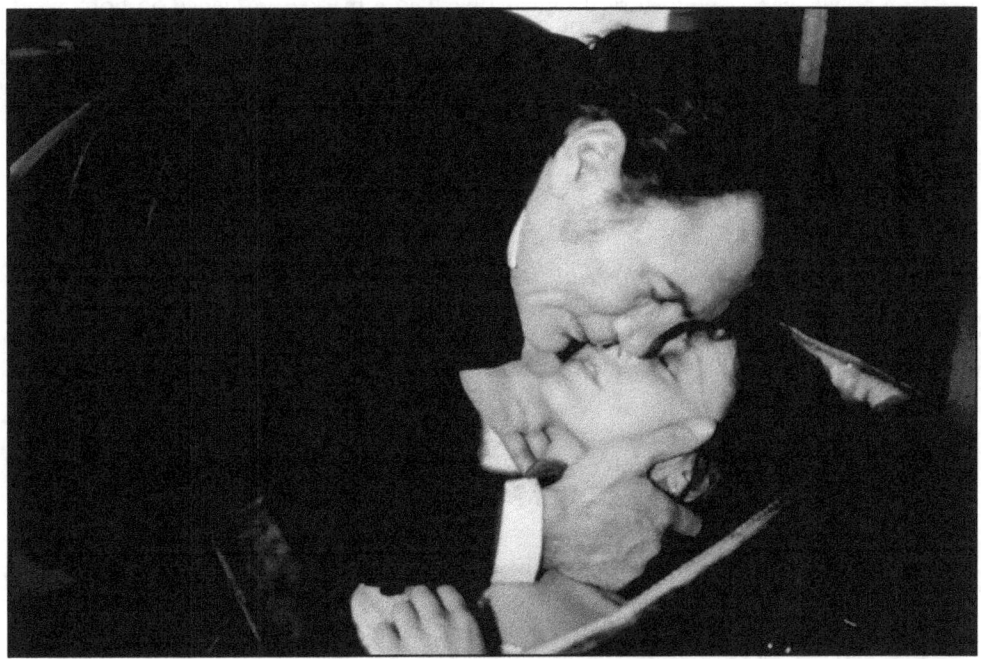

Dracula (1974): Jack Palance (*Bronk*) and Fiona Lewis (*Lisztomania*) play a frightening scene.

Cobert was given three weeks to write the music for Dracula. "That was a longer time than usual," he remembered.

> I usually got two weeks to write a movie score. I wrote the *Dracula* music at my beach house in the Hamptons. Writing it was a happy, rewarding experience. Whenever I did a movie with Dan, he and I sat down with a music editor, who took notes, and Dan showed me the movie. Then, we decided where the music should go. He'd say, "We need something here," and I'd say, "We need something there," and we worked it out. Dan said, "You gotta write something big for the death of Dracula," so I did. I ended with the theme for Dracula as the warrior and then the music box.[25]

The music, recorded by a 40-piece orchestra in London, was only one of many elements that made Curtis's *Dracula* an important addition to the nearly 200 film adaptations of Bram Stoker's novel since 1920. Of all of the actors who have portrayed the vampire, Jack Palance brought unique ferocity to the role and pioneered

Dracula's cinematic portrayal as Vlad the Impaler. Radu Florescu and Raymond McNally later noted Palance's portrayal of Vlad Dracula by declaring, "The best scene is where Dracula, upon finding that his long-lost love has been destroyed, groans like a wild animal as he smashes the funeral urns. In the final scene, Dracula is killed by a huge lance as the sun is coming up."[26] J. Gordon Melton, author of *The Vampire Book: The Encyclopedia of the Undead* (Visible Ink, 1994), added,

> Knowledge of the historical Dracula has had a marked influence on both Dracula movies and fiction. Two of the more important Dracula movies, *Dracula* (1974), starring Jack Palance, and *Bram Stoker's Dracula*, a recent [1992] production directed by Francis Ford Coppola, attempted to integrate the historical research on Vlad the Impaler into the story and used it as a rationale to make Dracula's actions more comprehensible.[27]

Dan Curtis confidently insisted that his, Matheson's, and Palance's film "is the best *Dracula* that was ever made! It was very erotic, without showing a hell of a lot, and very scary and done with a lot of classic style. We had a wonderful director of photography, Ossie Morris, and we shot it in England and Yugoslavia. It was a really good production."[28] *Variety* called it "a tribute to Palance, Curtis, and Matheson that it comes off as logically as it does." *Variety* continued,

> Curtis and Matheson, ignoring previous flourishes made out of Bram Stoker's Victorian novel, approach the tale with a fresh, realistic fashion, designed to chill. With Jack Palance turning in one of the finest performances of his career as the bloodthirsty nobleman, Matheson has brought out the essential elements of the story [. . .] Stoker, Sir Henry Irving's business manager as well as a novelist, would be delighted.[29]

Dracula benefits from beautiful cinematography by Oswald "Ossie" Morris (1915-2014), who recently had won the Academy Award for his cinematography of *Fiddler on the Roof* (1971). Morris imbued *Dracula* with gorgeous shots of the Yugoslavian countryside, high-angle shots of running wolves, and Curtis's trademark low-angle shots of the actors. Oswald Morris photographed *Dracula* around the time that he shot *The Man with the Golden Gun* (1974), the James Bond movie that co-starred another one of the best movie Draculas, Christopher Lee.

CBS reran *Dracula* in the mid-1970s, and A&E and local TV stations showed it in the 1980s. CBS re-aired it on Saturday 28 November 1992 in order to take advantage of the momentary upswing of interest in Dracula—especially Dracula as Vlad Tepes—because of the release of Francis Ford Coppola's *Bram Stoker's Dracula* (1992) on November 13. Fans were delighted to see 1992 end with a Dan Curtis classic to complement the new productions *Angie the Lieutenant* (February 1) and *Intruders: They Are Among Us* (May 17 & 19). When *Dracula* re-aired on November 28, Dan Curtis was busy filming *Me and the Kid* (1993).

As excellent as *Dracula* is as a two-hour movie, it would have been even more epic as the three-hour film that Curtis and Matheson had envisioned. Sadly, almost all of the extra, unused footage for a three-hour *Dracula* was lost some time in the 1980s. The MPI Blu-Ray of *Dracula* features the only remaining extra footage, "a few odd scraps" that Jim Pierson found "in a can of trailer outtakes" as he was restoring the film for the Blu-Ray release and a gala screening at the Vista Theatre in Los Angeles on Wednesday

30 April 2014.[30] The scraps reveal nothing new: they are soundless shots of Jack Palance posing as Dracula, Arthur and Van Helsing protecting Lucy as she sleeps, and Van Helsing hypnotizing Mina and staking Lucy and one of the brides.

Luckily, Matheson's three-act "screen treatment" (plot synopsis) and 140-page script (dated 7 August 1972) do exist and were published in Mark Dawidziak's 2006 book *Bloodlines: Richard Matheson's* Dracula, I Am Legend, *and Other Vampire Stories*. Dawidziak dedicated the Gauntlet Press book "to Dan [Curtis] and Darren [McGavin], both legends."[31]

Dracula (1974): **Nigel Davenport (*The Picture of Dorian Gray*) and Simon Ward (*The Four Musketeers*) portray Abraham Van Helsing and Arthur Holmwood, respectively.**

Matheson's typewritten script is that of a nearly three-hour-long film that very closely resembles the finished *two*-hour movie—with a few significant exceptions. In the first scenes at Castle Dracula, Matheson's script calls for Count Dracula to appear as an old man with his fingernails "cut to a point"[32] as in Bram Stoker's novel. It is only after biting Lucy that "Dracula now looks like a vigorous man in his forties."[33]

In the scene in which Dracula prevents his three wives from feeding on Jonathan, Dracula "has a moving sack in his hands."[34] The script calls for "a momentary glimpse of a half-dead little girl," upon whom "the hideous trio" pounces.[35] Next, the little girl's parents are standing outside the castle and screaming for Dracula to give them back their child. The vampire summons a pack of wolves to attack the parents.[36]

Other elements that do not transfer from script to screen are several more shots of Dracula's driving his carriage to and from the George Hotel, an image of the undead Lucy's tempting Arthur by showing her breasts to him, and a glimpse of Lucy's severed head. (Van Helsing does not cut off Lucy's or any vampire's head in the finished film.) In the scene in which Dracula bursts in to Mina and Mrs. Westenra's hotel room, Matheson calls for Mrs. Westenra's death at Dracula's hands, but Curtis leaves her alive.

A major difference between the script and the film is that Matheson, like Stoker, allows Jonathan Harker to escape from Castle Dracula. Other differences emerge at the end of the script when Arthur Holmwood and Abraham Van Helsing close in on the vampire at Castle Dracula. Matheson calls for the novel's horde of rats, as well as Dracula's gold coins that spill from his pockets after his impaled body begins "to atrophy as he dies."[37]

The script, as well as the movie, ends with crowd noises, the shot of Dracula's portrait, and the "crawl title" in red letters. Matheson and Curtis's film is largely faithful to Stoker's novel, but the additions of Old Dracula, Jonathan's escape (but *not* death), the rats, and the gold coins would have made the movie even *more* faithful.

What the typewritten script does *not* include is the creative input of director Dan Curtis. In Matheson's script, there is no scene in which Harker, now a vampire, attacks Holmwood and Van Helsing; there is no music box; there are no flashbacks to the life (brief love scene) and death (brief deathbed scene) of Dracula's long-lost love (Fiona Lewis); and there is no all-important moment (as in *Horror of Dracula* [1958] and several *Dark Shadows* episodes [1968 et al.]) when the vampire slayers flood the room with sunlight and stun the monster before they destroy him. Apparently, these scenes in the movie were devised by Dan Curtis (with input from Robert Cobert and Richard Matheson).

Mark Dawidziak's aforementioned *Bloodlines* book published Matheson's extremely detailed "screen treatment," which reveals the plot of the *three*-hour-long script and film that might have been. The treatment, too, first describes Count Dracula as "a tall, old man, clean-shaven except for a long, white moustache, [and] dressed entirely in black."[38] After Dracula goes to England and begins feeding on Lucy, he is "a very different Dracula, no longer old but seemingly, incredibly, becoming young again."[39] Later, after several nights when Arthur and his godfather Van Helsing prevent Lucy from going to Dracula, "the infuriated vampire [is] starting to age again."[40]

According to Dawidziak, Matheson lamented the shortening of his and Curtis's *Dracula* from three hours to two hours because (in Matheson's words) "it needed that extra hour" to be the nearly complete and definitive *Dracula* adaptation that Matheson had envisioned.⁴¹ If Matheson and Curtis had had that extra hour (for the Harker story arc, which included a hypnosis scene), a bigger budget (for the rats, the coins, Old Dracula, and other touches), and more freedom (for the horrifying moment with the little girl and her parents), *Dan Curtis's Dracula* (1974) would have been *the* definitive version of the oft-filmed story. As it is, it ranks with Gerald Savory and Philip Savile's *Count Dracula* (1977) and one or two other films as *one of* the most nearly definitive adaptations of *Dracula*. Like Curtis's mostly faithful versions of *The Strange Case of Dr. Jekyll and Mr. Hyde* and *The Picture of Dorian Gray*, Matheson and Curtis's *Dracula* is a major touchstone in horror television. According to Richard Matheson,

> I think it came as close as you could with just two hours, but there was quite a bit missing. I would have loved to have seen it at three hours. That would have been dandy. Then, we could have really done it to a fare-thee-well. But even at the shorter time, it still came off very well.⁴²

Five-and-one-half years later, Dan Curtis made a splash with his one-and-only Western epic. In 1979, during the crucial November-sweeps period, NBC aired the three-hour event, **The Last Ride of the Dalton Gang** (Tuesday 20 November), one of Curtis's personal favorites of his films. The film's VHS tape box described it as "an epic tale of outlaws running out of time."

In a 2005 DVD interview, Dan Curtis revealed that he "always loved Westerns." He added, "I always wanted to make a Western. I just love the whole feel of Westerns and the look of Westerns. At that point [1979], I had reached *my style* in terms of shooting, and my style was accommodated very nicely by the Western genre because I jammed frames with gun butts and everything that has dust in it!"⁴³

Curtis originally planned the production as a two-part, four-hour miniseries called *Raid on Coffeyville*, but he (not the network) decided to reshape it as a tighter, one-night feature. (The extra footage still exists.) Curtis remembered, "The only reason it ended up the length it was is I didn't think that the four hours would *hold* over two nights. It probably would have, and it was a mistake to cut it down, but the cut-down version was great, playing as three hours in one night."⁴⁴

The Last Ride of the Dalton Gang, produced by Joseph Stern (*Mrs. R's Daughter*) and written by future Oscar winner Earl W. Wallace (*Witness*), tells the often light-hearted story of the Dalton brothers' misadventures as deputy marshals-turned-horse thieves, train bandits, and bank robbers. Curtis mixes the rollicking tone of *Bonnie and Clyde* (1967) with the fatalism of *The Wild Bunch* (1969) and the nostalgia of classic Hollywood Westerns. He filmed the movie in and around Los Angeles, Columbia, Jamestown, Placerville, Sacramento, Sonora, and Stockton, California.

The Last Ride of the Dalton Gang (1979) features one of the best opening-credits sequences of all of Curtis's movies: a fast-moving montage of covers of Western pulp magazines, such as *The Pecos Kid Western, Ace-High Western Stories, Fifteen Western Tales, Ranch Romances,* and *Thrilling Western*. According to Curtis,

> The title sequence in this picture is one of my favorite things in the movie. The picture is very reminiscent of the feel that you get from reading those old pulp Westerns, and I used to love the covers of those pulp westerns. So in order to get that feel for this picture—let the

audience know what's coming—I thought if we took those covers and did a montage of those covers, doing camera moves on those covers, on those great paintings, it would tell the audience, "This is the kind of movie you're about to see," and the music that Cobert wrote to go with it really hammered that home.[45]

Over the last 130+ years, magazines and movies have transformed the real lives of the Dalton brothers and their accomplices into the stuff of pulpy Western adventure-romances. *The Last Ride of the Dalton Gang* focuses on five of the brothers. Don Collier briefly plays Frank Dalton (1858-1888), who became a Deputy U.S. Marshal but was killed in the line of duty three years later. Bronze Wrangler Award winner Randy Quaid plays Gratton Dalton (1861-1892), who also became a Deputy U.S. Marshal for a time. Mills Watson plays Bill Dalton (1866-1894), who ran for the California State Legislature but turned to a life of crime himself after the death of his brothers. Bronze Wrangler Award winner Cliff Potts plays Bob Dalton (1869-1892), the self-appointed leader of the Dalton Gang and the mastermind of the raid on Coffeyville. *CHiPs* star Larry Wilcox plays Emmett Dalton (1871-1937), who establishes the frame story of the movie by telling his life story to a newspaper reporter (Terry Kiser) in Hollywood, California, on 6 June 1934.

The Last Ride of the Dalton Gang (NBC, 1979) stars (standing, from left) Matt Clark, John Fitzpatrick, Cliff Potts, Sharon Farrell, Larry Wilcox, James Crittenden, Eric Lawson (and kneeling, from left), Bo Hopkins, Randy Quaid, and Dennis Fimple.

The real-life Bob and Emmett followed Grat's lead and became U.S. Deputy Marshals. They worked for the famous "Hanging Judge," Isaac Parker (1838-1896; Dale Robertson in the movie), but the brothers soon became disenchanted and decided that the other side of the law—outlawry—was the place where their talents and fortunes lay. They graduated from lesser crimes (1890-1891) to four spectacular train robberies (May 1891-July 1892), all the while being pursued by U.S. Marshal Heck Thomas (1850-1912; in Curtis's movie, only a minor character, played by Bill Jelliffe). The last ride of the Dalton Gang was into Coffeyville, Kansas, where Bob Dalton led his brothers and two of their confederates in a failed mission to rob *two* banks at the same time in broad daylight.

Before the Coffeyville raid, the actual Dalton Gang numbered ten or more as shown in the film. Other gang members included George "Bitter Creek" Newcomb (played by Matt Clark), Bill "Billy" Doolin (portrayed by Bo Hopkins), "Blackfaced" Charlie Bryant (played by Dennis Fimple), "Cockeye" Charley Pierce (not a character in the film), Bill McElhanie (called "Hugh MacElhenie" in the movie and portrayed by James Crittenden), Bill Power (called "Willie Powers" in the movie and played by Eric Lawson), and Dick Broadwell (called "'Texas Jack' Broadwell" in the movie and portrayed by John Fitzpatrick). All of the aforementioned outlaws met their deaths between 1891 and 1895; however, Dan Curtis and Earl Wallace take the liberty of allowing "Bitter Creek" Newcomb to live on and run in to Emmett Dalton on the street in Hollywood in 1934. They draw guns on each other, which attracts the attention of the reporter Mr. Nafius, but then they make peace and sit down with Nafius to talk about the infamous Dalton Gang of '92.

In reality, the five Dalton Gang members who rode into Coffeyville on Wednesday 5 October 1892 to rob the First National Bank and the C.M. Condon Bank were Bob, Emmett, and Grat Dalton; Bill Power; and Dick Broadwell. The men wore unconvincing fake beards and openly carried rifles as it was hunting season. Under their coats, each man carried two guns (most of them Colt .45 revolvers) except Bob Dalton, who carried a British Bulldog .38 in addition to his two Colts.[46] For years, there was a rumor of a sixth accomplice, possibly Bill Doolin, but there is little or no evidence of a sixth outlaw in Coffeyville that day.

The five outlaws assumed that they could breeze into town, rob the banks, and make a clean getaway, but the shrewd Coffeyville citizens immediately saw through their disguises and spread the word that the Daltons were striking the First National and the Condon. The townspeople—two shoemakers, a barber, a stable owner, Town Marshal Charles Connelly, and many others—quickly fetched their personal firearms or were quietly issued rifles from the Isham Hardware Store next door to the First National. The townsmen took up positions along the street, in windows, and on rooftops and waited for the robbers to emerge.

Bob and Emmett had stormed into the First National Bank while Grat, Bill Power, and Dick Broadwell had invaded the Condon Bank. Bob and Emmett efficiently stole more than $20,000 from the First National, but the tellers at the Condon Bank were giving their three robbers a harder time by gathering the silver coins very slowly and claiming that the vault where the paper money was kept was on a timed lock and could not be opened "for another 15 minutes." The townspeople outside the banks were making good use of those minutes and began shooting at the criminals when they ran out of the banks. The Dalton Gang returned fire.

Bo Hopkins (*The Kansas City Massacre, Supertrain*) portrays the often disgruntled Dalton Gang member Billy Doolin.

Photographs taken later that same day (5 October 1892) show the results of the huge gun battle that ensued: bank windows riddled with bullet holes, dead horses, and the corpses of Bill Power (who died first), Dick Broadwell, Bob Dalton, and Grat Dalton. Emmett Dalton, who tried to rescue his dead or dying brothers, was shot 23 times but did not die. In addition to the four dead outlaws and several dead horses, the smoky, hellish gunfight killed four Coffeyville citizens (including Town Marshal Connelly, shot by Grat) and wounded three.[47]

Emmett Dalton (1871-1937) lived to serve 14 years in prison and another 30 years as a free man. In 1907, he married Julia Johnson Dalton (played by Julie Hill in Curtis's movie) and settled in Los Angeles where he worked in real estate and filmmaking. He also wrote two books about his brothers and himself. Both of his books, *Beyond the Law* and *When the Daltons Rode*, were made into movies in 1918 and 1940, respectively.

In the 1940s and 1950s, several films, of varying quality and veracity, were made about the Dalton Gang. In his 2000 Castle book *Robbing Banks*, L.R. Kirchner singles out Gordon Douglas's *Doolins of Oklahoma* (1949) and Dan Curtis's *Last Ride of the Dalton Gang* (1979) as films that, while exaggerated, "have the distinctive Western feel of the time period and are legitimate movies as far as decent acting and scripts are concerned."[48]

Curtis's film, while historically accurate on many points, does not stick to the facts at all times. In addition to keeping "Bitter Creek" alive for the fictitious 1934 reunion, the movie has Bill Dalton running for governor of California. Judge Isaac Parker (Dale Robertson) is involved in the movie, but Heck Thomas is replaced by a new character, "U.S. Marshal Will Smith," played by Jack Palance. In this movie, "Smith" is the one who doggedly pursues the Dalton Gang and shows up in Coffeyville in time to shoot Emmett before Judge Parker shoots him. (In actuality, Heck Thomas was not present for the gun battle.) In a major (and perhaps unwise) deviation from reality, "Smith" brings 50 men with him to Coffeyville, and it is they, not the townspeople, who battle the Daltons.

Another major character in the film is (more or less) real: "Virginia Wade," a.k.a. Eugenia Moore, a.k.a. T. King, a.k.a. Flo Quick (Sharon Farrell), a schoolteacher-turned-"businesswoman" who falls for Bob Dalton, runs with the Dalton Gang, and forms her own gang of outlaws after the Coffeyville incident. Old Emmett tells the reporter that Flo and her gang "got killed robbin' a bank down in Las Cruces in '93." Sharon Farrell, a familiar face in 1960s and 1970s television, gives a multi-faceted performance as the tough madam whose heart melts for Bob Dalton.

Curtis's often light-hearted film begins with the playful legend, "What follows here is not intended to be an accurate re-creation of historical fact. Not that it matters." This disclaimer, along with the montage of pulp magazines and Robert Cobert's rollicking opening theme, effectively clues-in the audience. Curtis remarked, "As you see from the legend at the beginning of the film, that's basically the feeling that we had throughout the picture."[49] There are moments of hilarity along the way, and even a Buffalo Bill Wild West Show that the Dalton Gang disrupts, but the final gun battle, which took Curtis four days to shoot, packs an emotional punch. By then, the audience has come to know and care about the cocky Bob, the naïve Emmett, and the slow-witted Grat and their friends and lovers.

Sharon Farrell (*The Eyes of Charles Sand*, *The Cloning of Clifford Swimmer*) plays Flo Quick in Dan Curtis's *Dalton Gang* movie.

By 1979, Curtis, now having shot *Dracula, Burnt Offerings, Curse of the Black Widow,* and two Melvin Purvis crime dramas, had matured and refined his *auteur*'s style of filmmaking. Curtis explained,

> I was pretty ready to shoot this picture. I knew it was going to be loaded with action, but those Melvin Purvis movies I had done showed me that I could handle that stuff with ease. This picture was tougher than any movie I've ever made—including *The Winds of War* and *War and Remembrance*. It was supposed to be four hours long, a two-parter. I had a 31-day shooting schedule. It was the most difficult thing I've ever had to do because, as you see from the film, it was just loaded with action and loaded with texture and a million characters. It was a very difficult picture to make, but it turned out great.[50]

Despite stiff competition from *Happy Days, Three's Company,* and other ABC comedies, *The Last Ride of the Dalton Gang* was a ratings success on the night of Tuesday 20 November 1979. Judith Crist of *TV Guide* wrote,

> For those who delight in later Americana (strictly dime-Western, romantic version), there's *The Last Ride of the Dalton Gang,* produced and directed for TV by Dan Curtis, written by Earl W. Wallace, and offered with the warning that "What follows here is not intended to be an accurate re-creation of historical fact. Not that it matters." What follows is a boisterous, shoot-'em-up account of the law-manning, horse-stealing, train-and-bank-robbing career of the four of five brothers who "just couldn't stay on the right side of the law." Only Em Dalton (Larry Wilcox), who recounts their adventures to a reporter in 1934, died (in 1937) with his boots off. The virtue of this entertainment is that the outlaws, though appealing, are not glorified but are seen clearly as the not-too-bright hoodlums they were.[51]

The Last Ride of the Dalton Gang won the Western Heritage Bronze Wrangler Award, for Outstanding Fictional Television Program of 1979, from the National Cowboy Hall of Fame. "This picture really got me ready for *The Winds of War*," Curtis observed, because of its large cast, complex action sequences, and period detail.[52]

The National Cowboy Hall of Fame also honored composer Robert Cobert, whose *Dalton Gang* music score won the Bronze Wrangler Award for Best Western Music Score of 1979. Cobert's music is by turns playful, romantic, comedic, and suspenseful. Cobert achieves an authentic Western sound through his use of harmonica, guitar, snare drum, player piano, and sentimental strings. In an interview on the 2005 MPI Home Video *Dalton Gang* DVD that also includes 14 tracks (40 minutes) of Cobert's music, Dan Curtis declared,

> Cobert once again astounded me. It was our first Western, his *and* mine, and from a guy who had never written anything for a Western score, for a picture that was loaded with action and humor, it could be one of the greatest scores he's ever written. Every single cue in it was absolutely wonderful.[53]

Cobert's happy/sad music propels *The Last Ride of the Dalton Gang* from initial exuberance to ultimate catastrophe, and it unifies the shorter cut of the movie.

Director Dan Curtis and film editor Dennis Virkler's three-hour cut of the four-hour *Raid on Coffeyville* is tight, fluid, and engrossing. Virkler had edited *Burnt Offerings, Dead of Night, When Every Day Was the Fourth of July,* and other productions for Curtis. He later received Academy Award nominations for his work on *The Hunt for Red October* (1990) and *The Fugitive* (1993).

In 2015, *CHiPs* and *Dalton Gang* star Larry Wilcox called Dan Curtis "a very passionate director." He added,

> Dan became a kind of mentor for me as a director. He loved the low-angle shots (we call them the Hero Shot or the John Wayne Shot), and he was a strong believer in full-frame composition. His shots were staged to have lots of visual clutter in them, both foreground and background, to make a frame more interesting. He was a master of camera placement. [. . .] He loved directing, and he was very efficient. [. . .] He hired good actors, and he seemed to love the process of reading and casting actors. He was proud of "his team," and he enjoyed making his team a family during the shoot.[54]

In a 2005 DVD interview, Curtis stated that he felt that his *Dalton Gang* TV-movie could have been released theatrically, "as is," and succeeded. The film lives on through occasional showings on the Encore Western cable-TV channel and through its VHS and DVD releases. Who knows what a second Curtis Western would have been like? A clue, sure to delight fans of both Dan Curtis and Richard Matheson, awaits in this book's seventh chapter, "…What Might Have Been."

The 1970s saw Dan Curtis dominate television horror (*Dracula, Trilogy of Terror*) and experiment with Westerns (*The Last Ride of the Dalton Gang*). The 1980s propelled him even higher in the TV firmament as he became king of the miniseries. He spent almost the entire decade on the two greatest achievements of his career and two of the most impressive filmmaking feats in history: the ABC miniseries *The Winds of War* (1983) and *War and Remembrance* (1988, 1989), based on the best-selling novels by Herman Wouk (1915-2019).

In 1980, ABC executive Barry Diller asked Curtis to take on the Herculean task of bringing to television **The Winds of War**, Wouk's sprawling novel of an American Naval family in the years 1939–1941. Wouk himself was against the idea after being greatly displeased by Hollywood's filmings of his novels *The Caine Mutiny* in 1954 and especially *Marjorie Morningstar* in 1958 and *Youngblood Hawke* in 1964. Wouk felt that Hollywood had "trivialized" the latter two works, and he did not want to see a watered-down screen version of his 1971 masterpiece *The Winds of War*, an 888-page opus which he had begun researching in 1960.[55]

Nevertheless Curtis, once a Naval Reserve officer, and Wouk, a four-year naval officer on minesweepers, met and convinced each other to film *The Winds of War* from a screenplay by Wouk. Unaccustomed to writing for the screen, Wouk gladly accepted pointers from Curtis, by now a master at doctoring the scripts of his projects. Earl Wallace (*Curse of the Black Widow, The Last Ride of the Dalton Gang*) served as story editor. "We all worked closely on the screenplay," Curtis recalled, "with Herman having the final word on everything. He even told ABC how many commercials and *what kind of* commercials they could run during the thing!"[56]

Victoria Tennant, with novelist Herman Wouk (left) and director Dan Curtis, plays Pamela Tudsbury in *The Winds of War* (1983) and again in *War and Remembrance* (1988, 1989).

The miniseries's running time of nearly 15 hours (scheduled in an 18-hour block on ABC) was the equivalent of seven motion pictures. Curtis originally planned to direct only parts of the epic and use other directors to fill in the rest, but ABC wanted a single director—Curtis—and his singular *auteur's* vision. Curtis remembered,

> I kept thinking, "What am I going to do?" I talked to my wife about it, and then I said, "I'll just start directing this thing, and then when I start to wear myself out, I'll bring in other directors and fight about it then." Norma said, "As long as you promise me you won't direct the whole thing!" I said, "Promise you? There's no way I could direct the whole thing." Well, I directed the whole thing.[57]

Curtis filmed the $40 million production for more than one year (1 December 1980 to 8 December 1981) at 267 locations in six countries: the United States, England, West Germany, Austria, Italy, and Yugoslavia. "We shot as much as we could in Yugoslavia," Curtis explained in a DVD interview. He remembered,

> The people were wonderful in Yugoslavia. It was still a communist country, and the people were very impoverished. But it had this tremendous innocence. Wherever you went, people were happy to see you. We found quaint villages like where we shot the Jewish wedding, and we actually used the real rabbi and the real cantor. Ali [MacGraw] loved the flower markets and the food markets. The food was great.[58]

At that time the most enormous project in television or film history, *The Winds of War* consisted of 4000 camera set-ups, more than one million feet of film, and 1785 scenes in Wouk and Curtis's 962-page script. There were 285 speaking roles and thousands of extras spread across Europe.[59] Curtis had actualized the Old Hollywood expression, "a cast of thousands." Heading the cast, along with Ali MacGraw, were Robert Mitchum, Polly Bergen, Jan-Michael Vincent, Victoria Tennant, David Dukes, Peter Graves, Chaim Topol, Jeremy Kemp, and John Houseman. Character actors from Anton Diffring, Andrew Duggan, Jerry Fujikawa, and John Karlen to Charles Lane, Ferdy Mayne, Barry Morse, and Richard X. Slattery made appearances, and Ralph Bellamy reprised his 1960 *Sunrise at Campobello* role of President Franklin Delano Roosevelt. The narrator was William T. Woodson, whose voice was also heard on *The Invaders* and *The Odd Couple*.

Dan Curtis (left) directs Robert Mitchum as Victor "Pug" Henry in *The Winds of War* (1983) and again in *War and Remembrance* (1988, 1989). Both men hail from Bridgeport, Connecticut.

Playing Morse's on-screen wife was Barbara Steele, an icon of 1960s-era European cinema (*8½*, *The Hours of Love*, *Young Torless*) and Italian horror (*Black Sunday*, *The Horrible Dr. Hichcock*, *An Angel for Satan*). Steele was living in Los Angeles after the 1980 death of her husband, Oscar-winning screenwriter James Poe (*Around the World in 80 Days*; *Lilies of the Field*; *They Shoot Horses, Don't They?*). She met Curtis through a mutual friend, British ICM agent Maggie Abbott, and he hired her to peruse stock footage of World War II for possible use in *The Winds of War*. Curtis and Steele began a successful professional relationship that lasted until his death. Steele became associate producer of

The Winds of War, full producer of *War and Remembrance* and *Saving Milly*, co-producer of *Our Fathers*, and co-star of the 1991 *Dark Shadows* revival.

"*The Winds of War* and *War and Remembrance* were such vast projects of staggering complexity, covering all of World War II and the events leading up to it," Steele observed. She explained,

> This involved years of shooting, pre-production, and post-production. It was the equivalent of making 18 motion pictures back to back, involving so many people, countries, currencies, and shifting world events that it seemed unimaginable and even mad to me that one man could have the desire and the passion—let alone the energy—to be able to translate these two epic books to the screen with a commitment involving years and years of work. But Dan never faltered in his vision. He was like a rabid wolf in his intensity and determination. Of course, the whole operatic landscape suited his personality so perfectly; it's as if he were born for these projects. They were both beautiful and terrible.[60]

Robert Mitchum, who starred as Captain Victor "Pug" Henry, described Dan Curtis to reporters as a director of "complete and total ferocity."[61] In *People* magazine in 1983, Curtis called Mitchum "the biggest pro in the world."[62] Ali MacGraw, who played Natalie Jastrow Henry, told *Entertainment Tonight* that Dan Curtis was "the best director" with whom she had ever worked.[63]

Polly Bergen was well suited for the role of Rhoda Henry, Pug's restless wife. Bergen, a voracious reader, had read both *The Winds of War* and its 1042-page sequel, *War and Remembrance* (1978), and strongly desired to play Rhoda. She received Emmy nominations for her work in both miniseries. "I loved working with Dan," Bergen recalled. "He was enormously supportive, a terrific and very loud director, and I had complete trust in him. He could be very difficult, but he never was with me. I would work with him any day of the week."[64]

Singer-actress Polly Bergen (as Rhoda Henry) receives Emmy Award nominations for her work in both *The Winds of War* (1983) and *War and Remembrance* (1988, 1989).

Once fearful that he would tire of shooting *The Winds of War*, Curtis later declared, "It was the toughest thing I ever did, but I *never* got tired. I could have kept shooting forever. Making *The Winds of War* was one of the greatest experiences of my life. Recreating history where it actually happened was the most exciting experience."[65] Curtis remembered with special fondness shooting the meeting between Roosevelt (Ralph Bellamy) and Churchill (Howard Lang) aboard the *Prince of Wales* (actually the U.S.S. *Missouri*) and recreating the attack on Pearl Harbor (actually the Oxnard, California, naval base)—*on December 7* of 1981—two decades before Michael Bay's *Pearl Harbor* (2001) and well before the conveniences of CGI special effects.

Curtis's efforts paid off remarkably when *The Winds of War*, broadcast on ABC-TV on February 6-11 & 13 of 1983 (two or three hours each night), commanded more than 140 million viewers. It delivered a 38.6 rating and a 53 share, and it remains the third most-watched miniseries of all time, after *Roots* in 1977 and *The Thorn Birds* later in 1983.[66] *The Winds of War* appeared on more than 17 different magazine covers and made headlines around the world. "The reviews were phenomenal," Curtis beamed. "I'd never even *seen* reviews like the ones we got."[67] *Variety* called *The Winds of War* "striking television" and "an impressive look at history in the making" and praised its "enormous sweep" and "unerring ring of truth."[68] *Newsday* called it "really something extraordinary and special,"[69] and the *Philadelphia Enquirer* proclaimed it to be "television in its finest hour."[70] The *Detroit News* added,

> Producer-director Dan Curtis treads knowingly between the television form known as docudrama and the old movie romances. He tastefully employs 1940s movie conventions (the recurring, heavy love-theme music; the camera turning around the kissing couple), but he knows he's directing for the little screen, not the big one. His emphasis is on the telling close-up, the intimate set piece. His action sequences are just enough to convey cold or smoke or carnage. Some of the outdoor shots are beautiful—a delicately lighted Geneva, the Kremlin as seen from a frozen hill, the leafy richness of Sienna. The total effect is remarkably evocative of the period.[71]

Robert Cobert's music score, with its love theme, marches, waltzes, and ethnic music, ran longer than 2000 manuscript pages. The love theme has joined Cobert's equally haunting "Quentin's Theme" from *Dark Shadows* as a staple on what the broadcasting industry calls beautiful-music radio stations.

Writing for *The World of Dark Shadows* #36 (December 1983), I called *The Winds of War* "a grandiose tale" and added, "Herman Wouk's teleplay and Dan Curtis's direction did a marvelous job of explaining the situations, events, philosophies, cultures, and emotions which together hurled the planet into the awesome maelstrom that took years to resolve."[72]

The Winds of War was nominated for the Emmy Award for Outstanding Limited Series, and Dan Curtis was nominated for Outstanding Directing in a Limited Series or Special for his direction of "Into the Maelstrom," the seventh and final episode of the blockbuster miniseries. *The Winds of War* received 11 other Emmy nominations in various Limited-Series categories: cinematography, art direction, special visual effects, costumes, film editing, film sound editing, film sound mixing (three separate nominations), supporting actress (Polly Bergen), and supporting actor (Ralph Bellamy). Bergen and Bellamy lost to Jean Simmons and Richard Kiley, both of *The Thorn Birds*, and Curtis lost to director John Erman for *Who Will Love My Children?* The TV-movie, starring Ann-Margret, ran on ABC on Valentine's Day 1983, the night after the final episode of *The Winds of War*.

In one of the most startling upsets in Emmy history, *both* the high-profile *Winds of War* and *Thorn Birds* lost the Outstanding Limited Series award to the Royal Shakespeare Company's syndicated TV adaptation of Charles Dickens's *Nicholas Nickleby*, a production that ABC, CBS, and NBC had turned down. However, *The Winds of War* did win Emmy Awards for cinematography (Charles Correll), costumes (Tommy Welsh et al.), and special visual effects (Roy Downey et al.). Although it did not win any of its four Golden Globe nominations, the miniseries won Spain's TP de Oro award for best foreign series, and Dan Curtis himself received the Torch of Liberty award from the Anti-Defamation League.[73] *The Winds of War*, as well as its sequel, is available on VHS and DVD.

By the time that ABC-TV reran *The Winds of War* on September 7, 9-10, & 12-14 of 1986 (three hours each night) as a kick-off to its 1986–1987 season, Curtis was already two-and-one-half years into his work on the miniseries's even more staggering sequel, **War and Remembrance**, again based on a Herman Wouk novel. This time, Curtis and Earl Wallace wrote the dramatic, personal scenes involving the novel's characters, and Herman Wouk wrote the historical scenes. Returning as sole director was, of course, Dan Curtis, who remembered,

> When I finished *The Winds of War*, which turned out to be 18 hours, I swore I would never, ever do *War and Remembrance*. But *Winds* was such a huge hit that I knew *War and Remembrance* was going to be made. I wasn't going back into television. I figured I had done all the television I was ever going to do. I could never be able to top myself. I might as well get into the feature business, which is where I wanted to be. [ABC executive] Brandon Stoddard kept after me [to direct *War and Remembrance*], and I kept saying, no, no, no, no, no. One day, my wife and I were driving to Palm Springs. I was an unhappy guy, and she said to me, "You want to do *War and Remembrance*, don't you? I know you really want to do it." I said, "Yeah, maybe I do; I miss all the action and the excitement." Norma said, "Well, then, why don't you do it?"[74]

Curtis went to *War* again in early 1984 and began pre-production on the continuing story of the Victor Henry family in the years 1941–1945. This miniseries would recreate the most crucial events of World War II with stunning accuracy and power. History-making moments at Midway, Guadalcanal, Stalingrad, Yalta, El Alamein, the Battle of the Bulge, Babi Yar, Leyte Gulf, Iwo Jima, and Hiroshima would live again under Curtis's meticulous direction. The 21-month-long shooting schedule began in January 1986 in France and Poland and ended in September 1987 in Mobile, Alabama. A cast/crew wrap-party/dinner was held aboard the *Queen Mary* in Long Beach, California, on Friday, January 8, 1988.[75]

While viewers found the naval battle sequences thrilling, the submarine sequences technically impressive, and the characters' romantic entanglements satisfying, the defining segments of *War and Remembrance* were the devastating recreations of the Holocaust—filmed at one of the actual places where the genocide occurred. After two years of delicate negotiations with the Polish government, Curtis and his cast and crew were allowed to film harrowing Holocaust scenes at the Auschwitz concentration camp in January and May of 1986.[76]

"Auschwitz was the worst," Curtis admitted. "There's no way to describe the feeling" of recreating the unspeakable horrors of the Nazis' "final solution" on the very ground where it happened—and with some of the actual survivors.[77] As a boy, Curtis's associate producer Branko Lustig had been imprisoned in Auschwitz. Many of the extras who played the doomed Jews, herded naked into gas chambers, were also survivors of the camps. In January 1986, Herman Wouk himself visited Curtis in Poland and observed one night of the grueling filming at Auschwitz. The writer came away deeply moved and convinced that he and Curtis had captured the atrocity exactly as it must have happened.[78]

"When we do the extermination of 30,000 Jews at Babi Yar, you'll never see anything like it in your life," Curtis told the *Los Angeles Times* in September 1986. "As tough as it was for us, it was even tougher for the German crew because they couldn't come to terms with the fact that their forebears really did this."[79]

The Holocaust scenes were unflinching in their brutality, nudity, and horror. "One of the conditions that I had before I agreed to do *War and Remembrance*," Curtis stipulated, "was that ABC had to give me carte blanche." He insisted,

> I would not be *edited* in terms of pulling punches because I felt that to show the Holocaust in anything but its most brutal form would be a crime—and I didn't want to be part of that—so what I needed to know was there wasn't going to be anybody who was going to be censoring me or anybody who was going to stop me from doing what I had to do. ABC agreed to that. I met with the Standards and Practices people, and we had an understanding.[80]

While *The Winds of War* was the equivalent of seven motion pictures, *War and Remembrance*—more than 23 hours of footage spread across 29 hours of television—approximated 11 movies in one. The final cost of the gigantic miniseries was $140 million, at that time the most expensive motion picture ever made and exceeded only in later years by *Titanic* (1997) and various fantasy and super-hero films that have cost more than $200 million or even $300 million. Wouk, Curtis, and Wallace's 1492-page script contained 2070 scenes which took 1,852,739 feet of film to shoot.[81]

ABC touted the miniseries as having been filmed in more than ten countries: England, France, West Germany, Switzerland, Austria, Poland, Yugoslavia, Italy, Canada, the United States (including Hawaii), and the Bahamas. Although 757 sets were built and used, many scenes were filmed at the actual locations, such as The Eagle's Nest and The Wolf's Lair (two of Adolf Hitler's headquarters), the Paris Opera House, and the Auschwitz death camp. Rummaging through some filing cabinets at Auschwitz, Curtis found the actual blueprints and specifications for the death camp's crematoria, whose interiors were then rebuilt almost perfectly to scale on a soundstage.[82] Curtis and Wouk's goal was to tell the story of the Holocaust more vividly and accurately than ever before. "It's a way to make sure it never happens again," Curtis insisted.[83]

Academy Award winner John Gielgud is in his early 80s when he plays Aaron Jastrow in *War and Remembrance* (seen on ABC in 1988 and 1989).

Somewhere in Time star Jane Seymour portrays Natalie Jastrow Henry in Dan Curtis's *War and Remembrance* (1988, 1989).

Most of the principal actors of *The Winds of War* reprised their roles in *War and Remembrance*, and the several recastings were changes for the better, making a good cast great. Heading the cast were Robert Mitchum, Polly Bergen, Hart Bochner (replacing Jan-Michael Vincent), Jane Seymour (replacing Ali MacGraw), Victoria Tennant, David Dukes, Peter Graves, Chaim Topol, Jeremy Kemp, John Gielgud (replacing John Houseman), Sharon Stone (replacing Deborah Winters), Barry Bostwick (replacing Joseph Hacker), Steven Berkoff (replacing Gunter Meisner), and Ralph Bellamy. Once again, the supporting cast was a movie-and-TV who's who: Eddie Albert, Brian Blessed, Mike Connors, John Dehner, Howard Duff, Nina Foch, Pat Hingle, E.G. Marshall, Ian McShane, Robert Morley, Dennis Patrick, Addison Powell, William Prince, John Rhys-Davies, William Schallert, and others. William T. Woodson (*This Is Your FBI, Super Friends*) returned as the narrator. Robert Cobert made a cameo appearance as a bandleader in the third episode. In all, there were 358 speaking roles, 2257 bit players, and 41,720 extras. Counting the almost 1700 crew members, Dan Curtis commanded an army of 46,000 people marching across Europe and North America.[84] Curtis worked indefatigably with decommissioned or still-active ships, aircraft carriers, submarines, and planes; with 35-foot-long miniature ships on a "wet set" at Pinewood Studios in England; and with the thousands and thousands of extras playing the difficult roles of refugees, soldiers, prisoners, and corpses.

Producer Barbara Steele (who also played the small role of Elsa) had nothing but praise for the director. She remarked,

> There were moments when I thought the demands would kill all of us, but never Dan, because he was working from the center of his very big heart. It's as if we were living in Beethoven's Ninth Symphony. I don't believe there is another filmmaker on the planet who could have done [the two miniseries]. It was a moment of brilliant synchronicity, and it was wonderful to witness someone work at the height of his powers in a state of sustained enthrallment. Dan knew that this was his "moment," and he could put his signature so beautifully and powerfully on a devastating period of history.[85]

Polly Bergen added, "I don't think there is any other television show, movie, or miniseries that has captured the incredible scope and majesty of *The Winds of War* and *War and Remembrance*. Dan never received the kind of recognition that he deserved."[86] Auschwitz survivor and associate producer Branko Lustig declared, "Dan Curtis can be put in the category with Steven Spielberg and Ridley Scott. Nobody recreated the Holocaust better than Dan Curtis. He did it with his heart."[87] Lustig went on to produce Curtis's *Intruders* (1992), Spielberg's *Schindler's List* (1993), and six of Scott's films, including *Gladiator* (2000) and *American Gangster* (2007).

Also adding heart to *War and Remembrance* was the 11 hours of music—3500 manuscript pages—composed and conducted by Curtis's musical mainstay Robert Cobert. At ABC's request, Cobert repeated his *Winds of War* theme as the main-title theme of *War and Remembrance*; additionally, he composed what he called "everything from pure, romantic music to all kinds of military music to jazz."[88]

Dan Curtis (left) directs Ali MacGraw in a scene from *The Winds of War* (1983).

Despite Cobert's success with *The Winds of War* and essentially all of Dan Curtis's productions, Cobert initially was not guaranteed the job of scoring the sequel. In a DVD interview, the composer recalled,

> When they started *War and Remembrance*, they said, "Let's get Leonard Bernstein," or "Let's get John Williams." But Dan wanted me and *only me*. He called me up and said, "You're doing it!" Curtis asked me if I could write five minutes of music a day, and I thought about it and said, "Yeah, but I won't do it for free." When Dan told me that money was no object, I called my agent and said, "Go get 'em!"[89]

While many composers manage to perfect only one to three minutes of programmatic music per day, Cobert wrote five minutes of music each day. He dutifully worked 12 to 14 hours a day, seven days a week, from August through October 1988 in order to meet the deadline for the November 1988 episodes of *War and Remembrance*. With Curtis present in the recording studio and signing off on every note, Cobert conducted a 50-piece orchestra in the recording of his background music. Except for a few quibbles, Curtis enthusiastically approved of every theme.

"I think Cobert's a genius, no question about it," Curtis declared. "He has an incredible knack for writing clever background music that enhances my movies all the time. He stands up there with the greatest, and somebody should start to recognize him."[90]

Finally, after almost five years in the making, *War and Remembrance* aired on ABC-TV on November 13, 15-17, 20, & 22-23 of 1988 (parts 1–7), and May 7-10 & 14 of 1989 (parts 8–12, called *War and Remembrance: The Final Chapter*), between two and three hours each night. Because of the overwhelming length of the miniseries, its unwise division into two segments six months apart, and the ever-increasing alternative programming available on cable television, *War and Remembrance* attracted only about one-half of the 140 million viewers of *The Winds of War*. Nevertheless, commanding 55 to 75 million TV viewers is still impressive and admirable whether in 1988–1989, the 1990s, or the 21st century.

Once again, the reviews were spectacularly positive. The *Washington Post* called *War and Remembrance* "monumental," "mammoth," and "tremendous."[91] *Newsday* called it "super TV,"[92] and the *Newark Star Ledger* proclaimed the "masterwork" miniseries "very simply television's finest hours."[93] Newspapers from Los Angeles to Kansas City praised Dan Curtis's brilliant directing, and *TV Guide* singled out Curtis's "unparalleled combat footage."[94] Curtis especially enjoyed the Associated Press's assessment: "Curtis has himself a masterpiece of a war movie [...] the battle scenes are stunning [...] some of the best submarine scenes since *Das Boot*. The Battle of Midway [is] worthy of a theatrical film. The concentration-camp scenes are the most powerful such depictions television has ever seen."[95]

Curtis's personal goal with the submarine scenes was to top *Das Boot* (1981), and he also strove to surpass *Midway* (1976), all World War II movies, and NBC-TV's Emmy Award-winning *Holocaust* (16-19 April 1978). According to the *Kansas City Star*, "Curtis did not fail."[96]

Terror Train star Hart Bochner plays Byron Henry in Dan Curtis's *War and Remembrance* (seen on ABC in 1988 and 1989).

Howard Rosenberg of the *Los Angeles Times* concurred, "*War and Remembrance* takes its place at the top of all TV drama." Rosenberg added, "Volume one of ABC's *War and Remembrance* is more than just a dazzling achievement in historical storytelling. It is the best serialized drama in the history of American television. This is important, landmark TV—hard to take, but even harder to ignore. ABC should be proud."[97]

Indeed, in a rich American television landscape which had already produced *Rich Man, Poor Man* (1976); *Captains and the Kings* (1976); *The Moneychangers* (1976); *Roots* (1977); *Washington: Behind Closed Doors* (1977); *79 Park Avenue* (1977); *Roots: The Next Generation* (1979); *Shogun* (1980); *The Winds of War* (1983); and *The Thorn Birds* (1983), being canonized by the *Los Angeles Times* as the greatest serialized drama in the history of American television was perhaps the ultimate accolade.

Writing for *Lone Star Shadows* vol. 2, no. 7/8 (summer/fall 1989), I concurred that *War and Remembrance* was even better than *The Winds of War*, and I called Robert Cobert's new music "superb, possibly even better than his music for *The Winds of War*. [. . .] Cobert's *War and Remembrance* theme song has been recorded by the likes of easy-listening instrumentalist Lex de Azevedo and 1940s bandleader Ray Anthony."[98] I played those records, as well as "Quentin's Theme," many times on WAMB-AM & FM in Nashville from the 1980s to the 2010s.

In January 1989, the first half of *War and Remembrance* won three Golden Globe Awards. John Gielgud and Barry Bostwick, both of whose roles had been played by other actors in *The Winds of War*, tied for Best Supporting Actor in a TV Miniseries. In his acceptance speech, Bostwick, who had portrayed Lt. Carter "Lady" Aster, said,

> I accept this award not only for myself but also for the 357 other supporting players on *War and Remembrance*. We were supporting a dream—Dan Curtis's dream—of bringing to television 29 of its finest hours, a depiction of World War II so accurate and so moving that many of its images would be forever burned into our collective consciousness. I think he's done that. I thank Dan Curtis for allowing me to color in just a very small corner of his masterpiece.[99]

Although Curtis himself did not win a Golden Globe for his direction, his masterpiece won the award for Best TV Miniseries. In his acceptance speech, Curtis said, "A whole lot of people went to war about five years ago, and we're lucky to be standing up here right now. It's just a great joy to have it all appreciated and to mean something. Thank you from the bottom of my heart."[100] Two months later, *War and Remembrance* won the People's Choice Award for best miniseries.

In September 1989, *War and Remembrance* won another victory—on Emmy night. The miniseries was nominated for 15 Emmy Awards in various Outstanding-Miniseries categories: best miniseries, direction (Dan Curtis), lead actor (John Gielgud), lead actress (Jane Seymour), supporting actress (Polly Bergen), cinematography, special visual effects, film editing, sound editing, film-sound mixing, art direction, music composition (Robert Cobert), costumes, makeup, and hairstyling. Gielgud lost to James Woods for *My Name is Bill W.*, Seymour lost to Holly Hunter for *Roe Versus Wade*, and Bergen lost to Colleen Dewhurst for *Those She Left Behind*.[101]

The miniseries's most formidable competition was *Lonesome Dove* (CBS, February 5–8, 1989), the highest-rated TV miniseries since 1985's *North and South* and, like *War and Remembrance,* itself one of the finest programs in the history of American television. *Lonesome Dove* won seven Emmys, including awards for its director Simon Wincer and its composer Basil Poledouris, at that time both big names from the world of theatrical films. Wincer had directed *The Man from Snowy River* in 1982 and *Phar Lap* in 1983; Poledouris had scored *The Blue Lagoon* in 1980 and *Conan the Barbarian* in 1982. *Lonesome Dove* was considered to be the front-runner for Outstanding Miniseries, but in an upset equaling *Nicholas Nickleby*'s victory over *The Winds of War*, it was *War and Remembrance*, not *Lonesome Dove*, that was named the best miniseries of 1988–1989. In his acceptance speech, Dan Curtis admitted that the victory was "a major shock," and he thanked ABC "for having the guts to pony up the dough" to make *War and Remembrance*.[102] Ultimately, *War and Remembrance* won only three Emmys, for editing (Peter Zinner, John Burnett), special visual effects (William Schirmer et al.), and Outstanding Miniseries.[103]

Zinner and Burnett won the Eddie Award from the American Cinema Editors, and cinematographer Dietrich Lohmann won the A.S.C. Award. The U.S. TV Fan Association gave *War and Remembrance* awards for best miniseries, best director (Curtis), and best music score (Cobert). BMI (Broadcast Music, Incorporated) awarded Robert Cobert a certificate for writing the longest film score in history. (Two months earlier, BMI had given Cobert a certificate marking the one-millionth radio performance of "Quentin's Theme" from *Dark Shadows*.) Curtis won the Distinguished Service Award from the Simon Wiesenthal Center, and he was nominated for the Directors Guild Award in both 1989 and 1990. Curtis won the prestigious DGA Award in 1990, and eight years later he won the Golden Laurel Award from the Producers Guild of America.[104] Curtis had gone from filming PGA golfers at the beginning of his career to being honored by a very different PGA near the end of his career.

In May 1989, Curtis told the Associated Press, "I'm vastly relieved that I'm done with *War and Remembrance*, yet my heart is breaking. I'm so ambivalent I want to cry. I feel my mission is accomplished. I pray that the memory and impact of it will be there with us for a long time. I pray that it will make a difference."[105] He told the *Los Angeles Times*, "I feel so good about this show because I know we've accomplished something that won't be accomplished again."[106] Of course, films such as *Schindler's List* (1993), *Saving Private Ryan* (1998), and *Flags of Our Fathers* (2006) and TV miniseries such as *When Lions Roared* (1994), *Band of Brothers* (2001) and *Hitler: The Rise of Evil* (2003) have come along in the wake of *War and Remembrance,* but nothing has matched the epic, global scope of Curtis's work. As Robert Cobert bluntly put it, "We make *Schindler's List* look sick! Of course, they had only three hours, and we had 30 hours."[107]

Curtis himself stated the case more diplomatically, but just as firmly, in the 15 March 1997 edition of the *Los Angeles Times*. The director responded to a February 26 article about the NBC telecast of *Schindler's List*. Curtis's letter to the editor stated,

> As the executive producer/director of the 30-hour ABC-TV miniseries *War and Remembrance*, I think it important to demur to some points made by Howard Rosenberg in his February 26 column "NBC Can't Just Rest on Laurels." When he writes that NBC's airing of *Schindler's List* intact "marks a maturation high for network television" and "never within memory has one of the major networks shown such nudity or depicted so much violence so graphically," I feel compelled to comment.

The dehumanizing of victims, on arrival at their destination of doom, by forcing them to disrobe, was central to scenes in the miniseries. We received widespread commendation for those scenes, and ABC deserves much credit for taking a pioneering risk in first allowing me to film them and then broadcasting them without cutting a single frame.

Rosenberg himself wrote on November 23, 1988, "Never before in an American TV drama has the Holocaust been so graphically, uncompromisingly, and profoundly depicted. Tonight's scenes of rotting corpses at Auschwitz and the Nazi massacre of Jews at Babi Yar in the Soviet Union are excruciatingly and revoltingly real. This is important, landmark TV—hard to take, but even harder to ignore." The Babi Yar sequence involving the slaughter of hordes of naked Jews, which was a terrible task to film, did however evoke a protest from Nobel Laureate Elie Wiesel, who thought it unendurably graphic—an opinion I respect, but to my best ability I depicted the historic truth, nothing more.

War and Remembrance, which won the Emmy as best mini-series of 1988–1989, represents several years of my hardest work as a filmmaker. If I am proud of it, perhaps it is a pardonable pride. Certainly, no one is looking for bragging rights to graphic violence and nudity, but with regard to the memory of the horrors of the Holocaust, where we pioneered, I want the record to show it.

Signed, DAN CURTIS[108]

In 1992, after 25 years of exploring supernatural mysteries on TV and film, Dan Curtis turned to another one of life's greatest mysteries—unidentified flying objects—and executive-produced and directed **Intruders: They Are Among Us**, a four-hour miniseries seen on CBS-TV on Sunday 17 May and Tuesday 19 May. *Intruders* was Curtis's follow-up to his two massive *War* miniseries of the 1980s and his 1991 remake of *Dark Shadows*, the first four hours of which had run as a two-night miniseries. CBS proudly scheduled *Intruders* during the crucial May-sweeps ratings period opposite the NBC miniseries *Cruel Doubt*.

Intruders is based on a non-fiction book of the same name by the noted ufologist (UFO expert) Budd Hopkins, who studied more than 700 cases of alien abductions. In 1964, when he was 33 years old, Hopkins saw a UFO in broad daylight, and his lifelong interest in UFOs began. A dozen years later, he began writing about UFOs, and a dozen years after that, he was one of the world's leading experts in the field of ufology and especially alien abductions. Finally, Hopkins, who was also a painter and a sculptor, headed the Intruders Foundation, which documented cases of humans abducted by aliens. He died on Sunday 21 August 2011. In his 1987 Random House book *Intruders: The Incredible Visitations at Copley Woods,* Budd Hopkins wrote,

No aspect of this [UFO] phenomenon is as controversial—or as dramatic—as a so-called "abduction report" of the type I shall deal with in this book. Over the years, hundreds of otherwise credible people have described being somehow immobilized in their cars or homes or wherever and then taken by UFO occupants into landed UFOs for what appears to be a kind of physical examination conducted while the abductee is stretched out upon a table. What seems to be externally imposed amnesia usually prevents the abductee from recalling the full scenario of his or her experience, which generally lasts an hour or two. (Hypnosis has been the most useful method that investigators have employed to aid the victim's recollection.) Now, we would willingly dismiss any *one* of these accounts, taken alone, as nothing more than an intrinsically unbelievable aberration. But as we shall see, the overall patterns in these cases are so remarkably consistent, often down to tiny details, and the people reporting these experiences are often so inherently credible, that the phenomenon simply cannot be dismissed. However one wishes to theorize about these accounts—that they represent some strange new mass-psychological delusion or that they represent descriptions of real, physical experiences—something important is going on, something which demands open-minded, scientific investigation.[109]

Five years later, Dan Curtis co-executive-produced the film version of *Intruders* along with Robert O'Connor (*Frank Nitti: The Enforcer, Jack the Ripper*) and Michael Apted (*21 Up, Coal Miner's Daughter*). His writers were *Medical Center* scribe Barry Oringer, who had written for *The Invaders* (1967-1968) and *Planet of the Apes* (1974), and future *Sliders* writer Tracy Torme, who had investigated several abduction cases alongside Budd Hopkins and who had written for *Star Trek: The Next Generation* (1987-1994). Both Oringer and Torme were well suited for this alien fare, which Curtis directed with earnestness and restraint, docudrama-style, but with numerous scary jolts, accentuated by Robert Cobert's staccato brass and eerie synthesizer effects, similar to his music for the 1991 *Dark Shadows* series.

Psychiatrist Dr. Neil Chase (Richard Crenna) suddenly finds himself treating two new patients, Lesley Hahn (Daphne Ashbrook) in California and Mary Wilkes (Mare Winningham) in Nebraska, and noticing startling similarities in their hazy, traumatic memories of abduction and invasive examination by "little gray men" with "burning, black eyes." The fact that these phrases can be spoken by the actors in utter seriousness and without camp or unintentional humor is a testament to the verisimilitude that director Curtis brings to *Intruders*. The *Pennsylvania Patriot-News* noted that the production is "nicely, if sedately, acted" and is "an attempt to bring respectability to the kind of tale usually reserved for the tabloids."[110] Because the acting *is* so low-key, Curtis avoids turning *Intruders* into an overwrought melodrama or a typical invasion-from-outer-space thriller. It comes across just as rational and clinical as Dr. Chase himself, who goes from skepticism to belief as he works with Lesley and Mary.

Chapter Four: The Epics 123

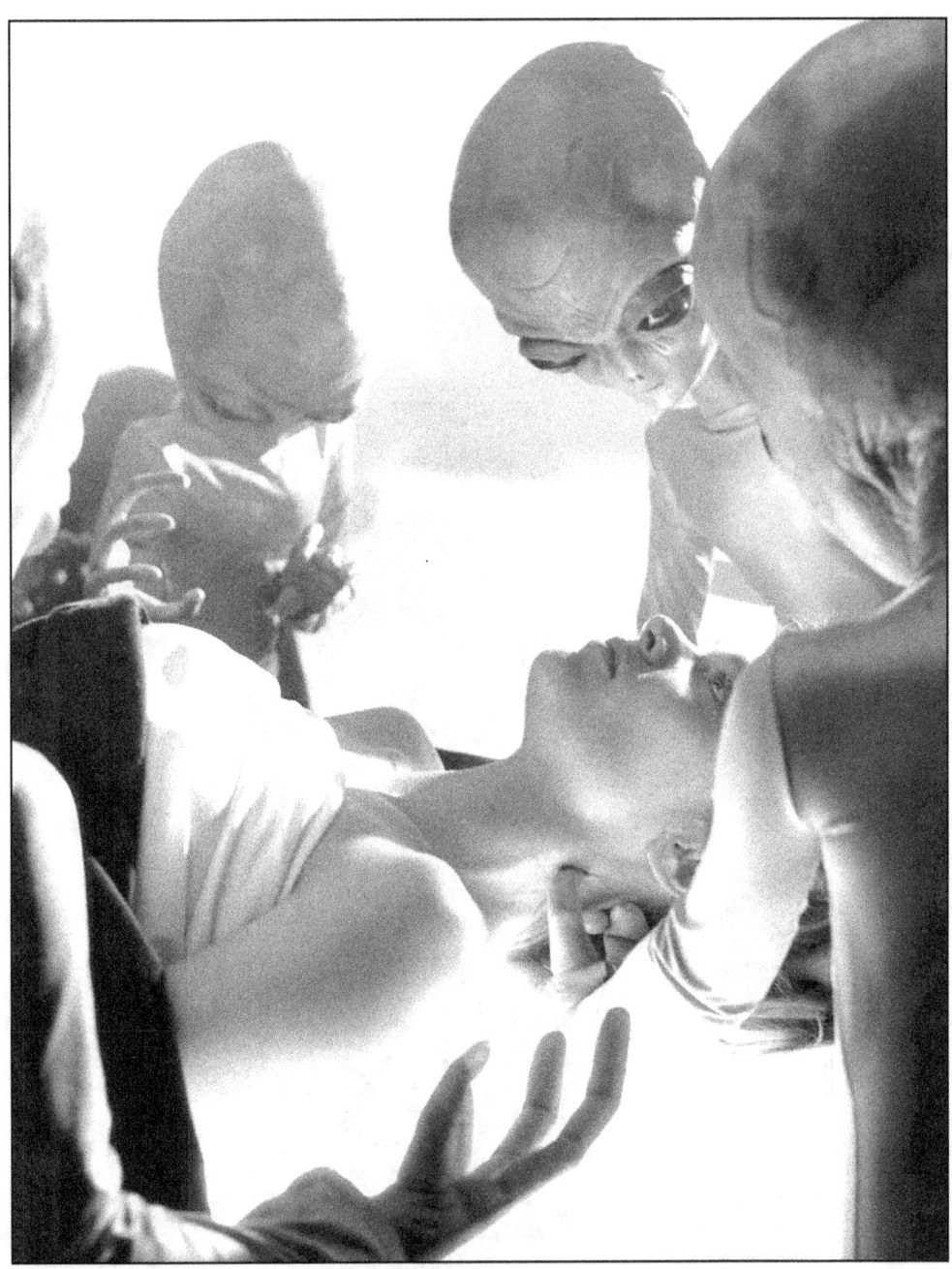

Intruders (1992): The aliens examine Daphne Ashbrook (as Lesley Hahn). In 2006, Ashbrook is a voice artist in Big Finish Productions' *Dark Shadows* CD audio drama *The Book of Temptation,* co-starring John Karlen and Kathryn Leigh Scott.

As the stories of Lesley Hahn and her boyfriend Ray Brooks (Jason Beghe) and Mary Wilkes and her husband Joe (Alan Autry), son Timmy (Christopher and Joseph Cousins), and sister Leigh Holland (Susan Blakely) unfold, a third case study seems to corroborate the women's stories. Dr. Chase interviews mental patient Gene Randall (Ben Vereen), a former Air Force officer who is haunted by an experience in New Mexico in 1973. In a stunning flashback sequence that is one of the highlights of *Intruders*, Randall witnesses the crash of a UFO and has very brief contact with the dying alien crew members before he is whisked away, pressured into signing a statement saying that he was "on something" hallucinogenic, and relegated to a mental hospital. Ben Vereen's powerful performance earned him an Emmy Award nomination for Best Supporting Actor in a Miniseries.

Intruders **(1992): Ben Vereen, as mental patient Gene Randall, is nominated for an Emmy Award for Best Supporting Actor in a Miniseries.**

As Neil Chase immerses himself in the cases of Lesley and Mary—and falls in love with Mary's sister Leigh—he comes to realize that this is no "terrestrial mystery" as he first believed but an ongoing cosmic event of immense importance. Through regressive hypnosis of the women, Chase learns that they have been visited many times by the intruders, and their lives (especially Mary's and her whole family's) are strongly intertwined with those of the visitors. When one of the women mysteriously becomes pregnant and then is robbed of her fetus, Dr. Chase realizes the extent to which the intruders are involved with the women of Earth.

Torme and Oringer's script does an excellent job of expressing the disparate views of science, religion, business, and government toward the idea of alien abductions. While, in another script, the psychiatrist (Crenna), the priest (John Snyder), the hospital administrator (Robert Mandan), and the Army general (G.D. Spradlin) would be mere stock characters, this script fleshes them out and gives them thought-provoking points to make. Spradlin is especially good—as are Crenna, Vereen, and Winningham—and Steven Berkoff of *War and Remembrance* has a couple of memorable scenes as a persuasive ufologist. The characters are so rich that a four-hour miniseries is not quite enough to give all of them ample screen time. *Intruders* could have succeeded as a five- or six-hour production.

In addition to Gene Randall's "origin story" and the women's hypnosis scenes, a highlight of *Intruders* is Dr. Neil Chase's and other characters' attendance at a meeting of ufologist Addison Leach's support group for women and men who have been abducted. Here again, a lesser script and a lesser director would have made such a scenario laughable, but *Intruders* approaches the subject matter with complete seriousness and compassion. A group member's lament, "They took *my* baby, too," is heartbreaking. Dr. Chase's feelings about alien abductions change so drastically that he commits "professional suicide" by speaking out about the phenomenon at a meeting of the State Psychiatric Association.

Richard Crenna's own attitudes underwent a change as he portrayed Dr. Neil Chase. In a May 1992 interview, Crenna spoke about his own "healthy curiosity and interest" in UFOs. He said,

> People who are very skeptical are not going to change their minds as a result of this film—and that's not the intention. But it does pose enough questions that if you're an inquisitive person at all, you're going to be tempted to probe beyond what you hear on this show. [. . .] I think it's rather presumptuous on our part to assume, in this galaxy of millions and millions of stars and planets, and in the extended universe of millions and millions of galaxies, that we are the only living beings of any sort. [. . .] I'm not absolutely convinced at this point except that I'm very open-minded to the whole idea of extraterrestrial beings. [. . .] The purpose of the movie is pure entertainment, but I think in the course of that entertainment, people are going to be turned on to these various possibilities.[111]

Mare Winningham was much more emphatic when she told *TV Host* magazine that, after playing the traumatized Nebraska housewife Mary Wilkes, "it's impossible for me *not* to believe!"[112] Her personal dedication contributed to her (in the words of *TV*

Guide) "winning performance"[113] which should have been nominated for an Emmy Award alongside Ben Vereen's.

Mare Winningham plays Mary Wilkes in *Intruders: They Are Among Us* (CBS, 1992). The miniseries is nominated for Emmy, Saturn, and American Society of Cinematographers awards.

Once again, a Dan Curtis production generated positive reviews. *TV Guide* complimented all of the "stellar talent" in *Intruders*,[114] and *People* magazine called the miniseries "well acted [with a] strong supporting cast" and "absorbing whether you regard UFO stories as hogwash or gospel."[115] The *Washington Post* insisted, "It won't matter if you believe or not. You'll still be wowed."[116]

Variety declared, "Scaremaster Dan Curtis applies his directorial skills to a two-part sci-fi adventure, and the first two hours are whizbang stuff ending with a surefire cliffhanger"[117] (an alien visitation to the Wilkeses' home). *Tune in Tonight* added, "*Intruders* is a likely favorite with viewers because of its tabloid-style subject matter— abduction by alien beings—and its classy treatment by a producer-director with a known talent for creating credible drama from essentially unbelievable material. [. . .] The [alien] beings are even better than those in the now-classic *Close Encounters of the Third Kind*" [1977]. The special effects are remarkable, and the story may even convince a few skeptics."[118]

Of course, one of the greatest assets of *Intruders* is its weird, unnerving alien creatures, the "little gray men" who exude both menace and a strange comfort. Even more striking are the half-human, half-alien beings that are the product of extraterrestrial impregnation of earth women. The special effects (Robert Short), visual effects (Mitch Suskin), makeup (Jim Kail), and otherworldly costuming (Deborah Lancaster) in *Intruders* are equal to the science-fiction feature films of the day. *USA Today* called this "mystery with horror aspects" (*Intruders*) "a cross of *Close Encounters*, *Rosemary's Baby*, *Mars Needs Women*, and any number of government-conspiracy flicks."[119]

Just as Dan Curtis's horror productions were in tune with their times (e.g. *The Norliss Tapes*, *Dead of Night*), or ahead of their time (e.g. *The Night Stalker*, *The Night Strangler*), the Saturn Award-nominated *Intruders* was at the forefront of the wave of the public's 1990s/2000s fascination with aliens. *Intruders* appeared ten years before M. Night Shyamalan's film *Signs*, six years before Melinda Metz's *Roswell High* novel series, five years before Barry Sonnenfeld's film *Men in Black*, three years before Paul Shapiro's *Invaders* TV miniseries with Roy Thinnes and Scott Bakula, and one year before Fox TV's smash-hit series *The X-Files* (1993-2002), which creator Chris Carter has often said was inspired by *The Night Stalker* (1972) and *The Night Strangler* (1973).[120] Just as the *Boston Globe* called *Night of Dark Shadows* (1971) "a horror film for people who don't really like horror films,"[121] *Intruders* is a movie for people who don't necessarily like movies about UFOs, aliens, and science fiction. At its heart, it is a human drama (like *Shadow of Fear* and *The Invasion of Carol Enders*) and a family drama (like *Burnt Offerings* and *Curse of the Black Widow*) about people caught up in a horrifying, fantastical mystery. Those who *do* love sci-fi and UFO dramas will scarcely find a better one than the understated, disturbing, and thought-provoking *Intruders*.

After *Intruders*, Dan Curtis still had a half-dozen more productions ahead of him, but none of them matched the epic scope of *Dracula*, the *Dalton Gang* Western, the two World War II miniseries, and *Intruders*. The great producer-director would prove that he could make huge entertainments (*The Winds of War*) and intimate dramas (*Saving Milly*) equally effectively.

Significa from the House of Dan Curtis: In 1986, Dan Curtis took a very short break from filming *War and Remembrance* to shoot a live performance of his good friend Dean Jones's one-man show **St. John in Exile**. Written by Don Berrigan and directed on stage by Lory Basham Jones, *St. John in Exile* presents Dean Jones as the 86-year-old last surviving Apostle, John, who tells his inspiring story while he is detained on the Greek island of Patmos. The *Arizona Republic* called *St. John in Exile* "magnificent! One is reminded of unforgettable roles played by Henry Fonda as Clarence Darrow and Hal Holbrook as Mark Twain." After directing a special live videotaping (in Van Nuys, California) of Dean Jones's *tour de force* as St. John, Dan Curtis called it "the best performance I've ever seen."[122] Dean Jones passed away on Tuesday 1 September 2015. His remarkable performance is available on VHS and DVD.

Significa from the House of Dan Curtis: In *Intruders,* when Mary and Joe Wilkes dine out in a restaurant, the background music is a new solo-piano arrangement of Robert Cobert's "Quentin's Theme." In Gene Randall's 1973 flashback sequence, Randall watches *The Carol Burnett Show* on a portable television set.

Several people in the alien-abduction support group are named after Dan Curtis Productions personnel, including producer Daniel Blatt, production assistant Margaret Hussey, and Curtis's long-time executive assistant Ruth Kennedy. In another scene, "Dr. Lustig" is named after Branko Lustig, who was the associate producer and assistant director of *War and Remembrance* (1988, 1989), the producer and assistant director of *Intruders* (1992), and one of the seven producers of Steven Spielberg's *Schindler's List* (1993).[123]

In *Intruders,* the exterior and interior of the scene taking place at General Hanley's house was filmed at Greystone mansion in Beverly Hills. The 55-room Tudor Revival mansion on 18 acres of land was built in 1928 by the oil millionaire Edward Doheny, who earlier in the 1920s had played a role in the Teapot Dome scandal. Doheny gave the mansion to his son Ned and daughter-in-law Lucy. Ned was murdered in the house in 1929; Lucy lived there until 1955. The city of Beverly Hills assumed ownership of Greystone in 1965, and since 1971 it has opened the grounds (but not the house) as a public park.

Since 1963, Greystone has been seen in countless movies and TV shows, including *Alias, All of Me, Arrow, Bare Essence, Batman and Robin, The Big Lebowski, The Bodyguard, The Bold and the Beautiful, Dark Mansions, The Day Mars Invaded Earth, Dead Ringer, The Disorderly Orderly, The Flash, General Hospital, Gilmore Girls, Hart to Hart, The Immortal, The Loved One, Mannix, The Mentalist, Mission: Impossible, Murder She Wrote, NCIS, The Phantom, Picture Mommy Dead, The Prestige, Revenge, The Social Network, Spider-Man, There Will Be Blood, The Trouble with Angels, War and Remembrance, The Winds of War,* and *The Young and the Restless.* Dan Curtis also used Greystone as Collinwood both in the 1991 *Dark Shadows* series and in the never-aired 2004 *Dark Shadows* pilot for the WB television network.[124]

Significa from the House of Dan Curtis: A case can be made that the year 1968 brought camp full-time to ABC-TV's *Dark Shadows.* Critic Harry M. Benshoff calls it "naïve camp," i.e. an outlandish tone achieved unintentionally instead of deliberately (as in Tim Burton's intentionally campy 2012 *Dark Shadows*).[125] The early Burke Devlin episodes, the phoenix storyline, the introduction of Barnabas, and the 1795 storyline usually were *not* campy (except for some occasional histrionics by a few characters), but the 1968 Adam/Eve/Nicholas storyline ushered in Julia's new haircut, Cassandra's loud dresses, some over-the-top performances of Dream Curse dreams, the arrival of Dr. Lang, the return of Willie, the antics of Adam, and the jarring sights of Barnabas riding in a car, wearing pajamas in the hospital, and toting a shotgun through the woods. The tone of *Dark Shadows* had changed—"quickly!"

CHAPTER V

The Dramas
Purvis, Coopers, Mrs. R, and More

When most television viewers think of Dan Curtis, they think of World War II and daytime, prime-time, and late-night horror, or they think of Barnabas Collins, Karen Black, and Carl Kolchak. They may not think of the emotional dramas from the production house of Dan Curtis—*Mrs. R's Daughter, The Long Days of Summer, The Love Letter, Saving Milly*, et al.—or Curtis's two gangster films.

Curtis's two-picture foray into gangster movies began with **Melvin Purvis, G-Man**, co-starring Dale Robertson as the Bureau of Investigation agent and Harris Yulin as Purvis's adversary Machine Gun Kelly. Released theatrically overseas as *The Legend of Machine Gun Kelly*, this Dan Curtis/AIP co-production was an outgrowth of American International Pictures' 1973 theatrical film *Dillinger*, co-starring Warren Oates as John Dillinger and Ben Johnson as Melvin Purvis. While *Dillinger* was not a Dan Curtis production, its art director was Trevor Williams, a Curtis regular who would serve as art director on Curtis's two Purvis films. Also, the movie's set decorator was Charles Pierce, who would dress the sets for three of Curtis's 1974 *Wide World Mystery* segments and for Curtis's second Purvis film in 1975.

Dale Robertson (*The Iron Horse*) stars as the real-life Bureau of Investigation agent, *Melvin Purvis, G-Man* (1974).

When ABC wanted to bring the story of Melvin Purvis (1903-1960) to television, the house of *Blacula* (AIP) joined with the house of *Dark Shadows* (DCP) to produce *Melvin Purvis, G-Man*, seen on the *ABC Tuesday Movie of the Week* on 9 April 1974. *Dillinger* writer-director John Milius (*The Wind and the Lion, Big Wednesday*) co-wrote the teleplay with William F. Nolan (*The Norliss Tapes, The Turn of the Screw*), and *Dillinger* production manager Elliot Schick served as executive production supervisor of *Melvin Purvis*. Donald C. Klune returned as assistant director. Dan Curtis produced and directed *Melvin Purvis*, with plenty of his trademark low-angle shots, and Robert Cobert, of course, composed the music, a change-of-pace mixture of rowdy bluegrass and melancholy solo harmonica.

Melvin Purvis, G-Man, which takes place in December 1933-January 1934, is a prequel to *Dillinger*, which is set mostly in the summer of 1934. Oddly, *Melvin Purvis* dramatizes events that actually occurred in July-September 1933 when George "Machine Gun" Kelly and his gang kidnapped Oklahoma City oil millionaire Charles Urschel and held him for ransom. In the telefilm, Kelly (Harris Yulin) kidnaps millionaire "Thatcher Covington" (Dick Sargent); collects a $500,000 ransom; releases Covington; but is captured by Purvis (Dale Robertson) in his sixth-floor room in the Monarch Hotel in Memphis, Tennessee (Kelly's hometown). In Curtis's remake of a scene from *Dillinger*, "Machine Gun" Kelly pleads, "Don't shoot me, G-man," and thereby gives Melvin Purvis and all Government men their catchy name. (In subsequent decades, the anecdote has been attributed to Kelly's wife Kate Thorne, Kelly himself, FBI publicity, or legend.)

An important difference between Milius's *Dillinger* and Nolan and Curtis's *Melvin Purvis* is in the portrayal of women. In *Dillinger*, Billie Frechette (played by Michelle Phillips) is passive and only slightly involved in John Dillinger's criminal activities. In *Melvin Purvis*, Kate Ryan Kelly (as Margaret Blye's fiery character is named) is a full-fledged member of the Kelly Gang. She can handle firearms more skillfully than some of the men in the gang, such as Anthony Redecci (John Karlen), and in the Monarch Hotel scene she is portrayed as the backbone behind her much softer husband and his doltish henchmen—"a collection of inept buffoons," in the words of TV-movie expert Alvin Marill.[1]

Noting this film's seriocomic tone, the *Los Angeles Herald-Examiner* called *Melvin Purvis, G-Man* "a whimsical throwback to 1930s gangsterdom, country style. It advances in a delightfully bouncy rhythm. It has more the effect of a sly, tongue-in-cheek folk tale than the ache of real bullet holes" as *Dillinger* had.[2] The *Los Angeles Times* went so far as to call "ABC's spunky, provocative" telefilm "far superior to *Dillinger*, the theatrical film that preceded it." The *L.A. Times* continued, "Here, motivation and character are made to count for much more than mere violence. Its development creates confrontations both revealing and ambiguous, which have been directed by Dan Curtis with a sense of edginess and insight."[3] Two of those confrontations are a very personal machine-gun "duel" between Kelly and Redecci and a tender exchange between an unusually compassionate Purvis and the wounded, frightened Kelly Gang member Thomas "Buckwheat" Longaker (played by Elliott Street of *The Harrad Experiment*).

Variety had similar praise for "AIP's first TV venture, and under the imaginative banner of Dan Curtis Productions." It reported, "Curtis's direction is creative [and] makes a strong script by John Milius and William F. Nolan come to life without tripping over [the] nostalgia theme."[4] While an exciting shoot-out between the Bureau agents and the Kelly Gang is a highlight, the centerpiece of *Melvin Purvis, G-Man* is Dale Robertson's charismatic, larger-than-life portrayal of the unflappable clothes-horse who spouts self-assured observations on human nature between tokes on his ever-present cigar. The telefilm ends with Purvis getting a shoe shine and chuckling to himself over his capture of Kelly and his new "G-man" moniker. Adding further flair to the proceedings are the aforementioned Karlen and Street as Redecci and "Buckwheat," Matt Clark as Charlie Parlmetter, David Canary as Gene Farber, and Don Megowan as a smart-aleck short-order cook.

Critic Leonard Maltin characterized *Melvin Purvis, G-Man* as "a wonderful send-up of the type of gangster movie they don't make any more."[5] A sequel followed on ABC one-and-one-half years later, but first *The Fugitive* creator Roy Huggins followed Curtis's lead by executive-producing the 1974 TV-movie *The Story of Pretty Boy Floyd* for ABC. Later in 1974, Quinn Martin, the *Fugitive* and *FBI* executive producer, joined the trend with *The FBI vs. Alvin Karpis, Public Enemy Number One* on CBS. *Melvin Purvis, G-Man*, as well as its follow-up, is available only on VHS.

That follow-up was another adventure of Melvin Purvis, G-man. ABC launched its 1975-1976 season with **The Kansas City Massacre** on Friday 19 September, and like *Trilogy of Terror* six months earlier, Curtis's new Purvis film carried a PARENTAL DISCRETION IS ADVISED warning because of its violent, mature subject matter. Dale Robertson returned as the epicurean fashion-plate to smoke out more public enemies in America's heartland—but also to stop and show compassion for a criminal's wife (Sally Kirkland) and young son (Ike Eisenmann).

The Kansas City Massacre, which is set in April, May, and June of 1933, once again moves backward in time from the events of *Melvin Purvis, G-Man* (December 1933-January 1934) and *Dillinger* (summer 1934). It dramatizes the watershed event that spurs on Purvis's efforts to round up the public enemies and that ushered in the important change of allowing Bureau of Investigation agents to carry firearms and make arrests.

A machine-gun attack on criminal Frank "Jelly" Nash and several law enforcers and bystanders occurs at the Union Station railroad depot in Kansas City, Missouri, on Saturday, June 17, 1933. According to Robertson's voice-over narration as Purvis,

> In addition to our prisoner, Frank Nash, and one of the gunmen, Solly Weissman, five officers were killed that morning at Union Plaza Station: Frank Hermanson and W.J. Grooms of the Kansas City Detective Bureau, Mike Fanning and Lyle Gage of the federal penitentiary, and Ed Martin of the Bureau. Twelve innocent bystanders were also seriously wounded in that violent exchange of gunfire which came to be known as the Kansas City Massacre.

American International Pictures had no involvement with *The Kansas City Massacre*, which was strictly a Dan Curtis production. *Norliss* and *Purvis* writer William F. Nolan co-authored the script with *Lawman* and *Laredo* writer "Bronson Howitzer" (Richard

Hardman), and Curtis script-doctored, produced, and directed. Curtis mixed his trademark low camera angles with some high shots (i.e. looking down from the tops of stairwells) and even a few crooked angles reminiscent of ABC-TV's *Batman* (1966-1968).

The Kansas City Massacre (1975): Scott Brady (as Hubert McElwaine), John Karlen (as Sam Cowley), and Dale Robertson (as Melvin Purvis) perform a scene in William F. Nolan and Dan Curtis's second Purvis film.

In *The Kansas City Massacre,* Purvis, along with his aide Sam Cowley (John Karlen), battles a veritable rogues' gallery of more than one dozen criminals, loosely organized as the "Karpis/Barker/Floyd Gang": Alvin Karpis (Morgan Paull), Doc Barker (Gary Sandy), Fred Barker (Hunter Von Leer), "Pretty Boy" Floyd (Bo Hopkins), Adam Richetti (Robert Walden), "Baby Face" Nelson (Elliott Street), Frank "Jelly" Nash (Mills Watson), Vernon Miller (Matt Clark), Homer Van Meter (Brion James), Harry Pierpont (Larry Manetti), Wilbur Underhill (W.T. Zacha), Larry DeVol (James Storm), and John Dillinger (William Jordon). This time, Harris Yulin plays crime boss Johnny Lazia, and Western and *film-noir* veteran Scott Brady portrays Commissioner Hubert Tucker McElwaine, who is not what he seems. Brady was one of Dan Curtis's favorite actors; he appeared in six of Curtis's productions.

Curtis's self-proclaimed "stock company" of actors was one of his *auteur* hallmarks. Just as Orson Welles and Alfred Hitchcock before him, Robert Altman and Woody Allen alongside him, and Joe Dante and Fred Olen Ray after him had done, Curtis populated his movies with many of the same actors time and again. Roy Thinnes (*The Norliss Tapes, Supertrain, Dark Shadows*) remarked, "Dan's honest, and he wants everyone around him to be honest, so he hires people and puts together this great repertory company. You see a lot of the same people working with him down the line—a faithful group"[6]—that included Scott Brady, Orin Cannon, Matt Clark, Anjanette Comer, Elisha Cook Jr., Nigel Davenport, David Dukes, Jo Ann Pflug, Peter Graves, John Karlen, Geoffrey Lewis, Jack Palance, James Storm, Mills Watson, Harris Yulin, and others.

The Kansas City Massacre (1975) has no shortage of fine actors as the *Los Angeles Times* noted when it declared, "The casting is inspired."[7] *Variety* added, "Splendid cast, with Robertson again portraying suave, humorless FBI Midwest chief, abetted by producer Dan Curtis's inventive direction, reconstructs era [of the 1930s] with relentless authenticity."[8]

Indeed, *The Kansas City Massacre* surpasses *Melvin Purvis, G-Man* in plot, characterization, action, music, and period detail. With a running time only eight minutes shorter than John Milius's *Dillinger,* Curtis's *Kansas City Massacre* has a longer time to establish plotlines than the shorter *Melvin Purvis* movie of the week. Although William F. Nolan and "Bronson Howizter" (Ric Hardman) seemingly overcrowd their teleplay with far more bad guys than are needed, their detailed script allows the audience to learn something about the character of each of them. The all-out firefight between the overzealous, bungling Oklahoma Highway Patrol and the outlaw legion concentrated at "Pretty Boy" Floyd's farmhouse tops the smaller-scale gunfight in *Melvin Purvis, G-Man.* Robert Cobert's music is an effective blend of bluegrass, Dixieland, and solo-clarinet cues, as well as the use of such vintage songs as "Life Is Just a Bowl of Cherries" and "If You Knew Susie." Lynn Loring's character Viola Moreland, as "Sally Strand," sings "Am I Blue?" at Johnny Lazia's nightclub. Adding to the period detail are striking 1930s-era clothes and cars, plus radio broadcasts of *Little Orphan Annie* and *The Shadow.* According to *TV Guide,* this "tongue-in-cheek retrospection makes for solid entertainment."[9]

This time, the criminals are much smarter and more fearsome, and the comic relief comes from the Oklahoma Highway patrolmen, led by future *Mary Hartman, Mary Hartman* star Philip Bruns as Captain Ralph "Jimbo" Jackson. A light note late in the film is that "Pretty Boy" Floyd escapes in Captain Jackson's automobile. Essentially, Purvis, who has captured the Kansas City Massacre's mastermind Vernon Miller, *allows* Floyd to escape because Purvis realizes that Floyd apparently was not responsible for, or even aware of, the impending massacre. Although this theory is backed up by certain historical findings, Purvis's actions here do not match the events of *Dillinger,* in which Purvis still blames Floyd for the massacre one year later. We fans of *Dark Shadows* and Dan Curtis movies can attribute this discrepancy to the notion that *Dillinger* takes place in parallel time and the two Curtis films occur in "our" time band.

The Kansas City Massacre is a rousing climax to the Milius/Curtis trilogy of Melvin Purvis adventures. Dan Curtis considered making a Melvin Purvis TV series, and William F. Nolan's detailed outline *The Legend of Johnny Dillinger* might have served as its pilot. However, no series materialized, but information about six unused "spec" scripts can be found at the end of this chapter. In July 2009, Purvis (Christian Bale), Floyd (Channing Tatum), Nelson (Stephen Graham), and Dillinger (Johnny Depp) lived again, this time in director Michael Mann's *Public Enemies* (not a Dan Curtis production).

When Every Day Was the Fourth of July (NBC *Big Event,* Sunday 12 March 1978) was the first of Curtis's two nostalgic, semi-autobiographical films about the

Cooper family of Bridgeport, Connecticut. In June of 1937, attorney Ed Cooper (Dean Jones) and his wife Millie (Louise Sorel) are the parents of Daniel (Chris Petersen) and Sarah (Katy Kurtzman). The character of young Daniel Cooper is based on Daniel Cherkoss (Dan Curtis) himself. Charles Aidman narrates the film as Daniel, remembering that turbulent summer when his father defended Sarah's friend, Albert "Snowman" Cavanaugh (Geoffrey Lewis), a brain-damaged Great War veteran, when "Snowman" was accused of murdering his employer.

When Every Day Was the Fourth of July **(1978): Katy Kurtzman (as Sarah Cooper) and Dean Jones (as Ed Cooper) pose in costumes designed by Winnie Brown and Joseph Roveto.**

All of the principals deliver fine performances in this successful combination family-and-courtroom drama. Scott Brady (*Shotgun Slade, The Kansas City Massacre*) is especially noteworthy as the unsympathetic character Officer Mike Doyle, based on an unsavory neighbor of the Cherkoss family. Geoffrey Lewis's kindly character Albert cannot speak, so Lewis performs eloquently with his face and body. After Lewis (*Dillinger, The Great Ice Rip-Off*) died on Tuesday 7 April 2015, his actress-daughter Juliette Lewis stated on *Facebook* that *When Every Day Was the Fourth of July* was one of her favorite performances of her father's. Writer Lee Hutson (*The Children Nobody Wanted*) scripted the film, from a story by Hutson and Curtis. Mr. Hutson's teleplay was nominated for an Edgar Award. Walter Scharf (*The Man from U.N.C.L.E.*) composed the music.

In Dan Curtis and Dean Jones's DVD commentary, Curtis explains that he wanted to film this highly personal movie in his actual Laurel Avenue neighborhood of Bridgeport, Connecticut, but the area had changed too much. Instead, Curtis found houses, stores, a factory, and a YWCA building in the Echo Park section of Los Angeles, all of which perfectly evoked 1930s Bridgeport. The courtroom was a set at the Samuel Goldwyn Studios. Many of the most powerful scenes in *When Every Day Was the Fourth of July* take place in the packed, sweltering courtroom where Ed Cooper (Jones) and D.A. Joseph Antonelli (Curtis mainstay Harris Yulin) argue Albert's case—a case that deeply affects the Cooper family. "I've got tears in my eyes watching this!" Curtis reveals in the DVD commentary. Dean Jones agrees that Curtis's film perfectly captures the nostalgia and emotions of the time.

In its glowing review of this telefilm, the *Los Angeles Herald-Examiner* declared, "It's an absolute gem. It will touch all of your emotions. It will grip you with suspense. It will amuse you. It will warm your heart."[10] The *Los Angeles Times* concurred that *When Every Day Was the Fourth of July* was "pretty wonderful."[11] Curtis told the *L.A. Times* that this was the movie that he had wanted to make for the last 20 years.[12] The film won the 1978 Golden Halo Award for Family Film Entertainment from the Southern California Motion-Picture Council, as well as a Certificate of Commendation from the Horizon House Institute in Philadelphia "for exemplary work in bringing mental-health issues to the American public."[13] Indeed, the film does explore issues of bigotry, bullying, alcoholism, and family dysfunction in ways that family members of all ages can appreciate. *When Every Day Was the Fourth of July* is available on VHS as well as DVD. It is one of the highlights of Curtis's *oeuvre*.

One-and-one-half years later, **Mrs. R's Daughter** (NBC, Wednesday 19 September 1979), developed and produced by Joseph Stern (*Supertrain*), showcased a *tour-de-force* performance by Cloris Leachman as a mother determined to bring her daughter's rapist to justice. The lives of Ellie Pruitt (Season Hubley), her mother Ruth Randall (Leachman), and her stepfather Frank Randall (Donald Moffat) are shattered when Ellie is beaten and raped. Mrs. Randall exclaims, "Her life's been changed—and *he* did it!" The punishment for serial rapist Carl Bergson (John Fitzpatrick) proves to be elusive even after his capture because of scared witnesses, continuances, and mistakes. The tenacious Mrs. Randall goes through several lawyers before Joseph Barron (Ron Rifkin) helps her bring Ellie's rapist to trial after a year-long delay. Emmy Award-winning writer George Rubino (*The Last Tenant*) based his teleplay on an actual incident.

Mrs. R's Daughter **(1979): Season Hubley of** *Family* **and Cloris Leachman of** *Phyllis* **play daughter and mother in Joseph Stern and Dan Curtis's bleak drama.** *TV Guide* **calls the telefilm "intense."**

As in his horror movies (especially *Burnt Offerings*), Curtis's extremely low camera angles in *Mrs. R's Daughter* effect a tone of claustrophobia and despair. Robert Cobert's somber music, augmented by Moog synthesizers, adds to the melancholy mood. *Mrs. R's Daughter* is available on VHS only.

The Cooper family of Bridgeport, Connecticut, returned in **The Long Days of Summer** (ABC, Friday 23 May 1980), another semi-autobiographical work, directed by Curtis, produced by Joseph Stern (*Mrs. R's Daughter*), and co-written by Lee Hutson (*Killing at Hell's Gate*) and Hindi Brooks (*Family*). Walter Scharf (*Mission: Impossible*) composed the music.

Dean Jones reprises his role of attorney Ed Cooper, husband to Millie (Joan Hackett) and father to Daniel (Ronnie Scribner) and Sarah (Louanne Sirota). Whereas

Sarah is one of the protagonists of *When Every Day Was the Fourth of July*, this sequel shifts the focus mostly to Daniel. Charles Aidman returns to narrate Daniel's memories of the summer of 1938.

The Long Days of Summer (1980): **Dean Jones (as Ed Cooper) smiles alongside Joan Hackett (as Millie Cooper).**

The Coopers, who are Jewish (like Curtis's own Cherkoss family of Bridgeport), confront anti-Semitism from the local German-American Club. The family is further distressed when Josef Kaplan (Donald Moffat), a German Jewish man, escapes to America and reveals Nazi Germany's growing atrocities against the Jews. Ed Cooper tries to help Kaplan, whose dire message falls on indifferent ears around town. A highlight of the film is a scene in which Ed's WASP employers (Andrew Duggan and Dave Shelley) pressure Ed to cut his ties with Kaplan. This film's historical subject matter—the Holocaust, a whistle-stop appearance by President Franklin Roosevelt (Stephen Roberts), the June 22 Joe Louis-Max Schmeling fight, and a Golden Gloves boxing match between young Daniel Cooper and an older boy (David Baron)—begins to evoke an era that Curtis, several years later, brought fully to life in his two epic *War* miniseries. *Dark Shadows* actors John Karlen and Michael McGuire play supporting roles, and Gloria Calomee returns as the Coopers' housekeeper Clementine.

Like its predecessor (*When Every Day Was the Fourth of July*), *The Long Days of Summer* received the Golden Halo Award for Family Film Entertainment from the Southern California Motion-Picture Council. The *Los Angeles Herald-Examiner* ranked the "extraordinarily good" film number three in the top ten television programs of 1980.[14] *The Los Angeles Times* declared that the film "has the sort of honesty and reality that is lacking in most TV series."[15] Once again, this sequel is not afraid to tackle difficult issues such as race, bigotry, politics, and ethics. Like the first Cooper family movie, *The Long Days of Summer* is available on VHS and DVD.

Dan Curtis (pictured) is remembered by producer Joseph Stern (*I Think I'm Having a Baby, The Big Easy*) as "a real original" with "a big heart."

On the afternoon of Tuesday 3 March 1981, after *Guiding Light*, CBS-TV's *Afternoon Playhouse* presented **I Think I'm Having a Baby**, a teenage drama starring David Birney, Shawn Stevens, Shane Sinutko, and several up-and-coming actresses: Jennifer Jason Leigh, Tracey Gold, Ally Sheedy, and Helen Hunt. Leigh plays a high-school student who fears that she is pregnant after one sexual experience with Stevens's character. David Birney is excellent as Mr. Fenning, a dynamic teacher who asks his students tough questions about life, love, and sex.

Although Dan Curtis did not produce or direct *I Think I'm Having a Baby*, the program was made under his Dan Curtis Associates banner. Joseph Stern (*The Long Days of Summer*) was the executive producer, Clare "Blossom" Elfman (*The Girls of Huntington House*) was the writer, and Arthur Allan Seidelman (*Children of Rage*) was the director. The music composer was Curtis mainstay Robert Cobert, who was nominated for a Daytime Emmy Award for his music score, which makes good use of flute and harp. Cobert lost the Emmy to Dick Hyman for "Sunshine's on the Way" (*NBC Special Treat*). Elfman won an Emmy for writing the show.[16] *I Think I'm Having a Baby* has never been released on VHS or DVD.

Seventeen years later, Curtis's 1998 drama became the seventh-highest-rated *Hallmark Hall of Fame* presentation in history when it was watched by 20,920,000 viewers.[17] **The Love Letter** (CBS, Sunday 1 February 1998) was a critically acclaimed adaptation of time-travel master Jack Finney's short story about kindred spirits who exchange heartfelt letters across two centuries. The story first appeared in the 1 August 1959 edition of *The Saturday Evening Post*.

In the updated film version, set in Massachusetts, Scotty Corrigan (Campbell Scott) lives in 1998 while the poet Elizabeth Whitcomb (Jennifer Jason Leigh) lives in 1863. Scott buys an antique desk that happened to belong to Elizabeth, and inside a secret compartment he finds a letter that Lizzie has written to her unknown soulmate, whoever, wherever, and *whenever* he is. Scott begins mailing letters to Lizzie at an 1857-era U.S. Post Office still in use. She sends letters to him by leaving them in the secret compartment of the desk that both of them own, 135 years apart.

Lizzie's father (Gerrit Graham) is forcing Lizzie into a marriage to Everett Reagle (Curtis regular David Dukes) until she flees to Boston and meets Colonel Caleb Denby (Campbell Scott) at the very moment that Scott, in 1998, has suffered a bicycling injury and is unconscious. Scott's fiancée Debra (Daphne Ashbrook) and his mother Beatrice (Estelle Parsons) wait for him to recover, and he does. Lizzie loses Colonel Denby in the Battle of Gettysburg, and Scott loses Debra to his obsession with Lizzie and her world. The final scene takes place at the grave of Elizabeth Whitcomb (1834-1901) as Scott Corrigan begins a new chapter in his life.

The Love Letter is exquisitely romantic and heartfelt, and Robert Cobert's music is especially wistful and sentimental. One of the most sublime moments occurs when Scott and Lizzie feel each other's presence when they traverse the same staircase in their respective times. *Love Letter* scriptwriter James Henerson (*Love on a Rooftop*, *The Second Hundred Years*) won the Writers Guild of America award for the Best Long-Form Screenplay of 1998.[18]

The Love Letter (1998): Between *Somewhere in Time* and *The Lake House,* there is Dan Curtis's love letter to romantic fantasy. Campbell Scott and Jennifer Jason Leigh co-star in one of the highest-rated *Hallmark Hall of Fame* presentations.

Curtis directed the Hallmark movie in and around Richmond, Petersburg, and Manakin, Virginia, during the fall of 1997. Lizzie's house was actually the Tuckahoe historic home in Manakin. Curtis admitted that he had wanted to film Finney's time-travel romance for two decades. *The Love Letter* "is the most magical love story I've ever come across," he uncharacteristically gushed. Curtis explained,

> It transcends time and will enchant the audience. It reaches into your heart because it's about two people yearning for each other, separated by almost 150 years, who exist simultaneously and communicate through letters. Watching this movie is going to be the equivalent of curling up in front of the fireplace on a winter's night with a wonderful, engaging romantic novel. You just know it's going to make you feel good, and that's what *The Love Letter* does. It tells us that romance is always possible in our lives—even though it may occur in very unusual ways![19]

USA Today observed, "Producer-director Curtis, who gingerly moved between time periods and parallel dimensions on the classic soap *Dark Shadows*, is up to his old tricks."[20] *Entertainment Weekly* awarded *The Love Letter* the grade of A- and added, "It's like that rarest of Hallmark cards: unabashedly romantic yet surprisingly light on cheese."[21] The *Christian Science Monitor* called *The Love Letter* "a delightful high romance; the movie spins a fantastic story of love that transcends time itself; beautifully acted and directed, it creates a world that is entirely engaging."[22] *Variety* praised the film's "well-executed script, based on a Jack Finney short story, that melds romance, fantasy, and quasi-time travel and is enhanced by endearing performances from its principals," including Scott, Leigh, Parsons, and Dukes. According to *Variety*,

> Director Dan Curtis keeps the pace brisk, knowing when to move the tale along or to slow down for some weepy moments that are crucial but never indulgent. He is aided by Eric Van Haren Norman's camerawork, which uses the striking shades of autumn to backdrop the story and its emotional underpinnings while soaking in Jan Scott's lush production design. Bill Blunden's editing makes it all seamless. The only quibble is this Hallmark card should have been saved for airing closer to Valentine's Day [instead of 13 days prior to the date].[23]

Jennifer Jason Leigh of *I Think I'm Having a Baby* and *The Love Letter* declared, "I love Dan Curtis. With everything he's done—all those huge miniseries like *War and Remembrance*—I mean, he's a legend. But he's got a great young attitude and a really sweet heart. He's got this tough-guy exterior and this deep, gruff voice, but he really is a marshmallow."[24] Many fans of *Somewhere in Time*, *The Lake House*, and *The Time Traveler's Wife* agree that *The Love Letter* is just as exquisite.

In the mid-2000s, Curtis's final two films recalled the heartrending drama of his two semi-autobiographical TV-movies and the issue-oriented fare of *Mrs. R's Daughter* (1979). **Saving Milly** (CBS, Sunday 13 March 2005; rerun Sunday 9 July 2006), filmed in Vancouver, British Columbia, was based on political journalist Mort Kondracke's non-fiction best-seller of the same name. As adapted by Jeff Arch (*Sleepless in Seattle*), *Saving Milly* is the story of Kondracke's 38-year love affair with his activist wife Millicent "Milly" Martinez Kondracke (d. 22 July 2004), who was diagnosed with an especially severe form of Parkinson's disease. Bruce Greenwood and Madeleine Stowe play Mort and Milly as they meet, fall in love, marry, raise two daughters, deal with his alcoholism, and face her devastating illness. The story is framed by Mort's testimony before a Congressional subcommittee on behalf of Parkinson's research, and it is tagged by remarks by Michael J. Fox (*Family Ties*) and the real-life Mort Kondracke (*The Beltway Boys*). Madeline Stowe, who gives a brilliant and breathtaking performance, won an Imagen Award for Best Television Actress. Arch's emotional script was nominated for the Humanitas Prize.[25] After Robert Cobert did only some preliminary work, Lee Holdridge (*Beauty and the Beast, The Dreamer of Oz*) composed the music heard in the telefilm.

Director Dan Curtis and *Back to the Future* star Michael J. Fox smile on the set of *Saving Milly* (2005). Fox appears as himself at the end of Curtis's next-to-last film.

Curtis admitted that he was drawn to the project because Alzheimer's disease had touched his family and he wanted to raise the public's awareness of all debilitating neurological diseases. "I'm usually never happy to hear about people crying," Curtis told *USA Today*. "This time, I am. *Saving Milly* is not a disease-of-the-week movie. If we can get the word out there, without it being a lesson or homework, and tell a great, moving love story, a ten-handkerchief picture, then I'll do it."[26] He did.

The *New York Daily News* called *Saving Milly* "challenging," "well-acted," and "tender," as well as "part passionate romance, part advocacy piece, and definitely worth a look."[27] The Parents Television Council named it "the best TV show of the week."[28] *The Hollywood Reporter* called *Saving Milly* "a beautifully acted, deeply moving film that manages to be at once inspirational and grueling."[29] Susan Stewart of *TV Guide* observed, "*Milly* may rely on the conventions and clichés of the issue movie, but it also boasts moments of unusual intimacy and candor. My score (0-10): 7."[30] *Saving Milly* has never been released on VHS or DVD except as a private VHS "screener" for Emmy voters.

Two months later, Curtis was back on television with another hard-hitting topical work—and his swan song. **Our Fathers** (Showtime, Saturday 21 May 2005), available on DVD, was a fact-based examination of the Boston Catholic diocese's sex-abuse scandal as it was first exposed in 2000. Christopher Plummer portrayed Cardinal Bernard Law and received Emmy and SAG Award nominations, and Ted Danson played Mitchell Garabedian, the real-life Boston attorney who represented some of the victims of alleged abuse by Boston-area priests. Brian Dennehy (as Father Dominic Spagnolia) also received an Emmy Award nomination.

Boston attorney Mitchell Garabedian (Ted Danson) organizes more and more victims of sexual abuse until 86 plaintiffs sue the diocese and Cardinal Law. Among the victims, now grown men, are Angelo DeFranco (Daniel Baldwin), Patrick McSorley (James Oliver), and Gary Bergeron (Thomas Mitchell). Garabedian interviews Mary Ryan (Ellen Burstyn), the mother of seven sons, *all* of whom were abused by Father John Geoghan (played by Damien Atkins [young] and Steven Shaw [old]). The elderly Geoghan is convicted, imprisoned, and ultimately murdered in his jail cell.

One of the highlights of the film is the scene in which another victim, Olan Horne (Chris Bauer of *The Wire*), confronts Cardinal Law at his residence and shames Law into facing the men in a support group for sex-abuse victims. The cast of *Our Fathers* also includes Kenneth Welsh, Jan Rubes, Will Lyman, Kathleen Laskey, Hugh Dillon, and Wayne Best. Colin Fox of *Strange Paradise* plays Law's advisor Daniel Kibbe.

Curtis's film was based on the book *Our Fathers: The Secret Life of the Catholic Church in an Age of Scandal*, by *Newsweek* writer David France (himself a victim of abuse). The screenplay, by Thomas Michael Donnelly (*Quicksilver*, *Talent for the Game*), was nominated for a Writers Guild of America award for Best Long-Form Adapted Screenplay. Robert Cobert composed the music. The film attracted attention and ratings to Showtime.[31]

Curtis sought to make a non-sensational, balanced look at both the church and the victims. "It had everything that I thought would make a really riveting picture," he noted. "Then comes the difficulty of doing something that's as touchy as this. How do you do it? It's kind of simple in a strange way. You just tell the truth."[32] Indeed, *USA Today* observed, "Curtis never allows a trace of salaciousness to enter the film. He sets the tone without showing anything explicit."[33] Nevertheless, the *Boston Herald* conceded, "If your heart hasn't already been broken by the priest sex-abuse scandal, then Showtime's strong film *Our Fathers* will finish the job."[34]

The San Jose *Mercury News* proclaimed that *Our Fathers* was "everything most TV docudramas about recent events are *not:* thoughtful, restrained without sacrificing emotion, and with a clear ring of truth to it."[35] The *News* added, "The real emotional core is the way *Our Fathers* handles the effect the abuse had on the victims. Without being explicit, the film captures the horror these young men went through as their innocence, faith, and trust were ripped away."[36] *TV Guide*'s Matt Roush noted, "Dan Curtis knows all about *Dark Shadows*, and there are plenty to be found in the conspiracy of silence that is shattered in *Our Fathers*, a forceful and sorrowful docudrama."[37] Ten years later, Stanley Tucci played Mitchell Garabedian, and Len Cariou played Cardinal Law, in Josh Singer and Tom McCarthy's film *Spotlight*, which won the Academy Award for the Best Picture of 2015.

On 22 April 2004, one year before the premiere of *Our Fathers,* Jim Pierson (left) and Dan Curtis attend the Museum of Television and Radio's tribute to Curtis on his 41st anniversary as a producer. Curtis holds the book that Pierson wrote about him.

Dramas from the house of Dan Curtis dealt with Depression-era family life and crime, as well as the present-day issues of disease, rape, teen pregnancy, and sexual abuse—plus real-life love (*Saving Milly*) and fantastical romance (*The Love Letter*). For those Curtis fans less familiar with these dramas, it is fortunate that all of them (except for *Milly* and *I Think I'm Having a Baby*) are available on VHS and/or DVD. The videocassettes of the Melvin Purvis movies and *Mrs. R's Daughter* are hard to find but worth the search.

Significa from the House of Dan Curtis: After the successes of *Melvin Purvis, G-Man* (1974) and *The Kansas City Massacre* (1975), Dan Curtis considered making more Purvis TV-movies and/or a weekly series, so he amassed numerous Melvin Purvis "spec" scripts from various writers. Between February and May 1975, Jock MacKelvie (*The Rookies*) submitted "Machine-Gun Kate" and "Death Wears a Baby's Face," Richard Guttman (*Back Door to Hell*) offered "The Legend of Bonnie and Clyde," and both Robert Lewin (*Bracken's World*) and Robert Schlitt (*The Monkees*) turned in scripts coincidentally titled "Mrs. Machine-Gun Kelly." As late as 1994, Earl Wallace (*The Last Ride of the Dalton Gang*) and Dan Curtis himself worked on "The Great Chicago Raid," which was inspired by William F. Nolan's 1974-1976 research and work on an epic script called *The Legend of Johnny Dillinger*.[38]

Significa from the House of Dan Curtis: The producer-director had such affection for his semiautobiographical dramas *When Every Day Was the Fourth of July* (1978) and *The Long Days of Summer* (1980) that he wished he could have starred the characters in a *Waltons*-style family TV series called *The Coopers*. Later in the 1980s and even in the 1990s, Dan Curtis and writer Lee Hutson kept alive hope for a *Coopers* series by preparing at least three episode scripts: "A Christmas Story" (by Curtis, Hutson, Tim Kring, and I.C. Rappaport), "For the Love of Ginger Parker" (by Rappaport), and "A Little Girl Across the Room" (by Hutson).[39]

Significa from the House of Dan Curtis: In mid-2004, Curtis directed a heartbreakingly beautiful PSA (**public-service announcement**) for the Alzheimer's Association. The four-minute film (available as an extra on a *Dark Shadows* DVD) depicts an elderly couple walking along a beach as Barbra Streisand's recording of Marvin Hamlisch's song "The Way We Were" is heard on the soundtrack. Home-movie-style flashback footage shows the woman and man much younger and living through the milestones of their lives. According to Jim Pierson, "Dan was frustrated as he never saw it shown anywhere. Ironically, the PSA's voice artist, Peter Falk, later suffered from Alzheimer's disease."[40] So did my mother, Sonia Anne Young Thompson, who passed away in May 2018 as I was preparing the revised second edition of *The Television Horrors of Dan Curtis* (McFarland, 2019).

CHAPTER VI

The Pilots
The Big Easy, Johnny Ryan,
Angie the Lieutenant, and More

Many prospective television series never make it past one episode—the pilot. Countless pilots go unaired, such as the 1967 *Dick Tracy* pilot for NBC (starring Ray MacDonnell of *The Edge of Night* and *All My Children*), the 1997 *Justice League of America* pilot for CBS (never telecast in the United States but aired in England), and the 2004 *Dark Shadows* pilot (rejected by the WB network and never officially seen anywhere except at the Dark Shadows Festival). In mid-2009, CBS shot pilots of new versions of the game shows *Pyramid* (with Robert Cobert's theme song), *Let's Make a Deal*, and *The Dating Game* before it selected *Let's Make a Deal* to replace the cancelled *Guiding Light*. In mid-2010, CBS considered replacing the cancelled *As the World Turns* with *Pyramid*. Instead, CBS launched *The Talk*.

Many other unsold pilots do air on television once (*Father on Trial, Just Desserts*) or even twice (*Bates Motel, Hardcase*). You may have seen *Baffled, Chain Letter, Computercide, Country Estates, The Covenant, Crash Island, Dare Devil, Dark Mansions, Doctor Strange, Down Delaware Road, Escapade, The Gifted One, In Search of America, Mockingbird Lane, The Mysterious Two, The Norliss Tapes, The Questor Tapes, The Spirit, Willow B: Women in Prison,* and/or Cathy Lee Crosby as *Wonder Woman* (but *not* Ellie Wood Walker as *Wonder Woman*—that pilot footage never aired on TV). In 1969, 1982, 1990, and 1992, the networks aired four unsold mystery pilots from Dan Curtis Productions.

For most of the 1960s, Dan Curtis Productions had provided CBS and ABC with plenty of daytime programming, first with the weekend *CBS Golf Classic*, beginning in December 1963, and then with the weekday *Dark Shadows*, beginning on ABC in June 1966. In January 1968, Curtis presented his first prime-time program, *The Strange Case of Dr. Jekyll and Mr. Hyde*, starring Jack Palance, on ABC. **Dead of Night: A Darkness at Blaisedon**, a pilot that aired on ABC in August 1969, was his second nighttime offering.

In 1968, after the Josette/Barnabas/Angelique storyline had made *Dark Shadows* a ratings powerhouse, ABC commissioned Dan Curtis Productions to make a pilot episode for a possible nighttime TV series about the supernatural. Curtis and his *Dark Shadows* writer Sam Hall co-created *Dead of Night*, featuring the adventures of the psychic investigator Jonathan Fletcher (Kerwin Mathews) and his Indian assistant Sajeed Rau (Cal Bellini). Even without the title card, A DAN CURTIS PRODUCTION, as part of the opening credits, viewers would have realized that *Dead of Night* was Curtis's attempt to recreate *Dark Shadows* at night.

In addition to Sam Hall, several *Dark Shadows* personnel worked on *Dead of Night*. They included composer Robert Cobert, costumer Ramsey Mostoller, stunt coordinator Alex Stevens, and assistant to the producer George DiCenzo. Trevor Williams, Curtis's art director on *Jekyll and Hyde,* served in the same capacity again and became a regular on Curtis's future productions for the next dozen years. The director was Lela Swift, Curtis's stalwart *Dark Shadows* director and mentor.

In the autumn of 1968, Swift directed *Dead of Night* at NBC Studios in Brooklyn, New York. The daytime serial *Another World* (1964-1999) was taped there, and Swift used some of the *Another World* personnel, such as technical director Heino Ripp, when she shot *Dead of Night* (on videotape, not film, except for one exterior scene). Dan Curtis produced the pilot, and Robert Cobert scored it with his tried-and-true *Dark Shadows* music cues, as well as some new compositions. According to film-music expert Jon Burlingame, "Cobert believed that his penchant for using vibraphone and percussion as suspense-generating devices originated with this project; the *Dead of Night* music cues resurfaced on *Dark Shadows*."[1] Indeed, the pilot's main-title theme later became the *Dark Shadows* cue associated with the disembodied head of Judah Zachery in the 1840 storyline in 1970.

Art director Trevor Williams created magnificent, multi-level sets, including the foyer, library, staircase, and other areas of Blaisedon, a Victorian mansion somewhere on the Hudson River, as well as the cottage of its caretaker (played by *Dark Shadows* star Thayer David, whose "Seth Blakely" was a close approximation of his initial *Dark Shadows* role as the surly caretaker Matthew Morgan). The split-level set of Jonathan Fletcher's Greenwich Village apartment would have appeared every week if *Dead of Night* had become a series.

Dark Shadows fans have often remarked that their favorite show featured almost every type of monster except a mummy. A mummy does appear in Paperback Library's *Barnabas, Quentin, and the Mummy's Curse* (April 1970), by Dan "Marilyn" Ross, and in Gold Key Comics' *Dark Shadows* #6 (August 1970), as well as in *Dead of Night* (not to mention *Ryan's Hope*, the serial that Lela Swift directed after *Dark Shadows*). As *Dead of Night* begins, Jonathan Fletcher and Sajeed Rau are studying an Egyptian mummy "from the sixth century B.C."—Sam Hall's indication that these characters have had adventures before this "first episode." Jonathan later reveals that he dropped out of law school and became a psychic investigator when his father's ghost appeared to him.

A Darkness at Blaisedon, which aired on ABC-TV on the night of Tuesday 26 August 1969, serves as the "origin episode" of the character who would have co-starred with the two men if *Dead of Night* had become a series. Angela Martin (played by Marj Dusay) starts out as the men's client, but by the end of the hour, she has decided to chuck her secretarial job in San Francisco and go ghost-hunting with her new friends. In the closing scene, Angela wears a gray Nehru suit.

Angela has inherited the great house of Blaisedon and wants to sell it but cannot because it is haunted by the vengeful ghost of Commodore Nicholas Blaise (*Dark Shadows* star Louis Edmonds) and his younger wife. Melinda Blaise died, apparently of influenza, in 1916 at age 28. Her husband, the Commodore, followed her in death one year later at age 64. Now, their ghosts haunt Blaisedon, and Lela Swift uses several high-angle shots to suggest that a presence is hovering over the house and watching Jonathan, Angela, and Sajeed.

Dead of Night: A Darkness at Blaisedon (1969): Marj Dusay, later of *Capitol* and *Guiding Light*, stars in Lela Swift and Dan Curtis's unsold pilot for a nighttime TV series about the supernatural.

In a reprise of the seminal *Dark Shadows* storyline—later reused in Curtis's *House of Dark Shadows* and *Dracula*—a living woman resembles another character's long-dead beloved. Angela Martin looks exactly like Melinda Blaise (as seen in a painting), and the Commodore's ghost covets her. At one point, Angela slips Melinda's ring on to her finger and becomes possessed by Melinda—a plot device that coincidentally was central to the initial months of the syndicated Canadian television serial *Strange Paradise* (1969-1970).

In *A Darkness at Blaisedon,* Sam Hall tries out a couple of ideas that would later shape his and Dan Curtis's script of *Night of Dark Shadows* (1971). Caretaker Seth Blakely, like housekeeper Carlotta Drake, is aware of the presence of the ghost in the house and seeks to assist its mission of controlling the living. Melinda Blaise, like Angelique Collins, is wrongfully accused of something. Just as Angelique is accused of being a witch but is not, Melinda is accused of infidelity when she actually has been faithful to the insanely jealous Commodore. Evidence that Jonathan Fletcher finds in a secret room and an opened grave bears this out.

Dead of Night echoes *Dark Shadows* not only in music, sets, and cast but also in the aforementioned grave-digging and secret-room plot points, as well as in a séance conducted by Jonathan, Angela, Sajeed, and the caretaker. Lela Swift shoots the actors, at their séance table, from above to show how their fingers are "touching at all times."

Viewers who happened to catch *Dead of Night: A Darkness at Blaisedon* in its one-and-only showing in late August 1969 were treated to an atmospheric and viable (if slow-moving) nighttime reincarnation of *Dark Shadows*. However, ABC passed on the pilot, and it did not become a series.

According to Jim Pierson, "Dan wanted to transfer *Dark Shadows*-style success to prime-time, but ABC decided *Blaisedon* wouldn't work in prime time with a *Dark Shadows* videotape format. It should have been half an hour, too," because of (in Pierson's words) the "padded story" that contributed to the program's slow-moving pace at times.[2]

Just think if *Dead of Night* had become a nighttime series in the fall of 1969. On Saturday nights in the 1969-1970 and 1970-1971 seasons, ABC signed off at 10:30 PM Eastern time instead of at the customary 11:00. A half-hour *Dead of Night* could have followed *Hollywood Palace* (in 1969-1970) or *Most Deadly Game* (a short-lived 1970-1971 mystery series about a trio of criminologists) in that 10:30 ET timeslot.

Another possibility is that *Dead of Night* could have capitalized on its serial look and feel and been telecast for 30 minutes twice weekly on ABC. In the mid-1960s, all three networks had experimented with multi-night continuing series. In the summer of 1965, CBS-TV's *Our Private World* (a nighttime spin-off of *As the World Turns*) aired on Wednesdays and Fridays. In the fifth and final season (1965-1966) of NBC-TV's *Dr. Kildare,* the series divided into half-hour Monday-and-Tuesday segments. ABC enjoyed the greatest such success with *Batman,* telecast twice a week in 1966 and 1966-1967, and, of course, with the twice-weekly *Peyton Place* (1964-1969), which, in its second season (1965-1966), topped *Dr. Kildare* by airing *three* nights per week. Perhaps, in some parallel band of time so familiar to *Dark Shadows* fans, *Dead of Night* enjoyed a two- or three-year run on some other ABC network.

In reality, it would be another two-and-one-half years before a Dan Curtis production was telecast in prime time. On the night of 11 January 1972, the *ABC Tuesday Movie of the Week* presented *The Night Stalker*, starring Darren McGavin. *Dead of Night: A Darkness at Blaisedon* disappeared from view until it was released on VHS in 1992 and on DVD in 2008.

The next unsold mystery pilot did not come along until 13 years later. ***The Big Easy*** (ABC, Sunday 15 August 1982) was executive-produced by Curtis, produced by Joseph Stern (*I Think I'm Having a Baby*), written by Lee Hutson (*When Every Day Was the Fourth of July*), and directed by Jud Taylor (*Then Came Bronson*). According to Jim Pierson, "Joe [Stern] reminded me that Dan was barely involved with it like *I Think I'm Having a Baby*. *The Big Easy* was Joe's project."³

If it had become a series, *The Big Easy* would have starred William Devane as New Orleans private investigator Jake Rubidoux, Nicholas Pryor as newspaperman Walker Garrett, Lane Smith as policeman Frank Medley, and Ja'net Dubois as nightclub owner Gloria Chenier. Between P.I. jobs, Jake plays clarinet in Gloria's French Quarter club, The Big Easy, "a lived-in joint that's been here for a while—like before the Louisiana Purchase," as Jake remarks in his ongoing voice-over narration. Mr. Hutson's teleplay effects a *film-noir* feel through this narration, Jake's wisecracking personality, and such hard-boiled lingo as "racket," "dough," "frail," "stiff," and "doll." Jake characterizes himself by observing, "Good thing I'm an easygoing guy," and by constantly referencing old movies (*The Postman Always Rings Twice, Desert Fury, Dial M for Murder, One-Eyed Jacks*) as if he and the people in his orbit could be a part of them.

William Devane (*Knots Landing*) and Ja'net DuBois (*Good Times*) co-star in *The Big Easy*, an unsold pilot. *The Big Easy* (1982) and *The Winds of War* (1983) come about through a production deal between Dan Curtis Productions and Paramount Pictures.

Rubidoux is hired by a client (Hugh Gillin) who claims to be Texas oilman Nunnally Hayes, the father of Cynthia Hayes (Mary Crosby), a woman who has gone missing. Only after Jake finds Cynthia with her gambler-boyfriend Jean Laveau (Crofton Hardester) and tells "Hayes" does he discover that "Hayes" is *not* Cynthia's father but a hit man hired to "chill" her. Adding to the intrigue is Cynthia's ex-boyfriend, gigolo Jeb Taylor (Jared Martin), who is being "kept"—and quite possessively—by Lorri Fitzgerald (Barbara Babcock), a *femme fatale* whom Jake compares to "the blonde in *Desert Fury*" (apparently, Lizabeth Scott). Along the way, director of photography Charles Correll (*The Long Days of Summer*) frames atmospheric shots of Bourbon Street, Jackson Square, Audubon Park, and the Superdome. Composer J.J. Johnson (*Lucan, CHiPs*) provides minimal background music but a pleasing main-title theme and plenty of source music (e.g. "Hello Dolly," "Love Letters," "The Nearness of You," "Tangerine," et al.).

After surviving a dramatic shoot-out with the hit-man at journalist Walker Garrett's house, Jake solves his case at Lorri Fitzgerald's home in the Garden District. NOPD Lt. Frank Medley asks Jake, "What are you going to do next?" and Rubidoux replies, "Take a nap."

Variety was complimentary of William Devane and *The Big Easy*. The trade paper declared, "A veteran actor and far more skilled than most TV stars, Devane demonstrated a capacity for the insouciant charm so necessary to carry off a private eye who spends his spare time in a New Orleans jazz joint. [. . .] If ABC comes up short some time in mid-winter, *The Big Easy* would be resurrected with profit."[4] If *The Big Easy* (1982) had become a successful television series, William Devane might never have starred on CBS-TV's *Knots Landing* from 1983 to 1993. The Edgar Award-nominated *Big Easy* (not to be confused with Jim McBride's 1986 theatrical movie) has never been released on VHS or DVD.

The next unsold pilot surfaced eight years later. Fourteen months after *War and Remembrance: The Final Chapter* (1989), the first post-*War* Dan Curtis production was the two-hour pilot movie **Johnny Ryan**, starring Clancy Brown. It aired on NBC on Sunday 29 July 1990 after the rerun of *A Family for Joe*, the February pilot movie that had launched *War* star Robert Mitchum's March-August 1990 situation comedy of the same name.

Dan Curtis served as executive producer of *Johnny Ryan* but left the producing to Christopher Chulack and the directing to Robert Collins. Chulack went on to produce and direct *Homefront, Third Watch,* and *ER* after *Johnny Ryan*. Collins had directed *Police Story, Gideon's Trumpet,* and *Savage Harvest* before *Johnny Ryan*. The teleplay was by Mark Rodgers, who had written for *Police Story, Eischied,* and *T.J. Hooker*.

Johnny Ryan, originally titled *Against the Mob*, pits a special NYPD task force against five crime families in 1949 New York City. Heading the squad is Detective Johnny Ryan (Clancy Brown), a former Marine who answers to New York's District Attorney, Frank S. Hogan (J. Kenneth Campbell). While Johnny Ryan is a fictional character, Frank Hogan (1902-1974) was New York's real-life, long-time DA from 1941 until his resignation (after a stroke) in late 1973. The inclusion of a few real-life personalities, such as the incorruptible Hogan and the gangsters Frank Costello (Victor Argo) and Meyer Lansky (Michael Fairman), gives *Johnny Ryan* a docudrama feel. Adding to the verisimilitude is the period detail of the clothes and the cars, as well as stock footage of Times Square from decades ago. Jack Benny is heard on the radio, and a "Sugar" Ray Robinson fight airs on an early television set in a bar.

The cast of *Johnny Ryan* (1990) includes (seated) Teri Austin and Clancy Brown and (standing, from left) Cameron Thor, Bruce Abbott, Eugene Clark, and Nestor Serrano.

Unfortunately, too much of a period-docudrama feel, along with the absence of Dan Curtis's more dynamic directing style, makes *Johnny Ryan* rather stodgy in places. Mark Rodgers's script, while well written, is a rehash of countless cops-and-robbers movies that had come before: the murder of an informant, a kindly old Irish cop who mentors Johnny Ryan, Johnny's unwise romantic entanglement with a gangster's girlfriend, the revelation of a "good" cop's collusion with the gangsters, etc. There is even a *Casablanca*-esque good-bye scene at an airport.

On the other hand, a well-done highlight of *Johnny Ryan* is an ambush and shoot-out on the road to Utica, New York. Other assets are the excellent performances of J. Kenneth Campbell as DA Hogan, Robert Prosky as Captain Miles Fitzgerald, and Julia Campbell as Eve Manion, the showgirl who has the bad luck of being caught between gangster/club owner Steve Lombardi (Paul Rossilli) and Johnny Ryan. Teri Austin of *Knots Landing* is underused as attorney Paula Westridge, a potentially interesting character. In the limited time that he appears, Jason Beghe of *Intruder*s also shines as Peter Howard, an alcoholic, suicidal police officer who ultimately helps Ryan and his partner Tom Kelly (Bruce Abbott) make their case against Lombardi and Anthony "Tough Tony" Cardini (Robert Miranda), who together threw an informant out of a window to his death.

A crucial element missing from *Johnny Ryan* is Robert Cobert's music. Director Bob Collins selected as his composer Chris Boardman, who had written the music for Collins's 1989 TV-movies *The Hijacking of the Achille Lauro* (NBC, Monday 13 February) and *Prime Target* (NBC, Friday 29 September). Boardman's music score is a mixture of *noir*-ish muted-trumpet and tenor-saxophone cues, big-band swing interludes, and vintage songs such as "Sing, Sing, Sing," which opens the film; "Satin Doll," to which Eve Manion and the other showgirls dance at Steve Lombardi's Havana Club; and "Body and Soul," which "Mel Torme" (actually a lookalike actor) sings at the club. Boardman's scores for *Achille Lauro* and *Johnny Ryan* were nominated for Emmy Awards but lost to the music from *Lonesome Dove* (Basil Poledouris) and *Stephen King's IT* (Richard Bellis), respectively. Poledouris won his Emmy over both Chris Boardman for *The Hijacking of the Achille Lauro* and Robert Cobert for *War and Remembrance*.

As the single Dan Curtis production between *War and Remembrance* (1988, 1989) and *Dark Shadows* (1991), *Johnny Ryan* (1990) is enjoyable but far from one of the strongest productions from the house of Dan Curtis. With Curtis's *auteur* directing and script-doctoring—and Cobert's music—*Johnny Ryan* possibly could have been another *Kansas City Massacre* (1975). Without them, it is an admirable but ordinary programmer. *TV Guide* gave the telefilm two stars (out of four). The pilot did not sell, and it was never released on VHS or DVD.

Angie the Lieutenant, the fourth and final unsold mystery/crime pilot from the production house of Dan Curtis, aired one-and-one-half years later in 1992. One of writer-producer-director Robert Collins's greatest accomplishments is his creation of the classic TV series *Police Woman* (NBC, 1974-1978), starring Angie Dickinson as Sgt. Suzanne "Pepper" Anderson. Bob Collins had written "The Gamble," the Tuesday 26 March 1974 episode of NBC-TV's *Police Story* that had introduced Angie Dickinson as a police officer named "Lisa Beaumont." The "Gamble" pilot was retooled, Earl Holliman was added to the cast, and *Police Woman* premiered on NBC on Friday 13

September 1974 (opposite "The Ripper," the debut episode of *Kolchak: The Night Stalker*, on ABC).

The aforementioned 1989 TV-movie *Prime Target*, which Collins wrote, executive-produced, and directed, starred Angie Dickinson as police sergeant Kelly Mulcahaney in an adventure based on the 1979 novel *No Business Being a Cop*, by Lillian O'Donnell, author of *The Phone Calls*, *Don't Wear Your Wedding Ring*, and more than one dozen other Norah Mulcahaney crime novels. Now, in early 1992, one year after the 1991 *Dark Shadows* had come and gone, Robert Collins and Angie Dickinson were together again as writer-producer-director and star, respectively, of *Angie the Lieutenant* (ABC, Saturday 1 February), executive-produced by Dan Curtis. *Angie* was the pilot for a potential half-hour dramatic series about Lt. Angela "Angie" Martin (Dickinson), a recently promoted Washington DC policewoman who assumes the leadership of a multicultural, all-male squad of plainclothes detectives. Under Lt. Martin's command are her old friend Carl Koenig (Michael MacRae), overachieving Georgetown graduate Elliott Chase (Jesse Dabson), Oliver Jackson (Harold Sylvester), and Ernesto Mendez (Geoffrey Rivas)—all of whom are disconcerted that their new boss is a woman.

Angie Dickinson becomes a police woman again for the unsold half-hour dramatic pilot *Angie the Lieutenant* (1992).

Providing local color are scenes of Washington DC landmarks and a cameo appearance by Congressman William D. Lowery (R-California), who was a member of the United States House of Representatives from 1981 to 1993. As the pilot episode begins, Lowery's statement to the press is being covered by newswoman Zee Campbell (Sarah Carson) of WDBX-TV 8 in Washington DC. Later, the reporter is raped, beaten, and left for dead in "Crack City" by a gang of four men—and Lt. Angie Martin and her detectives begin their first case together.

Angie Dickinson, certainly no stranger to playing gun-wielding policewomen, brings believability and a natural ease to her role. She is suitably authoritative, forceful, and even sarcastic when she needs to be. At other times, she adds a woman's touch to her work, such as bringing Zee Campbell's favorite TV makeup and a hairbrush to her bedside and suddenly embracing Det. Carl Koenig in order to hide his face from some crooks who would recognize him. Dickinson also wears three different stylish outfits in the episode, and in the final moments, she goes to the Capitol and meets an unnamed undersecretary (Michael Tolan) who is the man in Lt. Angie Martin's life.

Robert Collins's script, set to synthesized music by Stanley Clarke (*The Five Heartbeats*), is fast-paced and full of characterization, and his direction is much more energetic than that of the often languorous *Johnny Ryan*. Angela Bassett makes the most of her small role as Zee Campbell's nurse. A moment of hilarious comic relief is provided by Juanita Gallegos (Dyanna Ortelli), a self-proclaimed "streetwalker" whom Angie Martin recruits as an informant. "In my business," Juanita remarks, "you meet a lot of people, but you don't see much of their faces." To be convinced to become a "snitch," Juanita insists on having Angie's smart alligator purse. Upon closer examination of her new handbag, Juanita protests, "Hey, this isn't real alligator!" Angie matter-of-factly replies, "Oh, in our business, we learn to fake things, too, Juanita."

Perhaps one reason why the otherwise promising *Angie the Lieutenant* pilot did not sell is that audiences did not know what it was supposed to be. It aired on a Saturday night after *Perfect Strangers* and *Growing Pains*, and it was a half-hour show in which the star played a character with a first name that was the same as her own. That sounds just like a sitcom, does it not? The lackluster title, *Angie the Lieutenant*, sounds vaguely comedic and is only a slightly better name than *She's the Sheriff* (the title of Suzanne Somers's 1987-1989 syndicated sitcom). Perhaps, ABC was attempting another "dramedy" along the lines of *Hooperman; The Wonder Years; Doogie Houser, M.D.;* and *Cop Rock*. Even *The Commish*, Michael Chiklis's excellent series that *Angie the Lieutenant* pre-empted on Saturday 1 February 1992, blended comic elements with serious crime drama.

According to Jim Pierson, "*Angie* was a half-hour pilot idea for ABC to return to the old half-hour drama format like *Adam-12, Felony Squad,* etc. and was paired with Brian Keith's half-hour MGM TV pilot *The Streets of Beverly Hills* [not a Dan Curtis production]. Dan was only moderately involved with *Angie*."[5] *The Streets of Beverly Hills*, starring Brian Keith of *Family Affair* and Stan Kirsch of *Highlander* as a Los Angeles policeman and his son, finally aired on ABC on Monday 13 July 1992.

A return to half-hour dramas was a valid idea. In addition to *Adam-12* and *Felony Squad*, numerous half-hour dramas filled the TV schedules of yesteryear. *Dragnet,*

Flipper, Gentle Ben, The Green Hornet, Have Gun Will Travel, Honey West, Lassie, M Squad, NYPD, One Step Beyond, Peyton Place, Police Surgeon, The Protectors, The Rat Patrol, The Restless Gun, The Rifleman, Steve Canyon, The Twilight Zone, Werewolf, and *Zorro* packed plot, characterization, and action into their half-hour running times.[6] In the 2020s, 30-minute dramas such as *T.H.E. Cat* and *The Guns of Will Sonnett*—not to mention 90-minute dramas such as *The Virginian* and *The Name of the Game*—seem to be a thing of the past.

These four unsold pilots from the house of Dan Curtis—*Dead of Night: A Darkness at Blaisedon* (hour-long), *The Big Easy* (hour-long), *Johnny Ryan* (two-hour), and *Angie Lieutenant* (half-hour)—are certainly not Curtis's most famous, accomplished, or popular productions—very probably because "Dan was only moderately involved" with three of them[7]—and, except for *Blaisedon*, they have never been released on VHS or DVD. Nevertheless, all four of them have their merits and their own places among the output of Dan Curtis Productions. Watching any rare, unsold pilot tucked away on a Saturday night or thrown away in July or August is always fun because it is the one-and-only chance to see that premise and that cast of characters. In the words of the producer Steven Bochco (*Hill Street Blues, LA Law, NYPD Blue*), "Making pilots is fun. It's what happens after they sell where it gets ugly."[8]

Significa from the House of Dan Curtis: *Big Easy* composer and jazz trombonist J.J. Johnson (1924-2001) played in Benny Carter's and Count Basie's bands, and he also played with Illinois Jacquet and Kai Winding. In the 1970s, Johnson composed music for the television series *Buck Rogers in the 25th Century, CHiPs, Future Cop, Lucan, The Six-Million-Dollar Man,* and *Starsky and Hutch*.[9]

Significa from the House of Dan Curtis: *Angie the Lieutenant* composer and bass guitarist Stanley Clarke (b. 1951) wrote music for the 1990s films *Boyz N the Hood, Passenger 57, What's Love Got to Do with it, Poetic Justice, Higher Learning,* and *Down in the Delta*.[10]

Significa from the House of Dan Curtis: Twenty-three years apart, the leading characters of *Dead of Night: A Darkness at Blaisedon* (1969) and *Angie the Lieutenant* (1992) are coincidentally named Angela Martin (Marj Dusay of the *Star Trek* episode "Spock's Brain") and Angela Martin (Angie Dickinson of *One Shoe Makes it Murder*). Dickinson also starred in *The Norliss Tapes* (1973), which was intended as a pilot for a series starring Roy Thinnes. Both *The Norliss Tapes* and its sequel *The Return* are discussed in Chapter II. As mentioned at the end of Chapter V, Dan Curtis wished that *When Every Day Was the Fourth of July* (1978) and *The Long Days of Summer* (1980) could have piloted a *Waltons*-type series called *The Coopers*.

CHAPTER VII

The Mysteries
Wide World Mystery, The Great Ice Rip-Off, Supertrain, and What Might Have Been

In addition to conquering daytime television with *Dark Shadows* and making a huge impact on prime-time TV with *The Night Stalker, Trilogy of Terror,* and the two *War* miniseries, Dan Curtis made his presence known in late-night TV, that sleepy realm after the 11:00 news (10:00 PM Central). Granted, late-night was dominated (and deservedly so) by *The Tonight Show Starring Johnny Carson,* but in the mid-1970s, ABC made a valiant attempt to offer something different to the 11:30 audience. Dan Curtis Productions was a part of that difference.

Between early 1973 and the end of the decade, ABC's late-night schedule was a mixed bag of talk (Jack Paar, Dick Cavett), music (*In Concert, The Roger Miller Show*), reruns (*Mannix, The Streets of San Francisco*), and mystery. ABC-TV's *Wide World Mystery* anthology series of crime, mystery, science fiction, and horror aired on Tuesday nights (December 1973-January 1976) and later on Monday nights (January-September 1975) as well. Between January 1973 and September 1975, one-night or two-night *Wide World Mystery* episodes occasionally aired on *any* weeknight as the *ABC Late-Night Special* (later called the *Wide World Special*). *Wide World Mystery* reruns continued to air occasionally until 1978.

Only a few of the many fondly remembered *Wide World Mystery* segments are "Hard Day at Blue Nose" (John Astin and Patty Duke Astin; Tuesday 12 February 1974); "Legacy of Blood" (Clifton Davis, TSU's Moses Gunn; Tuesday 12 March 1974); "The Cloning of Clifford Swimmer" (Peter Haskell, Sharon Farrell; Friday 1 November 1974); "Please Call It Murder" (Bradford Dillman, Kathleen Widdoes; Tuesday 21 January 1975); "The Death Volley" (Beverly Garland, Sam Chew; Monday 27 January 1975); "The Two Deaths of Sean Doolittle" (George Grizzard, Grayson Hall; written by Sam Hall; directed by Lela Swift; Friday 4 April 1975); "The Norming of Jack 243" (David Selby, Leslie Charleson; directed by Gloria Monty; Tuesday 9 September 1975); "Too Easy to Kill" (Imogene Coca, Peter Coffield; Tuesday 14 October 1975); "Demon, Demon" (Juliet Mills, Billy Barty; Tuesday 11 November 1975); and "Alien Lover" (Kate Mulgrew, Pernell Roberts; directed by Lela Swift; Tuesday 25 November 1975; rerun Wednesday 29 March 1978).[1]

Dan Curtis produced seven *Wide World Mystery* programs in 1973 and 1974. He co-wrote one of them (*Frankenstein*), and he directed another (*The Turn of the Screw*). As producer, Curtis kept a close eye on each of these late-night programs which bore the stamp, A DAN CURTIS PRODUCTION. In a June 2006 DVD commentary, actor Robert Foxworth said of Curtis and his input, "As I recall, he got his two cents in!"

The first Curtis-produced *Wide World Mystery*—a two-night adaptation of **Frankenstein**, starring Foxworth—aired on Tuesday-Wednesday 16-17 January 1973. (Coincidentally, Curtis's TV-movie *The Night Strangler* had aired in prime time on the night of January 16.) Curtis co-wrote *Frankenstein* with Sam Hall and Richard Landau. Hall had been one of the head writers of *Dark Shadows* and co-writer of the two subsequent movies. Landau had co-written *The Quatermass Xperiment*, a.k.a. *The Creeping Unknown* (1955), and *Frankenstein 1970* (a 1958 Boris Karloff movie), among other films and TV episodes.

Curtis chose one of his protégés to direct *Frankenstein*. Glenn Jordan had directed only five TV movies (1969–1972) before *Frankenstein*, but he went on to direct *Les Miserables* (TV-1978), *Mass Appeal* (1984), *O Pioneers!* (TV-1992), and two of the three *Sarah, Plain and Tall* telefilms for *Hallmark Hall of Fame*. Even though Curtis did not direct *Frankenstein*, he put his distinctive stamp on the production through his work on the script and his careful management of the *Dark Shadows/Jekyll and Hyde* look of the movie.

Radu Florescu, author of *In Search of Frankenstein* (1975), observed of this "really first-class" adaptation of Mary Shelley's 1818 novel that "for the very first time, an attempt was made to try and stay reasonably close to Mary Shelley's original conception of the monster." Florescu continued,

> With Robert Foxworth as Victor Frankenstein and Susan Strasberg as Elizabeth, Bo Svenson emerged as a literate, well-spoken, and sensitive monster. Although the plot once again had the creature created electrically rather than biologically, director Glenn Jordan adhered to Shelley's desire to have her monster seek a mate in order to pacify his destructive impulses. Admittedly, the intricate flashback mechanism of the novel was again shunted aside, but at least a sincerely admirable linkage between printed page and movie (or TV, in this case) screen was attempted.[2]

The practice of using electricity to bring the creature to life is a deeply entrenched tradition in film versions of *Frankenstein*. Of the more than 230 filmings since 1910, one dozen of them even used the same electrical equipment, built by Kenneth Strickfaden for Universal's 1931 classic. Mary Shelley's novel avoids any concrete description of exactly how Dr. Victor Frankenstein brings his creation to life, but the author implies that the process involves chemistry, alchemy, and electricity. In fact, in chapter five Dr. Frankenstein remarks, "I collected the instruments of life around me that I might infuse *a spark* of being into the lifeless thing that lay at my feet."[3] Film audiences expect some sort of galvanic process in the obligatory creation scene, and Curtis and Jordan's *Frankenstein* does not disappoint.

Horror-film critic Paul O'Flinn concedes, "There is no such thing as *Frankenstein*; there are only *Frankensteins* as the text is ceaselessly rewritten, reproduced, refilmed, and redesigned."[4] He adds that "the shift of medium" from novel to film demands that the screenwriters "must inevitably obliterate and replace" elements of the novel in order to make the work more visual and filmable,[5] a mandate which had necessitated a few cinematic changes to Curtis's *Jekyll and Hyde* production several years earlier.

Chapter Seven: The Mysteries 161

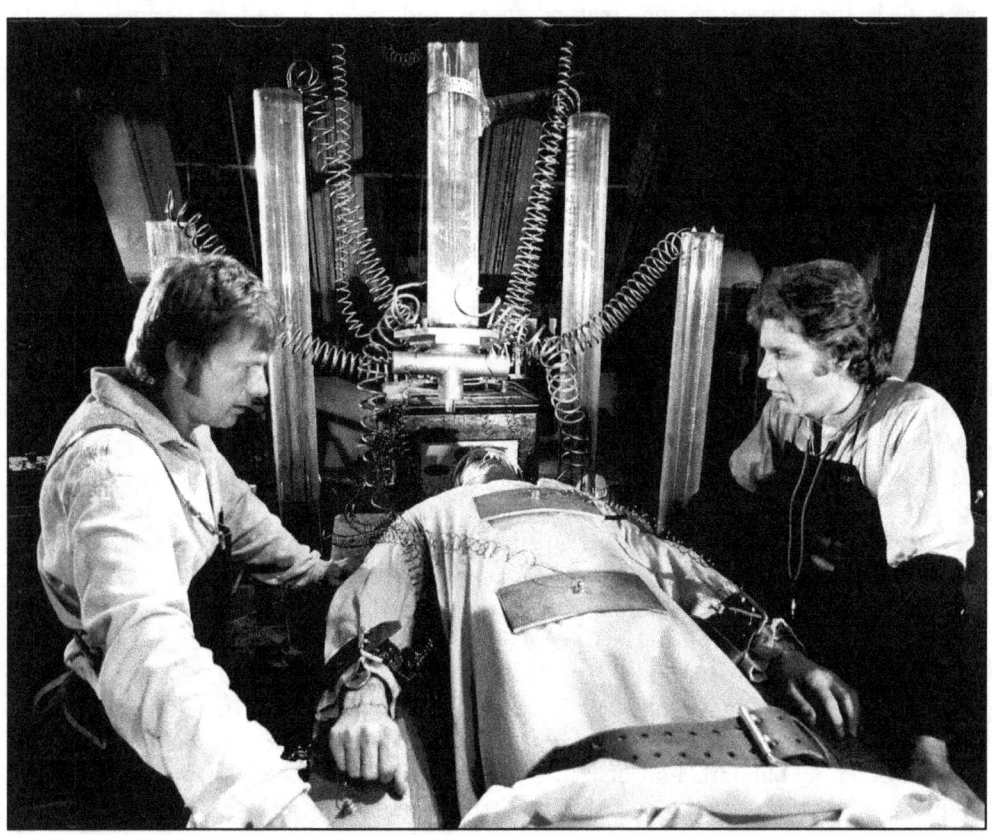

Frankenstein (1973): John Karlen (left), Bo Svenson (on table), and Robert Foxworth co-star in the two-night adaptation produced by Dan Curtis and directed by Glenn Jordan for ABC's *Wide World Mystery.*

Even after making such changes to their *Frankenstein,* writers Curtis, Hall, and Landau do succeed in remaining more nearly faithful to the spirit of Shelley's novel than previous movie versions. All of the major characters and plot threads are present and true to form except for Captain Robert Walton (and the framing device of Frankenstein's telling the story to him aboard his ship) and housekeeper Justine Moritz (and the subplot of her being wrongly accused of and hanged for William's murder). Most of the action takes place in Ingolstadt, Germany—for budgetary reasons, this version eschews Frankenstein's travels around Europe and to England and the Orkney Islands—and the year is now 1856, more than a half-century after the novel's time setting. The movie's primary focus is on Dr. Victor Frankenstein (Robert Foxworth), the Creature (Bo Svenson), and Agatha DeLacey (Heidi Vaughn). Secondary focus is on Alphonse Frankenstein (Philip Bourneuf), Elizabeth Lavenza (Susan Strasberg), and Dr. Henri Clerval (Robert Gentry), all of whom frequently question Frankenstein about his erratic, obsessive behavior.

For dramatic purposes, Dr. Frankenstein has two lab assistants, Hugo (George Morgan) and Otto (Curtis mainstay John Karlen). Frankenstein uses the mortally wounded Hugo's heart as the creature's heart, and the creature later accidentally kills Otto by hugging him much too strongly after Otto has thrown a ball with him and taught him the words "Otto" and "play." Dr. Frankenstein finds the puzzled creature standing over the dead man and begging him, "Otto, play?" This is the first of many instances of poignancy and sympathy for the monster. An important trait of many of Curtis's productions is a degree of sympathy for the evildoer—Barnabas Collins, Dr. Jekyll, the Night Strangler, Count Dracula, the crook Harry Banner in *Me and the Kid*, and others. Curtis reflected, "I try to find an additional dimension to the monster. Sometimes, you actually end up feeling sorry for him. We certainly did that with Barnabas Collins and Dr. Jekyll."[6] Curtis, Hall, Landau, and director Jordan achieve the same effect with the Giant (as Bo Svenson's character is called).

Although, as Florescu notes, the storyline aboard Robert Walton's ship is not included in this version, Curtis and the scriptwriters do offer a rich portrayal of the DeLacey family, the French exiles who unknowingly become the creature's family after he hides in their shed for months and learns about language, history, friendship, and love by listening to them through the walls. Monsieur Charles DeLacey (Jon Lormer), his grown children Felix (Brian Avery) and Agatha (Heidi Vaughn), and Felix's fiancée Safie (Malila Saint-Duval) play their same instructive roles from the novel, but with two changes. In this version, Safie is Spanish, not Turkish, and it is Agatha, not her father, who is blind. Curtis and his co-writers did not want to try to top the famous monster-meets-blind-man scene in James Whale's *The Bride of Frankenstein* (1935)—or even want to remind viewers of that outlandish meeting—in the middle of their serious adaptation of Shelley's novel. Plus, allowing the Giant to interact with a young blind woman instead of an old blind man injects more pathos and even a hint of love interest into the movie. Furthermore, the Giant's and Agatha's similar desire to have friends echoes Captain Robert Walton's selfsame desire for a friendly companion as expressed in his letters to his sister Margaret Walton Saville at the beginning of Shelley's novel—"I bitterly feel the want of a friend."[7]

Of the hundreds of actors who have portrayed the Frankenstein creature over the decades, Bo Svenson is one of the most successful at infusing the monster with pathos. When he hears Agatha tell Safie that talking with someone is the best way to learn a language, the scarred Giant carves a face onto a potato in the DeLaceys' shed and speaks to it. He later tells Agatha, "Sometimes, I wish the whole world was blind; then, everyone would be alike." Soon, the DeLacey men and Safie return home and recoil from the Giant. In two other moments that humanize the creature, the Giant kills young William Frankenstein (Willie Aames) by accident when he tries to stop the boy from crying out to Elizabeth, and the Giant desires to "learn forgiveness" just before his death (scored to Robert Cobert's death-of-Jekyll/death-of-Barnabas music).

Cobert did not write a new score for *Frankenstein*; instead, he used his tried-and-true music cues from *Dark Shadows*, as well as two cues from *The Strange Case of Dr. Jekyll and Mr. Hyde*. By January 1973, the time of the *Frankenstein* telecast, almost two years had elapsed since *Dark Shadows* fans had heard Cobert's famous TV music cues anywhere except on their well-worn 1969 *Dark Shadows* soundtrack record album (as of 2020 still one of the top 15 best-selling TV soundtracks of all time). Cobert's distinctive brand of (in his words) "great spook music"[8] instantly marked a program as A DAN CURTIS

PRODUCTION, and loyal *Dark Shadows*/Dan Curtis devotees eagerly sought out any television show that afforded them another example of Curtis and Cobert's work. (Dan Curtis was always well aware of his fan base. In later years, he closely monitored, but never attended, the Shadowcon and Dark Shadows Festival fan conventions.)

Frankenstein garnered more stellar reviews for Dan Curtis. Cecil Smith of the *Los Angeles Times* wrote, "*Frankenstein* is the best shot yet in ABC's ongoing war to woo the midnight audience. Despite a miniscule budget, [*Frankenstein*] is quite a handsome show, with huge, foreboding sets and a splendid array of special effects."[9] *Variety* called the production "extraordinary entertainment" and declared, "*Frankenstein* marks a decided step forward in late-night entertainment. It's really too good to relegate to the insomniacs."[10] Two years later, in his book *In Search of Frankenstein*, Radu Florescu paid Curtis the ultimate compliment when he wrote, "This 180-minute television film was probably the most faithful rendering the screen has yet seen."[11]

Unfortunately, *Frankenstein* did not receive the lasting recognition that it deserved because it aired late at night, it was shot on videotape, and it was quickly overshadowed by Jack Smight's *Frankenstein: The True Story* (NBC, November 30-December 1 of 1973; rerun December 30-31 of 1974) and Mel Brooks's *Young Frankenstein* (1974). The former, with its close relationship between Victor Frankenstein (Leonard Whiting) and his *handsome*, inquisitive creation (Michael Sarrazin), was one of Anne Rice's inspirations for her 1976 novel *Interview with the Vampire*. The latter, an uproarious spoof of Frankenstein movies, was one of Kenneth Branagh's inspirations as he filmed *Mary Shelley's Frankenstein* (1994), despite the two films' vast difference in tone. *Young Frankenstein*, of course, features a monster-meets-blind-man scene that has *never* been topped.

In October 2001, the *Journal of Frankenstein* noted that the acting in Dan Curtis's *Frankenstein* "was quite good. [*Frankenstein*] got good reviews from the critics and did well in the ratings. This version is pretty much forgotten, but it should not be. It is an admirable adaptation." [12]

Five years before the *Los Angeles Times* published Dan Curtis's letter putting *War and Remembrance* (1988, 1989) and *Schindler's List* (1993) into perspective, the *Times* published another of Curtis's emphatic statements, this one about *Frankenstein*. In the Monday 30 November 1992 edition, Curtis wrote,

> I read with interest the location piece filed from England by Jeff Kaye regarding TNT's *Frankenstein*. In it, Kaye says that "TNT is producing the most true-to-the-original-story version of *Frankenstein* that has ever been filmed." He further asks, "If the original story is so good, why hasn't anyone filmed it before?"
>
> The fact of the matter is that I produced a three-hour adaptation of Mary Shelley's classic work that ABC aired as part of its *Wide World of Mystery* late-night programming schedule in two parts on January 16-17, 1973. The production, starring Robert Foxworth as Dr. Frankenstein and Bo Svenson as the creature, received rave reviews and was highly rated.
>
> In fact, the *Los Angeles Times*'s television reporter, Cecil Smith, wrote glowingly of the production, the direction, the cast, and so forth. Smith

pointed out that "major departures were made from the *Frankenstein* we knew and loved in James Whale's great 1931 movie.

"Instead of the inarticulate, lumbering monster that Boris Karloff played so brilliantly, this adaptation, by producer Dan Curtis and writer Sam Hall, is truer to Mary Shelley's classic novel, in which Dr. Frankenstein produced in his laboratory a 'superhuman,' the strongest, most brilliant man on earth."

Although I eagerly await this new production of Shelley's enormously rich literary masterpiece, I feel compelled to recognize the extraordinary contributions of my colleagues to this earlier, groundbreaking television production. These include my co-adaptors, Sam Hall and Richard Landau; director, Glenn Jordan; music director, Robert Cobert; art director, Trevor Williams; and a wonderful cast, headed by Foxworth, Svenson, and Susan Strasberg.

Throughout my career, I have felt a deep kinship for this particular entertainment genre. Who knew that a show I created almost 30 years ago called *Dark Shadows* would become a major daytime cult hit?

Actually, it was only recently, while reviewing the press materials for the soon-to-be-released video library of my "scariest" productions, that I realized what a large percentage of my creative output has dealt with such matters as the occult, vampires, horror, and "things that go bump in the night."

The Strange Case of Dr. Jekyll and Mr. Hyde with Jack Palance (1968), Darren McGavin in *The Night Stalker* (1972), Lynn Redgrave in *The Turn of the Screw* (1974), and *Bram Stoker's Dracula* (1974), again with Palance, to name a few—all of my works in this field have in some way been informed and nourished by the literary and cinematic references that have preceded them. That's how a subject matter becomes a genre in the first place. I only wish Kaye had researched the television lineage of Mary Shelley's *Frankenstein* a little more assiduously.

Signed, DAN CURTIS[13]

Three months after *Frankenstein*, Curtis and Jordan returned to ABC-TV's late-night *Wide World Mystery* with **The Picture of Dorian Gray** (Monday-Tuesday 23-24 April 1973), written by John Tomerlin from the 1891 novel by Oscar Wilde. Tomerlin had written "Dark Legacy," the 30 May 1961 episode of *Boris Karloff's Thriller*, and "Number Twelve Looks Exactly Like You," the 24 January 1964 episode of *The Twilight Zone*, among other teleplays. Now, he submitted to Curtis a *Dorian Gray* adaptation that *The Hollywood Reporter* noted "adheres closely to the original."[14]

Curtis's *Dorian Gray* is more widely remembered than his *Frankenstein* because there have not been as many movie versions of Wilde's novel and because this *Dorian Gray* is considered to be one of the two best adaptations of the more than 30 treatments filmed since at least 1910. Although everyone from Lloyd Bochner (1954) and Helmut Berger (1970) to Stuart Townsend (2003) and Ben Barnes (2009) has played Dorian Gray, the two most widely remembered portrayals are those by Hurd Hatfield in Albert

Lewin's 1945 MGM feature and Shane Briant in Curtis's 1973 telefilm. Both the 1945 and 1973 adaptations take a few liberties with Wilde's text, but Curtis's production is the most faithful adaptation of *The Picture of Dorian Gray* ever filmed. Tomerlin's script retains many of Lord Henry Wotton and Dorian Gray's famous aphorisms about beauty, love, marriage, and temptation—and the movie is more revealing of Dorian Gray's omnisexuality than the more discreet versions made in the 1910s, the 1940s, and the 1960s.

Whereas the action of Wilde's 1891 novel (an expansion of his novella published in the 20 June 1890 issue of *Lippincott's Monthly Magazine*) takes place over the course of 18 years, the events of this adaptation stretch from 1891 to 1911. The film begins with a Wildean epigraph—"Those who go beneath the surface do so at their peril"—just as Curtis's *Frankenstein* begins with an epigram from John Milton's *Paradise Lost*. This *Picture of Dorian Gray* does especially well in faithfully bringing to the screen the novel's first and second chapters (Basil and Henry's conversation about Dorian and the introduction of Dorian himself) and chapter 16 (Dorian's visit to the opium den and his confrontation with Sybil's brother James). Artist Basil Hallward (Charles Aidman) is suitably protective (and enamored) of young, blond, androgynously handsome Dorian (Shane Briant), and Lord Henry Wotton (*Harry* Wotton in this adaptation) is charismatically witty, seductive, and Svengali-esque toward this new object of his affection.

The Picture of Dorian Gray (1973): Nigel Davenport (*Dracula*), Shane Briant (*Frankenstein and the Monster from Hell*), and John Karlen (*Dark Shadows*) perform a scene in Dan Curtis and Glenn Jordan's two-part *Wide World Mystery.*

The script offers a more expansive depiction of Dorian's scandalous activities than do other adaptations. Dorian is seen gambling, smoking opium, cavorting with female prostitutes, and courting Sybil Vane (Vanessa Howard), whom he pressures into having sex with him. After he drops her, Sybil kills herself (in this version by drowning herself, not by taking poison as in the novel). In a shocking scene that had to be reworked at the demand of the ABC censors, Dorian pays a prostitute extra to let him have sex with her unseen, underage daughter.

Also, after Lord Harry Wotton (Nigel Davenport of Curtis's *Dracula*) influences him, Dorian counts homosexual gratification among his "new interests." For example, Wotton offers to share his "young friends" with Dorian; Gray flirts with a handsome, young blond man at a party; and a rent boy is seen leaving Dorian's bedroom. Shane Briant explained,

> That was done to show Dorian's depravity though it's not actually suggested in Wilde's book. Both Glenn [Jordan] and I thought, if you're doing a show in 1973 and all Dorian does is go to bed with women—well, what's so depraved about that?! So he drinks a lot! So he smokes! So what? You had to do something that the audience considered depraved [at least, in 1973]."[15]

In this adaptation, Dorian's relationship with Alan Campbell (John Karlen again) is more overtly homosexual. In the novel, Dorian summons Alan, a scientist, after Gray stabs Basil to death, and he demands that Campbell dispose of the corpse for him. Dorian persuades Alan to do his bidding by handing him a note on which Dorian has written Alan's ghastly secrets (undisclosed in the novel but assumed to be homosexual liaisons). In this adaptation, Dorian does not call for Alan when he bludgeons Basil to death—two disreputable Burke and Hare-type fellows take the body away—but Dorian does summon him when he stabs James Vane (Tom McCorry) to death. Writer John Tomerlin changes James's accidental death in the novel to murder in order to provide Dorian with yet another sin of commission.

Callously lounging in his bed, Dorian now voices aloud a suggestion of Alan's secrets by calling the names of three men ("Brighton, Pembroke, Sir William Nolan"). Alan stops in his tracks and meekly agrees to do his estranged friend's grisly bidding. Similarly, Basil, in an earlier re-enactment of Wilde's chapter 12, has listed to Dorian three men whom Dorian has shamed.

The movie's most considerable departure from Wilde's novel is a plot device that writer-director Albert Lewin first used in his 1945 version. In that film, Basil has a young ward, Gladys, played as an adult by Donna Reed and invented as a latter-day love interest for Dorian Gray. Likewise, in Tomerlin's script, Basil has a niece, Beatrice, who as a five-year-old (Kim Richards) idolizes Dorian and who as a 25-year-old (Linda Kelsey) comes back into Dorian's life and becomes his fiancée. This plot device is a very effective way of showing the passage of time. Wotton has gone gray, Basil is long dead, and Beatrice has grown up—yet Dorian retains the beautiful, innocent countenance of a 20-year-old while Basil's portrait of Dorian depicts every debauch, excess, cruelty, sin, and murder committed by the Faustian playboy. Dorian declares that the hideous painting allows him "to read from the page of my own degradation."

Seventies-era movie-poster artist John Solie (*Soylent Green, Shaft's Big Score*) created six different portraits to trace the ruination of Dorian Gray's soul. Shane Briant revealed that he got to keep one of them (the beautiful one). Briant explained,

> On the last day, the prop man cut out the portrait—which was six feet long and four feet wide—and rolled it up and gave it to me, which was lovely. I went off to a party that Fionnula Flanagan was giving up in the [Hollywood] hills, and I left it in the back of the cab! I figured it was lost, [but] I rang up the cab company the next day, and they had it. So I still have it—but it hasn't changed! I used to stand in front of it and pray, "Please, I'm getting old! Isn't there something you can do?" But no, the picture is still as good as ever, and I'm getting old and wrinkled.[16]

The Picture of Dorian Gray, like Curtis's *Frankenstein*, was shot on videotape at the MGM Studios in Culver City, California. Briant remembered,

> We had eight days of rehearsal, and then we shot it in four. We did a three-hour program from start to finish in 12 days, which must be some kind of a record! We were really going! We rehearsed in the Culver City studios—not the ones now, but on the old *Gone with the Wind* lot, and then we shot it with four videotape cameras. We went from start to finish almost in order, from eight in the morning until eight at night, non-stop. Dan Curtis is a very strong character, strong-willed and a hard taskmaster. If he says you shoot it in four days, you shoot it in four days![17]

While Lewin's MGM movie with Hurd Hatfield, Angela Lansbury, and George Sanders was Old Hollywood's gold-standard adaptation of *Dorian Gray,* Curtis's 1973 production became the definitive version for the modern era. *Variety* declared,

> Oscar Wilde's world of entertainment (London, 1891), stylishly produced by Dan Curtis Productions, revives the horror tale with insights entirely in keeping with the theme of the original book. Hints of malevolence, sensuality, and decadence, all played out with fine restraint by exotic young actor Shane Briant, give the story freshness and suspense. Wilde knew what he was talking about, and Dan Curtis's production, handsomely mounted, handles the tale with respect and care. Everyone associated with this production deserves kudos.[18]

As produced by Curtis, the stories of Dr. Jekyll (discussed in Chapter II), Dr. Frankenstein (in this chapter), and Dorian Gray all point out man's dual nature. Jekyll, recognizing that man has the capacity for both good and evil, drinks his potion in the hope of bringing out the virtuous side of man—but he unleashes the monstrous side instead. Frankenstein and the Creature are two sides of the same coin. As a matter of fact, David Wickes's *Frankenstein* adaptation for TNT (13 June 1993) suggests that the monster (Randy Quaid) is the alter ego of Frankenstein (Patrick Bergin). Frankenstein creates a totally *innocent* monster who kills only after dreadful circumstances cause him to do so. The doctor begins as a knowledge-hungry student, and he turns *himself* into a monster because of his rejection of the creature, his depression, and his guilt. Dorian Gray constantly struggles with his feelings of righteousness and sinfulness, optimism and cynicism, heterosexuality and homosexuality, and hopefulness and hopelessness.

Dan Curtis's adaptations effectively capture these characters' dual natures through general fidelity to the texts, excellent performances, striking makeup (the pitiful visage of the Giant), impressive set design, and, of course, Robert Cobert's music. Again for *Dorian Gray*, Cobert does not compose new music but oversees the skillful use of his *Dark Shadows* cues, including several versions of "Quentin's Theme," as well as two cues from *The Strange Case of Dr. Jekyll and Mr. Hyde.* Cobert's emotional cue "Death of Hyde" has lived again at the deaths of Barnabas, Frankenstein and his creation, and now Dorian Gray. In Wilde's words,

> When they entered, they found, hanging upon the wall, a splendid portrait of their master as they had last seen him, in all the wonder of his exquisite youth and beauty. Lying on the floor was a dead man, in evening dress, with a knife in his heart. He was withered, wrinkled, and loathsome of visage. It was not 'til they had examined the rings that they recognized who it was.[19]

Curtis's five other *Wide World Mystery* productions aired between January and August of 1974. The four single-night episodes were shot on videotape at General Service Studios in Hollywood. The studio, now known as the Sunset Las Palmas Studio, has existed since 1919 and has been the home of such television series as *The Adventures of Ozzie and Harriet, Petticoat Junction,* and *The Newlywed Game.*

Far less expansive and atmospheric than *Frankenstein* and *Dorian Gray* but compelling nevertheless, Curtis's *Wide World Mystery* production **Shadow of Fear** (Monday 28 January 1974) is a contemporary, five-character mystery drama that has the look and feel of the daytime serials of the 1970s. Written by Larry Brody (*Bright Promise, The Bold Ones*) and directed by Herb Kenwith (*Star Trek, Strange Paradise*), *Shadow of Fear* concerns a man named Styron (Claude Akins), a former cop-turned-private investigator who tends to become too closely involved with his cases.

Styron comes to the aid of Danna Ballard Forrester (Anjanette Comer), the young wife of Pantronics Corporation president Martin Forrester (Jason Evers). Now that Styron has been thrown off the police force (Brody's script hints that Styron attacked or even killed one or more men who were seeing his wife Lil), he is working as the head of Pantronics plant security, and Martin Forrester asks for his help when Forrester's wife Danna appears to be the victim of a stalker. Styron uncovers the fact (omitted by Forrester) that Danna previously was hospitalized for D.I.D. (dissociative identity disorder) and suspects that, now, either Danna's malicious alter-ego "Donna" has returned, or someone is making it look that way.

When Forrester's artist-mistress turns up dead (off-camera), Styron tells his protégé Sgt. Lou Arnburg (Phil Carey), "This whole thing is an elaborate murder frame!" The story's final twist reveals exactly who is framing whom. The four actors who carry the show play well as an ensemble and make the most of their many sets (home, office, bank, police station, apartment, stairwell, etc.), which are the most lavish element of this otherwise small-scale production. A fifth character, Danna's friend Mark Brolin (Tom Selleck), appears only at the beginning and the end of *Shadow of Fear.*

Shadow of Fear (1974): Anjanette Comer (as Danna) is not sure whether Tom Selleck (as Mark) is her friend or her enemy in Dan Curtis and Herb Kenwith's late-night mystery.

Robert Cobert uses a solo-piano theme for Danna, and the rest of the background music in *Shadow of Fear* is Cobert's well-loved *Dark Shadows* music cues, most of them not heard on the 1969 soundtrack LP and therefore always a treat for fans to hear again in those days after the cancellation of the Gothic serial, before its spotty return in syndicated reruns, and long before its debut on VHS and DVD. Cobert's distinctive brand of (in his words) "great spook music"[20] is always an immediate signal to viewers that a program is A DAN CURTIS PRODUCTION, and Curtis himself was always the first to credit Cobert with contributing to the success of their many collaborations, whether large (*The Last Ride of the Dalton Gang*), small (*Shadow of Fear*), or gigantic (*War and Remembrance*).

One of Cobert's most haunting compositions, the harmonica theme from *Night of Dark Shadows* (1971), became the theme song of the next Curtis-produced *Wide World Mystery* episode, **The Invasion of Carol Enders** (Friday 8 March 1974), directed by Burt Brinckerhoff and written by Gene Raser Kearney from a story by Kearney and Merwin Gerard. Brinckerhoff, then a new director, went on to direct the controversial PBS program *Steambath* (1973) and television adaptations of *How to Succeed in Business without Really Trying* (1975) and *Brave New World* (1980). Gene Kearney had written and directed episodes of *Night Gallery* and *Kojak,* and Merwin Gerard had written for *M Squad* and *One Step Beyond.* Both writers were well suited to pen this supernatural—yet realistic—story of possession, set to Robert Cobert's *Dark Shadows* background music.

Meredith Baxter plays Carol Enders, who is assaulted and nearly dies. Elsewhere in the hospital where Carol has been taken, Diana Hastings Bernard (Sally Kemp), the new wife of Dr. Peter Bernard (Charles Aidman), *does* die of injuries from a suspicious car accident just as Carol is fading fast. Suddenly, Carol rallies miraculously and awakens with the consciousness of Diana Bernard. The spirit possessing Carol's body comes to realize that it is earthbound because Diana was murdered—perhaps by someone close to her—and Diana must use Carol to expose her murderer.

This clever plot—possibly the inspiration for at least one episode of *Medium* (not to mention the Lifetime TV series *Drop Dead Diva*)—may sound preposterous, but the excellent cast, led by Meredith Baxter and Christopher Connelly (as Carol's concerned fiancé Adam Reston), makes it believable and enthralling. Baxter succeeds in delivering lines such as, "I think I know who killed me," with complete seriousness and no camp or unintentional humor.

Another asset to the strong cast is, once again, John Karlen, who appeared in 14 of Dan Curtis's productions. A bit of 1970s-era social commentary occurs when Karlen's character, David Hastings, muses, "I was a space engineer making $30,000 a year when I married Diana. Then, the world got bored with the moon, and I got stuck in a field nobody needs. I liked what I did. There were some real thrills in those days." George DiCenzo, who appeared in four of Curtis's productions, plays Dr. Palmer, who is as baffled by the possession of Carol Enders as Lt. Carrea (Phil Pine) is.

Dan Curtis, who served as an uncredited director of portions of *The Invasion of Carol Enders*, knew the value of an accomplished cast. "If you've got good actors," he said in a DVD interview, "you don't have to tell them a damn thing."[21] The cast of *Carol Enders* makes this the best of Curtis's four single-night *Wide World* mysteries.

The Invasion of Carol Enders (1974): To enhance the unusual love story enacted by Christopher Connelly (as Adam) and Meredith Baxter (as Carol), composer Robert Cobert sets it to his haunting theme from *Night of Dark Shadows.*

The best of Curtis's three classic *Wide World* miniseries is the one that he himself directed. **The Turn of the Screw**, videotaped on location at Hennick House in Essex, England, was seen late-night on ABC-TV on Monday-Tuesday 15-16 April 1974. "While I was in England shooting *Dracula* and finishing *Dracula*," Curtis explained, "I was in pre-production on *Turn of the Screw*."73 Adapting Henry James's 1898 novel was fantasy novelist William F. Nolan, who wrote or co-wrote 15 scripts for Curtis. Before *The Turn of the Screw*, Nolan had written *The Norliss Tapes* (1973) and its never-produced sequel *The Return*, and he had co-written *Melvin Purvis, G-Man* (1974) and *The Kansas City Massacre* (1975). Nolan called *The Turn of the Screw* "one of my best scripts."22

The Turn of the Screw was one of Dan Curtis's favorite ghost stories. The director admitted,

> A good deal of it went into *Dark Shadows*. I first saw it as *The Innocents* as a play in some regional theatre in New Jersey, and it scared the hell out of me. I was always fascinated by it. Right after I saw the play, I read James's *Turn of the Screw* and was even more fascinated by it. Then, I saw Jack Clayton's *The Innocents* [1961], which I thought was absolutely brilliant, and I was still in love with the story. I thought if I ever got the chance, I would love to do my own version of it.23

Curtis chose Hennick House to embody the novel's Bly House. He cast Lynn Redgrave as the governess—named Miss Jane Cubberly in Nolan's script—and Megs Jenkins herself as Mrs. Grose. Jenkins had played Mrs. Grose in Clayton's 1961 film with Deborah Kerr and Michael Redgrave (Lynn Redgrave's father), and Curtis could visualize no actress in the role other than Jenkins. For Flora (age eight in the novel and nine in the script), Curtis cast Eva Griffith, who had just appeared with Elizabeth Taylor and Richard Burton in *Divorce His/Divorce Hers* (ABC, 6-7 February 1973).

The only casting problem was the role of Miles (ten in the novel but fourteen in Nolan's script). Curtis hired Mark Lester, the star of *Oliver!* (1968), and he and his castmates began the two-week rehearsal period. Very soon, Curtis, Redgrave, and Jenkins saw that the 15-year-old Lester was not succeeding in the part and would have to be replaced. "Mark Lester could not play Miles," Curtis admitted. "It was a tragedy. He couldn't walk and talk at the same time. He couldn't play an upper-class boy. As sad as it made me feel—and it really did hurt me—I had to let the kid go."24 Lester's last-minute replacement was the red-haired, quirkily talented Jasper Jacob, a 14-year-old who had appeared with Curtis's *Dorian Gray/Dracula* star Nigel Davenport in the 1972 BBC-TV miniseries *The Edwardians*.

As with *Jekyll and Hyde, Frankenstein,* and *Dorian Gray,* Curtis shot *The Turn of the Screw* on videotape. He had to use the early-1970s-era big, bulky cameras that barely fit into the rooms of Hennick House and were controlled by a mobile unit in a truck outside. "We didn't have anything back then," Curtis remarked about technology, but by ordering a special camera and a special dolly from the United States he managed to give *The Turn of the Screw* "that low-angle look that I always feel brings more intimacy and texture to the picture."25 Curtis enjoyed having a chance to perfect the soap-opera-style, live-on-tape, in-camera editing he had learned when he had directed 21 episodes of *Dark Shadows* in the late 1960s. Additionally, nine short scenes were filmed, not videotaped, for logistical or technical reasons. This mixture of film and tape was not uncommon in British television productions of the seventies (e.g. *Doctor Who; Blake's 7; Upstairs, Downstairs*). There was even one filmed exterior scene in Curtis and Lela Swift's otherwise videotaped *Dead of Night: A Darkness at Blaisedon* in 1969. Robert Cobert scored *The Turn of the Screw* (1974) with eerie music cues from *Dark Shadows* and *Night of Dark Shadows*.

William F. Nolan remembered that adapting Henry James's enigmatic novella was "difficult in that I had to 'extend' the material from a novelette to a two-night miniseries. I wanted to retain the mood and period atmosphere and to remain faithful to James's concept and characters. Apparently, I pulled it off because the critical reception to my teleplay was very positive."[26]

Nolan does remain faithful to the events of James's novel, from the governess's first-person narration to the overall authenticity of the characters' speech patterns to much of James's exact dialogue. For example, Miss Cubberly asks Mrs. Grose if Miles has the ability "to contaminate" or "to corrupt," James's words in chapter two.[27] Both on the page and on the screen, Mrs. Grose replies, "Are you afraid he'll corrupt *you*?"[28] Later, Nolan reproduces the governess's angry words to Miss Jessel in the schoolroom—"You terrible, miserable woman!" (Chapter 15)[29]—as, "You vile, miserable woman!" Later still, Nolan retains the governess's expression from Chapter 21 that Mrs. Grose's witnessing Flora's foul language "so justifies me"[30] in the governess's assertion that the ghost of Miss Jessel possesses Flora just as the ghost of Peter Quint controls Miles. Mrs. Grose admits, "I believe."[31] Finally, in a moment of foreshadowing, Nolan has Miss Cubberly say, "The boy's life—literally, his *soul*—was in my hands."

Since this TV production is a ghost story written for a master horror producer-director, Nolan, of course, makes the ghosts real. Because cinema and television are such visual media, all of the governesses in the 20-plus filmings of *The Turn of the Screw* since 1957 have encountered more or less real spectres. Benjamin Britten's 1954 opera and William Tuckett's 1999 ballet also present *The Turn of the Screw* as the ghost story that it is—at least on the surface.

The straightforward, so-called "apparitionist" interpretation of James's ambiguous novel is that the ghosts constitute a real supernatural threat to the children—as they certainly do in Curtis's quite literal interpretation of two *Turn of the Screw*-like scenarios on *Dark Shadows* (in 1968–1969 and mid–1970) when first the ghosts of Quentin and Beth and later the ghosts of Gerard and Daphne haunt the children. However, the "non-apparitionist" approach, most famously promoted by the early-20th-century critic Edmund Wilson, maintains that the ghosts exist only in the governess's hysterical mind and are a manifestation of the sexual repression of this naïve, 20-year-old daughter of an austere parson.[32]

In James's novel, when the governess meets with the handsome, dashing uncle of the children and he hires her to care for Flora and Miles (with no further input expected from him), the young woman becomes infatuated with this romantic figure. In Chapter 1, she gushes, "I'm rather easily carried away. I was carried away in London!"[33] It is possible that the governess's overactive imagination invents the ghosts and publicizes them to Mrs. Grose as a ploy to lure the children's uncle back to Bly House so that she can see him again.

In Chapter 3, which features the first appearance of Peter Quint, the governess is strolling alone through the gardens of Bly and dreamily wishing "suddenly to meet someone" (like the distant uncle) along the path. She wishes that "someone would appear there at the turn of a path and would stand before me and smile and approve."[34] As if on cue, Peter Quint materializes. In Chapter 15, when the governess considers leaving Bly, Miss Jessel makes her dramatic appearance in the schoolroom—only the governess sees her, of course—and the governess realizes that she must stay and fight for the souls of Flora and Miles. As the novel progresses, the governess becomes more and more dogmatic, shrill, and "pressing" (James's word) in her crusade to force Miles and Flora to admit that they see the ghosts. Neither ever admits such, and Mrs. Grose never sees what the governess sees. Finally, the governess's pressure on Flora makes the little girl ill, and Mrs. Grose leaves for London with Flora. At the climactic moment when the governess presses Miles to acknowledge Peter Quint's ghostly face at the window, all the boy does is enigmatically mention Miss Jessel and then say, "Peter Quint—you devil!"[35] before he dies of fright and exhaustion in the governess's arms. In life, and now perhaps in death, Peter Quint certainly has behaved like a devil, but was poor Miles calling *him* a "devil" or saying "you devil" to his *current* tormentor, the governess? Each reader must decide for herself or himself.

However, Nolan's script plays like the horror/ghost story that movie-and-TV audiences most often perceive *The Turn of the Screw* to be. Nolan increases the number of fleeting appearances of Peter Quint (James Laurenson) and Miss Jessel (Kathryn Leigh Scott of *Dark Shadows*), and he climaxes part one of the two-night production with a recreation of the governess's encounter with Quint on the stairs. In the novel, each ghost appears four times. Peter Quint materializes atop the tower (Chapter 3), at the window (Chapter 4), on the stairs (Chapter 9), and again at the window just before Miles's death (Chapter 24). Miss Jessel appears at the lake (Chapter 6), on the stairs (Chapter 10), in the schoolroom (Chapter 15), and again at the lake (Chapter 20). In Nolan's teleplay, Quint appears—always only to Jane Cubberly—at the base of the parapet atop which *she* is perched, then at the window, in a cemetery, on the stairs, again at the base of the parapet (in a scene reminiscent of one in *Night of Dark Shadows*), and finally on the stairs (instead of at the window) for the climactic confrontation with Miss Cubberly and Miles.

Peter Quint makes one additional appearance in a dream sequence scored to nightmarish music from *Night of Dark Shadows*. In Miss Cubberly's dream, the governess allows Quint to make love to her. Here, Nolan is implying the governess's sexual repression. Meanwhile, Miss Jessel makes her customary appearances at the lake (twice) and in the schoolroom (once), but Nolan also places her in the clock tower (near a trunk of Quint's belongings) and in the reflection of a mirror. Interestingly, Miss Cubberly sees Miss Jessel in the mirror in place of her own reflection, suggesting that Miss Cubberly and her "corrupt" predecessor may not be as different as she wishes to believe.

The Turn of the Screw (1974): Lynn Redgrave (as the governess) and Jasper Jacob (a last-minute replacement for *Oliver!* star Mark Lester) pose for a somber shot from Dan Curtis's two-part ABC *Wide World Mystery*.

Nolan augments the events of the novella with extra scenes in keeping with the spirit and realism of James's work. There are scenes of Miss Cubberly and the children in the schoolroom and on the grounds, roles for the groomsman Luke (Anthony Langdon) and his young son Timothy (Benedict Taylor), and a disturbing scene in which Miles and Flora, under the evil influence of Quint and Jessel, perform an unsettling theatrical for Miss Cubberly and Mrs. Grose. Flora plays Edvard Grieg's funeral march on the piano, and she and Miles recite the boy's morbid poem about death. In another invention, Nolan acknowledges the topical nature of Curtis's recent *Dracula* (1974) by having Miles say,

> Miss Cubberly, I've been reading a book about a prince in the 15th century in Transylvania who employed a unique method of punishment. When someone displeased him, he ordered him stripped naked and impaled on a stake. He would often eat his dinners surrounded by his victims. Nasty fellow withal, wouldn't you say?[36]

Nolan and Curtis's only two major deviations from James's novel occur at the very beginning and the very end of this adaptation. In the first scene, the children's uncle Mr. Fredricks is played unsympathetically by an older actor (John Baron), and Miss Cubberly (Lynn Redgrave) does not fall in love with him. Instead of a starry-eyed infatuation, Cubberly's reaction is frankly a much more realistic one, especially in the minds of late-20th-century audiences. Love is the last thing on this governess's mind; instead, she expresses outrage over Fredricks's callous, unfeeling desire to ditch his niece and nephew with a stranger and never to be bothered with their care again, other than sending money. Miss Cubberly takes the job because she realizes that Flora and Miles need someone to care for them—and because she can relate to the children's situation since she does not remember her late mother and her parson-father is stern and distant. Nolan subtly updates the governess's motivations for contemporary audiences.

In the final scene—since this is, after all, an actual ghost story—Nolan has Miles speak more definitively and declare, "Yes, yes, yes, damn you, woman! You want to hear me say it? *Peter Quint is here!*" In a 2002 interview, Dan Curtis spoke even more concretely of his and Nolan's ending of the story. The director mused, "Did the governess lose the boy to Peter Quint? Did she win? When he actually died, was his soul freed? What was the meaning of it? What did Henry James have in mind? I had my feelings about what happened, and I wanted to tell the story my way." Curtis continued,

> I knew it was a fight between the governess and Peter Quint for the soul of the boy, and I wanted to show that at the end when the boy was all alone in the house with her and Quint came to confront the governess and the boy. I put the governess at the top of the stairs, the kid in the middle, and Quint down below trying to draw the boy to him. The governess was telling him to turn his back on him and come to her. Finally, the kid turned and ran up the stairs to her, and she grabbed hold of him and held the kid in her arms. Suddenly, she looked, and it was no longer the kid. It was Quint, and he grabbed her head and smashed his lips onto hers. She screamed and pushed him back and pushed Quint

over the railing and went to look. The thunder crashed, and the lightning lit up the room. She looked down there, and instead of the "body" of the ghost of Quint, she saw the little, smashed body of Miles. She ran down the stairs, and she knelt over him, and she started to cry, and we slowly started to pull back, and that's the way we ended it. I believe that what that that meant was yes, the kid is gone—the kid is dead—but his soul is saved. He didn't end up with Quint and the evil, infamous Miss Jessel![37]

Lynn Redgrave had her own memories of *The Turn of the Screw*. She recalled,

Dan Curtis is a larger-than-life character with a smile so broad, so extraordinary, that when he says, "You must do this," you think, "But of course!" He brings such enthusiasm to his projects. Boy, did he really get involved in this—so involved in the Henry James story, in where the location would be, in the costuming, in the whole thing of how to show the spirits of Quint and Miss Jessel, who were possessing the young children. It was wonderful working with him. All sorts of peculiar things happened because it was the seventies and we were on location, but he always somehow made sure that everything ended up okay.[38]

Once again, Curtis's efforts to adapt 19th-century literature met with critical approval. The *Los Angeles Herald-Examiner* wrote, "The Henry James story can still exert a magnetic pull, as witness the two-parter that will be screened by ABC tonight. The Dan Curtis production—he directed also—bears the glossy token of its English make. The acting has the glisteningly fine finish of the English period film."[39] *Variety* added,

Dan Curtis traveled to England to produce and direct William F. Nolan's tele-adaptation of Henry James's chilling *Turn of the Screw*, two-parter late-night version. Curtis brings off several interesting touches, such as [Megs] Jenkins's explaining the evils of the house to Cubberly—without being heard [by the viewers]. Or the frightening appearances of Quint—and the insinuations of evil by the children as they half-mock Cubberly. It should hold late-night viewers who want their goosebumps served large.[40]

One month after *The Turn of the Screw* aired, Curtis produced **Come Die with Me** (Tuesday 14 May 1974), directed by Burt Brinckerhoff (*Lou Grant*, *ALF*, *Seventh Heaven*) and written by James Blumgarten (*Lights Out*, *True Story*, *Mister Rock and Roll*). In terms of cast, this claustrophobic drama is a treat for fans of *Route 66* (George Maharis), *Dark Shadows* (Kathryn Leigh Scott), *Batman* (Alan Napier), and *Blacula* (Charles Macaulay), but the main attraction is the outstanding performance by Eileen Brennan (*Laugh-In*) as Mary Thatcher, a repressed housekeeper who suddenly finds her manipulative side when she blackmails the rakish murderer Walter Burr (Maharis) into a love affair. Blumgarten's 1973 script describes Mary as "the housekeeper of this, the Burr homestead in Devon, Connecticut. Some years younger than Walter. A large-boned woman, asexually handsome, but suggesting glimmerings of a latent passion."[41]

Come Die with Me (1974): Eileen Brennan (as Mary) and George Maharis (as Walter) stand over Charles Macaulay (as Walter's brother Frank, whom Walter has murdered).

Kathryn Leigh Scott is equally fine as Burr's New York girlfriend, Suzy Pratt, who urges Walter to get out from under Mary's thumb—with disastrous results. Many of Suzy's scripted conversations with Walter are shortened in the final edit of *Come Die with Me*. Mostly, chit-chat about Suzy and Walter's New York society friends is cut. For example, as Walter's nemesis Lt. Jenkins (Philip Sterling) listens outside the door of Walter's New York apartment, Walter asks Suzy, "What's new?"

> SUZY
>
> Fatso didn't go on his dig. His mother's quite sick. Something terminal.
>
> WALTER
>
> I don't want to hear about death. What about Tony?
>
> SUZY
>
> He's dug up a lawyer. The fee's outrageous. Poor Tony's been hitting up everybody. Did you pay off your markers?
>
> WALTER
>
> That's just where I came from. Oh, yeah, while I was there, Santini told me something else. He said he's been seeing you with "a number of different gentleman friends."
>
> SUZY
>
> Were you worried?
>
> WALTER
>
> Curious.
>
> SUZY
>
> They were just friends. But now they're retired. It'll be just the two of us again. We'll be good; you'll see. You'll be good—
>
> WALTER
>
> I'm fine.
>
> SUZY
>
> But you'll be better. We'll pick up where we left off.[42]

Also cut are earlier scenes between Walter and Mr. Santini (John A. Zee), the club owner who puts pressure on Walter to pay him the $20,000 that Walter owes, and between Walter and Mary at Hammonnassett Beach after he reluctantly has become her lover. *Come Die with Me* is a fascinating study in the shifting power that people hold over each other, but after a well-written and well-acted build-up, the drama suffers from an unsatisfying, inconclusive ending.

In terms of music, *Come Die with Me* is a veritable Robert Cobert hit parade. Cobert scores the drama with his music from *Dark Shadows* and many other Dan Curtis productions, including party music from *House of Dark Shadows*, the piano theme from *Night of Dark Shadows*, the music-box theme from *Dracula* (1974), the piano theme from *Shadow of Fear*, and both sides of the Robert Cobert Orchestra's 1970 Roulette Records 45 RPM single ("Ode to Angelique" and "Missy").

Three months later (Tuesday 20 August 1974, my parents' 20th wedding anniversary), Dan Curtis produced the seventh and last of his ABC late-night mysteries. Based on a true story, **Nightmare at 43 Hillcrest** was directed by Curtis's frequent collaborator Lela Swift and written by novelist and lyricist William Katz. Part family drama and part crime story, *Hillcrest* effectively conveys the truly nightmarish situation of an innocent family terrorized, arrested, and persecuted as "heroin dealers" when, in fact, the police have *planted* eight bags of heroin in the house to cover up a colossal mistake. The officers have raided the house at 43 Hillcrest when they should have busted the house at 43 *North* Hillcrest. To cover their blunder, the ruthless, ambitious deputy police commissioner Clarence Hartog (Peter Mark Richman) orders Detective Sanford Bates (Don Dubbins) to plant the heroin in the home of Esther and Greg Leyden (Emmaline Henry, Jim Hutton) and their daughter Nancy (Linda Curtis, Dan Curtis's daughter, who died tragically in 1975). Even after the Leydens' attorney Richard Estabrook (Richard Stahl) gives up on them, Officer Frank Linwood (John Karlen again) and Assistant District Attorney Sharon Reischauer ("special guest star" Mariette Hartley) continue to try to prove the family's innocence to District Attorney Michael Doran (Walter Brooke, essentially reprising his *Green Hornet* role as the DA).

Robert Cobert's *Dark Shadows* music cues are minimal as much of *Nightmare at 43 Hillcrest* takes on a documentary feel, complete with closing crawls about the fates of the innocent and the guilty. The cast members give earnest performances, with Peter Mark Richman especially effective as the smarmy, arrogant Hartog. The highlight of the program is a long interrogation scene between the diligent assistant DA (Hartley) and the sexist Hartog, who is amazed and furious that a woman is making him squirm. The scene plays out like live theatre, an observation that Robert Foxworth (in a June 2006 DVD interview) made about his and Karlen's own *Frankenstein* miniseries.

Chapter Seven: The Mysteries

Nightmare at 43 Hillcrest **(1974) is the seventh and last** *Wide World Mystery* **episode produced by Dan Curtis (pictured).**

In the years 1973 and 1974, Dan Curtis seemed to own ABC as no less than 11 Dan Curtis productions aired in prime time or late-night—*The Night Strangler; Frankenstein; The Picture of Dorian Gray; Scream of the Wolf; Shadow of Fear; The Invasion of Carol Enders; Melvin Purvis, G-Man; The Turn of the Screw; Come Die with Me; Nightmare at 43 Hillcrest;* and *The Great Ice Rip-Off.* Curtis even accomplished the hat trick of presenting his material on the other two networks as well—*The Norliss Tapes* on NBC in February 1973 and *Dracula* on CBS in February 1974 (rescheduled from October 1973 because of a prime-time speech by President Richard Nixon). Although the late-night mysteries that Curtis produced are not as famous as the prime-time films that he directed, anyone who stayed up past his or her bedtime to watch *Wide World Mystery* knows that *any* production associated with Dan Curtis and Robert Cobert is guaranteed to entertain. In a 2004 DVD interview, Dan Curtis remarked that the "quirky little stories" and "fun stories" that he produced "just had to be entertaining, fun, good, scary, dramatic, whatever, and we made 'em fast, and we made 'em cheap, and it was a great period of time."[43]

Indeed, almost any production from the house of Dan Curtis is a satisfying ride, but **The Great Ice Rip-Off** is a literal one. Curtis's "nicely played comedy whodunit" (in the words on the extremely rare VHS tape box) carries viewers on a Greyhound bus tour from Seattle to San Francisco to Carmel to Los Angeles to San Clemente to San Diego in the company of four diamond thieves and a newly retired cop intent on foiling them.

Curtis's change-of-pace comedy-mystery, originally titled *A Break in the Ice,* aired in prime time as an *ABC Movie of the Week* on Wednesday 6 November 1974 and capped Curtis's impressive feat of presenting nine of his productions on television in that year (all but *Dracula* on ABC). Interestingly, his first movie of the year (*Scream of the Wolf,* Wednesday 16 January) and his last (*The Great Ice Rip-Off,* 42 weeks later) are two of his most unusual productions but two of his most inaccessible. *Scream of the Wolf* (discussed in Chapter II) is available only on random public-domain DVDs and videotapes, and *The Great Ice Rip-Off* has never been available on VHS or DVD in the United States. Long thought to be unreleased, the film actually did appear very briefly on VHS in Canada on "Star Video" (ABC Video Enterprises, Inc./Publishing & Broadcasting Video/CEL Communications & Entertainment Ltd.) circa 1981. This video release was so obscure that Dan Curtis himself never knew that *The Great Ice Rip-Off* had come out on video! I made the discovery in 2008 when I snapped up the vintage clamshelled video on *eBay.* Jim Pierson pointed out that in the late 1970s and especially the early 1980s, when home video was in its infancy, "ABC threw all kinds of product onto VHS"—albeit briefly, sometimes—just to see what would rent or sell.[44] *The Great Ice Rip-Off* was such a flash in the pan.

The film deserves much better. The script by Andrew Peter Marin (*Bad Ronald, The Million-Dollar Rip-Off, Black-Market Baby*) is clever, the music by Robert Cobert is innovative, and the cast is first-rate. "Special guest star" Grayson Hall joins two fine actors who, like Hall herself, really have no present-day equivalents—Lee J. Cobb and Gig Young. Dan Curtis's direction is sharp, and this time, he mixes his trademark low camera angles with some exciting high angles—aerial shots of the Greyhound bus as it travels downs the picturesque coastline.

Chapter Seven: The Mysteries 183

Grayson Hall, who had been directed by Norman Corwin, Tyrone Guthrie, John Huston, Robert Stevenson, and Lela Swift, was well aware of Dan Curtis's strengths and weaknesses as a new director of *House of Dark Shadows* (1970) and *Night of Dark Shadows* (1971). In 1974, when she reunited with Curtis for *The Great Ice Rip-Off*—after he had directed *The Night Strangler* (1973); *The Norliss Tapes* (1973); *Scream of the Wolf* (1974); *Dracula* (1974); *Melvin Purvis, G-Man* (1974); and *The Turn of the Screw* (1974)— Hall noticed how much his directorial prowess had advanced. According to her biographer R.J. Jamison, Grayson Hall declared, "Dear old Dan; I love him dearly, but he's *Dan!* [He's] learned a great deal, and I must give him full marks. I was terribly satisfied and pleased."[45]

The Great Ice Rip-Off (1974): Lee J. Cobb (as Willy), Grayson Hall (as Helen), and Gig Young (as Harkey) take a rest stop during their characters' bus trip down the California coast.

As Curtis was perfecting his craft as a director, he was creating one of his filmic trademarks that was as intrinsic to his movies as Robert Cobert's music scores. Curtis's effective use of the beauty and mystery of the Lyndhurst mansion in his two *Dark Shadows* films (especially *Night of Dark Shadows*) had begun his pattern of infusing his films with a palpable sense of place. Las Vegas and especially Seattle were characters in their own right in the Kolchak movies, and *The Norliss Tapes* created a definite sense of place through Curtis's use of San Francisco scenery, a dramatic Pacific Coast highway bridge, and Northern California local color. Watching a Dan Curtis movie inspires many viewers to want to visit Lyndhurst in Tarrytown, New York (*House of Dark*

Shadows, Night of Dark Shadows); Las Vegas (*The Night Stalker*); Seattle (*The Night Strangler*); Yugoslavia (*Dracula, The Winds of War*); or Dunsmuir House in Oakland, California (*Burnt Offerings*), because they feel almost as if they have already been there. Needless to say, Curtis's travelogue approach is in high gear in *The Great Ice Rip-Off* as the cross-country bus makes a half-dozen stops between Seattle and San Diego. (Actually, most of *The Great Ice Rip-Off* was filmed in and around Los Angeles and Malibu.)

Cobert's music score signals that *The Great Ice Rip-Off* is an unusual Dan Curtis production as baritone saxophone and low brass (in unison), muted trumpet, flute, and percussion create a main-title theme that is playful and Mancini-esque. After an opening sequence in which Curtis and Paul Lohman's camera focuses on close-ups of hands manipulating safety-deposit boxes, the quartet of diamond ("ice") thieves is revealed in seriocomic style.

Harkey Rollins (Gig Young), the suave ringleader, dresses as a gray-haired old woman and steals $1,000,000 in diamonds from Klein's Jewelers in Seattle. (The jewelry store is named for Norma Mae Klein Curtis.) Rollins, now back in his smart business suit, boards a Greyhound bus in Seattle and rides out of town with a briefcase full of "ice." Georgie (Matt Clark) poses as a security guard and steals $1,250,000 in diamonds from the San Francisco Museum of Modern Art. He, with the loot, boards the bus when it stops in San Francisco. Archie (Geoffrey Lewis) dresses as a machine-gun-toting mugger and holds up a Carmel society wedding for $1,500,000 in the guests' diamond jewelry. When the Greyhound bus stops in Carmel, Archie, with the swag, gets aboard. Checker (Robert Walden) poses as the night desk clerk at the Royal Palms Hotel in Pasadena and helps himself to $1,000,000 in diamonds from the hotel guests' safety-deposit boxes. Packing up the "ice" but running late, he takes a frantic cab ride from Pasadena to Hollywood and flags down the bus just in time to board. (A radio news report reveals that the head of security at the Royal Palms Hotel is one Daniel Cherkoss, which is the birth name of Dan Curtis.)

This clever and seemingly foolproof plan is marred by Willy Calso (Lee J. Cobb), a newly retired Seattle cop who, with his wife Helen (Grayson Hall), is riding the bus to his and Helen's new home in San Diego. Willy, along with Helen, latches on to Harkey, chats him up, plays cards with him, enlists his aid in foiling an unrelated on-board pickpocket, and even confides in Harkey his suspicions that the perpetrators of the systematic diamond thefts are on board this very bus. The interplay among Cobb, Hall, and Young is delightful and much more than enough to make an often static bus-ride scenario crackle with excitement. Grayson Hall's Helen Calso is warm to Harkey and solicitous of her cop-husband, who still has not processed the idea of retirement. Asking for the newspaper, Helen quips, "I want to see if Ann Landers can tell me how to handle retired husbands." Hall's biographer R.J. Jamison adds,

> The film [. . .] provides opportunities to observe the subtleties of Grayson's acting. Small yet significant actions such as Grayson removing a toothpick from Cobb's mouth to make a point or resting her head on his shoulder, unscripted actor-inspired moments, allow the viewers to believe they are actually watching a wife interact with her husband.[46]

Also, Helen brushes off her husband's coat and scolds him for loading up on Ellery Queen and John D. MacDonald mystery novels to read on the bus. Across the aisle from them, Harkey coolly reads *Poirot Investigates,* by Agatha Christie, and tries not to notice that the overzealous Willy Calso is coming closer and closer to ruining everything.

Dan Curtis was especially proud of this "quirky little story"[47] and was happy to see it generate good reviews. *The Hollywood Reporter* called *The Great Ice Rip-Off* "a caper picture that is highly entertaining."[48] *Variety* applauded the "light touch [. . .] applied by producer Dan Curtis at directorial reins of quadruple diamond caper. [. . .] Pic has enough sharp corners to keep viewers alert, and Curtis's eye for human foibles again manages to get yocks. [. . .] Curtis picks up credit for being able to derive amusement from a caper film after the onslaught of the genre in recent years."[49] In the months before this TV-movie's premiere, audiences had seen such theatrical capers as *The Hot Rock* (1972), *The Getaway* (1972), *The Sting* (1973), *Charley Varrick* (1973), *The Taking of Pelham One Two Three* (1974), and *Bank Shot* (1974). Nevertheless, producer-director Curtis, writer Marin, and composer Cobert manage to craft something fresh and delightful. Cobert even uses "Quentin's Theme" as the background Muzak in the coffee shop in the Carmel, California, bus station where Willy, Helen, and Harkey take a rest stop.

In the early 1990s, Cobert slipped "Quentin's Theme" in to another restaurant scene (this time in *Intruders*), and Curtis attempted to recapture his *Ice Rip-Off* telefilm's brand of caper humor in his little-seen Orion motion picture *Me and the Kid.* While those latter-day Dan Curtis productions are available on VHS and DVD, *The Great Ice Rip-Off* was screened at the 2006 Dark Shadows Festival in Brooklyn, New York, but otherwise remains as elusive as Harkey Rollins and his band of ice thieves. Maybe, *eBay* will offer up another rare VHS tape or two some day, for every Dan Curtis enthusiast ought to take this wild ride.

Another "ride" four-and-one-half years later turned out to be Dan Curtis's only real television flop. NBC-TV's **Supertrain** (Wednesday 7 February to Saturday 28 July 1979) was one of the most expensive and high-profile failures in the history of television—"the biggest money-loser in TV history at the time," according to Jim Pierson.[50] Designed as an answer to ABC-TV's *The Love Boat* (1977-1986), *Supertrain* was a prime-time anthology series of comedy, drama, and mystery about the passengers and crew of a futuristic, atomic-powered locomotive that crossed the country in 36 hours at a speed of 200 miles per hour. Some of the show's elaborate sets were of the train's 14' X 22' swimming pool, the gymnasium and steam room, and the seventies-style discotheque. The sets, along with detailed miniatures of the train, inflated the show's budget to ten million dollars.

Supertrain **(1979): Dan Curtis (conversing on the set) steers the multi-million-dollar vehicle through only the two-hour pilot "Express to Terror" and four subsequent hour-long episodes. Curtis—and many of the viewers—leave *Supertrain* before episodes 5-9 are made.**

"Frankly, I thought *Supertrain* was the worst idea I'd ever heard," Curtis remembered. "I thought they were out of their minds. But a good friend at NBC said, 'Everybody wants you to do this thing called *Supertrain*.' And they convinced me to do it—against my better judgment."[51]

Curtis executive-produced the first five of the show's nine episodes, but he directed only the February 7 pilot episode (later released on VHS as *Express to Terror*), featuring music by Robert Cobert. After that highly-rated debut episode (starring Steve Lawrence, Don Meredith, and Robert Alda), *Supertrain* plummeted in the ratings, and NBC pulled the show after only four more Wednesday-night episodes (February 14, 21, & 28 and March 14).

The guest stars in the five episodes executive-produced by Curtis included Stella Stevens and Vicki Lawrence in "Express to Terror" (February 7; never rerun); Dick Van Dyke and Barbara Rhoades in "And a Cup of Kindness, Too" (February 14; rerun June 2); Nehemiah Persoff and Paul Sand in "The Queen and the Improbable Knight" (February 21; rerun June 9); Roy Thinnes (in a dual role) and Scott Brady in "Hail to the Chief" (February 28; rerun June 16); and Bo Hopkins and Mills Watson in "Superstar" (March 14; rerun June 30).

Chapter Seven: The Mysteries

Don Meredith (left) is the guest star of "Express to Terror," the Dan Curtis-directed premiere episode (February 7) of *Supertrain* (1979).

Dick Van Dyke and Barbara Rhoades co-star in "And a Cup of Kindness, Too," the second episode (February 14) of *Supertrain* (1979).

At this point, Curtis left the show, and NBC brought back a slightly revamped *Supertrain* for four additional new episodes and eight reruns (7 April to 28 July 1979) on Saturday nights (opposite ABC's popular *Love Boat* companion, *Fantasy Island*). Jim Pierson observed, "NBC wanted *Supertrain* to be more escapism like *Love Boat*, but Dan wanted more mystery and intrigue with a touch of violence."[52] In later years, whenever anyone asked Dan Curtis about *Supertrain*, his reply was, "Super *what?*"[53] Curiously, in the 2010s, a super-fast train figured in the plots of episodes of *Human Target* and *Supergirl*. In June 2018, the long-lost Supertrain miniature seen on the 1979 TV series was found in a barn, and a *Supertrain* fan bought it for $25,000.

The fact that Dan Curtis was a great producer-director is no mystery. *The Great Ice Rip-Off,* certainly *Wide World Mystery,* and even *Supertrain* are of interest to Dan Curtis devotees, but so would be the dozens of Curtis productions that never were. There is a truism that the film and television projects that actually get produced are only a tiny fraction of all of the ideas, outlines, and scripts that float around Hollywood. Such is the case with Dan Curtis Productions. For every *Intruders,* there is an unproduced project called *The Bannerman Solution* (1991) or *Cut-Out* (1996). For every *Winds of War,* there is *Gunning for Glory* (1994), a never-produced World War I drama. For every trilogy that *was* produced, there is a 1974 *Stories of John O'Hara* anthology project that never becomes A DAN CURTIS PRODUCTION.

Over the years, Dan Curtis considered filming John Dickson Carr's 1946 mystery novel *He Who Whispers,* about a vampire hoax; Berton Roueche's 1971 horror novel *Feral* (a.k.a. *The Cats*), a *Birds*-like story of a horde of deadly felines; and Bob Mayer's 1996 thriller novel *Eternity Base,* about a secret U.S. military base in Antarctica. In 1999, Curtis considered making a new version of Joe David Brown's 1971 novel *Addie Pray,* which Peter Bogdanovich had filmed as *Paper Moon* (1973). None of these projects advanced to the stage of a finished script or a pitch to a studio.

In 1980, David Freeman (*Street Smart*) did turn in a finished script called *Tough Customers,* but it never was produced. Similarly, John Crowther (*Kill and Kill Again*) scripted *The Love Thieves,* based on Peter Packer's 1962 courtroom novel. In 1992, Susan Lambert (*On Guard*) wrote *Otto's Boy,* based on Walter Wager's 1985 crime novel. Seven years later, James Webb (*Cheyenne Autumn*) adapted *A Sense of Honor,* his 1981 novel of military life, as a possible Dan Curtis production.

Dan Curtis himself wrote or co-wrote several never-produced scripts, including *The Hoods* (a.k.a. *Noodles and Maxy*), *The Raid on 330 Park* (with Earl Wallace), and *The Last Summer* (with Barbara Steele). In 1989, 1999, and 2005, he prepared different versions of *Making It,* his most personal pet project. *Making It* was essentially *The Dan Curtis Story*—the saga of a showman who progresses from golf-show producer to king of the miniseries. According to Jim Pierson, "Every few years, Dan would get out the *Making It* script and work on it."[54]

In some parallel band of time, *Making It, The Last of the Crazy People,* and *RFK: Between the Gunshots* are the names of three Dan Curtis productions. Perhaps the two most significant Curtis shows-that-never-were are Richard Matheson's 1993-1998 work on a script for a four-hour version of his 1991 Western novel *Journal of the Gun Years* and *Elizabeth R* writer Julian Mitchell's 1979 adaptation of Emily Bronte's 1847 Gothic novel *Wuthering Heights*. The former would have been yet another Matheson/Curtis collaboration—and Curtis's second Western—and the latter would have added a sixth Curtis adaptation of classic Gothic literature to the prestigious DCP quintet of *Dracula, Frankenstein, The Picture of Dorian Gray, The Strange Case of Dr. Jekyll and Mr. Hyde,* and *The Turn of the Screw*. In the 1990s, Curtis also considered remaking *Dr. Jekyll and Mr. Hyde* on film (not videotape) and in England (not Canada).

Obviously, plans change. The September 1982 issue of *On Cable* magazine went so far as to announce that Paramount Pictures would launch a film called *The Godfather III*—and that it would be directed by Dan Curtis! Of course, a third *Godfather* film did not materialize until 1990, and it was directed by Francis Ford Coppola, but according to Jim Pierson, the *On Cable* report was "definitely true." Pierson explained,

> Dan had a production deal at Paramount, which is what *The Winds of War* came from, and the only other thing that got done was the *Big Easy* pilot. He also met with Diana Ross about a possible film. Dan was attached to several major theatrical films that he ended up not doing, [such as] *Once Upon a Time in America* (he did *Burnt Offerings* instead), *Damien—Omen II,* and *Godfather III*. Dan ultimately felt [that the] latter wasn't a great script and did *Winds of War* instead.[55]

Dan Curtis Productions constantly commissioned scripts for possible production, and while virtually every project that Curtis truly wanted to do got off the ground, many other scripts never made it out of development limbo. Below is information about a dozen of those never-realized scripts.

What might have been: if the 1982 pilot *The Big Easy,* starring William Devane (foreground), had become a successful television series, Devane might never have starred on *Knots Landing* from 1983 to 1993.

Command Performance,* a.k.a. *Parade Rest, by James Henerson (*The Love Letter*). 138-page treatment dated Wednesday 25 January 1995. Fort Hooker, a military base in San Lucas, California, is dealing with the possibility of being closed when a much more immediate problem rocks the base. Command Sergeant Major Jack Timmory is stabbed seven times to death, and Specialist Fourth Class Pegeen "Peggy" Reilly is arrested for the murder. At her court martial, Peggy Reilly is convicted and sentenced, but last-minute evidence reveals that although Peggy did stab Timmory when he attempted to rape her, someone else later found Timmory, still alive, and finished the job. The final scene takes place one year later when Sergeant Peggy Reilly attends Fort Hooker's decommissioning ceremony.

***Condemned,* Part I,** by Lee Hutson (*When Every Day Was the Fourth of July*). 92-page script dated Monday 11 June 2001. ***Condemned,* Part II,** by Lee Hutson (*The Long Days of Summer*). 108-page script dated Monday 25 June 2001. Inspired by a 9 June 2000 *Wall Street Journal* article about renewed interest in the 1913 Mary Phagan murder case, Hutson wrote this retelling of the case which had previously been filmed in 1937 as Warner Brothers' *They Won't Forget* (directed by Mervyn LeRoy) and (more accurately) in 1988 as NBC-TV's five-hour Emmy Award-winning miniseries *The Murder of Mary Phagan* (directed by Billy Hale and Daniel Petrie). In Mr. Hutson's teleplay, the events of 1913-1915 are narrated by Britt Craig, a reporter for the *Atlanta Constitution*. This miniseries script dramatizes the 26 April 1913 murder of the young factory worker Mary Phagan; the subsequent arrest, trial, and conviction of her supervisor, Leo Frank; the commutation of Frank's death sentence by Georgia governor John Slaton; and the 16 August 1915 lynching of Frank. The script concludes with a whatever-happened-to billboard that reveals the fates of other characters, gives an apparent solution to the murder mystery, and reports the State of Georgia's 1986 posthumous pardon (but not exoneration) of Leo Frank. Hutson's powerful, dramatic teleplay also utilizes the song "The Ballad of Mary Phagan."

***Deathwork*,** by Robert Carrington (*Wait Until Dark*). Based on the 1978 novel by James McLendon (*Eddie Macon's Run*). 167-page script dated 1992. In the 1970s, the State of Florida plans to electrocute four condemned prisoners on the same day. Through photo montages and journalist Lincoln Daniels's narration, the script details the lives of three-time poisoner Alice Fuller, serial rapist George Kruger, mad bomber Jose Santos, and triple murderer Charlie Parker. *Deathwork* climaxes with the on-screen executions of Fuller, then Kruger (who takes longer to die because of a malfunction in the electric chair), then Santos, and finally Parker, who offers the least resistance to his fate.

The Hoods,* a.k.a. *Noodles and Maxy, by Dan Curtis. Based on the 1952 novel by "Harry Grey," a.k.a. Harry Goldberg (*Portrait of a Mobster*). 125-page script submitted to Lou Rudolph of ABC-TV on Thursday 30 January 1975. In 1974-1975, both Dan Curtis and Sergio Leone began making plans to film Harry Grey's novel *The Hoods*. Curtis decided to film Robert Marasco's novel *Burnt Offerings* instead, and Leone finally completed his *Hoods* film version, called *Once Upon a Time in America*, a decade later in 1984. Curtis's *Hoods* script chronicles the violent lives of Noodles, his girlfriend Peggy Reilly, and his friends Maxy, Cockeye, Patsy, Pipy, and Goo-Goo in 1913, the 1920s, and 1933-1934. Most of the action takes place in New York City, but the final sequence, which offers a happy ending for Noodles and Peggy, occurs in Nyack, New York. (Coincidentally, the name "Peggy Reilly" is also used in Jim Henerson's *Command Performance* script.) Dan Curtis's meticulous *Hoods* script calls for wide shots, tight shots, P.O.V. shots, 9mm-lens shots, and, of course, plenty of low angles.

I Love Harrisburg in the Springtime, by Jack Finney ("The Third Level"). Based on Finney's 1960 short story "I Love Galesburg in the Springtime" and other stories. 83-page script submitted to Brandon Stoddard of ABC-TV on Tuesday 1 October 1974. Finney, who specialized in time-travel fiction (e.g. *Time and Again, From Time to Time, The Woodrow Wilson Dime*), wrote this sentimental, time-bending trilogy set in Harrisburg, Massachusetts (population 14,061), a seemingly sentient town that appears to be as enchanted as Collinsport, Maine. The trilogy's anchor character is *Harrisburg Blade-Tribune* reporter Oscar Mannheim, who remarks that the quaint town seems to be "fighting back" against progress. A long-extinct streetcar comes out of nowhere and scares away a businessman who wants to level much of Broad Street in order to build a factory, and a man who intends to cut down some of Harrisburg's old-growth trees is struck by a phantom 1916 Buick. Finney adapts three of his own stories: "Where the Cluetts Are" (1961), about how a house and its occupants slip backwards into time; "Second Chance" (1956), about a college student who drives a restored Jordan Playboy automobile out of the year 1968 and into the year 1926; and "The Love Letter" (1959), about a heartfelt exchange of letters between Jake Belknap in 1971 and Helen Elizabeth Worley in 1882. Although this script of Finney's was never used, Dan Curtis did include Richard Matheson's similar adaptation of "Second Chance" in the 1977 trilogy *Dead of Night*, and Curtis filmed James Henerson's expanded version of "The Love Letter" as a *Hallmark Hall of Fame* TV-movie in 1998.

Journal of the Gun Years, by Richard Matheson (*Shadow on the Sun*). Based on Matheson's 1991 novel. 22-page outline dated Monday 4 October 1993. ***Diary of a Gunfighter*, Part I**, by Richard Matheson (*Hunted Past Reason*). Based on Matheson's 1991 novel *Journal of the Gun Years*. 93-page script dated Thursday 29 January 1998. ***Diary of a Gunfighter*, Part II**, by Richard Matheson (*The Gunfight*). Based on Matheson's aforementioned novel. 93-page script dated Thursday 29 January 1998. Curtis's frequent collaborator Matheson spent some of the 1990s developing film scripts of his great epistolary Western novel that spans the years 1864-1876 and Marshal Clay Halser's diary entries therein. As early as October 1993, Matheson submitted an outline of more than 165 scenes. As late as January 1998, he finished revising a 186-page script for a TNT miniseries that never materialized. *Diary of a Gunfighter* (not as good of a title as the original *Journal of the Gun Years*) depicts the picaresque adventures of Clay Halser, a Union soldier, bartender, stagecoach driver, fugitive, card player, and City Marshal of Caldwell, Texas. Much of the story details Halser's tumultuous year as Marshal of Hays, Kansas, and the powerful Griffin family's vendetta against him. By the end of the story, Halser's wife Anne McConnell and daughter Melanie have left him, and he has become a drunken caricature of himself as he stars, as himself, in a preposterous stage play called *Hero of the Plains*. Although the novel *Journal of the Gun Years* ends with Halser still alive and hoping to become a silver miner, Matheson ends his *Diary of a Gunfighter* teleplay with an ironic death for Clay Halser as the camera pulls back and the picture goes to sepia-tone. Never producing this epic Western miniseries was a real missed opportunity for both Matheson and Curtis, as well as their fans.

Komine, Pike, and W.D. Baldry, by Jerry Renert (*M*A*S*H*), Jeff Wilhelm (*Supertrain*), and Dan Curtis. 119-page script. Undated. Bernie Komine, Gabe Pike, and Willie Baldry are World War I soldiers who run confidence games on their fellow soldiers. When the Great War ends in 1918, the men return to the United States and drive a dark blue Mercury Speedster through Arkansas and several other states as they pull scams and rob banks. Tiggy Riley is Willie Baldry's love interest who leaves him at the altar but returns to help the three men escape from Bridgeport, Nebraska, after a robbery. The script provides a happy ending for the foursome: although they lose the Bridgeport money, they make a clean getaway and head to Florida and a more peaceful existence. Curtis and his fellow scriptwriters call for the use of such vintage songs as "Turkey in the Straw," "Rasper Leonard and His Country Cousins," and "In the Good Old Summertime" as source music. This seriocomic caper film is reminiscent of Curtis's Melvin Purvis adventures and *The Great Ice Rip-Off*.

The Last of the Crazy People, by Timothy Findley (*Elizabeth Rex*). Based on Findley's 1967 novel. 124-page script submitted to Lou Rudolph of ABC-TV on Tuesday 6 April 1976. Revised 1998. As early as 1969 or 1970, Dan Curtis planned to film Findley's novel. The 3 June 1970 issue of *The Hollywood Reporter* even announced that Curtis would make *The Last of the Crazy People* as a follow-up to his film *House of Dark Shadows*. The 1 April 1976 issue of *The Hollywood Reporter* mentioned such plans again, but *The Last of the Crazy People* never became a Dan Curtis production. Findley's 1998 script details the years 1961-1962 in the lives of the troubled Winslow family: Hooker (10), Gilbert (25), their parents Nicholas and Jessica, their aunt Rosetta Winslow, and their maid Iris Browne. Jessica is mentally ill and stays in her bedroom most of the time. Hooker thinks of himself and his brother Gilbert as the last of a long line of crazy people. Ultimately, Gilbert kills himself, and young Hooker shoots his parents. Timothy Findley and director Laurent Achard (*More Than Yesterday*) finally made a film of this novel in 2006.

The Last Summer, by Dan Curtis and Barbara Steele. 122-page script. Undated. Recent Princeton graduates and good friends Jack Sherwood, from upstate New York, and Charlie McCall, from Leeds, Alabama, spend their last carefree summer traveling through Europe, first on motorcycles and then in an old convertible. In Paris, they meet Morgan, from England, and Lise, from France. The script details the growing attraction and love between Jack and Morgan—even though each is engaged to marry someone else. When their wedding days arrive, Jack and Morgan cannot go through with the ceremonies, and they find each other again at Heathrow Airport. The final scene shows the happy couple, along with their dog Bilbo (named for the J.R.R. Tolkien character), driving through the French countryside. As in many other Dan Curtis productions (*The Night Strangler, The Great Ice Rip-Off*, et al.), this unrealized script exudes a strong sense of place. *The Last Summer* follows the characters from Paris, France, to Olbia, Sardinia, to Venice, Italy, to Darien, Connecticut, to London, England.

The Raid on 330 Park, a.k.a. **The Raid on Root Tower,** a.k.a. **Smash Attack,** a.k.a. **Hostile Takeover,** by Earl Wallace (*Curse of the Black Widow*) and Dan Curtis. 108-page script dated Friday 27 August 1993. Revised 109-page script dated

Wednesday 1 September 1993. In this violent, hard-hitting hostage drama set at Technodyne, a defense/aerospace conglomerate, Vince Devereau is a former Technodyne employee who was framed and imprisoned for embezzling $100 million. Now, Devereau and an army of 50 men have come back and stormed the Technodyne International Tower at 330 Park Avenue in New York City. Devereau and his militia take 200 hostages and demand one billion dollars from Technodyne CEO Winfield Root, who is one of their captives. Ultimately, Devereau gets away but with only a fraction of the money. In this parallel New York City, the African-American mayor is patterned after David Dinkins but named "George Patterson" for the sheriff of Collinsport, Maine!

RFK: *Between the Gunshots,* Part I ("Return from Armageddon"), by Lee Hutson (*The Big Easy*). "Completed treatment" submitted to Lou Rudolph of ABC-TV on Thursday 13 May 1976. 146-page script is undated; **Part II** is missing. Despite its lurid but catchy title, *Between the Gunshots* is a stately, authentic historical drama focusing on the political life of Robert Fitzgerald Kennedy. After a prologue set in 1960, the bulk of this first half of the miniseries takes place between November 1963 (when Robert's brother, President John F. Kennedy, is assassinated) and January 1965 (when Robert and his brother Ted Kennedy are sworn in as U.S. Senators from New York and Massachusetts, respectively). Hutson's comprehensive teleplay involves dozens of major and minor figures from the political and popular-cultural worlds of the 1960s. Especially effective are the scenes featuring President Lyndon Johnson, from his bitter private conversations with his aides Walter Jenkins and James Rowe to his strained meeting with Bobby Kennedy when he informs RFK that he will not consider Bobby as his running mate in the 1964 election. The second half of the miniseries covers the years 1965-1968 and concludes with scenes of RFK's funeral train heading to Washington DC. On the side of the tracks, a young boy holds up a sign that reads SHALOM, BOBBY. Hutson's strong teleplay sidesteps the overexposed personal lives of RFK and JFK and places the brothers in a serious, historical context. The real-life newscaster Eric Sevareid is an important character near the end of Part I, and Kennedy aide and future Nashville *Tennessean* publisher John Siegenthaler Sr. is a character in a few brief scenes.

***Wuthering Heights*, Part I**, by Julian Mitchell (*The Mysterious Stranger*). Based on the 1847 novel by Emily Bronte. 159-page script dated Tuesday 23 October 1979. ***Wuthering Heights*, Part II**, by Julian Mitchell (*Vincent and Theo*). Based on the 1847 novel by Emily Bronte. 151-page script dated Tuesday 23 October 1979. *Inspector Morse* writer Mitchell's ambitious teleplay, spanning 1769-1802, begins with Cathy's ghostly appearance to Heathcliff at the window and then flashes back to 1769 when Mr. Earnshaw brings home the strange child Heathcliff, who changes his daughter Cathy's life forever. Part I climaxes with Cathy's 1784 death and burial and Heathcliff's confrontations with Hindley and Isabella. Part II begins in 1794 when Cathy and Edgar's daughter Catherine Linton is ten years old. As the years go by, Catherine marries Heathcliff's son Linton, who later dies. All the while, Heathcliff is haunted by Cathy's ghost: Mitchell's moody script superimposes Cathy's face over the faces of other characters in Heathcliff's eyes. At last, Cathy's phantom comes to Heathcliff at the moment of his death, and their spirits disappear together. Catherine marries

Hareton Earnshaw as the final shot reveals a row of three graves—Edgar's, Cathy's, and Heathcliff's—with the moors stretching behind them. Like Matheson's *Diary of a Gunfighter*, Mitchell's *Wuthering Heights* is an unrealized gem that could have become one of Curtis's greatest epics.[56]

Wuthering Heights also might have come to life—with a script by *Dark Shadows* writer Sam Hall—if Curtis's idea for a TV show called *The Classic Horror Theatre* had materialized. In the early 1970s, Curtis imagined a series that would adapt "The Body Snatcher," *Carmilla*, *Dracula*, "The Fall of the House of Usher," *Frankenstein*, *The House of the Seven Gables*, *Jane Eyre*, "Ligeia," *The Phantom of the Opera*, *The Picture of Dorian Gray*, *The Turn of the Screw*, "Viy" (previously filmed as *Black Sunday*, starring Barbara Steele), *The Werewolf of Paris*, and *Wuthering Heights*. Also in the 1970s, Curtis considered filming such modern classics as *This Rough Magic*, by Mary Stewart; *Lady of Mallow*, by Dorothy Eden; *The Dark Shore*, by Susan Howatch; and three novels by Victoria Holt: *The Bride of Pendorric*, *Mistress of Mellyn*, and *The Shadow of the Lynx*.[57] Curtis's fans would have loved all of those adaptations, but four of the adaptations (*Dracula*, *Frankenstein*, *Dorian Gray*, and *Turn of the Screw*)—plus 1968's *Dr. Jekyll and Mr. Hyde*—did get made.

At least, certain *elements* of some of the timeless stories mentioned above found their way into the storylines of ABC-TV's *Dark Shadows* (1966-1971) because of Dan Curtis's love of classic horror movies such as *Dracula* and *Frankenstein* (both 1931). *Dark Shadows* treated fans to male and female vampires, terrified governesses, a new Adam & Eve, a magical portrait, werewolves, and more. The Gothic serial concluded with a story reminiscent of *Wuthering Heights*, and it began with Carolyn Stoddard (in episode number three) jokingly welcoming Victoria Winters "to the House of Usher!"

Significa from the House of Dan Curtis: Andrew Peter Marin's working title of *The Great Ice Rip-Off* was *A Break in the Ice*. The serial number on the back of the Greyhound bus used in the TV-movie is 2032. In the story, the value of the bus is $47,000.

Two years later, Marin and director Alexander Singer essentially remade *The Great Ice Rip-Off* as *The Million-Dollar Rip-Off* (NBC, Wednesday 22 September 1976), starring Freddie Prinze as a crook who, with his four female accomplices, steals money from the Chicago Transit Authority but runs afoul of a nosy detective (Allen Garfield). Andrew P. Marin based his script on a screenplay by future *Knots Landing* stars John Pleshette and William Devane.[58]

Significa from the House of Dan Curtis: Although Thayer David (*Dark Shadows*, *Nero Wolfe*) did not appear in either of Dan Curtis's Melvin Purvis movies, he did play Connelly opposite Mickey Rooney as Nelson in Don Siegel's *Baby Face Nelson* (1957). In that film, Homer Van Meter was played by Elisha Cook Jr. (*The Night Stalker*, *Dead of Night*), and John Dillinger was played by Leo Gordon (*The Winds of War*, *War and Remembrance*). Ten years later, when Thayer David was on *Dark Shadows*, he remarked, "Dan Cutis, our producer, has the idea that people like to see a stock company of actors."[59]

In Curtis's television mysteries and crime dramas, "stock company" actors Charles Aidman, Orin Cannon, Matt Clark, Anjanette Comer, Joan Hackett, Jim Hill, Norman Honath, Don Megowan, Dale Robertson, Elliott Street, Roy Thinnes, Robert Walden, and Harris Yulin appeared in two or more of them. Mills Watson appeared in five Dan Curtis productions, including *The Kansas City Massacre* and *Supertrain*, and Scott Brady appeared in six, including *The Night Strangler* and *The Last Ride of the Dalton Gang*.

Dark Shadows actors who worked with Dan Curtis again included Thayer David (*Night of Dark Shadows*), George DiCenzo (*The Norliss Tapes*), Louis Edmonds (*Dead of Night: A Darkness at Blaisedon*), Ivor Francis (*The Night Strangler*), Grayson Hall (*The Great Ice Rip-Off*), John Harkins (*The Winds of War*), Michael McGuire (*The Winds of War*), Dennis Patrick (*War and Remembrance*), Addison Powell (*War and Remembrance*), Kathryn Leigh Scott (*Wide World Mystery: Come Die with Me*), and Abe Vigoda (*Me and the Kid*). James Storm (*Wide World Mystery: The Invasion of Carol Enders*) appeared in five additional Dan Curtis productions after *Dark Shadows,* and John Karlen (*Wide World Mystery: Nightmare at 43 Hillcrest*) appeared a record 13 more times after *Dark Shadows.* In his talk at the 2005 Dark Shadows Festival, Karlen quipped, "Dan knew a good actor when he saw one!"[60]

Significa from the House of Dan Curtis: The *Paradise Lost* epigraph that begins Dan Curtis's *Frankenstein* is from Book X of John Milton's masterpiece: "Did I request thee, Maker, from my Clay/To mould me Man? Did I solicit thee/From darkness to promote me, or here place/In this delicious Garden?" (lines 743-746). Most of this quotation appears on the title page of the original 1818 edition of *Frankenstein; or, The Modern Prometheus,* by Mary Shelley.[61]

Dan Curtis (middle) directs Jane Seymour and John Gielgud in a scene from *War and Remembrance* (1988, 1989).

CONCLUSION

From *Dark Shadows* to Today

Dan Curtis won the Saturn Award and the Medalla Sitges en Oro de Ley for directing *Burnt Offerings*, the Bronze Wrangler Award for directing *The Last Ride of the Dalton Gang*, and the Emmy Award for producing *War and Remembrance*. (He was Emmy-nominated for directing *The Winds of War* and *War and Remembrance* and for producing *The Strange Case of Dr. Jekyll and Mr. Hyde*.) After *War and Remembrance*, Curtis won the Distinguished Service Award from the Simon Wiesenthal Center and the Career Achievement Award from the Television Critics Association. He was nominated for the prestigious award from the Directors Guild of America in both 1989 and 1990, and he *won* the DGA Award in 1990. In 1998, he won the Golden Laurel Award from the Producers Guild of America. Curtis had gone from filming PGA golfers at the beginning of his career to being honored by a very different PGA near the end of his career.[1]

After *Challenge Golf* and *The CBS Golf Classic*, there was, of course, *Dark Shadows*. The Daytime Emmy Awards did not come into existence until after *Dark Shadows* was off the air, but one wonders how many Emmys Dan Curtis, his series, and his cast and crew would have collected. Surely, music composer Robert Cobert (b. 1924) and set designer Sy Tomashoff (1922-2019) would have won for their distinctive work on the show. (In 1968, *Dark Shadows* star Joan Bennett was nominated for a special-class Emmy Award but did not win.) After *Dark Shadows* came many more horror and mystery productions, including *Trilogy of Terror* and *The Kansas City Massacre*.

No one book can sum up the impact on television and popular culture that Dan Curtis wielded in the 1960s with *Dark Shadows* and *The Strange Case of Dr. Jekyll and Mr. Hyde*, in the 1970s with his numerous horror classics and his one Western, in the 1980s with his unsurpassed World War II epics, or in the 1990s with *Dark Shadows* and *Intruders*. In the 2000s, as his output was slowing down, he finally was gaining a richly deserved reputation as an elder statesman of television horror and drama. At the end of his career, *Our Fathers*, one of his finest dramas, became his swan song before his rapid decline and death, just 20 days after the passing of his beloved wife Norma.

Joseph Stern, the future *Law & Order* and *Judging Amy* executive producer who worked with Dan Curtis in the late 1970s (*Mrs. R's Daughter*) and early 1980s (*The Big Easy*), remembered Curtis as "a real original" with "a big heart." According to Stern, "Dan always said, 'Basically, I work alone,'" but at the same time, Curtis valued his "stock company" of actors whom he hired again and again. "He and I became very close friends near the end of his life," Joe Stern told me in a 2018 phone conversation.[2] In the early 2000s, Curtis's daughter Tracy worked as the film editor on 32 of Stern's *Judging Amy* episodes.

On 22 April 2004, Dan Curtis (then 76 years old) poses for a picture at the Museum of Television and Radio in Los Angeles. Curtis is at the museum to be honored for his 41 years as a producer—from *Challenge Golf* '63 to *Dark Shadows* '04.

In his foreword to Jim Pierson's book *Produced and Directed by Dan Curtis* (Pomegranate Press, 2004), Herman Wouk (1915-2019) wrote of his experiences "as a writer of the teleplays" of *The Winds of War* and *War and Remembrance*. "Film is not my medium," Wouk confessed, "but, guided by Dan Curtis, I tried to do a workmanlike job, and he was always the man in charge, start to finish, on the script as well as in the colossal task of shooting the movies. Once, my New York literary editor aptly compared Dan Curtis to a battlefield general. Dan likes to call me 'the Professor,' I suppose, because of the way I insisted on the historical accuracy of the films. Well, the general and the professor emerged from the great task as lifelong friends. I salute Dan and congratulate him on this well-deserved tribute to his colorful career of making movies, from Gothic mysteries and bang-up Westerns to the Battle of Midway and the Holocaust."[3]

William F. Nolan, who wrote 15 scripts for Curtis, including the two Melvin Purvis films and *The Turn of the Screw*, observed, "Horror does not work until you have the mood and the atmosphere to go with it. The material is one thing, but it's how you treat the material, and Dan has always done that very well. *The Norliss Tapes* was great—he kept it raining all through the movie."[4] Nolan continued,

> I've been on hand for several location shoots with Dan relating to my scripts. The one I remember best was in Sacramento for *Melvin Purvis, G-Man*, for the big shoot-out scene at the roadhouse. Dan knew I was itching to fire a Thompson submachine gun. "Okay, give Nolan a Tommy," he told the prop man. "He can die on the roof with the rest of the gang." So I happily fired my Thompson down at Purvis and his G-men and fell dead at the proper moment. Finally, when I thought the scene was over, [and I was] peering toward the camera, Dan, still shooting, yelled, "Nolan, for Christ's sake, get out of the shot! You're supposed to be dead!" [. . .] That's what made Dan so much fun to work with—his sense of humor. He can be stern and tough, but most people don't realize just how much Dan loves to laugh. We shared a lot of laughs together.[5]

The *Logan's Run* author told me, "What a dynamic man he was! What energy! We were good pals. I recall the last time I saw him at his office; he threw an arm around my shoulder and said to a production man who was there: 'Nolan and I have been through a helluva lot together.' He said it with genuine affection. I was touched."[6]

On Wednesday 12 August 2015, what would have been Curtis's 88th birthday, William F. Nolan wrote on Facebook, "In all, I have had some 20 TV or film projects produced, but *Burnt Offerings* remains at the top of the list. It holds up. I am proud of the screenplay. [. . .] At 87, I ain't slowing down! With much ahead. And *Logan* still runs!"[7]

Burnt Offerings collaborators and friends William F. Nolan (left) and Dan Curtis smile for the camera at the Museum of Television and Radio in Los Angeles in April of 2004.

On the same day, filmmaker Ansel H. Faraj wrote on Facebook, "Happy birthday to a man who taught me so much, without my ever meeting him—Dan Curtis." Faraj is an *auteur* writer-producer-director who often casts *Dark Shadows* stars in his atmospheric thrillers, such as *Doctor Mabuse* (2013), *Doctor Mabuse: Etiopomar* (2014), *The Last Case of August T. Harrison* (2015), *The Job Interview* (2016), *The Night-Time Winds* (2017), *Will & Liz* (2018), and *Loon Lake* (2019).[8]

Emmy Award winner John Karlen (*Dark Shadows, Wide World Mystery*) declared, "Dan was a creative genius and was always passionate about his work. He loved making thrillers, and he was also an incurable romantic. When he merged those two themes, he was in his element, and over a 40-year career, he was responsible for some of the most popular and important entertainment in television history, ranging from *The Night Stalker* to *War and Remembrance*. No one was happier telling stories than Dan, and I'm happy that I was a part of his magical and mysterious world."[9]

Golden Globe Award winner Karen Black (*Trilogy of Terror, Burnt Offerings*) revealed,
I had never worked with anyone quite like Dan. He was ferocious and forthcoming. He had a very big heart and large intentions—and he was going to get that shot *right* no matter *what*—and it was usually a low shot. [. . .] He was really *with* the actor; he was very supportive of me. He was very open and very loving with me. Dan Curtis had a huge impact on my career. [. . .] When he was on his way [i.e. near death], he had a brain tumor, and he couldn't speak. Jim Pierson was very kind. He let me go and see Dan. Dan was lying on a couch, but he was still *Dan*. I knelt by him, and he held my hand and stroked my hair. He was just as feisty and

as beautiful as ever. We had a lovely good-bye. I don't know if you believe in energy or whether you believe people become air or you believe people become another lifetime, but if you are ever in your backyard and this huge gust of air—*wind*—comes around you, or if you feel a sudden, really strong, electric, outrageous burst of energy, or if you see a little baby who's kicking up a horrible fuss, then you can say hello—to Dan.[10]

At the Museum of Television and Radio on 22 April 2004, *Trilogy of Terror* **star Karen Black and her husband Stephen Eckelberry (middle) converse with** *Dark Shadows* **'04 associate producer Jim Pierson.**

Ansel Faraj (center) directs Kathryn Leigh Scott (left), David Selby (right), and others on the Minnesota set of *Loon Lake*. Image courtesy of Round Town Productions.

Afterword

Ansel Faraj

Lately, when I have found myself in a tough spot, I've caught myself muttering, "Help me, Dan," under my breath. The world of filmmaking—or rather, the *business* side of "the biz"—is truly a roller coaster which might jump the track at any moment. Navigating this world is nothing short of a magic trick.

There's definitely a difference between the Hollywood of 2020 and the Hollywood of 1970. Technology—specifically, how we receive our entertainment—is faster and exponentially broader in selection. As a result, the movies filling the big screen are massive, expensive, explosive blockbusters because technology has let loose the "small film" to our other screens. Everything is in a state of flux, and as a result, nobody knows what to do or what the audiences want. With no real training in "the art of Hollywood," filmmakers must stick to their guns and deeply trust their instincts.

Dan Curtis was not a filmmaker by trade. He was an ad man. He was also a shrewd businessman who found himself on the filmmaking playing field, where he wasted no time in grabbing a bullhorn and shouting to his troops—as he was known to do—instructions for how to bring his vision to life.

He stuck to his guns about the need for the ABC network to produce a risky half-hour daytime Gothic mystery instead of another tried-and-true game show. He barely had any directing experience when he helmed his first MGM theatrical blood-and-thunder horror show, *House of Dark Shadows*, but he trusted his instincts and did things his way, and rather successfully, too. He navigated the business and was able to bring his own haunted visions to life, on his terms. And his visions stuck with people. You can't scroll through Instagram without catching sight of the Zuni doll attacking Karen Black or Barnabas Collins leering out of the shadows of the Old House.

I've just completed a folk horror thriller titled *Loon Lake*. It was a pretty epic film for me, shot on location in Southwest Minnesota (instead of in my garage), with a minimal, but very real, crew (instead of just me). We still had no money, but we had gumption and luck, plus a thousand acres of farmland on which to run rampant. David Selby was with us on set for eight days, playing a dual role. Kathryn Leigh Scott flew in for two days to play her historical scenes in a real parsonage from the 1880s, instead of against the blue screen in my garage.

It took 30 days to shoot and two years of work overall from inception to completion. And not a day went by when I didn't think of Dan Curtis running rampant through Tarrytown, drowning Nancy Barrett and Jonathan Frid in fake blood and hanging Lara Parker from a Lyndhurst tree. Almost 50 years later, here I was with

David, who was sporting a very Quentin-looking cloak, prowling around a witch's bonfire in the woods. We were putting on a show ourselves, just like Dan and his troops did back in 1970.

And all throughout the lengthy and complicated process of post-production and securing distribution, as I learned new tricks and business "wheeling and dealing," my admiration for Dan has only grown. There are so many decisions to make, so many doors to walk through. How can a filmmaker differentiate the right door from the myriad wrong doors? The lesson I've learned is one that Dan lived by: you have to really listen to and trust your gut. Hollywood is a tough town, but Dan played the business game better than anyone. He managed to produce the content he wanted on his terms while turning a profit and always remaining prolific and reliable.

As I write this today, September 19, 2019, Warner Bros. has just announced plans to bring *Dark Shadows* back to life yet again in *Dark Shadows: Reincarnation*, a sequel to the original TV series, taking place in the Collinsport of 2020. Whether this new show comes to light or not is not the point. The point is that Dan's vision—Dan's world—endures. Dan stuck to his guns and did what he wanted. He didn't care that everyone said putting a vampire on daytime television was a dumb idea. He had a feeling it just might work—and what else was there to lose? All these years later, we're still talking about it. That tells you something about listening to yourself and trusting your gut. There's power there.

Rondo Award-nominated *auteur* filmmaker **Ansel H. Faraj** has been making movies since he was six years old. He is the writer-producer-director of *The Rising Light* (2013), *Doctor Mabuse: Etiopomar* (2014), *Whatever Happened to Detective Adam Sera?* (2015), *The Job Interview* (2016), *The Night-Time Winds* (2017), *Will & Liz* (2018), and *Loon Lake* (2019). His 2012 film *Brother Drop Dead* won an award for comedic writing at the Buffalo Niagara Film Festival. Ansel Faraj lives in Los Angeles, and his official Internet website is **www.hollinsworthproductions.com**.

Chapter Notes

Introduction

01 qtd. in *Stalker Interview*
02 Ibid.
03 Graham, email 26 April 2010
04 qtd. in Thompson, *Television Horrors,* 1st ed., 2, 52

Chapter I (*Dark Shadows*)

01 Thompson, *Nights,*1st ed., 220
02 qtd. in *Behind*
03 Ibid.
04 qtd. in *A Novel*
05 Thompson, *Television Horrors,* 1st ed., 56-57
06 Ibid.
07 Scott and Pierson, *Almanac,* Millennium ed., 104
08 qtd. in *Collection 11*
09 Scott and Pierson, *Almanac,* Millennium ed., 104
10 qtd. in *Inside*
11 Ibid.
12 qtd. in *Behind*
13 qtd. in Pierson, *Produced* 205
14 qtd. in Pierson, *Produced* 14
15 qtd. in Pierson, *Produced* 205
16 qtd. in Stewart 11
17 qtd. in *Behind*
18 Jenkins, *Textual* 137
19 qtd. in "Director/Co-Producer" 11
20 Ibid.
21 qtd. in Pierson, *Produced* 21
22 qtd. in *Collection 16*
23 Ibid.
24 qtd. in Robin, 54/55: 15
25 Benshoff 99
26 Muir, *Terror Television* 296
27 qtd. in Pierson, *Produced* 180
28 Ibid.
29 Ibid.
30 Ibid.
31 qtd. in Pierson, *Resurrected* 9
32 Gross, "Staked!" 64
33 qtd. in Gross, "Staked!" 64
34 Ibid.
35 qtd. in Gross, "Staked!" 65
36 Ibid.
37 qtd. in Gross, "Staked!" 82
38 Burr
39 Chang
40 Burr
41 "Vampire, Thirsty"
42 Chang
43 Burr
44 Logan, "Vamp Camp"
45 Stone D-1
46 Kennedy 7-A
47 Robin, 122/123: 34
48 qtd. in Robin, 122/123: 34
49 Ibid.
50 all quotations from *Master of Dark Shadows*
51 Thompson, *House,* 1st ed., 137
52 Thompson, *Television Horrors,* 2nd ed., 137

Chapter II (horrors)

01 Showalter 197
02 Stevenson 79
03 Stevenson 77
04 Stevenson 55
05 qtd. in Pierson, *Produced* 16
06 qtd. in Pierson, *Produced* 43
07 qtd. in Pierson, *Produced* 44
08 Ibid.
09 qtd. in Burlingame
10 qtd. in Pierson *Produced* 11
11 O'Neil 124-128
12 qtd. In Pierson, *Produced* 44
13 King 224
14 qtd. in Robin, 81:11
15 Ibid.
16 qtd. in Dawidziak, *Stalker* 21
17 qtd. in Burlingame
18 qtd. in Dawidziak, *Stalker* 21
19 qtd. in Burlingame
20 qtd. in Pierson, *Produced* 66

21 Ibid.
22 Ibid.
23 qtd. in Dawidziak, *Stalker* 83
24 qtd. in McCarty, "Nolan Looks"
25 Knowles
26 qtd. in Pierson, *Produced* 73
27 Ibid.
28 Ibid.
29 qtd. in Pierson, *Produced* 208
30 qtd. in McCarty, "Curtis Continues"
31 Nolan, personal interview 28 Feb. 2010
32 Deal 48
33 qtd. in Pierson, *Produced* 205
34 qtd. in Bosco
35 Ibid.
36 qtd. in *Trilogy* DVD commentary
37 qtd. in *Three Colors Black*
38 qtd. in Pierson, *Produced* 109
39 qtd. in Pierson, *Produced* 114
40 qtd. in Thompson, *Television Horrors*, 1st ed., 6
41 qtd. in Pierson, *Produced* 126
42 Deal 27
43 qtd. in Pierson, *Produced* 24
44 qtd. in McCarty, "Nolan Looks"
45 qtd. in Robin, 78:10
46 qtd. in Robin, 79:9
47 Ibid.
48 Ibid.
49 Ibid.
50 qtd. in McCarty, "Nolan Looks"
51 Nolan, personal interview 28 Feb. 2010
52 qtd. in *Master of Dark Shadows*
53 Pierson, email 7 May 2009
54 Dawidziak, *Stalker* 194

Chapter III (features)

01 qtd. in Thompson, *Television Horrors*, 2nd ed., 107
02 Scott and Pierson, *Movie Book* 20
03 qtd. in *Inside*
04 qtd. in Scott and Pierson, *Movie Book* 22
05 Ibid.
06 qtd. in Pierson, *Produced* 52
07 Glut 305
08 Thompson, *Television Horrors*, 2nd ed., 5
09 qtd. in *Collection* 16
10 Ibid.
11 Benshoff 96
12 qtd. in Pierson, *Produced* 57
13 Lucas, "*House*" 67
14 qtd. in Pierson and Scott, *Movie Book* 26
15 Weiler
16 qtd. in Pierson, *Produced* 57
17 Ibid.
18 Ebert, "*Night*"

19 Scott and Pierson, *Almanac*, Millennium ed., 162
20 qtd. in Thompson, *Television Horrors*, 1st ed., 86
21 qtd. in *Burnt* DVD commentary
22 Ibid.
23 Marasco 55
24 Marasco 226
25 "Not So Very" 6-D
26 qtd. in Pierson, *Produced* 120
27 Ibid.
28 "Outstanding Terror"
29 qtd. in Pierson, *Produced* 120
30 qtd. in Thompson, *Television Horrors*, 2nd ed., 205
31 qtd. in *Burnt* DVD commentary
32 "Outstanding Terror"
33 qtd. in Pierson, *Produced* 120
34 Ibid.
35 qtd. in McCarty, "Nolan Looks"
36 LaVoo 7
37 qtd. in LaVoo 100
38 qtd. in *Burnt* DVD commentary
39 qtd. in *Trilogy* DVD commentary
40 qtd. in Robin, 61:15
41 Ibid.
42 Ibid.
43 Ibid.
44 Ibid.
45 Ibid.
46 Thompson, *House*, 1st ed., 146-147
47 qtd. in Thompson, *House*, 1st ed., 136
48 Thompson, *Television Horrors*, 2nd ed., 207

Chapter IV (epics)

001 Thompson, *Television Horrors*, 2nd ed., 145
002 Thompson, *Nights*, 1st ed., 129
003 qtd. in Pierson, *Produced* 21
004 Stoker 320
005 qtd. in *Macabre*
006 Benshoff 101
007 qtd. in *Macabre*
008 qtd. in Pierson, *Produced* 85
009 Ibid.
010 qtd. in *Macabre*
011 Glut 293
012 Melton, *Vampire Book*, 2nd ed., 758-764
013 Stoker 29
014 Stoker 30
015 Stoker 30-31
016 Stoker 241-242
017 Melton, *Vampire Book*, 2nd ed., 702-703
018 Melton, *Vampire Book*, 2nd ed., 603-604
019 Melton, *Vampire Book*, 1st ed., 669
020 Stoker 303-304
021 Thompson, *Dracula* liner notes
022 qtd. in Burlingame

023 Thompson, *Dracula* liner notes
024 Ibid.
025 Ibid.
026 McNally and Florescu 273
027 Melton, *Vampire Book*, 1st ed., 670
028 qtd. in *Macabre*
029 qtd. in Pierson, *Produced* 86
030 Pierson, email 30 July 2015
031 Dawidziak, *Bloodlines* 5
032 Dawidziak, *Bloodlines* 71 (script, p. 13)
033 Dawidziak, *Bloodlines* 102 (script, p. 46)
034 Dawidziak, *Bloodlines* 88 (script, p. 29)
035 Dawidziak, *Bloodlines* 89 (script, p. 29)
036 Dawidziak, *Bloodlines* 90-91 (script, pp. 31-32)
037 Dawidziak, *Bloodlines* 195 (script, p. 134)
038 Dawidziak, *Bloodlines* 34
039 Dawidziak, *Bloodlines* 41
040 Dawidziak, *Bloodlines* 43
041 Dawidziak, *Bloodlines* 22
042 Ibid.
043 qtd. in *Daltons*
044 Ibid.
045 Ibid.
046 "Dalton Gang Raid"
047 Ibid.
048 Kirchner 225
049 qtd. in *Daltons*
050 Ibid.
051 Crist A8-A9
052 qtd. in *Daltons*
053 Ibid.
054 qtd. in Thompson, *Nights*, 1st ed., vii-viii
055 qtd. in *A Novel*
056 Ibid.
057 qtd. in "Director/Co-Producer" 11
058 qtd. in *Making The Winds of War*
059 Pierson, *Produced* 156
060 qtd. in Pierson, *Produced* 208
061 qtd. in Thompson, "*Winds*"
062 qtd. in Seymoure 74
063 qtd. in Thompson, "*Winds*"
064 qtd. in Pierson, *Produced* 205
065 qtd. in *Making The Winds of War*
066 Robin, 41:5
067 qtd. in *Making The Winds of War*
068 qtd. in Pierson, *Produced* 156
069 Ibid.
070 Ibid.
071 Ibid.
072 qtd. in Thompson, "*Winds*"
073 O'Neil 299-300, 303-307
074 qtd.. in *Making of War and Remembrance*
075 Robin, 41:5
076 *Making of War and Remembrance*
077 Gendel 10-F
078 Robin, 47:7
079 Gendel, 10-F
080 qtd. in *Making of War and Remembrance*
081 Pierson, *Produced* 168
082 Ibid.
083 DuBrow 4-F
084 Pierson, *Produced* 168
085 qtd. in Pierson, *Produced* 208
086 qtd. in Pierson, *Prodcued* 205
087 qtd. in Pierson, *Produced* 206
088 qtd. in Stewart 13
089 qtd. in *Making of War and Remembrance*
090 qtd. in Stewart 13
091 qtd. in Pierson, *Produced* 169
092 Ibid.
093 Ibid.
094 Ibid.
095 Ibid.
096 Ibid.
097 Pierson, *Produced* 168
098 Thompson, "Miniseries to Remember" 8
099 qtd. in Robin, 46:9
100 Ibid.
101 O'Neil 396, 400-406; Pierson, *Produced* 168
102 O'Neil 396
103 O'Neil 400-406
104 Robin, 82:10
105 Robin, 47:7
106 Ibid.
107 qtd. in *Making of War and Remembrance*
108 Curtis, "Remember *Remembrance*"
109 Hopkins 4-5
110 qtd. in Robin, 61:15
111 Ibid.
112 Ibid.
113 Ibid.
114 Ibid.
115 Ibid.
116 qtd. in Pierson, *Produced* 188
117 Ibid.
118 qtd. in Robin, 61:15
119 Ibid.
120 Dawidziak 13-18; Karol 5; Robin, 82:10; Robin, 108:8
121 qtd. in Pierson, *Produced* 57
122 Thompson, *Nights*, 1st ed., 86
123 Thompson, *House*, 1st ed., 156
124 Thompson, *Television Horrors*, 2nd ed., 106
125 Benshoff 72-77

Chapter V (dramas)

01 Marill, *Movies 1964-2004*, vol. 1, 147
02 qtd. in Pierson, *Produced* 94
03 qtd. in Pierson, *Produced* 93
04 Ibid.

05 qtd. in Pierson, *Produced* 94
06 qtd. in Pierson, *Produced* 208
07 qtd. in Pierson, *Produced* 114
08 Ibid.
09 Ibid.
10 qtd. in Pierson, *Produced* 132
11 Ibid.
12 qtd. in Pierson, *Produced* 24
13 qtd. in Pierson, *Produced* 131
14 qtd. in Pierson, *Produced* 145-146
15 qtd. in Pierson, *Prodcued* 156
16 O'Neil 275
17 Robin, 82:10
18 qtd. in Pierson, *Produced* 202
19 qtd. in Robin, 82:10
20 Ibid.
21 Ibid.
22 qtd. in Pierson, *Produced* 202
23 Ibid.
24 qtd. in Pierson, *Prodcued* 206
25 Pierson, *Produced* 213
26 Robin, 104:11
27 Ibid.
28 qtd. in Pierson, *Prodcued* 213
29 Ibid.
30 Stewart 57
31 Pierson, *Produced* 215-216
32 qtd. in Robin, 106:9
33 Ibid.
34 qtd. in Pierson, *Produced* 216
35 qtd. in Robin, 106:9
36 Ibid.
37 Ibid.
38 Thompson, *Television Horrors*, 2nd ed., 228
39 Ibid.
40 Thompson, *Nights*, 1st ed., 112

Chapter VI (pilots)

01 Burlingame
02 Pierson, email 20 June 2009
03 Pierson, email 23 August 2009
04 qtd. in Pierson, *Produced* 151
05 Pierson, email 7 May 2009
06 Thompson, *House*, 1st ed., 144
07 Ibid.
08 qtd. in Winkle
09 Thompson, *House*, 1st ed., 146
10 Ibid.

Chapter VII (mysteries)

01 Thompson, *House*, 1st ed., 113
02 Florescu 198

03 Shelley 58
04 O'Flinn 114
05 O'Flinn 115, 120
06 qtd. in Pierson, *Produced* 19
07 Shelley 19
08 qtd. in Burlingame
09 qtd. in Pierson, *Produced* 69
10 Ibid.
11 Florescu 236
12 qtd. in Thompson, *Television Horrors*, 2nd ed., 140
13 Curtis, "A Frank Explanation"
14 qtd. in Pierson, *Produced* 75
15 qtd. in Shinnick 49
16 qtd. in Shinnick 51
17 qtd. in Shinnick 50
18 qtd. in Pierson, *Produced* 75
19 Wilde 254
20 qtd. in Burlingame
21 qtd. in *Collection* 8
22 qtd. in McCarty, "Nolan Looks"
23 qtd. in *Macabre*
24 Ibid.
25 Ibid.
26 qtd. in McCarty, "Nolan Looks"
27 James 12
28 Ibid.
29 James 58
30 James 75
31 James 76
32 Wilson 385-406
33 James 8
34 James 15
35 James 86
36 Nolan, *Turn of the Screw* script
37 qtd. in *Macabre*
38 qtd. in *Macabre*
39 qtd. in Pierson, *Produced* 99
40 Ibid.
41 Blumgarten 4
42 Blumgarten 62-63
43 qtd. in *Stalker Interview*
44 Pierson, email 27 June 2008
45 Jamison 174
46 Jamison 175
47 qtd. in *Stalker Interview*
48 qtd. in Pierson, *Produced* 107
49 Ibid.
50 Pierson, email 22 Oct. 2007
51 qtd. in Pierson, *Produced* 25
52 Pierson, email 22 Oct. 2007
53 qtd. in Robin, 107:22
54 Pierson, email 13 Sept. 2009
55 Pierson, email 12 Nov. 2009
56 Thompson, *House*, 1st ed., 157-162
57 Thompson, *House*, 1st ed., 170
58 Thompson, *House*, 1st ed., 136

59 Thompson, *House,* 1st ed., 112
60 Thompson, *House,* 1st ed., 106; Thompson, *Nights,* 1st ed., 174
61 Thompson, *House,* 1st ed., 130; Thompson, *Television Horrors,* 2nd ed., 161

Conclusion

01 Thompson, *Nights,* 1st ed., 202
02 Thompson, *Television Horrors,* 2nd ed., 235-236
03 qtd. in Pierson, *Produced* 9
04 qtd. in *Burnt* DVD commentary
05 qtd. in Pierson, *Produced* 207
06 Nolan, letter 17 Jan. 2010
07 qtd. in Thompson, *Nights,* 1st ed., 220
08 Ibid.
09 qtd. in Thompson, *House,* 1st ed., 1
10 qtd. in Thompson, *House,* 1st ed., 90

House of Dan Curtis author Jeff Thompson (left) and *Dark Shadows* star David Selby pose for a picture at the 2008 Dark Shadows Festival in Burbank, California.

Bibliography

Alzheimer's Association public-service announcement. Dir. Dan Curtis. 2004.
Angie the Lieutenant. Dir. Robert Collins. Prod. Dan Curtis. Perf. Angie Dickinson, Nicholas Pryor, Jesse Dabson, Angela Bassett. RLC Productions & Dan Curtis Productions & MGM/UA Television, 1992.
Barthel, Joan. "Out in Detergent Land: A Hard Day's Fright." *New York Times* (30 July 1967). Web.
Barton, Kristin M., and Jonathan M. Lampley, eds. *Fan Culture: Essays on Participatory Fandom in the 21st Century.* Jefferson, NC: McFarland, 2014.
Beahm, Justin. "Tim Burton Steps into the Shadows." *Famous Monsters of Filmland* no. 261 (May-June 2012): 62-69.
Beaumont, Charles. *Perchance to Dream: Selected Stories.* New York: Penguin Books, 2015.
Benshoff, Harry. *Dark Shadows.* Detroit: Wayne State UP, 2011.
Bianculli, David. *The Platinum Age of Television.* New York: Anchor Books, 2016.
The Big Easy. Dir. Jud Taylor. Prod. Dan Curtis. Perf. William Devane, Mary Crosby, Ja'net Dubois, Barbara Babcock. Dan Curtis Productions & Paramount Television, 1982.
Birnes, William. *The UFO Magazine UFO Encyclopedia.* New York: Pocket Books, 2004.
Black, Karen. DVD interview. *Three Colors Black.* Dir. David Gregory. *Trilogy of Terror.* Dark Sky Films, 2006. DVD.
Black, Karen and William F. Nolan. DVD commentary. *Trilogy of Terror.* Dark Sky Films, 2006. DVD.
Black, Karen; Dan Curtis; and William F. Nolan. DVD commentary. *Burnt Offerings.* MGM Home Entertainment, 2003. DVD.
Bloch, Robert. *Psycho.* New York: Crest Books, 1959.
Blumgarten, James. *Come Die with Me.* Unpublished script for Dan Curtis Productions. Last revised 4 Dec. 1973.
Boedeker, Hal. "Dan Curtis Thought Big." *Orlando Sentinel Blog.* 28 March 2006. Web. 3 Sept. 2006.
Borzellieri, Frank. *The Physics of* Dark Shadows: *Time Travel, ESP, and the Laboratory.* New York: Cultural-Studies Press, 2008.
Bosco, Scott. Liner notes. *Trilogy of Terror.* Anchor Bay Entertainment, 1999. Videocassette.
Breznican, Anthony. "Into the Shadows." *Entertainment Weekly* no. 1206 (11 May 2012): 30-36.
Brooks, Tim and Earle Marsh. *The Complete Directory to Prime-Time Network and Cable-TV Shows 1946-Present.* 8th ed. New York: Ballantine Books, 2003.
Brosnan, John. *The Horror People.* New York: Plume Books, 1976.
Brown, Mary Ellen. *Soap Opera and Women's Talk.* London: Sage, 1994.
Burlingame, John. Liner notes. *The Night Stalker and Other Classic Thrillers.* Composed and conducted by Robert Cobert. Varese Sarabande, 2000. CD.
Burnt Offerings. Dir. Dan Curtis. Perf. Karen Black, Oliver Reed, Bette Davis, Lee Montgomery. United Artists, 1976.
"*Burnt Offerings* Is an Outstanding Terror Movie." *New York Times Online* 30 Sept. 1976. Web. 11 August 2006.
"*Burnt Offerings* Not So Very Well Done." *The* [Nashville] *Tennessean* 19 Nov. 1976: 6-D.
Burr, Ty. "*Dark Shadows.*" *Boston Globe* 10 May 2012. Web. 10 May 2012.
Cameron, Ian. *A Pictorial History of Crime Films.* London: Hamlyn, 1975.
Capley, Vance. "Shades of Darkness: An Interview with Dr. Jeff Thompson." *Monster Magazine* no. 4 (Feb. 2019): 11-16.
Carroll, David and Kyla Ward. "The Horror Timeline." *Tabula Rasa.* 2005. Web. 22 July 2006.
Cast and Characters. Dir. Donald Beck. *The Winds of War, Part V.* Paramount DVD, 2004. DVD.
CBS Golf Classic. Dir. Frank Chirkinian. Prod. Dan Curtis. CBS-TV, 1963-1973.
Challenge Golf. Prod. Dan Curtis. ABC-TV, 1963.

Chang, Justin. "*Dark Shadows.*" *Variety* 10 May 2012. Web. 10 May 2012.
Clover, Carol. "Her Body, Himself." *The Horror Reader*. Ed. Ken Gelder. London: Routledge, 2000. 294-307.
---. *Men, Women, and Chainsaws: Gender in the Modern Horror Film*. Princeton, NJ: Princeton UP, 1992.
Cobert, Robert. DVD interview. *The Music of War and Remembrance*. Dir. Donald Beck. *War and Remembrance: The Final Chapter, Parts XI-XII*. MPI Home Video, 2003. DVD.
---. Liner notes. *War and Remembrance*. Composed and conducted by Robert Cobert. MPI Music, 2003. CD.
Come Die with Me. Dir. Burt Brinckerhoff. Prod. Dan Curtis. Perf. Eileen Brennan, George Maharis, Kathryn Leigh Scott, Charles Macaulay. Dan Curtis Productions, 1974.
Creed, Barbara. "Kristeva. Femininity, and Abjection." *The Horror Reader*. Ed. Ken Gelder. London: Routledge, 2000. 64-70.
Crist, Judith. "This Week's Movies." *TV Guide* 17-23 Nov. 1979: A8-A9.
Culhane, Michael. "Welcome to Collinwood: *Dark Shadows* 101." *Famous Monsters of Filmland* no. 261 (May-June 2012): 32-33.
Curse of the Black Widow. Dir. Dan Curtis. Perf. Anthony Franciosa, Donna Mills, Patty Duke Astin, Roz Kelly. ABC Circle Films, 1977.
Curtis, Dan. DVD commentary. *War and Remembrance: The Final Chapter, Parts XI-XII*. MPI Home Video, 2003. DVD.
---. DVD interview. *Dan Curtis and the Daltons*. Prod. Jim Pierson. *The Last Ride of the Dalton Gang*. MPI Home Video, 2005. DVD.
---. DVD interview. *Directing The Night Strangler*. Prod. & dir. Greg Carson. *The Night Stalker & The Night Strangler*. MGM Home Entertainment, 2004. DVD.
---. DVD interview. *Inside the Shadows*. Prod. Jim Pierson. *Dark Shadows Special Edition*. MPI Home Video, 1999. DVD.
---. DVD interview. *The Night Stalker: Dan Curtis Interview*. Prod. & dir. Greg Carson. *The Night Stalker & The Night Strangler*. MGM Home Entertainment, 2004. DVD.
---. DVD interview. Prod. Jim Pierson. *The Dan Curtis Macabre Collection*. MPI Home Video, 2002. DVD.
---. DVD interview. Prod. Jim Pierson. *Dark Shadows DVD Collection 2*. MPI Home Video, 2002. DVD.
---. DVD interview. Prod. Jim Pierson. *Dark Shadows DVD Collection 8*. MPI Home Video, 2003. DVD.
---. DVD interview. Prod. Jim Pierson. *Dark Shadows DVD Collection 11*. MPI Home Video, 2004. DVD.
---. DVD interview. Prod. Jim Pierson. *Dark Shadows DVD Collection 16*. MPI Home Video, 2005. DVD.
---. DVD interview. Prod. Jim Pierson. *Dark Shadows DVD Collection 24*. MPI Home Video, 2006. DVD.
---. Foreword. *Dark Shadows Resurrected*. By Jim Pierson. Los Angeles: Pomegranate Press, 1992. 9.
---. "Frank Explanation of Producer's Version." Rpt. in *Shadowgram* no. 63 (Jan. 1993): 10.
---. "Remember *Remembrance*." Rpt. in *Shadowgram* no. 79 (May 1997): 9. Print.
Curtis, Dan and Lynn Redgrave. DVD interviews. Prod. Jim Pierson. *The Dan Curtis Macabre Collection*. MPI Home Video, 2002. DVD.
"Dalton Gang Raid." *Investigating History*. Prod. Bill Kurtis. Kurtis Productions, 2004. DVD.
"Dan Curtis Legacy Award." *Saturn Awards Organization*. 1 July 2018. Web. 5 July 2018.
Dark Shadows. Dir. Dan Curtis, Lela Swift, et al. Perf. Joan Bennett, Jonathan Frid, Grayson Hall, Louis Edmonds. ABC-TV, 1966-1971.
Dark Shadows. Dir. Dan Curtis, Rob Bowman, et al. Perf. Jean Simmons, Ben Cross, Barbara Steele, Roy Thinnes. NBC-TV, 1991.
Dark Shadows. Dir. P.J. Hogan. Prod. Dan Curtis. Perf. Blair Brown, Alec Newman, Kelly Hu, Martin Donovan. Filmed for the WB television network in April 2004 but never aired.
Dark Shadows. Dir. Tim Burton. Prod. David Kennedy. Perf. Michelle Pfeiffer, Johnny Depp, Helena Bonham Carter, Jonny Lee Miller. Warner Brothers, 2012.
Dark Shadows Behind the Scenes. Prod. Jim Pierson. *Dark Shadows Special Edition*. MPI Home Video, 1999. DVD.
Dark Shadows Reunion: 35th Anniversary Celebration. Prod. Jim Pierson. MPI Home Video, 2003. DVD.
Dawidziak, Mark. *Bloodlines: Richard Matheson's* Dracula, I Am Legend, *and Other Vampire Stories*. Colorado Springs: Gauntlet Press, 2006.
---. *The* Night Stalker *Companion: A 25th Anniversary Tribute*. Los Angeles: Pomegranate Press, 1997.
Dead of Night. Dir. Dan Curtis. Perf. Ed Begley Jr., Patrick Macnee, Joan Hackett, Lee Montgomery. Dan Curtis Productions, 1977.
Dead of Night: A Darkness at Blaisedon. Dir. Lela Swift. Prod. Dan Curtis. Perf. Kerwin Mathews, Marj Dusay, Thayer David, Louis Edmonds. Dan Curtis Productions & Donnybrook Productions, 1969.

Deal, David. *Television Fright Films of the 1970s*. Jefferson, NC: McFarland, 2007.
Del Valle, David. "Memories of Dan Curtis." *Films in Review*. 28 March 2006. Web. 14 June 2006.
Dillinger. Dir. John Milius. Perf. Ben Johnson, Warren Oates, Michelle Phillips, Richard Dreyfuss. American International Pictures, 1973.
"Director/Co-Producer Dan Curtis." *Drama-Logue* 14 Oct. 1993: 10-11.
Dracula. Dir. Dan Curtis. Perf. Jack Palance, Nigel Davenport, Simon Ward, Penelope Horner. Dan Curtis Productions, 1974.
DS Halloween Party. Dir. Joe Integlia. *Vista Theatre DS Events*. JT Video, 2006. DVD.
DuBrow, Rick. "*Winds of War II*: The Saga Continues." *Los Angeles Herald-Examiner* 17 May 1984: 4-F.
Durbano, Art. "This Week's Movies." *TV Guide* 28 July-3 Aug. 1990: 34-35.
Dwyer, Jessica. "*Dark Shadows*: A *Horror Hound* Retrospective." *Horror Hound* March-April 2012: 26-33.
---. "The Man Who Built Collinwood: Dan Curtis." *Horror Hound* March-April 2012: 52-53.
Dyess-Nugent, Phil. "How *Kolchak: The Night Stalker* Developed an Early Model for Television Horror." *A.V. Club*. 14 Feb. 2014. Web. 22 Aug. 2015.
Ebert, Roger. "*House of Dark Shadows*." *Chicago Sun-Times Online*. 6 Oct. 1970. Web. 11 August 2006.
---. "*Night of Dark Shadows*." *Chicago Sun-Times Online*. 21 Sept. 1971. Web. 11 August 2006.
Epstein, Dwayne. "Clint Walker: Larger Than Life!" *Filmfax* no. 150 (December 2017-February 2018): 60-65, 78-79.
Everson, William. *Classics of the Horror Film*. Secaucus: Citadel Press, 1974.
Express to Terror. Dir. Dan Curtis. Prod. Rod Amateau. Perf. Robert Alda, Edward Andrews, Steve Lawrence, Don Meredith. Dan Curtis Enterprises, 1979.
"Featured Filmmaker—Dan Curtis—The Career of the Man Behind *Dark Shadows* and Kolchak." *Film Force*. 8 July 2003. Web. 27 May 2006.
Finney, Jack. "Second Chance." *The Third Level*. New York: Dell, 1959. 153-172.
Florescu, Radu. *In Search of Frankenstein*. Boston: New York Graphic Society, 1975.
Florescu, Radu and Raymond McNally. *Dracula: Prince of Many Faces*. Boston: Little, Brown, and Co., 1989.
Frankenstein. Dir. Glenn Jordan. Prod. Dan Curtis. Perf. Robert Foxworth, Bo Svenson, Susan Strasberg, Heidi Vaughn. Dan Curtis Productions, 1973.
Gendel, Morgan. "ABC at *War* Again with Miniseries, Maxi-Sequel." *Los Angeles Times* 6 Sept. 1986: 10-F.
Gerani, Gary. "The Many Horrors of Dan Curtis." *Weird Tales of the Macabre* vol. 1, no. 1 (Jan. 1975): 24-30.
"Ghoul Show." *Newsweek* 21 Aug. 1967: 60.
Gibron, Bill. "Character over Carnage: Dan Curtis." *Pop Matters*. 3 April 2006. Web. 27 May 2006.
"Giddy Gothic." *TV Guide* 3-9 Dec. 1966: 12-13.
Gifford, Denis. *A Pictorial History of Horror Movies*. London: Hamlyn, 1973.
Glut, Donald J. *Classic Movie Monsters*. Metuchen: Scarecrow, 1978.
---. *The Dracula Book*. Metuchen: Scarecrow, 1975.
Graham, Ed. Email to the author. 26 April 2010.
---. Email to the author. 26 August 2018.
---. Personal interview. 1 August 2018.
Great Ice Rip-Off. Dir. Dan Curtis. Perf. Gig Young, Lee J. Cobb, Grayson Hall, Robert Walden. Dan Curtis Productions & ABC Circle Films, 1974.
Gross, Darren. "Closed Rooms in the *House of Dark Shadows*." *Video Watchdog* no. 40 (1997): 26-31.
---. "*Dark Shadows* Staked!" *Fangoria* no. 239 (Jan. 2005): 62 +.
---. "Illuminating *Night of Dark Shadows*." *Video Watchdog* no. 40 (1997): 32-45.
Gross, Edward. "Dan Curtis." *Dark Shadows Tribute*. Las Vegas: Pioneer Books, 1990.
---. "Dan Curtis: His 'Dream' Started It All." *The Dark Shadows Interviews*. Las Vegas: Schuster & Schuster, 1988.
Hobson, Dorothy. *Soap Opera*. Cambridge: Polity Press, 2003.
Hogan, Ron. *The Stewardess Is Flying the Plane! American Films of the 1970s*. New York: Bullfinch Press, 2005.
Hopkins, Budd. *Intruders: The Incredible Visitations at Copley Woods*. New York: Random House, 1987.
House of Dark Shadows. Dir. Dan Curtis. Perf. Joan Bennett, Jonathan Frid, Grayson Hall, Louis Edmonds. MGM, 1970.
"*House of Dark Shadows* Stresses the Sinister." *New York Times Online*. 29 Oct. 1970. Web. 31 May 2006.
Howard, Douglas, and David Bianculli. *Television Finales: From* Howdy Doody *to* Girls. Jefferson, NC: McFarland, 2018.
Howard, Malia. *Jonathan Frid: An Actor's Curious Journey*. Fort Worth: Howard Books, 2001.

Intruders: They Are Among Us. Dir. Dan Curtis. Prod. Branko Lustig. Perf. Richard Crenna, Mare Winningham, Ben Vereen, Daphne Ashbrook. Osiris Films, CBS Entertainment Productions, and Dan Curtis Productions, 1992.

Invasion of Carol Enders. Dir. Burt Brinckerhoff. Prod. Dan Curtis. Perf. Charles Aidman, Meredith Baxter, Christopher Connelly, John Karlen. Dan Curtis Productions, 1974.

I Think I'm Having a Baby. Dir. Arthur Allan Seidelman. Prod. Joseph Stern. Perf. Jennifer Jason Leigh, David Birney, Shawn Stevens, Helen Hunt. Dan Curtis Associates, 1981.

James, Henry. *The Turn of the Screw.* New York: Dover, 1991.

Jamison, R.J. "*Dark Shadows* Resurrected." *Screem* no. 24 (2012): 2-5.

---. *Grayson Hall: A Hard Act to Follow.* New York: iUniverse, 2006.

Javna, John. *Cult TV.* New York: St. Martin's Press, 1985.

Jenkins, Henry. *Convergence Culture: Where Old and New Media Collide.* New York: New York UP, 2006.

---. *Textual Poachers: Television Fans and Participatory Culture.* New York: Routledge, 1992.

Johnny Ryan. Dir. Robert Collins. Prod. Dan Curtis. Perf. Clancy Brown, Bruce Abbott, Teri Austin, Christine Moore. Dan Curtis Productions & MGM/UA Television & NBC Productions, 1990.

Joslin, Lyndon. *Count Dracula Goes to the Movies: Stoker's Novel Adapted, 1922-1995.* Jefferson, NC: McFarland, 1999.

Just, Ward. "Images of War: How America Re-creates the 'Blood and Darkness.'" *TV Guide* 29 Jan.-4 Feb. 1983: 2-4.

Kane, Tim. *The Changing Vampire of Film and Television: A Critical Study of the Growth of a Genre.* Jefferson, NC: McFarland, 2006.

Kansas City Massacre. Dir. Dan Curtis. Perf. Dale Robertson, Bo Hopkins, John Karlen, Sally Kirkland. Dan Curtis Productions & ABC Circle Films, 1975.

Karol, Michael. *The ABC Movie of the Week: A Loving Tribute to the Classic Series.* New York: iUniverse, 2005.

Katz, Ephraim. *The Film Encyclopedia.* 5th ed. New York: Harper Collins, 2005.

Kawin, Bruce. "Children of the Light." *Film Genre Reader II.* Ed. Barry Keith Grant. Austin: U of Texas Press, 1995. 308-329.

Kennedy, Lisa. "Burton and Depp's *Dark Shadows* Casts Its Comedic Lot amid the Details." *Denver Post* 11 May 2012: 7-A.

Kersey, Nancy, and Helen Samaras, eds. *Remembering Jonathan Frid.* West Hempstead, NY: Evil Twin Publications, 2014.

King, Stephen. *Stephen King's Danse Macabre.* New York: Berkley Books, 1981.

Kirchner, L.R. *Robbing Banks: An American History, 1831-1999.* Edison, NJ: Castle Books, 2003.

Knowles, Christopher. "The Norliss Tapes." *Weekend Matinee* 7 Oct. 2012. Web. 24 Oct. 2012.

Kristeva, Julia. *Powers of Horror: An Essay on Abjection.* New York: Columbia UP, 1982.

Kuttner, Henry. "The Graveyard Rats." *Dying of Fright.* Ed. Les Daniels. New York: Scribner's, 1976. 189-195.

Labbe, Rod. "Directing in the Shadows." *Fangoria* no. 313 (May 2012): 45-46.

---. "From Bruce to Barnabas." *Fangoria* no. 313 (May 2012): 46-47.

Ladnier, Curt. "*Strange Paradise:* Offbeat Supernatural Serial or *Dark Shadows* Clone?" Unpublished manuscript, 2010.

Lampley, Jonathan. *Women in the Horror Films of Vincent Price.* Jefferson, NC: McFarland, 2011.

Lampley, Jonathan; Ken Beck; and Jim Clark. *The Amazing, Colossal Book of Horror Trivia.* Nashville: Cumberland House, 1999.

Last Ride of the Dalton Gang. Dir. Dan Curtis. Perf. Jack Palance, Cliff Potts, Randy Quaid, Larry Wilcox. Dan Curtis Enterprises & NBC Productions, 1979.

LaVoo, George. "*Burnt Offerings* Filmbook." *The Old, Dark House* no. 1 (winter 1976-1977): 4-13.

Lemire, Christy. "Restraint Proves Biggest Enemy of Dillinger Film." *The* [Nashville] *Tennessean* 3 July 2009: 12-D.

Loban, Leila and Richard Valley. "The Pictures of Dorian Gray." *Scarlet Street* no. 41 (2001): 36 +.

---. "The Pictures of Dorian Gray, Part II." *Scarlet Street* no. 42 (2001): 52 +.

---. "The Pictures of Dorian Gray, Part III." *Scarlet Street* no. 43 (2001): 48 +.

Logan, Michael. "*Children* on the Move." *TV Guide* (24-Aug.-6 Sept. 2009): 78.

---. "Vamp Camp." *TV Guide* 7-20 May 2012: 42-43.

Long Days of Summer. Dir. Dan Curtis. Perf. Dean Jones, Joan Hackett, Ronnie Scribner, Louanne. Dan Curtis Associates, 1980.

Love Letter. **Dir. Dan Curtis. Perf. Campbell Scott, Jennifer Jason Leigh, David Dukes, Estelle Parsons. Hallmark Hall of Fame Productions, 1998.**
Lucas, Tim. "*Dracula.*" *Video Watchdog* no. 15 (Jan.-Feb. 1993): 11-12.
---. "*House of Dark Shadows* and *Night of Dark Shadows.*" *Video Watchdog* no. 22 (March-April 1994): 65-67.
MacAndrew, Elizabeth. *The Gothic Tradition in Fiction.* New York: Columbia UP, 1970.
MacGraw Ali. *Moving Pictures.* New York: Bantam Books, 1991.
MacKenzie, Robert. "Review: *The Winds of War.*" TV Guide 29 Jan.-4 Feb. 1983: 15.
Making of War and Remembrance. Dir. Donald Beck. *War and Remembrance: The Final Chapter, Parts V-VII.* MPI Home Video, 2003. DVD.
Making The Winds of War. Dir. Donald Beck. *The Winds of War, Part V.* Paramount DVD, 2004. DVD.
Maltin, Leonard, ed. *Leonard Maltin's 2010 Movie Guide.* New York: Plume, 2009.
Manning, Stuart. "Remembering Dan Curtis." *Dark Shadows Journal.* 28 March 2006. Web. 20 May 2006.
Marano, Michael. "Family Values." *Sci-Fi* June 2012: 36-39.
Marasco, Robert. *Burnt Offerings.* New York: Delacorte Press, 1973.
Marill, Alvin. *Movies Made for Television 1964-1979.* Westport, CT: Arlington House, 1980.
---. *Movies Made for Television 1964-1984.* New York: New York Zoetrope, 1984.
---. *Movies Made for Television 1964-2004.* 5 vols. Lanham, MD: Scarecrow Press, 2005.
Markovitz, Adam. "Johnny Depp, Tim Burton on Board for *Dark Shadows.*" *EW.com.* 25 June 2009. Web. 26 June 2009.
Master of Dark Shadows. Dir. David Gregory. Prod. Jim Pierson. Perf. Ian McShane. MPI Media Group, Severin Films, & Dan Curtis Productions, 2019.
Matheson, Richard. DVD interview. *Richard Matheson: Terror Scribe.* Dir. David Gregory. *Trilogy of Terror.* Dark Sky Films, 2006. DVD.
---. *I Am Legend.* Garden City, NY: Nelson Doubleday, 1954.
---. *Journal of the Gun Years.* New York: Berkley Books, 1992.
---. "The Likeness of Julie." *Shock II.* New York: Dell, 1964. 79-90.
---. "Needle in the Heart," a.k.a. "Therese." *Shock Waves.* New York: Dell, 1970. 109-111.
---. "No Such Thing as a Vampire." *Shock II.* New York: Dell, 1964. 27-38.
---. "Prey." *Shock Waves.* New York: Dell, 1970. 119-131.
---. *Shock!* New York: Dell, 1961.
---. *Shock III.* New York: Dell, 1966.
McCarty, Michael. "Dan Curtis Continues to Thrive in the *Dark Shadows.*" *Sci-Fi.* 2002. Web. 14 June 2006.
---. "William F. Nolan Looks Back at the Legacy of *Logan's Run* and Looks Forward to Bryan Singer's Remake." *Sci-Fi.* 2005. Web. 21 July 2006.
McKenna, Michael. *The ABC Movie of the Week: Big Movies for the Small Screen.* Lanham, MD: Scarecrow Press, 2013.
McNally, Raymond and Radu Florescu. *In Search of Dracula.* New ed. Boston: Houghton Mifflin, 1994.
McNeil, Alex. *Total Television.* 4th ed. New York: Penguin Books, 1996.
Me and the Kid. **Dir. Dan Curtis. Perf. Danny Aiello, Alex Zuckerman, Cathy Moriarty, David Dukes. Dan Curtis Productions, 1993.**
Meikle, Denis. *A History of Horrors: The Rise and Fall of the House of Hammer.* Lanham, MD: Scarecrow Press, 1996.
Melton, J. Gordon. *The Vampire Book: The Encyclopedia of the Undead.* Detroit: Visible Ink Press, 1994.
---. *The Vampire Book: The Encyclopedia of the Undead.* 2nd ed. Detroit: Visible Ink Press, 1999.
---. *Vampires on Video.* Detroit: Visible Ink Press, 1997.
Melvin Purvis, G-Man. **Dir. Dan Curtis. Perf. Dale Robertson, Harris Yulin, John Karlen, Steve Kanaly. American International & Dan Curtis Productions, 1974.**
Meyer, Moe, ed. *The Politics and Poetics of Camp.* New York: Routledge, 1994.
Modleski, Tania. *Loving with a Vengeance.* Hamden, CT: Archon Books, 1982.
"Monster Revival." *Newsweek* 7 Jan. 1991: 58-59.
Mrs. R's Daughter. **Dir. Dan Curtis. Perf. Cloris Leachman, Season Hubley, Donald Moffat, Stephen Elliott. Dan Curtis Enterprises & NBC Productions, 1979.**
Muir, John Kenneth. *Horror Films of the 1970s.* 2 vols. Jefferson, NC: McFarland, 2002.
---. *Terror Television: American Series, 1970-1999.* 2 vols. Jefferson, NC: McFarland, 2001.
Mulvey, Laura. *Fetishism and Curiosity.* Bloomington: Indiana UP, 1996.
---. *Visual and Other Pleasures.* Bloomington: Indiana UP, 1989.

---. "Visual Pleasure and Narrative Cinema." *Norton Anthology of Theory and Criticism.* Ed. Vincent Leitch. New York: W.W. Norton, 2001. 2181-2192.

Nahmod, David-Elijah. "Ladies of the Shadows." *Famous Monsters of Filmland* no. 261 (May-June 2012): 56-61.

Nance, Scott. *Bloodsuckers: Vampires at the Movies.* Las Vegas: Pioneer Books, 1992.

Newman, Kim. Foreword. *The Vampire Archives: The Most Complete Volume of Vampire Tales Ever Published.* Ed. Otto Penzler. New York: Vintage Books, 2009. xi-xiv.

Nightmare at 43 Hillcrest. Dir. Lela Swift. Prod. Dan Curtis. Perf. Peter Mark Richman, Jim Hutton, Mariette Hartley, John Karlen. Dan Curtis Productions, 1974.

Night of Dark Shadows. Dir. Dan Curtis. Perf. David Selby, Kate Jackson, John Karlen, Grayson Hall. MGM, 1971.

Night Stalker. Dir. John Llewellyn Moxey. Prod. Dan Curtis. Perf. Darren McGavin, Simon Oakland, Carol Lynley, Barry Atwater. ABC Circle Films, 1972.

Night Strangler. Dir. Dan Curtis. Prod. Dan Curtis. Perf. Darren McGavin, Simon Oakland, Jo Ann Pflug, Richard Anderson. ABC Circle Films, 1973.

Nolan, William F. *Impact 20.* New York: Paperback Library, 1963.

---. Letter to the author. 17. Jan. 2010.

---. *Logan's Search.* New York: Bantam Books, 1980.

---. *Logan's World.* New York: Bantam Books, 1977.

---. Personal interview. 28 Feb. 2010.

---. Unpublished *Turn of the Screw* script for Dan Curtis Productions. 1973.

Nolan, William F. and George Clayton Johnson. *Logan's Run.* New York: Dial Press, 1967.

Norliss Tapes. Dir. Dan Curtis. Perf. Roy Thinnes, Don Porter, Angie Dickinson, Nick Dimitri. Dan Curtis Productions & Metromedia, 1973.

Novel for Television. Dir. Donald Beck. *The Winds of War, Part V.* Paramount DVD, 2004. DVD.

O'Flinn, Paul. "Production and Reproduction: The Case of *Frankenstein.*" *The Horror Reader.* Ed. Ken Gelder. London: Routledge, 2000. 114-127.

O'Hallaren, Bill. "He's the Only Gary Cooper Still Alive." *TV Guide* 29 Jan.-4 Feb. 1983: 8-11.

O'Neil, Thomas. *The Emmys.* 3rd ed. New York: Berkley, 1998.

On Location. Dir. Donald Beck. *The Winds of War, Part V.* Paramount DVD, 2004. DVD.

Our Fathers. Dir. Dan Curtis. Perf. Ted Danson, Christopher Plummer, Brian Dennehy, Ellen Burstyn. Dan Curtis Productions, Peach Arch Entertainment Group, and Showtime, 2005.

Palance, Jack. DVD interview. Prod. Jim Pierson. *The Dan Curtis Macabre Collection.* MPI Home Video, 2002. DVD.

Panitt, Merrill. "Review: *War and Remembrance.*" *TV Guide* 12-18 Nov. 1988: 40.

Parks, Tim. "Burton: *Dark Shadows* Will Be a Challenge." *Digital Spy.* 22 July 2009. Web. 26 July 2009.

Pattison, Barrie. *The Seal of Dracula.* New York: Bounty Books, 1975.

Peer, Kurt. *TV Tie-Ins: A Bibliography of American TV Tie-In Paperbacks.* Tucson, AZ: Neptune Publishing, 1997.

Picture of Dorian Gray. Dir. Glenn Jordan. Prod. Dan Curtis. Perf. Shane Briant, Nigel Davenport, Charles Aidman, Linda Kelsey. Dan Curtis Productions, 1973.

Pierson, Jim. "The Blood Lust Goes Way Back." *Los Angeles Time On-Line.* 14 June 2009. Web. 19 June 2009.

---. *Dark Shadows Festival Memory Book 1983-1993.* Maplewood, NJ: Dark Shadows Festival, 1994.

---. *Dark Shadows Resurrected.* Los Angeles: Pomegranate Press, 1992.

---. Email to the author. 30 July 2006.

---. Email to the author. 22 Oct. 2007.

---. Email to the author. 27 June 2008.

---. Email to the author. 7 May 2009.

---. Email to the author. 20 June 2009.

---. Email to the author. 12 July 2009.

---. Email to the author. 25 July 2009.

---. Email to the author. 23 August 2009.

---. Email to the author. 13 Sept. 2009.

---. Email to the author. 12 Nov. 2009.

---. Email to the author. 16 July 2015.

---. Email to the author. 30 July 2015.

---. Email to the author. 4 Aug. 2015.

---. Email to the author. 7 Sept. 2015.

---. Email to the author. 27 Nov. 2017.
---. Email to the author. 19 March 2018.
---. Email to the author. 1 Aug. 2018.
---. Email to the author. 20 Aug. 2018.
---. Email to the author. 15 Aug. 2019.
---. Liner notes. *Dark Shadows: The 30th Anniversary Collection*. Composed by Robert Cobert. Varese Sarabande, 1996. CD.
---. Liner notes. *House of Dark Shadows and Night of Dark Shadows*. Composed and conducted by Robert Cobert. Turner Classic Movies Music, 1996. CD.
---. Personal interview. 24 July 2018.
---. *Produced and Directed by Dan Curtis*. Los Angeles: Pomegranate Press, 2004.
Pilato, Herbie J. *Dashing, Daring, and Debonair: TV's Top Male Icons from the 50s, 60s, and 70s*. Lanham, MD: Taylor Trade Publishing, 2016.
Pinedo, Isabel. "Recreational Terror: Postmodern Elements of the Contemporary Horror Film." *Journal of Film and Video*, vol. 48, no 1/2 (spring-summer 1996): 17-31.
---. *Recreational Terror: Women and the Pleasure of Horror-Film Viewing*. Albany: State U of NY Press, 1997.
Public Enemies. Dir. Michael Mann. Perf. Christian Bale, Johnny Depp, Marion Cotillard, Billy Crudup. Universal, 2009.
Purvis, Alston and Alex Tresniowski. *The Vendetta: Special Agent Melvin Purvis, John Dillinger, and Hoover's FBI in the Age of Gangsters*. New York: Public Affairs, 2005.
Ramsland, Katherine. *Prism of the Night: A Biography of Anne Rice*. 2nd ed. New York: Plume, 1994.
Rathbun, Mark and Graeme Flanagan. *Richard Matheson: He Is Legend*. Chico, CA: Rio Lindo, 1984.
Raw, Laurence. *Adapting Henry James to the Screen: Gender, Fiction, and Film*. Lanham, MD: Scarecrow, 2006.
Real Untouchables: Melvin Purvis. Prod. Anthony Geffen. Dir. James Fothergill. Atlantic Productions, 2001. Videocassette.
Redgrave, Lynn. DVD interview. Prod. Jim Pierson. *The Dan Curtis Macabre Collection*. MPI Home Video, 2002. DVD.
"Reel World." *Enigma* 10 May 2012: 16.
Resch, Kathleen, and Marcy Robin. *Dark Shadows in the Afternoon*. New York: Image Publishing, 1991.
Rice, Jeff. *The Night Stalker*. New York: Pocket Books, 1973.
---. *The Night Strangler*. New York: Pocket Books, 1974.
Robin, Marcy, ed. "Dan Curtis News." *Shadowgram* no. 41 (Feb. 1988): 5.
---. "Dan Curtis News." *Shadowgram* no. 46 (April 1989): 9.
---. "Dan Curtis News." *Shadowgram* no. 47 (August 1989): 7.
---. "Dan Curtis News." Shadowgram no. 54/55 (Jan. 1991): 2.
---. "Dan Curtis News." *Shadowgram* no. 61 (August 1992): 15.
---. "Dan Curtis News." *Shadowgram* no. 67 (Jan. 1994): 15.
---. "Dan Curtis News." *Shadowgram* no. 78 (Feb. 1997): 10-11.
---. "Dan Curtis News." *Shadowgram* no. 79 (May 1997): 9.
---. "Dan Curtis News." *Shadowgram* no. 81 (Nov. 1997): 11.
---. "Dan Curtis News." *Shadowgram* no. 82 (Feb. 1998): 10.
---. "Dan Curtis News." *Shadowgram* no. 87 (Nov. 1999): 10.
---. "Dan Curtis News." *Shadowgram* no. 94 (Nov. 2001): 10.
---. "Dan Curtis News." *Shadowgram* no. 96 (June 2002): 9.
---. "Dan Curtis News." *Shadowgram* no. 97 (Oct. 2002): 10.
---. "Dan Curtis News." *Shadowgram* no. 104 (April 2005): 11.
---. "Dan Curtis News." *Shadowgram* no. 106 (Oct. 2005): 8-9.
---. "Dan Curtis News." *Shadowgram* no. 107 (April 2006): 12-13, 22-23.
---. "Dan Curtis News." *Shadowgram* no. 108 (June 2006): 8-10.
---. "*Dark Shadows* News." *Shadowgram* no. 54/55 (Jan. 1991): 15-16.
---. "*Dark Shadows*: the 2012 Movie." *Shadowgram* no. 122/123 (Jan. 2014): 7-10.
---. "Robert Cobert News." *Shadowgram* no. 49 (Jan. 1990): 9.
Robinson, Bruce. *They All Love Jack: Busting the Ripper*. London: Fourth Estate, 2015.
Ross, Marilyn. *Barnabas, Quentin, and the Mummy's Curse*. New York: Paperback Library, 1970.
Rossen, Jake. "14 *Dark Shadows* Facts with Bite." *Mental Floss*. 15 Oct. 2015. Web. 17 Oct. 2015.

Samaras, Helen, ed. *Fangs for the Memories: Memoirs of Dark Shadows Fans and Cast Members*. West Hempstead, NY: Evil Twin Publishing, 1996.

Saving Milly. **Dir. Dan Curtis. Perf. Madeleine Stowe, Bruce Greenwood, Robert Wisden, Claudia Ferri. 2 Dans Productions, 2005.**

Schow, David and Jeffrey Frentzen. *The Outer Limits: The Official Companion*. New York: Ace Science-Fiction Books, 1986.

Scott, Kathryn Leigh. *The Dark Shadows Companion*. Los Angeles: Pomegranate Press, 1990.

---. *Dark Shadows Memories*. Los Angeles: Pomegranate Press, 2001.

---. Letter to the author. 15 June 2006.

---. *My Scrapbook Memories of Dark Shadows*. Los Angeles: Pomegranate Press, 1986.

Scott, Kathryn Leigh and Jim Pierson, eds. *Dark Shadows Almanac*. Los Angeles: Pomegranate Press, 1995.

---. *Dark Shadows Almanac*. Millennium ed. Los Angeles: Pomegranate Press, 2000.

---. *Dark Shadows Movie Book*. Los Angeles: Pomegranate Press, 1998.

---. *Dark Shadows: Return to Collinwood*. Los Angeles: Pomegranate Press, 2012.

Scott, Lesley. "The Vamp in the Mirror: How Popular Culture's Obsession with the Undead Reveals What We're Really Afraid Of." *Stitch* vol. 1, no. 4 (Dec. 2003): 104-109.

Scream of the Wolf. **Dir. Dan Curtis. Perf. Peter Graves, Clint Walker, Jo Ann Pflug, Philip Carey. Dan Curtis Productions & Metromedia, 1974.**

"Screening Room." *TV Guide* 5-11 Feb. 1983: A-3.

Selby, David. *In and Out of the Shadows*. New York: Locust Grove Press, 1999.

Seymore, James. "Rough, Tough, and Rowdy: Robert Mitchum." *People Weekly* (14 Feb. 1983): 72 +.

Shadow of Fear. **Dir. Herbert Kenwith. Prod. Dan Curtis. Perf. Claude Akins, Anjanatte Comer, Jason Evers, Philip Carey. Dan Curtis Productions, 1974.**

Shelley, Mary. *Frankenstein, or The Modern Prometheus*. London: Penguin, 1992.

Shinnick, Kevin. "Come Back, Shane Briant." *Scarlet Street* no. 42 (2001): 46 +.

"Ship of Ghouls." *Time* 20 Aug. 1968: 66.

Showalter, Elaine. "Dr. Jekyll's Closet." *The Horror Reader*. Ed. Ken Gelder. London: Routledge, 2000. 190-197.

Silver, Alain and James Ursini. *The Vampire Film*. 2nd ed. New York: Limelight Editions, 1993.

Simpson, Robert. "Collinwood Calling: The Life of *Dark Shadows*." *Diabolique* no. 11 (July-August 2012): 20-27.

Skal, David. *The Monster Show: A Cultural History of Horror*. 2nd ed. New York: Faber and Faber, 2001.

Smith, Robert Barr. *Daltons! The Raid on Coffeyville, Kansas*. Norman, OK: Oklahoma UP, 1996.

Sontag, Susan. "Notes on Camp." *A Susan Sontag Reader*. New York: Vintage Books, 1983. 105-120.

Sosnowski, Matthew. "Stevenson and Curtis: Masters of the Macabre." Paper. U of Hartford, 2011.

Sragow, Michael. "Depp Unleashes Inner Outlaw in *Public Enemies*." *Baltimore Sun* (on-line). 30 June 2009. Web. 2 July 2009.

Stern, Joseph. Personal interview. 1 August 2018.

Stevenson, Robert Louis. *The Strange Case of Dr. Jekyll and Mr. Hyde*. New York: Books, Inc., n.d.

Stewart, Susan. "Hits and Misses." *TV Guide* 13-19 March 2005: 57.

Stewart, Zan. "Bob Cobert Scores His Own Victory in *War and Remembrance*." Rpt. In *Shadowgram* no. 45 (Jan. 1989): 13.

St. John in Exile. **Dir. Dan Curtis. Perf. Dean Jones. DJ Productions, 1986.**

Stoker, Bram. *Dracula*. New York: Signet Classic, 1992.

Stone, Jay. "*Dark Shadows* Stylish But Tedious." *The* [St. John, New Brunswick] *Telegraph-Journal* 11 May 2012: D-1—D-2.

Storm, James. Email to the author. 8 August 2019.

Strange Case of Dr. Jekyll and Mr. Hyde. **Dir. Charles Jarrott. Prod. Dan Curtis. Perf. Jack Palance, Denholm Elliott, Billie Whitelaw, Tessie O'Shea. Dan Curtis Productions & CBC-TV, 1968.**

"Sunday Previews." *TV Guide* 12-18 Nov. 1988: A-45.

Supertrain. **Dir. Dan Curtis, Rod Amateau, et al. Perf. Edward Andrews, Robert Alda, Steve Lawrence, Don Meredith. NBC-TV, 1979.**

Swaim-Robb, Connie. "Vampires Becoming More Romantic Through the Years." *Antique Week* vol. 44, no. 2256 (29 Oct. 2012): 1, 25.

"Terror on TV: 1969-1983." *The Terror Trap*. 1998. Web. 22 July 2006.

"Thayer David Quotes." *Brainy Quotes*. 2006. Web. 14 June 2006.

Thomas, Kevin. "Familiar Look to *Shadows* Sequel." *Los Angeles Times* (1971). Web.

Thompson, Jeff. "Barnabas, Quentin, and the Prolific Author: The *Dark Shadows* Novels of Dan 'Marilyn' Ross." *Paperback Parade* no. 43 (August 1995): 80-91.

---. "Breathing Down Our Necks: The 1970 Leviathan Storyline." *The Music Box* no. 9 (summer 1993): 21-23.

---. "*Burnt Offerings.*" *Movie Club* no. 12 (autumn 1997): 14-15.

---. "*Burnt Offerings.*" Presentation at TPA academic conference. Columbia, TN, 6 Feb. 2004.

---. "*Burnt Offerings.*" *You're Next! Loss of Identity in the Horror Film.* Ed. Anthony Ambrogio. Baltimore: Midnight Marquee Press, 2008.

---. "Dark Dreamer: Dan Curtis and Television Horror." Diss. Middle Tennessee State U, 2007.

---. *Dark Shadows Comic Books.* Los Angeles: Joseph Collins Publications, 1988.

---. "*Dark Shadows* Episode 1,245." *Television Finales: From Howdy Doody to Girls.* Eds. Douglas Howard and David Bianculli. Syracuse: Syracuse UP, 2018. 78-83.

---. "*Dark Shadows* Fandom, Then and Now (1966-2013)." *Fan Culture: Essays on Participatory Fandom in the 21st Century.* Eds. Kristin M. Barton and Jonathan M. Lampley. Jefferson, NC: McFarland, 2014.

---. "*Dark Shadows* in the 1970s: Best Episodes." *Shadows of the Night.* 20 Jan. 2006. Web. 20 July 2006.

---. *The Dark Shadows Memorabilia Slide Show.* Slide program. 1985-1992.

---. "*Death at Love House.*" *You're Next! Loss of Identity in the Horror Film.* Ed. Anthony Ambrogio. Baltimore: Midnight Marquee Press, 2008.

---. "*Die! Die! My Darling!*" *Midnight Marquee* no. 57 (summer 1998): 13.

---. "Effective Use of Actual Persons and Events in the Historical Novels of Dan Ross." Thesis. Tennessee State U, 1991.

---. "Films of Barbara Steele." *Movie Club* no. 7 (summer 1996): 40-41.

---. "Four-Color Shadows: The *Dark Shadows* Comic Books and Newspaper Comic Strip." Part 1. *Southern Fandom Update* no. 6 (June 2009): 9-15. Web. 10 June 2009.

---. "Four-Color Shadows: The *Dark Shadows* Comic Books and Newspaper Comic Strip." Part 2. *Southern Fandom Update* no. 8 (August 2009): 7-13. Web. 1 August 2009.

---. "Four-Colour Shadows: The Gold Key Comics." *Dark Shadows Journal.* 19 March 2006. Web. 20 March 2006.

---. "Gold Key *Dark Shadows* Comic Books." Presentation at PCAS popular-culture conference. New Orleans, 8 Oct. 2004.

---. "History of the East Coast Dark Shadows Festivals, 1983-1993." *Dark Shadows Festival Memory Book, 1983-1993.* Ed. Jim Pierson. Maplewood, NJ: Dark Shadows Festival,1994. 93-99.

---. *House of Dan Curtis: The Television Mysteries of the Dark Shadows Auteur.* 1st ed. Nashville: Westview, 2010.

---. "*House of Dark Shadows.*" *You're Next! Loss of Identity in the Horror Film.* Ed. Anthony Ambrogio. Baltimore: Midnight Marquee Press, 2008.

---. "In Memoriam: Dan Curtis." *Scoop.* 2002. Web. 31 March 2006.

---. "Introduction: *Dark Shadows*: A Final Look at the Comics." *Dark Shadows: The Complete Original Series.* Vol. 5. Ed Daniel Herman. Neshannock, PA: Hermes Press, 2012.

---. "Introduction: *Dark Shadows*: A Look at the Comics." *Dark Shadows: The Complete Original Series.* Vol. 2. Ed Daniel Herman. Neshannock, PA: Hermes Press, 2011.

---. "Introduction: *Dark Shadows*: A Look at the Comics." *Dark Shadows: The Complete Original Series.* Vol. 3. Ed Daniel Herman. Neshannock, PA: Hermes Press, 2011.

---. "Introduction: *Dark Shadows*: A Look at the Comics." *Dark Shadows: The Complete Original Series.* Vol. 4. Ed Daniel Herman. Neshannock, PA: Hermes Press, 2012.

---. "Introduction: *Dark Shadows* and the Comics." *Dark Shadows: The Complete Original Series.* Vol. 1. Ed Daniel Herman. Neshannock, PA: Hermes Press, 2010.

---. "Introduction: The Best of *Dark Shadows.*" *Dark Shadows: The Best of the Original Series.* Ed Daniel Herman. Neshannock, PA: Hermes Press, 2011.

---. "Introduction: The *Dark Shadows* Newspaper Strip." *Dark Shadows: The Complete Newspaper Strips.* Neshannock, PA: Hermes Press, 2018.

---. "Introduction: *Dark Shadows*: The Story Digest." *Dark Shadows: The Original Series Story Digest.* Ed Daniel Herman. Neshannock, PA: Hermes Press, 2011.

---. "*Intruders*, Directed by Dan Curtis: Alien Abduction as Family Drama." Presentation atPCAS popular-culture conference. New Orleans, 7 Oct. 2011.

---. "Life from a Coffin: How *Dark Shadows* Has Affected My Life." *Fangs for the Memories: Memoirs of Dark Shadows Fans and Cast Members.* Ed. Helen Samaras. West Hempstead, NY: Evil Twin Publishing, 1996. 61-64.

---. Liner notes. *Burnt Offerings.* Composed by Robert Cobert. Counterpoint, 2011. CD.
---. Liner notes. *Dracula.* Composed by Robert Cobert. Varese Sarabande, 2014. CD.
---. "Matinee." *Science-Fiction Invasions.* Ed. Don Dohler. Baltimore: Movie Club, 1998. 29-30.
---. "Mary Shelley's *Frankenstein* at 200 and Dan Curtis's *Frankenstein* at 45." Presentation at TPA academic conference. Cookeville, TN, 23 Feb. 2018.
---. "Mary Shelley's *Frankenstein* at 200 and Dan Curtis's *Frankenstein* at 45." Presentation at PCAS popular-culture conference. New Orleans, 5 Oct. 2018.
---. "Melvin Purvis, G-Man: Fact and Fiction." Presentation at PCAS popular-culture conference. Savannah, GA, Oct. 2010.
---. "Melvin Purvis, G-Man: Fact and Fiction." Presentation at TPA academic conference. Nashville, 22 Feb. 2014.
---. "Night of Dark Shadows." *You're Next! Loss of Identity in the Horror Film.* Ed. Anthony Ambrogio. Baltimore: Midnight Marquee Press, 2008.
---. *Nights of Dan Curtis: The Television Epics of the* Dark Shadows *Auteur.* 1st ed. Nashville: Ideas, 2016.
---. *Nights of Dan Curtis: The Television Epics of the* Dark Shadows *Auteur.* 2nd ed. Nashville: Ideas, 2019.
---. "Overview of *Dark Shadows* Fandom." *Southern Fandom Bulletin* no. 8 (January 1991): 18-21.
---. "Soap and Sorcery: Lara Parker." *Femme Fatales* vol. 4, no. 1 (summer 1995): 28-31 ff.
---. "*Somewhere* in Class." *INSITE* vol. 25, no. 3 (mid-2014): 12-14.
---. "The Strange Possession of Mrs. Oliver." *You're Next! Loss of Identity in the Horror Film.* Ed. Anthony Ambrogio. Baltimore: Midnight Marquee Press, 2008.
---. *Television Horrors of Dan Curtis:* Dark Shadows, The Night Stalker, *and Other Productions, 1966-2006.* 1st ed. Jefferson, NC: McFarland, 2009.
---. *Television Horrors of Dan Curtis:* Dark Shadows, The Night Stalker, *and Other Productions, 1966-2006.* 2nd ed. Jefferson, NC: McFarland, 2019.
---. "Timeless Loves: *Titanic* and *Somewhere in Time.*" *Scarlet Street* no. 28 (mid-1998): 29-31.
---. "*Trilogy of Terror.*" *You're Next! Loss of Identity in the Horror Film.* Ed. Anthony Ambrogio. Baltimore: Midnight Marquee Press, 2008.
---. "*Trilogy of Terror II.*" *You're Next! Loss of Identity in the Horror Film.* Ed. Anthony Ambrogio. Baltimore: Midnight Marquee Press, 2008.
---. "Visit with Marilyn and Dan Ross." *Dark Shadows Lives!* Ed. James Van Hise. Las Vegas: Schuster & Schuster, 1988. 57-67.
---. "*War and Remembrance*: A Miniseries to Remember." *Lone Star Shadows* vol. 2, no. 7/8 (summer/fall 1989): 8.
---. "Warm Acquaintance." *Remembering Jonathan Frid.* Eds. Nancy Kersey and Helen Samaras. West Hempstead, NY: Evil Twin Publications, 2014.
---. "Winds of War." *The World of Dark Shadows* no. 36 (Dec. 1983): 52-53.
Thomson, David. *The Moment of* Psycho: *How Alfred Hitchcock Taught America to Love Murder.* New York: Basic Books, 2009.
Toland, John. *Adolf Hitler.* New York: Doubleday & Company, 1976.
Trilogy of Terror. Dir. Dan Curtis. Perf. Karen Black, Robert Burton, John Karlen, George Gaynes. Dan Curtis Productions & ABC Circle Films, 1975.
Trilogy of Terror II. Dir. Dan Curtis. Perf. Lysette Anthony, Geraint Wyn Davies, Matt Clark, Geoffrey Lewis. Dan Curtis, Power Pictures, and Wilshire Court Productions, 1996.
"Tuesday Previews." *TV Guide* (19-25 Nov. 1988): A-91.
Tulloch, John, and Henry Jenkins. *Science-Fiction Audiences: Watching* Doctor Who *and* Star Trek. London: Routledge, 1995.
Turan, Kenneth. "The Fallen Star Battles Back." *TV Guide* 29 Jan.-4 Feb. 1983: 12-14.
"Turned-On Vampire." *Newsweek* 20 April 1970: 102-103.
Turn of the Screw. Dir. Dan Curtis. Perf. Lynn Redgrave, Megs Jenkins, Jasper Jacob, Eva Griffith. Dan Curtis Productions, 1974.
"TV Terror: Dan Curtis." *The Terror Trap.* 1998. Web. 27 May 2006.
"Vampire, Thirsty and Bewildered." *New York Times* 10 May 2012. Web. 10 May 2012.
Wallace, Marie. *On Stage and in Shadows.* New York: iUniverse, 2005.
Waller, Gregory. "Introduction to *American Horrors.*" *The Horror Reader.* Ed. Ken Gelder. London: Routledge, 2000. 256-264.
War and Remembrance. Dir. Dan Curtis. Perf. Robert Mitchum, Polly Bergen, Hart Bochner, Jane Seymour. Dan Curtis Productions & ABC Circle Films, 1988, 1989.

War and Remembrance: Behind the Scenes. Exec. Prod. Jim Pierson. *War and Remembrance: The Final Chapter, Parts XI-XII.* MPI Home Video, 2003. DVD.

Warren, Elaine. "Replacements Rushed to the Front Lines." *TV Guide* 12-18 Nov. 1988: 33-38.

Waters, Harry. "New Sins in Soapland." *Newsweek* 9 Dec. 1968: 100-104.

Weiler, A.H. "*Night of Dark Shadows* Arrives." *New York Times Online.* 14 Oct. 1971. Web. 31 May 2006.

Wells, Paul. *The Horror Genre: From Beelzebub to Blair Witch.* London: Wallflower, 2000.

"What a Doll!" *TV Guide* (1 March 1975): 12-13.

Wheatley, Helen. *Gothic Television.* Manchester: Manchester UP, 2006.

***When Every Day Was the Fourth of July.* Dir. Dan Curtis. Perf. Dean Jones, Louise Sorel, Chris Peterson, Katy Kurtzman. Dan Curtis Productions, 1978.**

Wiater, Stanley; Matthew Bradley; and Paul Stuve, eds. *The Richard Matheson Companion.* Colorado Springs: Gauntlet Press, 2008.

---, eds. *The Twilight and Other Zones: The Dark Moods of Richard Matheson.* New York: Citadel Press, 2009.

Wilcox, Larry. Email to the author. 28 Sept. 2015.

---. Email to the author. 2 Nov. 2015.

---. Email to the author. 6 Feb. 2016.

---. Email to the author. 31 July 2018.

Wilde, Oscar. *The Picture of Dorian Gray.* New York: Modern Library, 2004.

Williams, Linda. "When the Woman Looks." *Re-Vision: Essays in Feminist Film Criticism.* Eds. Mary Anne Doane, Patricia Mellencamp, and Linda Williams. Frederick, MD: American Film Institute Monograph Series, University Publications of America, 1984. 83-99.

Wilson, Edmund. "The Ambiguity of Henry James." *Hound and Horn* VII (April-June 1934): 385-406.

Windolf, Jim. "The Young and the Lifeless." *Vanity Fair* April 2012: 156-157.

***Winds of War.* Dir. Dan Curtis. Perf. Robert Mitchum, Polly Bergen, Jan-Michael Vincent, Ali McGraw. Dan Curtis Productions & Paramount Television, 1983.**

Winkle, Michael. "The Measure of Success." *Geocities.* 1999. Web. 21 July 2006.

Wolcott, James. "The Undead Don't Like to Leave Anything Undone." *Vanity Fair.* 24 Oct. 2012. Web. 24 Oct. 2012.

Wolf, Leonard, ed. *The Essential Dracula.* 3rd ed. New York: iBooks, 2004.

Wood, Robin. "The American Nightmare: Horror in the 1970s." *Horror, the Film Reader.* Ed. Mark Jancovich. London: Routledge, 2002. 25-32.

---. *Hollywood: From Vietnam to Reagan.* New York: Columbia UP, 1986.

Wouk, Herman. *War and Remembrance.* Boston: Little, Brown, and Co., 1978.

---. *The Winds of War.* Boston: Little, Brown, and Co., 1971.

Zacharek, Stephanie. "*Public Enemies.*" *Salon Arts & Entertainment.* 1 July 2009. Web. 2 July 2009.

Zahl, Paul. "A Sad but Important Week." *Trinity Episcopal School for Ministry.* 3 April 2006. Web. 21 July 2006.

Zaiman, Farihah. "How *Dark Shadows* Brought the Supernatural to Television Drama." *A.V. Club.* 31 Oct. 2012. Web. 22 Aug. 2015.

Zicree, Marc Scott. *The Twilight Zone Companion.* New York: Bantam Books, 1982. Print.

Index

A&E 96
Aames, Willie 162
ABC (American Broadcasting Company) 5, 6, 7, 8, 11, 12, 13, 16, 23, 35, 37, 38, 41, 46, 47, 49, 50, 55, 57, 62, 66, 69, 74, 77, 106, 107, 110, 111, 112, 115, 117, 118, 120, 121, 130, 131, 132, 136, 147, 148, 150, 151, 152, 155, 156, 159, 163, 164, 166, 172, 177, 180, 182, 185, 188, 190, 191, 192, 193, 203
ABC Movie of the Week 47, 68, 151, 182
Abbott, Maggie 108
Abbott, Bruce **153**, 154
Academy Awards 40, 45, 46, 62, 94, 96, 99, 106, 108, 113, 144
Ace-High Western Stories 99-100
Achard, Laurent 192
Adam-12 156
Addie Pray 188
Adventures in Paradise 22
Adventures of Ozzie and Harriet 168
Adventures of Robin Hood 43
Against the Mob 152
Aiello, Danny 84, **85**
Aiello, Rick 84
Aidman, Charles 134, 137, 165, 170, 195
AIP (American International Pictures) 129-130, 131
Akins, Claude 53, 55, 168
Albert, Eddie 115
Alda, Robert 186
Alexander, Geoffrey 44
ALF 177
Alias 128
Alice in Wonderland 35
Alien Lover 159
Allen, Woody 132
All My Children 22, 147
All of Me 128
Allyson, June 62, 64, 66
Altman, Robert 132
Alzheimer's Association PSA 10, 16, 145
Amadeus 45

Ambrogio, Anthony 8
"Amelia" 9, 57-58, **59**, 67
American Cinema Editors 120
American Gangster 115
American Society of Cinematographers 120, 126
Ancier, Garth 30
"And a Cup of Kindness, Too" 186, **187**
Anderson, Barbara 47
Anderson, Judith 47
Anderson, Richard 50
Angel for Satan 108
Angie the Lieutenant 6, 10, 16, 96, 154-**155**, 156-157
Ann-Margret 111
Another World 13, 148
Anthony, Lysette 26, 66, **67**, 68
Anthony, Ray 119
Anti-Defamation League 111
Antwerp Film Festival 83
AP (Associated Press) 117, 120
Apted, Michael 122
Arch, Jeff 141-142
Argento, Dario 30, 37
Argo, Victor 152
Arizona Republic 127
Around the World in 80 Days 108
Armchair Theatre 43
Armstrong Circle Theatre 12, 22
Arrow 128
Arsenault, Jeffrey 8
Ashbrook, Daphne 122, **123**, 139
Assassination Bureau 80
As the World Turns 13, 147, 150
Astin, John 159
Astin, Mackenzie 66
Astin, Patty Duke 12, 64, 66, 159
Astin, Sean 66
Astredo, Humbert Allen 17, **18**, 19, 62
Atkins, Damien 143
Atlanta Constitution 190
Atwater, Barry 47, 48

Aubrey, James 7-8, 76, 77
August, John 32
Austin, Teri **153**, 154
Autry, Alan 124
Avengers 61, 62
Avery, Brian 162
Azevdeo, Lex de 119

Babcock, Barbara 152
Baby Face Nelson 194
Back Door to Hell 145
Back to the Future 142
Bad Ronald 182
Bad Seed 62
Baffled! 147
Bain, Conrad 12
Bakula, Scott 127
Baldwin, Daniel 143
Bale, Christian 133
Baltimore Sun 46
Band of Brothers 120
Bank Shot 185
Bannerman Solution 188
Bare Essence 128
Barker, Doc 132
Barker, Fred 132
Barnabas, Quentin, and the Mummy's Curse 148
Barnes, Ben 164
Baron, David 137
Baron, John 176
Barovic, Dick 8
Barrett, Nancy 12, 16, 19, 22, 38, 40, 47, 72, 76, 203
Barty, Billy 159
Barzman, Paolo 44
Basie, Count 157
Bass Emory 19
Bassett, Angela 156
Bates Motel 147
Batman 7-8, 132, 150, 177
Batman Returns 32
Batman Forever 68
Batman and Robin 128
Batman vs. Dracula 91
Bauer, Chris 143
Baxter, Meredith 170, **171**
Bay, Michael 110

BBC (British Broadcasting Corporation) 43, 89, 172
Beaumont, Charles 75
Beauty and the Beast 24, 142
Beethoven, Ludwig 115
Beghe, Jason 124, 154
Begley Jr., Ed **60**, 61
Bellamy, Ralph 108, 109, 111, 115
Bellini, Cal 147
Bellis, Richard 154
Beltway Boys 142
Bennett, Joan 12, 16, 17, 19, 28, 197
Benny, Jack 153
Benshoff, Harry M. 8, 128
Bergen, Polly 108, **109**, 111, 115, 119
Berger, Helmut 164
Bergin, Patrick 167
Berkoff, Steven 115, 125
Bernau, Christopher 19
Bernstein, Leonard 117
Bernt, Eric 27
Berrigan, Don 127
Best, Wayne 143
Beyond the Law 103
Big Easy 6, 10, 16, 138, **151**-152, 157, **189**, 193, 197
Big Event 133
Big Finish Productions 8, 11, 29, 36-37, 39, 123
Big Fish 32
Big Lebowski 128
Big Wednesday 130
Billboard magazine 16
Birds 188
Birney, David 139
Black, Karen 37, 56, 57, 58-**59**, 60, 66, 79, **80**, 83, 88, 129, 200-**201**, 203
Blackburn, Clarice 17
Black Hawk Down 115
Black-Market Baby 182
Black Scorpion 62
Black Sunday 108, 194
Blacula 130, 177
Blakely, Susan 124
Blake's 7 173
Blatt, Daniel 128
Blees, Robert 62
Blessed, Brian 115

Index

Bloodline 29
Bloodlines: Matheson's Dracula 97, 98-99
Bloodlust 29
"Blood Sun" 89
Blue Lagoon 120
Bloch, Robert 8
Blumgarten, James 177
B.L. Stryker 24
Blunden, Bill 141
Blye, Margaret 130
BMI (Broadcast Music, Incorporated) 120
Boardman, Chris 154
"Bobby" (1977) 62, **63**, 68
"Bobby" (1996) 66-**67**, 68
Bochco, Steven 157
Bochner, Hart 115, **118**
Bochner, Lloyd 164
Bodyguard 128
"Body Snatcher" 194
Bogdanovich, Peter 188
Bold and the Beautiful 1, 128
Bold Ones 51, 168
Bonnie and Clyde 99
Book of Temptation 123
Boorstin, Jon 24
Boris Karloff's Thriller 164
Boston Globe 32, 33, 35, 46, 76, 77, 127
Boston Herald 143
Bostwick, Barry 115, 119
Bourneuf, Philip 161
Bowman, Rob 23, 28, 30, 31
Boyz in the Hood 157
Bracken's World 145
Bradbury, Ray 61
Bradley, Edson 41
Bradley, Matthew
Brady, Scott 87, **132**, 133, 135, 186, 195
Bram Stoker's Dracula 91, 92, 96
Branagh, Kenneth 163
Brando, Marlon 37
Brave New World 170
Break in the Ice 182, 194
Brennan, Eileen 177, **178**
Briant, Shane 164-**165**, 166, 167
Bride of Frankenstein 162
Bride of Pendorric 194
Bright Promise 168

Brinckerhoff, Burt 77, 170, 177
Briscoe, Don 17, 18
Britten, Benjamin 173
Broadwell, Dick 101, 103
Brockman, Michael 38
Brody, Larry 168
Bronk 95
Bronte, Charlotte 11, 14, 194
Bronte, Emily 14, 21, 188-189, 193-194
Bronze Wrangler Awards 100, 105, 197
Brood 62
Brooke, Walter 180
Brooklyn Horror-Film Festival 40
Brooks, Mel 163
Brother Drop Dead 204
Brotherhood of Satan 74
Brown, Blair 28
Brown, Clancy 152, **153**
Brown, Joe David 188
Brown, Murray 89
Brown, Pamela 89
Brown, Winnie 134
Bruns, Philip 133
Bryant, Charlie "Blackfaced" 101
Bucholz, Horst 62
Buck Rogers in the 25th Century 157
Buffalo Niagara Film Festival 204
Bureau of Investigation 129, 130, 131, 133
Burlingame, Jon 8, 148
Burnett, John 120
Burnt Offerings (Marasco) 79, 80, 81, 88
Burnt Offerings 6, 10, 60, 62, 79, **80**, 81-**82**, 83, 94, 105, 106, 127, 136, 184, 189, 190, 197, 199, 200
Burr, Ty 33, 35
Burstyn, Ellen 143
Burton, Richard 172
Burton, Robert "Skip" 57, 64
Burton, Tim 8, 16, 31, 33, 34, 35, 36, 128
Bushman, David 40
Butler, Josephine 32
Byron, George Gordon 15

Caesar, Sid 62, 64
Caine Mutiny 106
Caldwell, Joe 22, 38
Calomee, Gloria 137

Cameron, James 94
camp 33, 35, 122, 128, 170
Campanelli, Linda 24
Campbell, J. Kenneth 152, 154
Campbell, Julia 154
Canary, David 131
Cannon, Orin 62, 133, 195
Capitol 149
Captains and the Kings 28, 119
Career Achievement Award 197
Carey, Denise 41
Carey, MacDonald 12
Carey, Philip 55, **56**, 168
Cariou, Len 144
Carmilla 194
Carol Burnett Show 128
Carpenter Karen 32
Carpenter, Richard 32
Carr, John Dickson 188
Carradine, John 51
Carrie 62
Carrington, Robert 190
Carson, Johnny 159
Carson, Sarah 156
Carter, Benny 157
Carter, Chris 127
Carter, Helena Bonham 32
Case, David 55
"Case of Charles Dexter Ward" 75
Casablanca 154
Casino Royale 29
Castle books 103
Cats 188
Cavett, Dick 159
CBC (Canadian Broadcasting Corporation) 46
CBS (Columbia Broadcasting System) 6, 7, 8, 13, 22, 74, 76, 83, 89, 91, 96, 111, 119, 121, 126, 139, 141, 147, 150, 152, 182
CBS Golf Classic 6-7, 10, 11, 38, 147, 197
CBS Late Movie 87
Chain Letter 147
Challenge Golf 6, 10, 197, 198
Champ 84
Chaney Jr., Lon 75
Chang, Justin 33, 35
Changeling 24
Charleson, Leslie 159

Charley Varrick 185
Charlie and the Chocolate Factory 35
Chastain, Jessica 28
Cherkoss, Dan see Curtis, Dan
Cherkoss, Edward 6
Cherkoss, Mildred 6
Chermak, Cy 48, 49, 51
Chew, Sam 159
Cheyenne Autumn 188
Chicago Sun-Times 26, 77,
Chiklis, Michael 156
Children Nobody Wanted 135
Children of Rage 139
Chiller channel 27
Chinatown 64
CHiPs 5, 100, 106, 152, 157
Chirkinian, Frank 7
Cloning of Clifford Swimmer 104, 159
Christian Science Monitor 141
Christie, Agatha 185
"Christmas Story" 145
Chulack, Christopher 152
Churchill, Winston 110
Cinefantastique 67, 74
cinema verite 48
Clark, Dale 23
Clark, Eugene **153**
Clark, Matt 66, **100**, 101, 131, 133, 184, 195
Clarke, Frederick S. 74
Clarke, Stanley 156, 157
classic horror 40, 48-49, 50, 51, 54
Classic Horror Theatre 194
Classic Mystery Ghost Stories 68
Clayton, Jack 172
Cleveland Plain Dealer 47
Close Encounters of the Third Kind 126, 127
Coal Miner's Daughter 122
Cobert, Robert 8, 9, **15**-16, 23, 27, 30, 32, 35, 37, 38, 46, 50, 51, 53, 56, 58, 62, 66, 73-74, 77, 81-82, 84, 94-95, 98, 100, 103, 105, 110, 115, 117, 119, 120, 122, 128, 130, 133, 136, 139, 142, 143, 147, 148, 154, 162-163, 164, 168, 170, 171, 173, 180, 182, 183, 184, 185, 186, 197
Cobb, Lee J. 182, **183**, 184
Coca, Imogene 159
Cody, Kathy 20, 21
Cody, William 103

Coffield, Peter 159
Cohen, Stanley 83-84
Collier, Don 100
Collins, Robert 152, 154, 155
Collinsport Call 5
Combs, Jeffrey 87
Come Die with Me 5-6, 10, 77, 94, 177-**178**, 179-180, 182, 195
Comer, Anjanette 62, 133, 168, **169**, 195
comic books 5, 8, 11, 23, 27, 36, 148
Command Performance 190, 191
Commish 156
Computercide 147
Conan the Barbarian 120
Concentration 13
Condemned 190
Connelly, Charles 101, 103
Connelly, Christopher 170, **171**
Connors, Mike 115
Coppola, Francis Ford 91, 92, 96, 189
Cop Rock 156
Cook Jr., Elisha 133, 194
Cooper, Alice **33**
Cooper, Mary 22
Coopers 145, 157
Corey, Jeff 62, 64
Corman, Roger 75
Corpse Bride 32
Correll, Charles 111, 152
Corwin, Norman 183
Costello, Frank 152
Costello, Robert **12**
Costner, Kevin 84
Count Dracula 99
Country Estates 147
Cousins, Christopher 124
Cousins, Joseph 124
Covenant 147
Cowley, Samuel 132
Cox, Wally 51
Crash Island 147
Crawford, Terrayne 18
Creeping Unknown 160
Crenna, Richard 122, 125
Crist, Judith 105
Crittenden, James **100**, 101
Crosby, Cathy Lee 147

Crosby, Mary 152
Cross, Ben **24**, 25, 26, 30, 40
Crothers, Joel 12, 16, 17, 41,
Crow 87
Crowther, John 188
Cruel Doubt 121
Curse of Dark Shadows 77
Curse of the Black Widow 5, 10, 62, 64, **65**, 66, 105, 106, 127, 192
Curtis, Cathy 6, 13, 31, 38, 79
Curtis, Dan
  auteur 5, 38, 105, 107, 132, 154
  birth 6
  death 6, 31, 197
  funeral 5
  illness 6, 31, 197
  live-theatre effect in his films 180
  low camera angles in his films 48, 56, 57, 58, 62, 66, 81, 96, 106, 130, 132, 136, 172, 182, 191, 200
  memorial service 5
  personal life 6, 38, 79, 134-135, 142
  photographs 7, 12, 15, 42, 82, 85, 86, 107, 108, 116, 138, 142, 144, 181, 186, 187, 196, 198, 200
  sense of place in his films 46, 50, 51, 55, 183-184, 192
  stock company of actors in his films 106, 132-133, 194-195, 197
  sympathy for the monster in his films 91, 162
Curtis, Linda 6, 13, 79, 180
Curtis, Norma Mae Klein 6, 31, 38, 79, 107, 111, 184, 197
Curtis, Tracy 6, 13, 31, 38, 62, 64, 79, 83, 84, 197
Cut-Out 188
CW network 91, 204
Czuchry, Matt 28

Dabson, Jesse 155
Dallas 28
Dalton, Bill 100, 103
Dalton, Bob 100, 103
Dalton, Emmett 100, 103, 105
Dalton, Frank 100
Dalton, Gratton 100, 101, 103
Dalton, Julia 103
Damien—Omen II 81, 189
Dan Curtis Associates 6, 139

Dan Curtis Productions 3, 6, 8, 37, 129-130, 131, 147, 151, 157, 159, 167, 188, 189
Daniels, Dorothy 13
Danson, Ted 143
Dante, Joe 51, 132
Dare Devil 147
Dark Destroyer 62
Dark Mansions 128, 147
"Darkness at Blaisedon" 5, 10, 22, 147-**149**, 150, 157, 173, 195
Dark Shadows (1966-1971) 1, 3, 5, 6, 7, 8, 10, 11-**14**, 15-**18**, 19-23, 25, 27, 28, 30, 32, 33, 35, 38, 39, 40, 41, 43, 46-47, 50, 51, 66, 69, 71, 72, 73, 74, 76, 77, 81-82, 87, 88, 91, 94-95, 98, 110, 120, 123, 128, 133, 137, 141, 144, 145, 147-148, 150, 159, 160, 162-163, 164, 165, 170, 172, 173, 174, 177, 180, 191, 193, 194, 195, 197, 200, 203, 204
Dark Shadows (1991) 8, 9, 10, 23-**24**, **25**, 26-27, 28, 30, 32, 33, 40, 43, 55, 66, 79, 109, 121, 122, 128, 132, 154, 155, 197
Dark Shadows (2004) 8, 10, 26, 27-**29**, 30-**31**, 32, 40, 43, 66, 128, 147, 198, 201
Dark Shadows (2012) 8, 25, 31-**33**, **34**, 35-37, 40, 128
Dark Shadows Festival 8, 9, 11, 30, 31, 77, 147, 163, 185, 195, 210
Dark Shadows: Reincarnation 204
Dark Shadows Resurrected 27
Dark Shore 194
Darrow, Clarence 127
Das Boot 117
Dating Game 13, 147
Davenport, Nigel 89, **97**, 133, **165**, 166, 172
David, Thayer 12, 16, 18, 19, 41, 72, **73**, 148, 194, 195
Davies, Geraint Wyn 66
Davis, Alexander Jackson 87
Davis, Bette 60, 79, 81, 83
Davis, Clifton 159
Davis, Roger 17, 19, 38, 73
Davis Jr., Sammy 7
Dawidziak, Mark 8, 30, 47, 97, 98-99
Day Mars Invaded Earth 26, 128
Day of the Locust 80
Days of Our Lives 12
DC Comics 8, 147, 188
Dead of Night: A Darkness at Blaisedon 5, 10, 22, 147-**149**, 150, 157, 173, 195

Dead of Night (1977) 10, **60**, **61**, 62, **63**, 66, 68, 89, 106, 127, 191, 194
Dead Ringer 128
Deadwood 37
Deal, David 56-57, 66
Death Becomes Her 33
Death Volley 159
"Death Wears a Baby's Face" 145
Deathwork 190
Decades network 5, 11, 40-41
Deep Red 30
Defenders 43
Dehner, John 115
Del Valle, David 8
Demon Demon 159
Dennehy, Brian 143
Denver Post 35-36
Depp, Johnny 32, 35, 133
Desert Fury 151, 152
Desperate Housewives 31
"detective jazz" 50, 51, 66
Detroit News 110
Devane, William **151**, 152, **189**, 194
Dewan Tatum, Jenna 30
Dewhurst, Colleen 119
Dial M for Murder 151
Diary of a Gunfighter 191, 194
Diffring, Anton 108
DGA (Directors Guild of America) 5, 120, 197
DiCenzo, George 148, 170, 195
Dick, Philip K. 68
Dick Tracy 147
Dickens, Charles 111
Dickinson, Angie 53, 54, 154-**155**, 156, 157
Diller, Barry 106
Dillinger, John 129, 130, 132, 194
Dillinger (1973) 129-130, 131, 133, 135
Dillman, Bradford 159
Dillon, Hugh 143
Dimitri, Nick 53, **54**
Dinkins, David 193
Discovery 41
Disorderly Orderly 26, 128
Distinguished Service Award 120, 197
Divorce Hers 172
Divorce His 172
Doctor Mabuse 200

Doctor Mabuse: Etopomar 200, 204
Doctors 16
Doctor Strange 147
Doctor Who 5, 173
Doheny, Edward 26, 128
Doheny, Lucy 26, 128
Doheny, Ned 26, 128
Donnelly, Thomas Michael 143
Donnybrook Productions 147-150
Donovan 32
Donovan, Martin 28
Don't Wear Your Wedding Ring 155
Doogie Howser, M.D. 156
Doolin, Bill 101, 102
Doolins of Oklahoma 103
Douglas, Gordon 103
Douglas, Sarah 91
Douglas Fairbanks Presents 6
Down Delaware Road 147
Down in the Delta 157
Downey, Roy 111
Dracula (Stoker) 13, 40, 89-99, 194
Dracula (1931) 40, 48, 194
Dracula (1974) 10, 11, 57, 82, 89-**90**, 91-**95**, 96-**97**, 98-99, 105, 106, 127, 150, 162, 164, 165, 166, 172, 176, 180, 182, 183, 184, 189, 194
Dracula (2007) 93
Dracula: A Biography of Vlad the Impaler 92
Dracula Book 74, 92
Dracula in Istanbul 92
Dracula's Daughter 14
Dragnet 6, 156
Dr. Christian 43
Dr. Cyclops 66
Dream Lover 24
Dreamer of Oz 142
Dr. Jekyll and Mr. Hyde (1920) 41
Dr. Kildare 150
Dr. Phibes Rises Again 62
Drop Dead Diva 170
Dubbins, Don 180
DuBois, Ja'net 151
Duel 67
Duff, Howard 115
Duggan, Andrew 108, 137
Duke, Patty 12, 62, 64, 66, 159
Dukes, David 84, 108, 115, 133, 139, 141

Du Maurier, Daphne 75
Dune 30
Dunsmuir, Alexander 88
Dunsmuir House 79, 82, 88, 184
Durkin, Betsy 17
Dusay, Marj 148, **149**, 157
Dusty and Sweets McGee 74
Dynasty 23

Eastwood, Clint 84
eBay 182, 185
Ebert, Roger 77
Eckelberry, Stephen **201**
Eddie Award 120
Eddie Macon's Run 190
Eden, Dorothy 194
Edgar Awards 44, 47, 135, 152
Edge of Night 13, 22, 147
Edmiston, Walker 58
Edmonds, Louis 12, 16, 17, 19, 22, 41, 72, 148, 195
Edwards, Blake 76
Edward Scissorhands 68
8½ 108
Eis, Elizabeth 20
Eischied 152
Eisenmann, Ike 131
Elektra 30
Elfman, Clare "Blossom" 139
Elfman, Danny 16, 32
Elizabeth R 188
Elizabeth Rex 192
Elizabeth the Queen 47
Ellen 36
Elliott, Denholm **42**, 44
Ellis, Ralph 22
Emmy Awards 7, 15, 22, 27, 47, 68, 109, 110-111, 117, 119-120, 121, 124, 126, 135, 139, 143, 154, 190, 197, 200
Empire Strikes Back 26
Encore Western channel 106
Entertainment Tonight 109
Entertainment Weekly 36, 141
ER 28, 152
Erman, John 111
Escapade 147
Eternity Base 188

Evers, Jason 168
Every Little Crook and Nanny 74
Exorcist movies 45, 62
"Express to Terror" **186, 187**
Eyes of Charles Sand 104

Facebook 135, 199-200
Fairman, Michael 152
Falk, Peter 145
"Fall of the House of Usher" 194
Family 136
Family Affair 156
Family for Joe 152
Family Plot 88
Family Ties 142
Fantasy Island 188
fanzines 5, 23, 36, 110, 119
Faraj, Ansel H. 5, 8, 200, **202**, 203-204
Farrell, Sharon **100**, 103, **104**, 159
Fatal Attraction 36
Father on Trial 147
"Father-Thing" 68
FBI 131
FBI vs. Alvin Karpis 131
Fein, Rita 38
Feke, Steve 24
Felony Squad 156
feminism 176
Fengriffin 55
Fenwick, Gillie 44
Feral 188
Fiddler on the Roof 96
Fifteen Western Tales 99-100
film noir 47, 50, 64, 66, 68, 132, 151, 154
Films in Review 81, 83
Fimple, Dennis **100**, 101
Findley, Timothy 192
Finney, Jack 60, 61, 139, 141, 191
Fitzpatrick, John **100**, 101, 135
Five Heartbeats 156
Flags of Our Fathers 120
Flame in the Wind 22
Flanagan, Fionnula 167
Flash 128
Flesh and the Fiends 46
Flipper 157
Florescu, Radu 92, 96, 160, 162, 163

Floyd, "Pretty Boy" 132
Foch, Nina 115
Fonda, Henry 127
Ford, David **12**, 16, 17
"For the Love of Ginger Parker" 145
Fort Worth Star-Telegram 26, 81
Four Musketeers 97
Fowkes, Conard 12
Fox network 27, 127
Fox, Colin 143
Fox, Michael J. **142**
Foxworth, Robert 159-160, **161**, 163, 164, 180
France, David 143
Francis, Ivor 195
Franciosa, Anthony 62, 64, **65**
Frank, Leo 190
Frankenstein (Shelley) 17, 88, 167-168, 194, 195
Frankenstein (1931) 160, 164, 194
Frankenstein 1970 (1958) 160
***Frankenstein* (1973)** 5, 10, 46, 55, 159, 160-**161**, 162-164, 165, 166, 168, 172, 180, 182, 189, 194, 195
Frankenstein: The True Story (1973) 163
Frankenstein and the Monster from Hell (1974) 165
Frankenstein (1993) 163, 167
Frankenstein (2004) 30
Franklin, Hugh 12
Frank Nitti: The Enforcer 122
Frechette, Billie 130
Freeman, David 188
Frees, Paul 37
Freund, Karl 41
Frid, Jonathan 13-**14**, 15, 17, **18**, 20, 21, 25, 30, **33**, **34**, 35, 38, 40, 41, 43, 71, **72**, 74, 203
Friday the 13th The Final Chapter 87
Frogs 62
From Time to Time 61, 191
Fugitive 106, 131
Fujikawa, Jerry 108
"Funeral" 89
Future Cop 157
Fry, Dwight 33
Fyfe, Jim 25

Gail, Max 62, 64
game shows 13, 16, 147, 168, 203
Garabedian, Mitchell 143, 144

Garfield, Allen 194
Garfunkel, Art 32
Garland, Beverly 159
Gauntlet Press 97
Gaynes, George 57
gender 46, 130, 155, 180
General Hospital 26, 128
General Service Studio 168
Genesis II 47
Genn, Leo 44
Gentle Ben 157
Gentry, Robert 161
George, Anthony 17
Gerard, Merwyn 170
Getaway 185
Ghost in Monte Carlo 26
Ghost Whisperer 31
Gideon's Trumpet 152
Gielgud, John **113**, 115, 119, **196**
Gierasch, Stefan 24
Gifted One 147
Gillin, Hugh 152
Gilmore Girls 128
Girls of Huntington House 139
Gladiator 115
Gloria 87
Glut, Donald F. 74, 92
Godfather movies 45, 189
Going, Joanna **25**, 26
"Goin' to Mexico" 84
Gold, Tracey 139
Goldberg, Harry 190
Goldberg, Leonard 38
Goldberg, Whoopi 40
Golden Globe Awards 111, 119, 200
Golden Halo Awards 135, 137
Golden Laurel Award 120, 197
Goldenthal, Eliot
Gold Key Comics 5, 23, 148
Goldthwait, Bobcat 87
Gomer Pyle, USMC 74
Gone with the Wind 167
Good Times 89, 151
Good Year 115
Goodyear TV Playhouse 22
Gordon, Leo 194
Gordon-Levitt, Joseph 24, **25**

Gould, Alexander 28, 87
Gould, Anna 87
Gould, Dana 87
Gould, Jay 87
Graham, Ed 7-8
Graham, Gerrit 139
Graham, Stephen 133
Grahame-Smith, Seth 32. 35
Grammy Awards 47
Graves, Peter 55, **56**, 108, 115, 133
"Graveyard Rats" 9, 66, 68
Gray, William 24
"Great Chicago Raid" 145
Great Ice Rip-Off 6, 10, 38, 84, 94, 135, 182-**183**, 184-185, 192, 194, 195
"great spook music" 162, 170
Green, Eva 29, 32
Green Hornet 157, 180
Greenley, Howard 41
Greenwood, Bruce 141-142
Gregory, David 8, 37, 38, 68
Gremlins 51
Greystone mansion 26, 28, 128
Grieg, Edvard 176
Griffith, Eva 172
Grizzard, George 159
Gross, Darren 8, 77-78
Growing Pains 156
Guiding Light 139, 147, 149
Gunfight 191
Gunn, Moses 159
Gunning for Glory 188
Guns of Will Sonnett 157
Guttman, Richard 145
Guthrie, Tyrone 183

Hackett, Joan 62, **63**, 66, 136, **137**, 195
"Hail to the Chief" 186
Haggerty, H.B. 64
Hale, Billy 190
Haley, Jackie Earle 32
Hall, Grayson **14**, 15, 17, 19, 38, 41, 71, 72, **73**, **75**, 76, 159, 161, 182, **183**, 184, 195
Hall, Matthew 24
Hall, Sam 22, 24, 71, 74-75, 77, 147, 150, 159, 160, 162, 164, 194
Hallmark Channel 30

Hallmark Hall of Fame 47, 139, **140**, 141, 160, 191
Halloween 62
Hamilton, Margaret 51
Hamlisch, Marvin 145
Hannibal 115
Happy Days 65, 105
Hardcase 147
Hard Day at Blue Nose 159
Hardester, Crofton 152
Hardman, Richard 131-132, 133
Hard Times of R.J. Berger 32
Harkins, John 20, 195
Harrad Experiment 130
Harris, Richard A. 94
Harrison, Gregory 57
Haskell, Peter 159
Hart to Hart 26, 128
Hartley, Mariette 180
Hatfield, Hurd 164-165, 167
Haunted 43
Haunted Palace 75
Have Gun, Will Travel 157
Heathcote, Bella 32
Heckart, Eileen 79, 80,
Heiress 16
Henerson, James 139, 190, 191
Henesy, David 12, 16, 19, 20
Hennick House 172
Henry, Emmaline 180
Herrmann, Bernard 16
Hessler, Gordon
Heston, Charlton 47
"He Who Kills" 67-68
He Who Whispers 188
High Anxiety 66
Higher Learning 157
Highlander 156
Highlander: Endgame 27
Highlander: The Search for Vengeance 91
Hijacking of the Achille Lauro 154
Hill, Jim 195
Hill, Julie 103
Hill, Nathan 44
Hill Street Blues 157
Hingle, Pat 115
Hitchcock, Alfred 16, 79, 88, 132
Hitler, Adolf 112

Hitler: The Rise of Evil 120
Hoffman, Dustin 72
Hogan, Frank S. 152, 154
Hogan, P.J. 30, 31
Holbrook, Hal 127
Holdridge, Lee 142
Holliman, Earl 154
Hollinsworth Productions 204
Holmes, Rupert 27
Hollywood Palace 150
Hollywood Reporter 26, 47, 51, 54, 61, 68-69, 143, 164, 185, 192
Holt, Victoria 194
Home Alone 84
Homefront 152
homosexuality 43-44, 46, 165, 166, 167
Honath, Norman 195
Honey West 157
Hoodlum Priest 7
Hoods 188, 190-191
Hooper, Tobe 72
Hoooperman 156
Hopalong Cassidy 6
Hopkins, Bo **100**, 101, **102**, 132, 186
Hopkins, Budd 121-122
Horizon House Institute 135
Horner, Penelope 89
Horrible Dr. Hichcock 108
horror *see* classic horror; modern horror
Horror of Dracula 48, 98
Hostile Takeover 192-193
Hot Rock 185
Houdini, Harry 41
Houghton Mifflin 92
Hours of Love 108
"House" 22, 38
Houseman, John 108, 115
House of Dark Shadows 6, 10, 20, 24, 25, 28, 40, 46, 48, 50, 71, **72**, **73**, 74, 76, 77, 79, 83, 87, 94, 160, 162, 168, 180, 183-184, 192, 203
House of Dracula 15
House of Frankenstein 15
House of Terror 68
House of the Seven Gables 194
House That Would Not Die 47
Howard, Vanessa 166
Howatch, Susan 194

Index

Howitzer, Bronson 131-132, 133
How to Succeed in Business 170
Hu, Kelly 28, 30
Hubley, Season 135-**136**
Huggins, Roy 131
Humanitas Prize 142
Human Target 188
Hungary in Ancient…Times 93
Hunt, Helen 139
Hunted Past Reason 191
"Hunter" 55
Hunter, Holly 119
Hunter, Ian McLellan 43-44, 46, 47
Hunt for Red October 106
Hussey, Margaret 128
Huston, John 183
Hutson, Lee 135, 136, 145, 151, 190, 193
Hutton, Jim 180
Hyman, Dick 139

ICM (International Creative Management) 108
I Am Legend 47, 67, 89
Ideas into Books 5, 8
"I Love Galesburg in the Springtime" 191
I Love Harrisburg in the Springtime 191
Imagen Awards 142
Immortal 128
"I'm Gonna Dance for You" 46-47
In Concert 159
Incredible Shrinking Man 9, 47, 67,
Inferno 30
Inner Sanctum 61
Innocents 62, 172
Innovation Comics 27
In Search of America 147
In Search of Dracula 92
In Search of Frankenstein 160, 163
Inside the Old House 23
Inspector Morse 193
Instagram 203
Interview with the Vampire 15, 163
"Into the Maelstrom" 110
Intruders Foundation 121
Intruders: The Incredible Visitations at Copley Woods 121-122

Intruders: They Are Among Us 10, 11, 26, 66, 79, 89, 96, 115, 121-**123**, **124**, 125-**126**, 127, 128, 154, 185, 188, 197
Invaders 53, 108, 122, 127
Invasion 31
Invasion of Carol Enders 1, 5, 10, 77, 127, 170-**171**, 182, 195
Iron Horse 129
Ironside 47, 51
Irving, Henry 96
Irving, Washington 87
I Think I'm Having a Baby 10, 138, 139, 141, 145, 151
It's Alive 62
Ivan the Terrible 92

Jack the Ripper 122
Jackson, Kate 20, 28, 75, 76
Jackson, Shirley 21-22
Jacob, Jasper 172, **175**
Jacquet, Illinois 157
James, Anthony 81
James, Brion 132
James, Henry 23, 172-177, 194
Jamison, R.J. 183, 184
Jane Eyre 11, 14, 194
Jarrott, Charles **42**, 43, 46, 47
Jaws 83
Jekyll and Hyde (2008) 44
Jelliffe, Bill 101
Jenkins, Henry 16
Jenkins, Megs 172, 177
Jennifer Eight 30
Job Interview 200, 204
John, Elton 32
Johnny Ryan 6, 10, 16, 152-**153**, 154, 156, 157
Johnson, Ben 129
Johnson, J.J. 152, 157
Johnson, Lyndon B. 193
Jones, Dean 127, **134**, 135, 136, **137**
Jones, Lory Basham 127
Jordan, Glenn 160, 162, 164, 165, 166
Jordon, William 132
Journal of Frankenstein 163
Journal of the Gun Years 188-189, 191-192, 194
Judging Amy 197
"Julie" 57

Julliard School of Music 16
Just Desserts 147
Justice League of America 147

Kail, Jim 127
Kanaly, Steve
Kansas City Massacre 1, 10, 94, 102, 105, 129, 131, **132**, 133, 135, 145, 154, 172, 182, 192, 194, 195, 197, 199
Kansas City Star 117
Kaplan, Henry 22
Karlen, John 5, 8, 17, 19, 21, 22, 25, **31**, 38, 57, 72, 76, 84, 108, 123, 130, 131, **132**, 133, 137, **161**, **165**, 166, 170, 180, 195
Karloff, Boris 160, 164
Karpis, Alvin 132
Katz, William 180
Kaye, Jeff 163-164
Kearney, Gene R. 170
Keith, Brian 156
Kelly, Grace 6
Kelly, George "Machine Gun" 129, 130
Kelly, Roz 62, 64, **65**
Kelsey, Linda 166
Kemp, Jeremy 108, 115
Kemp, Sally 170
Kennedy, David 31-32
Kennedy, John F. 193
Kennedy, Lisa 35-36
Kennedy, Robert F. 193
Kennedy, Ruth 128
Kennedy, Edward M. 193
Kenwith, Herbert 168, 169
Kernochan, James 41
Kerr, Deborah 172
Kid 84
Kiley, Richard 111
Kill and Kill Again 188
Killing at Hell's Gate 136
Kilmer, Val 37
King, Burton L. 41
King, Stephen 3, 47
Kingdom of Heaven 115
Kirchner, L.R. 103
Kirkland, Sally 131
Kirsch, Stan 156
Kiser, Terry 100

Klune, Donald C. 130
Klute 30
Knots Landing 151, 152, **153**, 154, 189, 194
Knowles, Christopher Loring 53
Kojak 87, 170
Kolchak Tapes 53
Kolchak: The Night Stalker 48, 49, 51, 155
Komine, Pike, and W.D. Baldry 192
Kondracke, Millicent M. 141-142
Kondracke, Mort 141-142
Kring, Tim 145
Kurtzman, Katy **134**
Kuttner, Henry 66, 68

Lacy, Jerry 17, 19, 21, 26, 38
Lady of Mallow 194
Lair 91
Lake House 140, 141
L.A. Law 157
Lambert, Susan 188
Lancaster, Deborah 127
Land Beyond the Forest 93
Landau, Richard 160, 161, 162, 164
Landers, Ann 184
Lane, Charles 108
Lang, Howard 110
Langdon, Anthony 176
Lansbury, Angela 167
Lansky, Meyer 152
Laredo 131
Laskey, Kathleen 143
Lassie 157
Last Case of August T. Harrison 200
Last Child 47
Last of Sheila 62
Last of the Crazy People 188
Last Ride of the Dalton Gang 5, 6, 10, 11, 27, 62, 79, 87, 89, 99-**100**, 101-**102**, 103-**104**, 105-106, 127, 145, 170, 195, 197, 199
Last Summer 188, 192
Last Tenant 135
Laszowska, Emily Gerard 93
Late-Night Horror 89
Laugh-In 177
Laurenson, James 174
LaVoo, George 83
Law, Bernard 143, 144

Index

Law & Order 197
Lawman 131
Lawrence, Steve 186
Lawrence, Vicki 186
Lawson, Eric **100**, 101
Leachman, Cloris 135-**136**
Lee, Christopher 32, 37, 96
Legacy of Blood 159
"Legend of Bonnie and Clyde" 145
Legend of Johnny Dillinger 133, 145
Legend of Machine Gun Kelly 129
"Legend of Sleepy Hollow" (Irving) 87
Legend of Sleepy Hollow (1949) 87
Leigh, Jennifer Jason 139, **140**, 141
Leone, Nola 40
Leone, Sergio 190
LeRoy, Mervyn 190
Les Miserables 160
Lester, Mark 172, 175
Let's Make a Deal 13, 147
Lewin, Albert 164-165, 166, 167
Lewin, Robert 145
Lewis, Al 51
Lewis, Fiona 89, **95**, 97
Lewis, Geoffrey 66, 133, 134, 135, 184
Lewis, Juliette 135
Lifetime 170
"Ligeia" 194
Lights Out 177
"Likeness of Julie" 57
Lilies of the Field 108
Lincoln 25
Lindley, Barbara 91
Linus! the Lion-Hearted 6, 7-8
Lippincott's Monthly Magazine 165
Lisztomania 95
Little Big Man 72
Littlefield, Warren 27
Little Game 62
"Little Girl Across the Room" 145
Little Orphan Annie 133
Locke, Rosanna 64
Lockhart, June 62
Lockwood-Mathews Mansion 73
Logan, Michael 35
Logan's Run 68, 199
Lohmann, Dietrich 120

Lohmann, Paul 66, 184
Lonesome Dove 119-120, 154
Lone Star Shadows 5, 119,
Long Days of Summer 6, 10, 16, 48, 61, 129, 136-**137**, 138, 139, 141, 145, 152, 157, 190
Long Hot Summer 53
Look at Monaco 6
Loon Lake 5, 200, **202**, 203-204
Lord of the Rings 192
Loring, Lynn 133
Lormer, Jon 162
Los Angeles Herald-Examiner 130, 135, 137, 177
Los Angeles Times 23, 51, 85, 91, 112, 119, 120-121, 130, 133, 135, 137-138, 163
Lost 31
Lost Souls: The Doomed Journey 37
Lottery 21-22
Lou Grant 177
Louis, Joe 137
Love Boat 185, 188
Lovecraft, H.P. 75
Loved One 26, 128
"Love Letter" 61, 191
Love Letter 6, 10, 61, 85, 129, 139-**140**, 141, 145, 190, 191
Love Machine 76
Love of Life 22
Love on a Rooftop 139
Love Thieves 188
Love Trap 66
Lowery, William D. 156
Lucan 152, 157
Lucas, Donna 77, 78
Lucas, Tim 77, 78
Lugosi, Bela 40, 91
Lustig, Branko 111, 115, 128
Lyman, Will 143
Lynch, Paul 23
Lyndhurst 38, 71, 74, **75**, 77, 87, 183-184, 203

MacArthur, Douglas 58
MacCaulay, Charles 177, **178**
MacDonald, John D. 185
MacGraw, Ali 107, 108, 109, 115, **116**
"Machine-Gun Kate" 145
MacKelvie, Jock 145
Macnee, Patrick **61**, 62

MacRae, Michael 155
Maharis, George 177, **178**
Making It 188
Maltese Falcon 64
Maltin, Leonard 131
Mancini, Henry 50, 182, 184
Mandan, Robert 125
Manetti, Larry 132
Man from Beyond 41
Man from Snowy River 120
Man from U.N.C.L.E. 135
Mann, Michael 133
Mannix 26, 128, 159
Man with the Golden Gun 96
Marasco, Robert 79, 80, 190
March, Fredric 46
Marill, Alvin 130
Marin, Andrew Peter 182, 185, 194
Marjorie Morningstar 106
Marmorstein, Malcolm 22, 38, 40
Mars Attacks! 32
Marshall, E.G. 115
Mars Needs Women 127
Martin, Ben 21
Martin, Jared 152
Martin, Quinn 131
Marvel Comics 112, 128, 147
Mary Hartman, Mary Hartman 60, 133
Mary Shelley's Frankenstein 163
M*A*S*H 192
Mass Appeal 160
Master of Dark Shadows 8, 37-40, 68, 87
Masterpiece Theatre 93
Mastroianni, Armand 23, 40
Matheson, Richard 8, 9, 37, 47, 48, 50, 51, 55, 56, 57, 61, 62, 66-67, 68, 83, 89, 91, 92, 93-94, 96, 97, 98-99, 106, 188-189, 191-192, 194
Mathews, Kerwin 147
Matinee 51
Mayer, Bob 188
Mayne, Ferdy 108
MCA (Music Corporation of America) 6
McBride, Jim 152
McCarthy, Tom 144
McCorry, Tom 166
McDonnell, Ray 147
McDowell, Charlie 41

McElhanie, Bill 101
McFarland books 5, 26, 56-57, 66, 145
McGavin, Darren 47, **49**, 50, 51, **52**, 53, 97, 151, 164
McGrath, Gulliver 25, 32
McGuire, Michael 21, 137, 195
McKechnie, Donna 19
McLendon, James 190
McNally, Raymond T. 92, 96
McRae, Frank
McShane, Ian 37, 115
Me and the Kid 6, 10, 83-**85**, 86, 96, 162, 185, 195
Medalla Sitges en Oro de Lay 83, 197
Medical Center 122
Medium 31, 170
Meet-Up 9
Megowan, Don 131, 195
Meisner, Gunter 115
Melton, J. Gordon 8-9, 96
Melvin Purvis, G-Man 6, 10, 94, 105, **129**, 130-131, 133, 145, 172, 182, 183, 192, 194, 199
Men in Black 127
Mentalist 128
Mephisto Waltz 53
Mercury News 144
Meredith, Burgess 79, 80, 83
Meredith, Don 186, **187**
Merritt, George 87
Metromedia 61
Metz, Melinda 127
MGM (Metro-Goldwyn-Mayer) 8, 23, 71, 74, 76, 83, 164-165, 166, 203
Miami News 55
Midway 117
Milicevic, Ivana 28, **29**
Milius, John 130, 131, 133
Millay, Diana 13, 16, 19, 77
Miller, Jonny Lee 32
"Millicent and Therese" 57
Million-Dollar Rip-Off 182, 194
Mills, Donna 62, 64
Mills, Juliet 159
Milton, John 165, 195
"Mimsy Were the Borogroves" 66
Miranda, Robert 154
Miskatonic Institute of Horror Studies 40

Index

Mission: Impossible 128, 136
Missouri 110
"Missy" 180
Mister Rock and Roll 177
Mistress of Mellyn 194
Mitchell, Julian 188-189, 193-194
Mitchell, Thomas 143
Mitchum, Robert **108**, 109, 115, 152
Mockingbird Lane 147
modern horror 40, 48-49, 50, 51, 54
Moffat, Donald 135, 137
Moltke, Alexandra 12, 16, **18**, **37**
Moneychangers 119
Monkees 145
Montgomery, Lee Harcourt 62, 81, **82**
Monty, Gloria 159
Moody Blues 32
Moore, M.M. Shelly 24
Moore, Roger 88
Moretz, Chloe Grace 32
Morgan, George 161
Morgan Creek Productions 68-69
Moriarty, Cathy 84
Morley, Robert 115
Morris, Anita 84
Morris, Oswald 96
Morrow, Vic 62, 64
Morse, Barry 108
Most Deadly Game 150
Mostoller, Ramsey 148
Moxey, John Llewellyn 47, 48, 49
Mozart, Wolfgang Amadeus 95
MPAA (Motion-Picture Association of America) 76
MPI Home Video 8, 37, 96, 105
Mr. District Attorney 43
"Mrs. Machine-Gun Kelly" 145
Mrs. R's Daughter 6, 10, 99, 129, 135-**136**, 141, 145, 197
M Squad 157, 170
Muir, John Kenneth 26
Muktar, Mehmet 92
Mulgrew, Kate 159
multiculturalism 30, 155
Mummy 41
Murder of Mary Phagan 190
Murder She Wrote 128

Murray, Don 7-8
Museum of Television and Radio 68, 144, 198, 200, 201
My Music 5
My Name Is Bill W. 119
Mysterious Stranger 193
Mysterious Two 147

Naldi, Nita 41
Name of the Game 65, 157
Napier, Alan 177
Nash, Frank "Jelly" 131, 132
Nashville 66
Nashville State Community College 9
National Cowboy Hall of Game 1005, 105
NBC (National Broadcasting Company) 6, 7, 12, 13, 22, 23, 24, 26, 27, 53, 61, 99, 111, 117, 120, 121, 133, 135, 147, 148, 150, 152, 154, 182, 185, 186, 188, 190, 194
NBC Saturday Night at the Movies 88
NBC Special Treat 139
NCIS 128
"Needle in the Heart" 57
Nelson, "Baby Face" 132
Nelson, Byron 6
Nelson, Mary Catharine 8, 9
Nero, Franco 37
Nero Wolfe 194
Netflix 41
Neverending Story 87
Newark Star Ledger 117
Newcomb, George "Bitter Creek" 101, 103
Newlywed Game 13, 168
Newman, Alec 28, **29**, 30, 40
Newsday 110, 117
Newsweek 74, 143
New York Daily News 68, 143
New York Times 35, 50, 51, 77, 81, 83
Nickerson, Denise 18, 19
Nicholas Nickleby 111, 120
Night Before 77
Night Gallery 170
Night Killers 51
Nightlife 24
Nightmare at 43 Hillcrest 6, 10, 180, 181, 182, 195
Night of Dark Shadows 1, 6, 10, 23, 27, 28, 35, 36, 40, 47, 66, 74, **75**, 76-**77**, 78-79, 83, 87,

127, 150, 160, 170, 171, 173, 174, 180, 183-184, 195
Nights of Dan Curtis 5
Night Stalker 3, 10, 47-**49**, 50, 51, 53, 54, 55, 64, 66, 68-69, 127, 151, 159, 164, 183, 184, 194, 200
Night Stalker (2005) 69
Night Strangler 10, 48, 49, 50-**52**, 53, 54, 55, 64, 66, 127, 160, 162, 182, 183, 184, 192, 195
Night-Time Winds 200, 204
Nixon, Richard 182
No Business Being a Cop 155
Nolan, William Francis 9, 40, 53, 55, 57, 66, 67, 68, 79, 83, 130, 131, 132, 133, 145, 166, 172, 173, 174, 176, 177, 199, **200**
Nolte, Nick 68
Noodles and Maxey 188, 190-191
Norliss Tapes 10, 53, **54**, 55, 127, 130, 131, 132, 147, 157, 172, 182, 183, 195
Norman, Eric Van Haren 141
Norming of Jack 243 159
North and South 119
Nosferatu 48
"No Such Thing as a Vampire" **61**-62, 89
NYPD 157
NYPD Blue 157

Oakland, Simon 48, **49**, 50, 51
Oak Ridge 13
Oates, Warren 129
O'Connor, Robert 122
Odd Couple 108
"Ode to Angelique" 180
O'Donnell, Lillian 155
O'Flinn, Paul 160
O'Hara, John 188
Oklahoma Crude 89
Old, Dark House 83
O'Leary, Mary 40
Oliver! 172, 175
Oliver, James 143
Omen 83
On Cable 189
Once Upon a Time in America 189, 190
One-Eyed Jacks 151
One Life to Live 13, 22
One Shoe Makes It Murder 157
One Step Beyond 157, 170

On Guard 188
Opera 30
O Pioneers! 160
Orange County Register 85
Oringer, Barry 122, 125
Orion Pictures 83, 85, 185
Ornitz, Arthur 74
Ortelli, Dyanna 156
O'Shea, Tessie 46, 47
Other 62
Otto's Boy 188
Our Fathers 10, 31, 79, 85, 109, 143-144, 197
Our Fathers: The Secret Life 143
Our Private World 150
Outsiders 27

Paar, Jack 159
Packer, Peter 188
Paget, Debra 75
Palance, Jack 43, 44, **45**, 46, 47, 57, 68, 89, **90**, 91-92, **95**-96, 97, 103, 133, 147, 164
Paley Center for Media 40
Palmer, Arnold 6
Pantoliano, Joe 84
Paperback Library 13, 23, 38, 148
Paper Moon 188
Parade Rest 190
Paradise Lost 165, 195
parallel time 20, 21-22, 23, 74, 75, 133, 141, 150, 188
Parallel Times 5
Paramount Pictures 27, 151, 189
Parents Television Council 143
Parker, Isaac 101, 103
Parker, Lara 13, 17, **18**, 21, **34**, 35, 38, 41, 71, 76, **77**, 203, **210**
Parsons, Estelle 139, 141
Passenger 57 157
Patrick, Dennis 17, 19, 115
Patty Duke Show 12
Paul, Adrian 27
Paulding, William 87
Paull, Morgan 132
Pearl Harbor 110
Peckinpah, Sam 76
Pecos Kid Western 99-100
Penn, Arthur 72

Pennock, Christopher 19, 20, 21, 38
Pennsylvania Patriot-News 122
People magazine 109, 126
People's Choice Awards 119
Perfect Strangers 156
Perfect World 84
Perlman, Ron 37
Persoff, Nehemiah 186
Peter Gunn 50
Peter Pan 30
Peterson, Chris 134
Petrie, Daniel 190
Petticoat Junction 168
Petty, Dee-Dee 27
Peyton Place 22, 150, 157
Pfeiffer, Michelle 32
PGA (Producers Guild of America) 5, 120, 197
PGA (Professional Golfers' Association) 120, 197
Phagan, Mary 190
Phantasm 88
Phantom 128
Phantom of the Opera 194
Phantom of the Paradise 87
Phar Lap 120
Philadelphia Enquirer 110
Pflug, Jo Ann 51, 55, **56**, 133
Phillips, Fred 53
Phillips, Michelle 130
Phone Calls 155
Phyllis 136
Picture Mommy Dead 128
Picture of Dorian Gray (Wilde) 19, 23, 167-168, 194
Picture of Dorian Gray (1945) 164-168
Picture of Dorian Gray (1973) 5, 10, 46, 55, 97, 99, 164-**165**, 166-168, 172, 182, 189, 194
Pierce, Charles 129
Pierce, "Cockeye" Charley 101
Pierpont, Harry 132
Pierson, Jim 3, 5, 8, 9, 27, 31, 38, 61, 68, 78, 87, 96, **144**, 145, 150, 151, 156, 182, 185, 188, 199, 200, **201**
Pine, Phil 170
Pinewood Studios 34, 115
Plague Town 37
Planet of the Apes 122
Plan 9 from Outer Space 87
Player, Gary 6

Playhouse 90 47
Playroom 57
Please Call It Murder 159
Pleshette, John 194
Plummer, Christopher 143
Poe, Edgar Allan 194
Poe, James 108
Poetic Justice 157
Poirot Investigates 185
Poledouris, Basil 120, 154
Police Story 152
Police Surgeon 157
Police Woman 154-155
Pomegranate Press 27, 199
Porter, Don 53
Portrait of a Mobster 190
Postman Always Rings Twice 151
Potts, Cliff **100**
Pouget, Ely 25
Powell, Addison 17, 41, 115, 195
Powell, Hall 24
Power, Bill 101
Prentice, Keith 21
Prentiss, Paula 37
Prestige 128
"Prey" 57-**59**, 67
Price, Vincent 75
Price Is Right 16
Prime Target 154, 155
Prince, William 115
Prince of Wales 110
Prinze, Freddie 194
Produced and Directed by Dan Curtis 144, 199
Prosky, Robert 154
Protectors 157
Pryor, Nicholas 151
Psycho 79
Public Enemies 133
Purvis, Melvin 129, 130, 133
Pyramid 147

Quaid, Randy **100**, 167
Quantum Leap 23
Quatermass Xperiment 160
"Queen and the Improbable Knight" 186
Queen, Ellery 185

"Quentin's Theme" 9, 38, 46-47, 77, 110, 119, 120, 128, 168, 185
Queen Mary 111
Questor Tapes 147
Quick, Flo 103
Quicksilver 143

Raid on Coffeyville 99, 106
Raid on Root Tower 192-193
Raid on 330 Park 188, 192-193
Rampling, Charlotte 37
Ranch Romances 99-100
Random House 121-122
Rappaport, I.C. 145
Rat Patrol 157
Ray, Fred Olen 91, 132
Re-Animator 87
Rebecca 33, 75
Redford, Robert 41
Redgrave, Lynn 57, 164, 172, **175**, 176, 177
Redgrave, Michael 172
Reed, Donna 166
Reed, Oliver 60, 79, **80, 82**, 83
Reed, Rex 81, 83
Reiner, Carl 6
Renert, Jerry 192
Resch, Kathy 9, 23
Restless Gun 157
Return 55, 157, 172
Revenge 128
Reversal of Fortune 87
Reyes, Amanda 40
RFK: Between the Gunshots 188, 193
Rhoades, Barbara 186, **187**
Rhys-Davies, John 115
Rifkin, Ron 135
Rice, Anne 15, 163
Rice, Jeff 47, 48, 51
Rich, Monica 76
Richards, Kim 166
Richards, Lisa 19
Rich Man Poor Man 119
Richman, Peter Mark 180
Rifleman 157
Ripp, Heino 148
Rising Light 204
Rivas, Geoffrey 155

Robards, Jason 43
Robbing Banks 103
Roberts, Michael D. 30
Roberts, Pernell 159
Roberts, Stephen 137
Robertson, Dale 101, 103, **129**, 130, 131, **132**, 133, 195
Robin, Marcy 9, 23, 36
Robinson, "Sugar" Ray 153
Rodan, Robert 17, **18**
Rodgers, Mark 152, 154
Roe vs. Wade 119
Roger Miller Show 159
Romeo Must Die 27
Rondo Awards 204
Rookies 145
Rooney, Mickey 194
Roosevelt, Franklin 108, 110, 137,
Roots 110, 119
Roots: The Next Generation 119
Rose, Reginald 47
Rosemary's Baby 62, 127
Rosenberg, Howard 119, 120-121
Ross, Dan 5, 9, 13, 23, 39, 148
Ross, Diana 189
Ross, Marilyn 5, 9, 13, 23, 39, 148
Rossilli, Paul 154
Roswell High 127
Roth, Peter 28
Roueche, Berton 188
Roulette Records 180
Round Town Productions 202
Roush, Matt 144
Route 66 177
Routledge books 16
Roveto, Joseph 134
Royal Shakespeare Company 111
Rubes, Jan 143
Rubino, George 135
Rudolph, Lou 190, 192, 193
Russell, Gordon 22, 24, 71, 74
Russell, Ken 37, 76
Ryan, Mitchell 12, 16
Ryan's Hope 22, 148

Sacramento Union 46
SAG (Screen Actors Guild) 143

Index

Saint-Duval, Malila 162
Salve Regina University 41
Samuel Goldwyn Studios 135
Sand, Paul 186
Sanders, George 167
San Francisco Examiner 77
Sarah Plain and Tall 160
Sargent, Dick 130
Sarrazin, Michael 163
Saturday Evening Post 139
Saturn Awards 27, 60, 80, 83, 126, 127, 197
Savage Harvest 152
Savile, Philip 99
Saving Private Ryan 120
Saving Milly 6, 10, 16, 31, 79, 85, 109, 127, 129, 141-**142**, 143, 145
Savory, Gerald 99
Scarecrow books 74, 92
Scarlet Pimpernel 16
Schallert, William 115
Scharf, Walter 135, 136
Schick, Elliot 130
Schindler's List 115, 120-121, 128, 163
Schlitt, Robert 145
Schirmer, William 120
Schmeling, Max 137
Schofield, Frank 12, 16
Schott, Bob 53, **54**,
Sci-Fi Channel 5, 27, 30, 41
Scott, Campbell 139, **140**, 141
Scott, Geoffrey 19
Scott, Jan 141
Scott, Kathryn Leigh 9, 12, 14, 16, 17, 19, 21, 28, **34**, 35, 38, **39**, 71, 72, 87, 123, 174, 177, 179, 195, **202**, 203
Scott, Lizabeth 152
Scott, Ridley 115
Scream of the Wolf 1, 10, 55, **56**, 57, 62, 94, 130, 182, 183
Scribner, Ronnie 136
Scrooged 87
Search for Tomorrow 13
Seattle Underground 50, 52
Seaview Terrace 12, **37**, 41, 87
"Second Chance" **60**, 61, 191
Second Hundred Years 139
"Secret Room" 32

Secret Storm 13
Sedwick, John 22
Seidelman, Arthur Allan 139
Selby, David 13, 18, **33**, **34**, 35, 38, 47, 71, **75**, 76, 79, 159, **202**, 203-204, **210**
Selleck, Tom 168, **169**
Sense of Honor 188
Serling, Rod 43
Serrano, Nestor **153**
Sevareid, Eric 193
Seventh Heaven 177
79 Park Avenue 119
Severin Films 37
Seymour, Jane **114**, 115, 119, **196**
Shadow 133
Shadowgram 23, 36
Shadow of Fear 5, 10, 127, 168-**169**, 170, 180, 182
Shadow of the Lynx 194
Shadow on the Sun 191
Shadows of the Night 5
Shaft's Big Score 166
Shakespeare, William 13, 111
Shapiro, Paul 127
Shaw, Jason 30
Shaw, Steve 143
Sheedy, Ally 139
Shelley, Dave 137
Shelley, Mary 17, 160-164, 167-168, 194, 195
Shell's Wonderful World of Golf 7
Shelton, Marley 28
Shepard, Helen Gould 87
She's the Sheriff 156
She Waits 22
Shipman, Herbert 41
Shipman, Judith Bradley 41
Shirley, Ray 32
Shine on Harvest Moon 22
Shogun 119
Short, Robert 127
Shotgun Slade 135
Showalter, Elaine 43
Showtime 143
Shrinking Man 47, 67
Shyamalan, M. Night 127
Siegel, Don 194
Siegenthaler Sr., John 193

Sigismund I of Hungary 92
Signs 127
Simmons, Jean 24, 28, 111
Simon, Paul 32
Simon, Ron 40
Simon Wiesenthal Center 120, 197
Simpsons 66
Singer, Alexander 194
Singer, Josh 144
Sinutko, Shane 139
Sirota, Louanne 136
Sitges-Catalonian Film Festival 83, 197
Six-Million-Dollar Man 157
16 magazine 40
Slaton, John 190
Slattery, Richard X. 108
"Slaughter House" 68
Sleepless in Seattle 141
Sleepy Hollow International Film Festival 87
Sliders 122
Small Soldiers 51
Smallville 28
Smash Attack 192-193
Smight, Jack 163
Smith, Cecil 163-164
Smith, Dick 45, 46, 72
Smith, Lane 151
Smyth Lentz, Sharon 17
Snyder, John 125
soap operas 1, 11, 112, 13, 16, 22, 26, 35, 41, 71, 73, 74, 128, 139, 147. 148, 149, 150, 168, 172
Sobel, Mark 23
Social Network 128
Solie, John 167
Somers, Suzanne 156
Somerset 74
Somewhere in Time 47, 67, 114, 140, 141
Sonnenfeld, Barry 127
Sorel, Louise 134
Soylent Green 166
Space for Hire 53
Spider Lady 62
Spider-Man 128
Spielberg, Steven 25, 115, 128
Spirit 147
Spotnitz, Frank
Spradlin, G.D. 125

Sproat, Ron 22, 38
Sragow, Michael
Staab, Rebecca 24
Stahl, Richard 180
Stan Against Evil 87
Starsky and Hutch 157
Star Trek 5, 157, 168
Star Trek: The Next Generation 23, 122,
Star Trek (2009) 24
Star Video 182
Steambath 170
Steele, Barbara 9, 25, 37, 38, 40, 108-110, 115, 188, 192, 194
Steenburgen, Mary 41
Stein, Ben 84
Stephen King's IT 154
Sterling, Philip 179
Stern, Joseph 83-84, 99, 135, 136, 138, 139, 151, 197
Steve Canyon 157
Stevens, Alex 20, 148
Stevens, Shawn 139
Stevens, Stella 186
Stevenson, Robert 183
Stevenson, Robert Louis 20, 43-47, 74, 167-168, 194
Stewart, Fred Mustard 53
Stewart, Mary 194
Stewart, Susan 143
Sting 185
St. John in Exile 10, 127
Stoddard, Brandon 111, 191
Stoker, Bram 13, 40, 194
Stone, Jay 35
Stone, Sharon 115
Storm, James 1, 9, 20, 38, 64, 76, 132, 133, 195
Stories of John O'Hara 188
Story of Pretty Boy Floyd 131
Stowe, Madeleine 141-142
Strange Case of Dr. Jekyll and Mr. Hyde (Stevenson) 20, 43-47, 74, 167
Strange Case of Dr. Jekyll and Mr. Hyde 10, 13, 22, 38, **42**, 43-**45**, 46-47, 66, 73, 74, 99, 147, 148, 160, 162, 164, 167-168, 172, 189, 194, 197
Strange Game of Hyde and Seek 44
Strange Paradise 22, 143, 150, 168
Stranger Within 62

Index

Strasberg, Susan 160, 161, 164
Stratton, Rick 68
Street, Elliott 130, 131, 132, 195
Street Smart 188
Streets of Beverly Hills 156
Streets of San Francisco 159
Streisand, Barbra 145
Strickfaden, Kenneth 160
Stroka, Michael 21
Studio One 22, 47
Sullivan, Susan 28
Sunrise at Campobello 108
Sunset Las Palmas Studio 168
'Sunshine's on the Way" 139
Super Friends 115
Supergirl 188
Supernatural 31
"Superstar" 186
Supertrain 6, 10, 24, 38, 55, 62, 102, 132, 135, 186-**186, 187**, 188, 192, 195
Susann, Jacqueline 76
Suskin, Mitch 127
Suspiria 30
Svenson, Bo 160, **161**, 162, 163, 164
Swann, Francis 22
Swift, Lela 22, 148, 149, 150, 159, 173, 180, 183
Sydney, Sylvia 81
Sylvester, Harold 155
Syndicated 36
Syracuse University 6

Taking Gary Feldman 83-84
Taking of Pelham One Two Three 185
Talent for the Game 143
Tales from the Darkside 23
Talk 147
Tannenbaum, Richard 84
Tarantino, Quentin 3
Tartikoff, Brandon 23, 27
Tattered Web 22
Tatum, Channing 133
Taub, Bill 24
Taxi 105
Taylor, Benedict 176
Taylor, Don 81
Taylor, Elizabeth 172
Taylor, Jud 151

Telegraph-Journal 35
Television Critics Association 197
Television Fright Films of the 1970s 56-57, 66
Television Horrors of Dan Curtis 5, 145
Tennant, Victoria **107**, 108, 115
Tennessean 193
Tennessee State University 9, 84-85, 159
Tepes, Vlad 89, 92-94, 96, 176
Terror Television 26
Terror Train 118
Texas Chainsaw Massacre 62, 72
Textual Poachers 16
Theatre Bizarre 37
T.H.E. Cat 157
Then Came Bronson 151
There Will Be Blood 128
They Shoot Horses, Don't They? 108
They Won't Forget 190
Thinnes, Roy 24, **25**-26, 53, 54, 55, 127, 132-133, 157, 186, 195
"Third Level" 61, 191
Third Watch 152
This Is Your FBI 115
This Rough Magic 194
Three's Company 105
Thrilling Western 99-100
Thomas, Heck 101, 103
Thomas, Kevin 51
Thomas, Robin 84
Thompson, E.D. 9, 180
Thompson, Howard 51,
Thompson, Jeff 5, 7, 8-9, 50, 55, 68, 78, 79, 84-85, 110, 119, 180, 182, 197, 199, **210**
Thompson, Sonia 9, 145, 180
Thor, Cameron **153**
Thorn Birds 110, 111, 119
Thorne Kelly, Kate 130
Thorpe, Alexis 28
Those She Left Behind 119
Time After Time 66
Time and Again 61, 191
Timecop 28
Time Killer 50
Time magazine 74
Time Traveler's Wife 141
Titanic 94, 112
T.J. Hooker 152

TNT (Turner Network Television) 27, 163, 167, 191
Tolan, Michael 156
Tolkien, J.R.R. 192
Tomashoff, Sy 9, 12, 41, 197
Tomerlin, John 164, 165, 166
Tonight Show 159
Tony Awards 47
Too Easy to Kill 159
Topol, Chaim 108, 115
Torch of Liberty award 111
Torme, Mel 154
Torme, Tracy 122, 125
To Tell the Truth 16
Tough Customers 188
Townsend, Stuart 69, 164
TP de Oro award 111
T. Rex 32
Trauma 30
Traveling Executioner 74
Trilogy of Terror 1, 3, 5, 10, 56, 57-**59**, 60, 62, 66, 67, 68, 83, 106, 131, 159, 197, 200
Trilogy of Terror II 10, 57, 66, **67**, 68, 85
Trouble with Angels 128
True Story 177
Tucci, Stanley 144
Tuckahoe mansion 141
Tuckett, William 173
Tune In Tonight 126
Turn of the Screw (James) 23, 172-177, 194
Turn of the Screw 5, 10, 57, 130, 159, 164, 172-**175**, 176-177, 183, 189, 194, 199
Turquand, Todd 81
TV Guide 35, 105, 117, 125-126, 133, 136, 143, 144, 154
TV Host 125
Twain, Mark 127
21 Up 122
Twilight Zone 23, 47, 157, 164
Two Deaths of Sean Doolittle 159
"Twonky" 66

UFOs 121-128
Underhill, Wilbur 132
Unholy 25
Union Pacific 6
United Artists 60, 79, 80, 83, 88

Universal movies 14-15, 40, 41, 48, 160, 162, 164, 194
UPI (United Press International) 81
Upstairs Downstairs 173
Urschel, Charles 130
USA Network 66, 67
USA Today 67-68, 127, 141, 142-143
U.S. TV Fan Association 120

Vamberry, Arminius 93
Vampire Book 8-9, 96
Vampire Diaries 91
Van Dyke, Dick 186, **187**
Van Gelder, Lawrence 83
Van Meter, Homer 132, 194
Variety 26, 33, 35, 54-55, 60, 85, 96, 110, 126, 131, 133, 141, 152, 162, 167, 177, 18
Vaughn, Heidi 161, 162
Vendettas 32
Venturi, Ken 6
Vereen, Ben **124**, 125, 126,
Verheiden, Mark 28, 30, 40
Vestoff, Virginia 21
Viacom 68
Victory at Sea 6
Video Watchdog 77, 78
View-Master 11
View to a Kill 88
Vigoda, Abe 84, 195
Village of the Damned 62
Vincent, Jan-Michael 108, 115
Vincent and Theo 193
Virginian 51, 157
Virkler, Dennis 106
Visible Ink Press 96
Vista Theatre 38, 96-97
"Viy" 194
Vogue 81
Von Buelow, Erick 58
Von Leer, Hunter 132

Wager, Walter 188
Wait Until Dark 190
Walden, Robert 132, 184, 195
Walker, Clint 55, 56,
Walker, Ellie Wood 147
Wallace, Art 22, 33, 38

Wallace, Earl W. 55, 62, 99, 101, 105, 111, 112, 145, 188, 192-193
Wallace, Marie 9, 17, 19, 28, 38
Wall Street Journal 190
Walnum, Sven **82**
Waltons 145, 157
WAMB-AM & FM 9, 119
Wandrey, Donna 20
War and Remembrance 3, 5, 6, 10, 11, **15**, 23, 26, 37, 40, 58, 62, 79, 84, 89, 105, 108, 109, 111-**113**, **114**, 115-**116**, 117-**118**, 119-121, 125, 127, 128, 129, 137, 141, 152, 154, 159, 163, 170, 194, 195, **196**, 197, 199, 200
Ward, Simon 89, **97**
Warner Brothers 28, 30, 36, 79, 190, 204
Washington: Behind Closed Doors 119
Washington Post 117, 126
Watkins College of Art, Design, & Film 9
Watson, Mills 100, 132, 133, 186, 195
Wayne, John 106
WB network 27-31, 40, 66, 128, 147
Web 22
Webb, James 188
Wednesday Play 43
Weekend Matinee 53
Weiler, A.H. 77
Weir, Peter 62
Weird Tales 66, 68
Weiss, Michael 26
Welch, Raquel 37
Welles, Violet 22
Wells, John 28, 30
Welsh, Kennneth 143
Welsh, Tommy 111
Werewolf 157
Werewolf of Paris 194
Western Heritage Awards 100, 105, 197
Westview books 5
West Wing 28
Wetherell Bates, Virginia 91
WGA (Writers Guild of America) 139, 143
Whale, James 162, 164
Whatever Happened to Detective Adam Sera? 204
What's Love Got to Do with It 157
Wheeler, Ellen 26
When a Stranger Calls 24

When Every Day Was the Fourth of July 6, 10, 16, 48, 61, 106, 133-**134**, 135, 137, 141, 145, 151, 157, 190
When Lions Roared 120
When the Daltons Rode 103
"Where the Cluetts Are" 191
White, Barry 32
Whitelaw, Billie 46, 47
Whiting, Leonard 163
Whitney, Phyllis A. 13
Who Will Love My Children? 111
Wicker Man 62
Wickes, David 167
Widdoes, Kathleen 159
Wide World Mystery 1, 5-6, 22, 55, 77, 129, 159-**161**, 162-**165**, 166-**169**, 170-**171**, 172-**175**, 176-**178**, 179-180, 181, 182, 188, 195, 200
Wide World of Sports 7
Wiesel, Elie 121
Wilcox, Larry 5, 9, **100**, 105, 106
Wild Bunch 99
Wilde, Oscar 19, 23, 164-168, 194
Wilhelm, Jeff 192
Will & Liz 200, 204
Williams, John 117
Williams, Trevor 129, 148, 164
Willow B: Women in Prison 147
Wilson, Demond 84
Wilson, Edmund 173
Wincer, Simon 120
Wind and the Lion 130
Winding, Kai 157
Winds of War 3, 6, 9, 10, 11, 26, 40, 62, 79, 83-84, 89, 105, 106-**107**, **108**, **109**, 110-111, 112, 115, **116**, 117, 119, 120, 121, 127, 128, 129, 137, 151, 152, 159, 184, 188, 189, 194, 195, 197, 199
Winningham, Mare 122, 125-**126**
Winston, Daoma 13
Winters, Deborah 115
Winter's Tale 87
Wire 143
Witness 62, 99
woman-in-jeopardy subgenre 13, 56, 67
Wonder Woman 147
Wonder Years 156
Woodrow Wilson Dime 61, 191
Woods, James 119

Woodson, William T. 108, 115
World of Dark Shadows 5, 23, 110
Worst Witch 87
Wouk, Herman 3, 62, 106, **107**, 108, 110, 111, 112, 199, **201**
Wuthering Heights (Bronte) 14, 21, 188-189, 193-194
Wuthering Heights (1970) 14

X-Files 127

Young, Gig 182, **183**, 184
Young and the Restless 128

Youngblood Hawke 106
Young Frankenstein 163
Young Marrieds 16
Young Torless 108
Yulin, Harris 129, 130, 132, 133, 135, 195

Zacha, W.T. 132
Zee, John A. 180
Zinner, Peter 120
Zorro 157
Zuckerman, Alex 84, 85

www.ingramcontent.com/pod-product-compliance
Lightning Source LLC
Chambersburg PA
CBHW081428070526
44586CB00020B/2520